# RISKY TRANSACTIONS

# RISKY TRANSACTIONS

## Trust, Kinship, and Ethnicity

Edited by
Frank K. Salter

*Berghahn Books*
New York • Oxford

First published in 2002 by

**Berghahn Books**

www.berghahnbooks.com

Editorial offices:
604 West 115th Street, New York NY 10025, USA
3 NewTec Place, Magdalen Road, Oxford OX4 1RE, UK

© 2002 Frank Salter

**Library of Congress Cataloging-in-Publication Data**

Risky transactions : trust, kinship, and ethnicity / edited by Frank K. Salter.
    p. cm.
    Includes bibliographical references and index.
    ISBN 1-57181-710-7 (cl. : alk. paper) -- ISBN 1-57181-319-5 (pb. : alk. paper)
    1. Sociobiology. 2. Kinship. 3. Ethnicity. 4. Risk-taking (Psychology).
    5. Altruism. I. Salter, Frank K.

GN365.9 .R57 2002
304.5--dc21

2001052719

**British Library Cataloguing in Publication Data**

A catalogue record for this book is available
from the British Library.

Printed in the United States on acid-free paper.

ISBN 1–57181–710–7 (hardback)
ISBN 1–57181–319–5 (paperback)

# CONTENTS

## Risky business, illicit and licit

## Oppressed families and minorities

## AIDS, the U.S. Supreme Court, and Tourism

## Evolutionary syntheses

# LIST OF FIGURES

# MAP

# LIST OF TABLES

# ACKNOWLEDGEMENTS

The symposium lying behind this book would not have been possible without the gracious assistance of Wulf Schiefenhövel, who not only suggested a meeting soon after hearing the risky transaction idea, but lent his organizational talents to make it a reality. I also wish to thank the Werner Reimers Foundation who sponsored the meeting at their elegant headquarters in Bad Homburg, near Frankfurt, Germany, from 23–25 September 1996. The late Werner Reimer, an industrialist, saw the need for a better understanding of human behaviour, and endowed an independent organization to further research in that direction. Thanks are due to the Reimer board and especially Herr von Krosigk and his staff at the Reimers headquarters. I also wish to thank Dr Gebhard Geiger of the Technological University, Faculty for Economics and Social Science, Munich, for his helpful comments on some chapters.

# NOTES ON CONTRIBUTORS

## (IN ALPHABETICAL ORDER, BY FIRST AUTHOR, AND GROUPED BY CHAPTER)

**Pierre van den Berghe** is Professor Emeritus of Sociology and Anthropology at the University of Washington, Seattle. He carried out extensive fieldwork in Sub-Saharan Africa and Latin America, and specializes in kinship, ethnicity, tourism, genocide, and human biocultural evolution. Among his twenty-two books are *Race and racism* (1967), *Human family systems* (1979), *The ethnic phenomenon* (1981), and *Stranger in their midst* (1989).

**Anton Blok** is Professor of Cultural Anthropology at the University of Amsterdam. His publications include *The Mafia of a Sicilian village* (Oxford 1974) and *Honour and violence* (Cambridge 2001).

**Eugene Burnstein** is a professor of psychology at the University of Michigan and Senior Research Scientist at the Institute of Social Research. **Christine Branigan** is a doctoral student in the department of pyschology at the University of Michigan. **Grazyna Wieczorkowska** is a professor of psychology at Warsaw University and director of the Institute for Social Studies. All three are social psychologists interested in the psychological mechanisms implicated in evolutionary models such as kin selection and foraging theory and how these mechanisms operate in modern environments. Publications include:

Wieczorkowska, G., and Burnstein, E. (1999). Adapting to the transition from socialism to capitalism in Poland: The role of screening strategies in social change. *Psychological Science*, **10**, 98–105.

Burnstein, E., and Branigan, C. (2001). Evolutionary analyses in social psychology. In *Blackwell handbook of social psychology: intraindividual processes,* (eds A. Tesser and N. Schwartz). Blackwell, London.

**Janet Tai Landa** is Professor of Economics at York University, Toronto, Canada. She specializes in the New Institutional Economics of exchange institutions in developed and less- developed economies. She has published extensively on Chinese trading networks (see e.g. A theory of the ethnically homogeneous middleman group: An institutional alternative to contract law, *Journal of Legal Studies,* **10,** 2; June 1981, 349–62). Her book, *Trust, ethnicity, and identity: Beyond the New Institutional Economics of ethnic trading networks, contract law, and gift-exchange,* was published by the University of Michigan Press, Ann Abor in 1994 (second printing, 1998). She is the Editor-in-Chief of a new interdisciplinary journal, *Journal of Bioeconomics,* published by Kluwer Academic Publishers.

**Kevin MacDonald** is Professor of Psychology at California State University-Long Beach, Long Beach, CA 90840–0901, U.S.A. His research has focused on developing evolutionary perspectives in developmental psychology and ethnic relations. He has authored four books on these themes: *Social and personality development: An evolutionary synthesis* (Plenum, New York, 1988); *A people that shall dwell alone: Judaism as a group evolutionary strategy* (Praeger, Westport, CT,1994); *Separation and its discontents: Toward an evolutionary theory of anti-Semitism* (Westport, CT, 1998); and *The culture of critique: An evolutionary analysis of Jewish involvement in twentieth-century intellectual and political movements* (Westport, CT, 1998).

**Peter Meyer** is a professor of sociology at the Institute of Socioeconomics, University of Augsburg, Germany. His main interests are in applications of evolutionary theory to social theory. His publications include: *Evolution und Gewalt,* P. Parey, Berlin/Hamburg, 1981; *Soziobiologie und Soziologie,* Luchterhand, Darmstadt, 1982; co-author with N. Thornhill, A. Maryanski, J. Tooby, L. Cosmides, and J.H. Turner of 'Evolutionary theory and human social institutions: Psychological foundations', in *Human by nature,* (P. Weingart et al.). Erlbaum, Mahwah, NJ, 1998; 'The sociobiology of human cooperation: The interplay of ultimate and proximate causes', in *The Darwinian heritage and sociobiology,* (eds J.M.G. van der Dennen, D. Smillie, and D.R. Wilson). Praeger, Westport, CT, 1999.

**Frank Salter** is a political ethologist attached to the Max Planck Institute in Andechs, Germany. He studies political phenomena using the methods and concepts of behavioural biology in addition to conventional approaches. His research centres on social power in the form of command hierarchies and ethnic competition. Publications include *Emotions in command: A naturalistic study of institutional dominance* (Oxford University Press, 1995) and 'Indoctrination as institutionalized persuasion: Its limited variability and cross-cultural evolution', in *Indoctrinability, ideology, and warfare: Evolutionary perspectives,* which he edited with Irenäus Eibl-Eibesfeldt (Berghahn, 1998).

**James N. Schubert** is Professor of Political Science at Northern Illinois University with primary research interests in evolutionary political psychology. **Margaret Ann Curran** is Research Associate and Assistant Director at the Office of Research, Evaluation and Policy Studies at Northern Illinois University. **Steven A. Peterson** is Director of the School of Public Affairs at Penn State Harrisburg. **Glendon Schubert** is Professor of Political Science at the University of Hawaii. **Stephen L. Wasby** is Professor of Political Science at the Statue University of New York at Albany.

**Carmen Strungaru** is Lecturer in Human Ethology in the Department of Animal Physiology, Ethology and Biophysics, Faculty of Biology, University of Bucharest. Her research interests include the ethology of mate-choice behaviour, grooming, birthing, and street-begging.

**X.T. Wang** is associate professor in the Psychology Department at the University of South Dakota, U.S.A. He was also a visiting scientist at the Max Planck Institute in Berlin, German. He has published empirical findings on human decision making in social, managerial, and cross-cultural contexts; risk perception and management; probability judgement; hemispheric mechanisms of risky choice; and theoretical analysis of evolutionary and ecological rationality. He has published his findings in various journals, including *Cognition*; *Journal of Behavioral Decision Making*; *Organizational Behavior and Human Decision Making Processes*; *Evolution and Human Behavior*; *Brain, Behavior and Evolution*; *Psychophysiology*; *Behavioral and Brain Sciences*; and *American Behavioral Scientist*.

**Polly Wiessner** received her PhD from the University of Michigan, Ann Arbor in 1977 and is currently a Professor of Anthropology at the University of Utah. She has conducted long-term fieldwork among the !Kung Bushmen on risk, reciprocity, exchange networks and style in artefacts and among the Enga of Papua New Guinea on ethnohistory, exchange networks, warfare and rituals. Her major publications include *Food and the status quest* (edited together with Wulf Schiefenhövel), *Historical vines: Enga networks of exchange, ritual and warfare in Papua New Guinea* (co-authored with Akii Tumu), plus numerous articles.

# INTRODUCTION

## CHAPTER 1

# FROM MAFIA TO FREEDOM FIGHTERS

## QUESTIONS RAISED BY ETHOLOGY AND SOCIOBIOLOGY

### *Frank K. Salter*

❧ ❧

## Introduction

The efflorescence of ethnic mafias and nationalism in the twilight and night of the Soviet Union raises a question that has long haunted the Enlightenment imagination: Why is national identity so difficult to extinguish and so explosive in its capacity to galvanize intragroup solidarity and intergroup conflict?

This collection began with my curiosity about the prominent roles played by kinship and ethnicity in structuring the risky transactions conducted by organized criminals. This is a recurring theme in media reports from China to Sicily, from Australia to California. It is also the subject of scholarly research (e.g. Blok in this volume; Ianni 1972, 1974; Simis 1982). What had caught my attention was not news out of Sicily but reports of extensive Mafia operations in Russia following the decline of the Communist regime. Williams (1996, p. 13) notes that ethnicity has been one of the most important structuring principles of Russian organized crime, and makes his point by quoting from *Izvestia* (21 September 1995, p. 5):

> The largest and most influential groups have claimed the principal spheres of activity. For example, the Solntsevo gang "runs" the gambling business; the Kazan gang is

in charge of loans; the Chechens handle exports of petroleum, petroleum products and metals, banking operations, and the trade in stolen cars; Azerbaijani groups are into the drug business, the gambling business and trade; Armenian gangs deal in car theft, swindling and bribery; the Georgians are partial to burglary, robbery and hostage-taking; the Ingush's areas are gold mining, trade in precious metals, and weapons deals; and the Dagestanis are involved in rape and theft.

*Izvestia*'s account should not be taken as complete. Much organized crime in Russia is committed by ethnic Russians such as displaced Communist *apparatchiks* and unemployed KGB officers. Kin and ethnic groups do not monopolize organized crime, but they are nevertheless salient. This is interesting in its own right but carries an added theoretical interest for students of evolution when conjoined with the riskiness of illegal activity. Crime tends to be riskier to liberty and sometimes to life than legitimate business, so it is all the more important for criminals to trust their associates. Trusting kin and, under some circumstance, fellow ethnics, makes good sense from an evolutionary perspective.[1]

Modern biology is unified by "neo-Darwinian" evolutionary theory, the synthesis of Darwin's theory of natural selection and Mendel's discovery of the genetic transmission of traits (Fisher 1958/1930; Wilson 1975). According to this synthesis all humans, whatever their racial or cultural background, share the majority of their evolutionary history and thus share a species-typical repertoire of behaviours and motivations, usually called human nature.[2]

The aspect of human nature that inspired this book is risk-taking on behalf of kin. Risk-taking for kin lies at the heart of modern evolutionary theory of social behaviour, sometimes called evolutionary ecology but better known as sociobiology. The sociobiological revolution in evolutionary theory began with an insight by the great geneticist J.B.S. Haldane,[3] who noted that since siblings share half of one another's genes and cousins share one eighth, it would be adaptive to risk one's life to save three siblings or nine cousins from drowning.[4] Haldane's student William Hamilton formalized this insight beginning with the special case of social insects, which posed an insuperable problem for Darwin's original individual-based theory. The problem was that Darwin had assumed that individuals and groups were the units of selection in evolution, in which case self-sacrificial behaviour necessarily weeded out the altruist and left only selfish individuals after a few generations.[5] Yet altruism is manifest in humans, who risk themselves for kin and tribe. Altruism is much more extreme in social insects. Suicidal behaviour is common among social bees and wasps, whose "fearsome reputation ... is due to their general readiness to throw their lives away upon slight provocation" (Wilson 1975, p. 59).

How could evolution by differential reproduction of the most fit have produced individuals that cannot even reproduce? Hamilton showed that even the sterile castes of workers and soldiers could be explained by Darwinian theory when combined with knowledge of genes. His mathematics showed that genes coding for sacrificial behaviour need not be weeded out of the gene pool if the behaviour in question helps close kin to reproduce. The sterile castes help their sister queens to reproduce by tending her eggs and defending the nest, and this altruistic behaviour is adaptive because it efficiently reproduces the sterile members' genes in the next generation. Hamilton's theory is known as kin selection or inclusive fitness theory, and is basic to sociobiology, itself the dominant theory of social behaviour in non-human animals since the appearance of E.O. Wilson's *Sociobiology* in 1975.

Sociobiological theory converged on classical ethology, the latter having developed in the tradition established by Konrad Lorenz and Niko Tinbergen. At the beginning of the 1970s Irenäus Eibl-Eibesfeldt (1970), a colleague of Lorenz, proposed that the phylogeny of affiliative behaviour began with parenting. In birds and mammals solicitude, nurture, protection, and self-sacrifice are all behaviours that proved adaptive as unreciprocated parental acts toward offspring. In some species parental altruism later spread to form the basis of generalized kin altruism found in humans. Both sociobiology and ethology point to kinship as the evolutionary origins of trust.

What about trust between co-ethnics? Could there be a common explanation for both kin and ethnic group involvement in crime? Kinship and ethnic altruism have received unified theoretical treatment by Pierre van den Berghe in *The ethnic phenomenon* (1981). His ethnic nepotism theory proposes that ethnicity is an attenuated form of kinship. In this theory not only do co-ethnics perceive each other to be distant kin, but in fact they usually *are* distant kin at the genetic level; i.e., they share more of their genes by common descent than do individuals belonging to different ethnic groups. Van den Berghe's theory is promising as an explanation of the role of kin and ethnic ties in conducting risky business. Yet despite a wide-ranging analysis his book does not treat crime or mafias or kinship strategies for mitigating risk (although he does discuss the role of ethnicity in risk-taking among tourists in this volume). An evolutionary theory of preference for kin and ethnic partners in risk-sharing ventures follows directly from van den Berghe's sociobiological theory.

Familial- and ethnic group-cohesion are based on altruism (van den Berghe 1978a, 1981, 1995; Campbell 1965; Eibl-Eibesfeldt 1970, 1989, 1998), which in the case of criminal families and criminal groups of co-ethnics is often turned to aggression against outsiders. Illicit activities are risky because of police and competition from other criminals. A major risk is that of defectors who inform to police or competitors. This risk makes trust a valuable resource for partners in crime. The evolutionary theory of kin altruism offers some insights into the nature of trust. The theory of "kin selection" or "inclusive fitness" states that since close kin share a significant proportion of their distinctive genes, they have a joint interest in cooperating and, under certain conditions, in sacrificing personal gain or security for each other. Furthermore, humans have been selected to behave in this manner, and it is a universal component of human nature. No wonder that families figure so prominently in conducting transactions that require mutual trust but are not protected by contract law. As for ethnicity, kin selection theory could be relevant if ethnicity is an extended form of kinship, as argued by van den Berghe (1981; Salter 2001).

It is one step from this line of thought to the idea that evolved kin and ethnic altruism might play a part in mitigating the risk of other activities besides crime. Where else is kinship or ethnicity an important organizing principle? Does kin altruism help explain the workings of that principle? Are kin and ethnic relationships favoured when the relationship itself poses a serious risk?

Several colleagues expressed interest in these questions, and a meeting was held on the subject of "Risky Transactions: Kinship, ethnicity and trust" in September 1996, hosted by the Werner Reimers Foundation in Bad Homburg, Germany. The attending scholars were asked to address the following theme.

What kinds of social ties exist between people who conduct risky transactions together? Such transactions include illicit business such as trading in drugs, the expression of forbidden beliefs by dissidents in authoritarian societies, illegal political activities, or the conduct of tabooed or illegal sexual practices. In all cases participants are exposed to substantial risk to status, resources, freedom or even life. There is evidence pointing to social bonds, especially those of kinship and ethnicity, as important facilitators of risk-prone exchange (e.g. Bonacich 1973; Hess 1990; Ianni 1972; Landa 1981), in addition to economic and other social controls (Arlacchi 1988). The central role of kinship in structuring social security networks in hunter-gatherers indicates an evolutionary origin of this recurring pattern (Wiessner 1982). Kinship continues to underpin mutual support networks in all traditional societies. A considerable body of ethological and sociobiological theory predicts such a role for kinship, whether biological or socially defined. But the idea has never been systematically scrutinized.

The proposed symposium will seek to answer the following questions.

1. Ethological, ethnographic and sociological description. What are the main types of relationship in which risky transactions are embedded?
2. Induction to risky transaction relationships. How are kin, biologically or socially defined, recruited and indoctrinated? Do ties that mitigate transaction risk differ in their modes of initiation from those that do not? What is the importance of kinship, real or defined, in proofing relationships against defection?
3. Social control mechanisms. How do loyalty ties fit in the gamut of social control methods applying to different sorts of transactions? For example, mafias are characterized not only by real or defined familiarity but threaten would-be defectors with dire punishment. But dissident groups must often rely on nothing but the loyalty of members and their altruism under duress to maintain secrecy.
4. Religion. Are there religions especially adapted to mitigating the risk of transactions between members?
5. Game theory and economics. Do trusting relationships hinge on preventing defection when a member is confronted by the prisoner's dilemma? This is a plausible interpretation in the case of Mafia and dissident members who do not inform under duress or when cooperation with the authorities would be rewarded by leniency.

Answers to these questions are distributed across the following chapters, though usually not on a one-to-one basis. In the remainder of this chapter I summarize and comment on these contributions in the order in which they appear in the book.

## Ethnography

### Chapter 2

The starting point for any empirical test of an evolutionary theory is to describe the species in question in its natural condition. No human group remains in pristine evolutionary condition, but approximations are offered by societies that presently or until recently lived by hunting and gathering, the means of subsistence pursued by *Homo sapiens* for most of its evolutionary history. This mode of existence forces groups to remain small and mobile, and retain social ties able to mitigate risks from the environment and the predations of other groups. In Chapter 2, Polly Wiessner reports on how the social ties of the !Kung Bushmen of the Kalahari have fared under the impact of rapid social change occasioned by the Namibian Government's provision of stable water points allowing a sedentary lifestyle. Wiessner has been documenting !Kung exchange networks for over twenty years. Her original studies confirmed the importance of kin ties in mitigating risk of defection from exchange relationships, allowing the !Kung's "social security" net to extend over large distances. The present longitudinal extension of her research traces the development of these ties, whose *raison d'être* of providing security against famine and conflict was undermined by an era of relative plenty and stability. In her paper she presents new findings. Exchange ties are valuable and difficult to replicate once lost. In a process analogous to bequeathing land, elderly Bushmen also pass on their exchange ties to children. Thus, low-risk exchange ties are inherited from one's parents and grandparents. Wiessner's research also contributes to the debate over "fictive" versus "socially-constructed" kinship. The debate hinges on the question, how easy is it to manipulate humans into treating non-kin like real kin? Some theorists such as van den Berghe (1981) argue that ethnic groups have a genetic component to their identity, and that despite some exceptions people usually direct altruism towards groups with which they are the most closely related genetically. Others argue in the opposite direction, that ethnic groups and nationalism are social constructs with little or no genetic reality (e.g. Masters, forthcoming). Wiessner shows that in Bushmen society, fictive kinship based on shared names has some influence on patterns of exchange, but that delayed reciprocal arrangements – a riskier type of transaction than that yielding immediate returns – are made with closer genetic kin. What of non-hunter-gatherer societies, including present-day mass societies? Wiessner surmises that the hunter-gatherer heritage of kin-based risk-mitigating social techniques was selectively carried over to deal with risky transactions in the large, more anonymous societies that predominate in the modern world.

## Psychological mechanisms

### Chapter 3

X.T. Wang's chapter is an argument for the importance of "domain specific" cognitive mechanisms as the responsible agents for making decisions regarding risks to different kinds of groups. The human brain is not rational in the normative sense of generally giving equivalent answers to equivalent problems. Wang's evidence for this is the fact that individuals respond differently to logically identical problems that are put to them in different words – the framing effect. The chapter pays special attention to framing effects generated by perceived kinship and non-kinship. Respondents show greater concern for groups of kin than for groups of non-kin. As Wang puts it, his "findings suggest that decision making rationality is kinship specific…. [The result] argues against an all-purpose viewpoint and indicates that human choice mechanisms automatically distinguish kinship from pseudo-kinship or quasi-kinship." Wang also finds ethnic difference. Mainland Chinese subjects treat much larger hypothetical groups as kith and kin, compared with American subjects.

## Chapter 4

Eugene Burnstein, Christine Branigan and Grazyna Wieczorkowska-Nejtardt report psychological research on how risk-taking behaviour is influenced by kinship. They review experimental evidence indicating that kin altruism is a powerful motivation in decisions to run risks for others, but also show that such decisions are made in light of costs and benefits to the actor's inclusive fitness. The evidence suggests that humans follow the rule of thumb (the "heuristic"): "Help those most closely related to you, especially when the cost and benefits are large." For example, kinship altruism is more likely to motivate behaviour when a close relative is in peril than when he requests an everyday favour. Life and death emergencies are especially likely to release self-sacrificial altruism, and Burnstein et al. cite the extraordinary example of a fatal hotel fire on the Isle of Man in 1973 that trapped and killed fifty people (Sime 1983). An analysis of the emergency found that families had stuck together and exited or died as a group while friends and acquaintances had separated. Finally, Burnstein et al. speculate that ethnicity can probably elicit the same discrimination in times of threat to the ingroup. They end by expressing the hope that these evolved propensities do not make ethnic strife a permanent affliction, recalling Sherif's (1951) experimental discovery that a superordinate goal tends to produce cooperation by healing the wounds of past conflict, regardless of ethnic commonalities or differences.

## Risky business, illicit and licit

## Chapter 5

Anton Blok's chapter on the Sicilian Mafia reports field-work on the social organization of that best known of ethnic crime groups. His analysis of how biological kinship and metaphorical "shared blood" serve to bind together members of crime "families" and "brotherhoods" strongly confirms the evolutionary approach. "Given its preeminence in Mafia coalitions, agnatic kinship in Sicily, as in other Indo-European kinship systems, provides for relationships of 'diffuse, enduring solidarity' [citation]. If in the absence of effective state control trust can be found anywhere, it is primarily in the bonds between agnatic kinsmen, that is, 'blood' relatives." While biological kinship forms the core of Mafia families, alliances between intermarried families are also important, with sets of brothers-in-law often forming the core of groups of Mafia families. The bond is cemented with rituals that establish metaphorical brotherhood. The resulting relationships are more trusting than contracts. Kinship, both real and socially defined, is an economic and political asset because it facilitates the taxing of local businesses and trading in drugs. These practices are risky because of competition from other Mafia clans and because they are illicit and thus vulnerable to police informers.

## Chapter 6

One clear example of kinship acting to reduce the risk of transactions is ethnically homogeneous middleman groups. Janet Landa wrote one of the earliest analyses of this world-wide phenomenon, describing how ethnic-Chinese business people in Malaysia preferentially extend credit to family and ethnic members, rather than to ethnic Malays. Such is the trust that exists between family and ethnic members that credit is extended on the basis of a handshake. In the present volume, she reformulates the theoretical basis for her analysis. The new theory is still grounded in the New Institutional Economics (NIE, see Landa 1994) but now incorporates the cognitive anthropology of Mary Douglas. The NIE has ignored the cognitive and classificatory foundations of social institutions. Yet Landa argues convincingly that classification is such a central aspect of human social cognition that our species might be renamed "Homo classificus". Humans are compulsive classifiers, sorting other individuals into demographic and behavioural categories. Prominent among these social categories are kinship and ethnicity, the latter corresponding to the tribal boundaries within which the species evolved. When a person categorizes someone as close kin or fellow-ethnic, that person becomes a candidate recipient of greater altruism and trust, as Landa illustrates with her remarkable ethnographic data on Chinese middleman groups in Malaysia. These successful business-men and -women categorize their social worlds into seven nested circles of kinship and ethnicity, beginning with the nuclear family. Trust and loyalty then go, in decreasing intensity, to more distant kinsmen from the extended family and lineage, then to clansmen, fellow villagers, dialect group from the same province in China, Chinese speaking a different dialect; and finally to non-Chinese. A broader phenomenon in need of Landa's theory is that of the ethnic economy. Ethnic economies play important roles in even the most developed economies, such as the United States (Light and Karageorgis 1994).

## Oppressed families and minorities

### Chapter 7

Carmen Strungaru describes the powerful totalitarian social controls used by communist Romania until the early 1990s to dissuade and crush dissidents. A key strategy was to turn group members against one another by deceiving them to believe that some members had informed to the authorities. Special methods were adopted to bring families under surveillance, as revealed in the archives of the security services released in the 1990s. Dissidents not only received personal punishments, but saw their entire families persecuted. The result was to harness kin altruism for the suppression of dissident speech. Strungaru concludes that organized dissident movements were effectively prevented or crushed, even those based on family circles. Yet kinship and friendship did show their strength by being the last refuge for interpersonal trust between dissidents. One celebrated dissident intellectual is reported in the Security Archives as cutting all contacts with colleagues, but continuing to complain to his family about the lack of freedom in Romania. Strungaru's chapter is important for adding to knowledge of the social technologies of totalitarian social control and how it can compromise even kinship bonds with intense surveillance and punishment.

## Chapter 8

Jews, perhaps more than any other religious or ethnic group, have had to face persecution for maintaining their traditions, including distinctive communal associations and economic activities. Merely belonging to a Jewish community has often constituted a risky transaction, as has Jews' frequent middleman status. For example, when Frederick the Great of Prussia was close to bankruptcy after fighting the Seven Years' War, he had the Jewish officials who ran the royal mint inflate the Prussian currency with new coins containing less silver. The business was profitable and helped create a new Jewish business elite in Northern Europe, but it also risked a backlash from those who suffered from the resulting inflation (Blumenthal 1998). The Jewish diaspora has survived intermittent persecution for two millennia, more than sufficient time to develop cultural patterns adapted to mitigate the risks inherent in maintaining a separate minority identity. Kevin MacDonald is the author of a three-volume evolutionary analysis of diaspora Judaism as a group strategy for maintaining continuity and economic competitiveness (1994), anti-Semitic responses to Judaism (1998a), and Jewish criticisms of Gentile culture (1998b). For this anthology I asked him to analyse Jewish social-organizational and cultural responses to anti-Semitism. The resulting essay is a testament to our species' ability as "flexible strategizers" (Alexander 1979). Jewish communities have adopted strategies ranging from defensive assimilation to assertive legal and cultural manoeuvres as means for disarming their critics and persecutors.

## Miscellaneous – AIDS, the U.S. Supreme Court, and tourism

### Chapter 9

This chapter provides a disconfirming case for the hypothesis that co-ethnics are preferred as partners for risky transactions. James Schubert and Margaret Curran undertook to test a hypothesis that emerged from discussion of the risks of the AIDS virus. If people really show a heightened preference for physiognomic similarity in choosing a partner with whom to conduct risky relationships, then the AIDS epidemic might have resulted in reduced cross-ethnic homosexual partnering. Schubert and Curran focused on the incidence of HIV infection between the time that information about "Gay-related immunodeficiency disease" was publicized and the time that the HIV virus and its modes of transmission and prevention were discovered. They examined time series data on AIDS incidence rates in the United States for

Whites, Blacks and Hispanics, broken down by geographic region. It is well established that the AIDS epidemic initially took off within the White population. On this basis, Schubert and Curran operationalize the hypothesis as a slow-down in the spread of HIV to minority populations. But no such effect was found. The disconfirmation provided by Schubert and Curran stands as an exception to the pattern of ethnic trust that began with the observation of ethnic mafias. Schubert and Curran also report an intriguing and tragic difference between White and minority incidence of AIDS. White homosexuals appear to have reduced multiple partnering behaviour prior to knowledge about HIV transmission, while Black and Hispanic homosexuals evidently did not for approximately a two-year period. Instead of a lag in the spread of the disease, this resulted in a two-year rapid increase in these minority groups, probably due to differential access to information about risk.

## Chapter 10

James Schubert, Steven Peterson, Glendon Schubert, and Stephen L. Wasby find ethnic bias in speech behaviour of Supreme Court justices during oral argument. The hypothesized bias is not in the Court's judgments but in the justices' paralinguistic behaviour during the important oral argument phase of proceedings, although the authors do not rule out indirect effects on rulings. The authors based their hypothesis on the symposium theme of preference for ethnically similar partners in risky transactions. When Supreme Court judges hear weighty cases, namely those that require interpretation of the Constitution, a risk is posed to the reputation of the Court as well as to the reputation of individual judges. The hypothesis was that during these higher-risk proceedings judges would show greater anxiety in their questioning of lawyers who exhibited differently accented English, and be more relaxed in questioning lawyers who shared their own accent. Anxiety was operationalized as reduced questioning of lawyers during oral argument. The logic is that judges must concentrate more on lawyer's words when they are spoken in a novel accent. Greater concentration means greater cognitive effort, itself anxiety-producing in the adversarial context of court hearings. All this places a premium on detecting any attempts at deception in evaluating communications. Cues to veracity, however, are more opaque when presented by speakers using an unfamiliar accent or dialect, creating a degree of uncertainty and hence anxiety. For the purposes of their study the authors compared judges' behaviour towards lawyers with standard American idiom and those with a Southern idiom. Eighteen cases of the Southern accent were observed out of one hundred and sixty randomly sampled cases. They also compared judges' behaviour towards women and men, to control for the possibility that other than linguistic differences were causing the changes in speech behaviour. The results confirmed the hypothesis. Justices spoke less in questioning lawyers who had a Southern accent, but their volubility actually increased when questioning female lawyers, indicating less anxiety with female than with male lawyers.

## Chapter 11

Pierre van den Berghe's chapter takes an anthropological look at the real and imagined risks of tourism and how these risks are conditioned by ethnicity. Tourism in strange cultural settings is a microcosm of the global village, in which jumbo jets bring people together across continents in unprecedented numbers. Servicing this thirst for the exotic yielded a 1990 turnover of U.S.\$2.4 trillion. This quest for foreign looks, tastes and smells is countered by the feelings of security that come from the company of co-ethnics and familiar environments. Most tourists prefer to sample foreign experiences rather than undergo prolonged immersion. Sallying forth for several hours at a time from the ethnic redoubt of a five-star hotel or vetted hostel is more the rule than is "going native". And expeditions are usually conducted with kith-and- kin from the home country. The links between tourism, kinship and ethnicity is an important and fascinating theme, approached by the author with an anthropological eye appropriate for a transcultural phenomenon.

# Evolutionary syntheses

## Chapter 12

Peter Meyer seeks to redress social theorists' obsession with modernity. The ahistorical tunnel vision that dwells on the last few centuries of human existence has resulted in a marked failure to explain or predict the tenacity of ethnic and nationalist solidarity in the modern era. Neither has this narrow perspective predicted the continuing role of ethnicity, kinship and quasi-kinship in exploiting risky economic niches, including illicit and middleman businesses. This failure has been due to the absence of evolutionary insights about the ways humans pursue their vital interests, which centre around modes of cooperation. Meyer argues from a broad biological perspective for the need to incorporate biobehavioural variables in social theory, such as the role of emotions underpinning cooperative, trusting groups. Intimate small groups are so important for emotional well-being that ostracism is a universal form of social control. Understanding the emotional basis of social behaviour is advanced by analysing neurophysiology – such as the role of the neurotransmitter serotonin. It is also advanced by adopting an evolutionary perspective, for example by analysing the role of emotions as solutions to perennial problems occurring in hunter-gatherer ecologies, in which humans have spent most of their evolutionary history. He concludes that humanity's emotional make-up favours small-group living among trusted, familiar individuals, including kin and fellow ethnics. The large, complex and anonymous societies that now predominate tend to fragment into ethnic groups when those societies can no longer guarantee the security of their members.

## Chapter 13

Frank Salter argues that ethnic solidarity can be turned to offensive as well as defensive purposes because loyalty mitigates the risk of both kinds of group enterprises. He develops this thesis using the literature on ethnic mafias, nationalist fighters, ethnic middleman groups, and ethnic dissidents. There appears to be a hierarchy of tie strengths, strongest between close kin, weak between co-ethnics, and weakest between different ethnic groups. The role of culture in mobilizing groups for defence and offence raises the hopeful prospect of structuring societies so that they gain the benefits of solidarity without the costs of aggressive behaviour towards minorities and other societies. That hope is raised by an evolutionary perspective on ethnic solidarity, which indicates that solidarity is mobilized more spontaneously for defensive than for offensive purposes.

## Significance of this collection

The growth of Mafia networks and ethnic nationalism in Eastern Europe and the Balkans since the demise of communist rule has focused attention once again on the destructive potential of selective loyalties. Any theoretical advance in these vexed subjects is potentially of practical importance, not least by shedding light on underlying social patterns of organized crime but also on the dynamics of ethnonationalism, multicultural societies, and commercially important phenomena such as tourism. This book is designed to test the evolutionary theory that humans are phylogenetically adapted to seek security in relationships with kin and ethnic groups, the latter conceptualized as extended kin groups. We hope to make this test a stringent one by putting the spotlight on relationships that survive in the face of various types of risk.

In many places this book offers support for van den Berghe's (1981) ethnic nepotism theory, which explains ethnic solidarity as an extended form of nepotism. Several contributors discuss the connection between kin and ethnic solidarity. Meyer groups them together as primordial loyalties. Wang's finding that familial loyalty extends across larger group sizes in China than in America leads him to suggest a larger role for fictive kinship in Chinese ethnic culture. Burnstein, Branigan, and Wieczorkowska-Nejtardt conclude their report of kin altruism by suggesting that ethnic solidarity is based on the same evolved psychological processes. In his chapter on the Sicilian Mafia, Blok describes how the symbolism of blood relationships acts to bind gang members into trusting relationships. Although he does not discuss ethnicity, Blok endorses the idea that kinship altruism can be extended to non-kin groups by socially defining them as kin. If one adds to this the premise that ethnicity is, at its root, real or putative shared descent, then the homology of kinship and ethnic bonds becomes a reasonable hypothesis. In her analysis of ethnic trading networks, Landa connects kinship and ethnicity by placing them on the same scale of trustworthiness in business dealings. Merchants of Chinese extraction doing business in Malaysia grade other merchants into seven nested levels of descending trustworthiness, the most trustworthy being kin and clan, followed by local dialect group, Chinese of all dialects, and finally descending to non-Chinese. Salter fits the concept of ethnic nepotism into a cultural theory of group solidarity. The sociobiological component of this synthesis offers an ultimate explanation for the innate hierarchy of tie strengths, descending from close kin to ethnic and non-ethnic groups. The cultural component, formulated as social technology theory, is needed to explain how particular strata of tie strength are magnified or dampened.

One hypothesis generated from evolutionary theory was not supported. Schubert and Curran found that homosexual partnering in the United States did not become more intra-ethnic and less inter-ethnic when the cause of the AIDS epidemic became known in the early 1980s. This is indirect evidence that co-ethnics are not accorded greater trust, at least in homosexual partner choice, disconfirming ethnic nepotism theory. However, the theory was confirmed by Wiessner's finding of preference for kin partners in long-range exchange relationship among the Bushmen, Wang's experimental study of kith-and-kin rationality in risky choices, the review by Burnstein et al. of social psychological studies indicating that humans make decisions according to a kin selection heuristic sensitive to the costs and benefits of helping, Blok's analysis of the centrality of kinship and ethnicity in organizing the Sicilian Mafia, Landa's study of Chinese ethnic middlemen in Malaysia, the finding by Schubert et al. of procedural ethnic bias on the part of Supreme Court justices, and by van den Berghe's analysis of kin and ethnic preferences of tourists.

Several chapters are useful reminders of the limits of kin and ethnic solidarity. These ties can be broken by oppressive regimes (Strungaru) and forced underground (MacDonald).

This volume opens some interesting lines of inquiry into the role of kinship and ethnicity in negotiating risky transactions. Clearly the need remains for more complete theory and empirical research, and both will benefit from the interdisciplinarity demonstrated in the following chapters.

# References

Alexander, R.D. (1979). *Darwinism and human affairs.* University of Washington Press, Seattle.

Arlacchi, P. (1988). *Mafia business: The Mafia ethic and the spirit of capitalism.* Oxford University Press, Oxford.

Berghe, P.L. van den (1978a). Race and ethnicity: A sociobiological perspective. *Ethnic and Racial Studies,* 1(4), 401–11.

Berghe, P.L. van den (1978b). Bridging the paradigms: Sociobiology and the social sciences. *Society,* **15**(6), 42–9.

Berghe, P.L. van den (1981). *The ethnic phenomenon.* Elsevier, New York.

Berghe, P.L. van den (1990). Why most sociologists don't (and won't) think evolutionarily. *Sociological Forum,* 5(2), 173–85.

Berghe, P.L. van den (1995). Does race matter? *Nations and Nationalism,* 1(3), 357–68.

Blumenthal, W.M. (1998). *The invisible wall: Germans and Jews, a personal exploration.* Counterpoint, New York.

Bonacich, E. (1973). A theory of middleman minorities. *American Sociological Review,* **38**, 583–94.

Campbell, D.T. (1965). Ethnocentric and other altruistic motives. In *Nebraska symposium on motivation, Vol. 13,* (ed. D. Levine), pp. 283–311. University of Nebraska Press, Lincoln.

Darwin, C. (1978/1859). Neuter insects. In *The sociobiology debate: Readings on the ethical and scientific issues concerning sociobiology*, (ed. A.L. Caplan), pp. 17–22. Harper & Row, New York.

Degler, C. (1991). *In search of human nature: The decline and revival of Darwinism in American social thought*. Oxford University Press, Oxford.

Eibl-Eibesfeldt, I. (1970). *Liebe und Hass. Zur Naturgeschichte elementarer Verhaltensweisen [Love and hate. The natural history of behaviour patterns]*. Piper, München.

Eibl-Eibesfeldt, I. (1989). *Human ethology*. Aldine de Gruyter, New York.

Eibl-Eibesfeldt, I. (1998). Us and the others: The familial roots of ethnonationalism. In *Indoctrinability, ideology, and warfare: Evolutionary perspectives*, (eds I. Eibl-Eibesfeldt and F.K. Salter). Berghahn, Oxford and New York, pp. 21–53.

Fisher, R.A. (1958/1930). *The genetical theory of natural selection*. (2nd edn). Dover, New York.

Fox, R. (1989). *Search for society: Quest for a biosocial science and morality*. Rutgers University Press, New Brunswick, NJ.

Haldane, J.B.S. (1932). *The causes of evolution*. Longmans, London.

Hamilton, W.D. (1964). The genetic evolution of social behavior, parts 1 and 2. *Journal of Theoretical Biology*, **7**, 1–51.

Hamilton, W.D. (1971). Selection of selfish and altruistic behavior in some extreme models. In *Man and beast: comparative social behavior*, (eds J.F. Eisenberg and W. S. Dillon), Smithsonian Institute Press, Washington, DC.

Hess, H. (1990). Die sizilianische Mafia: ein Beispiel der Männerwelt des organisierten Verbrechens. In *Männer Bande Männe Bünde. Zur Rolle des Mannes im Kulturvergleich*, (ed. G. Völger and K. v. Welck), pp. 113–20. Rautenstrauch-Joest-Museum Köln, Köln.

Ianni, F.A.J. (1972). *A family business: Kinship and social control in organized crime*. Russell Sage Foundation, New York.

Ianni, F.A.J. (1974). *Black Mafia: Ethnic succession in organized crime*. Simon and Schuster, New York.

Landa, J.T. (1981). A theory of the ethnically homogeneous middleman group: an institutional alternative to contract law. *Journal of Legal Studies*, **10**(June), 349–62.

Landa, J.T. (1994). *Trust, ethnicity, and identity. Beyond trading networks, contract law, and gift-exchange*. Michigan University Press, Ann Arbor.

Light, I. and Karageorgis, S. (1994). The ethnic economy. In *The handbook of economic sociology*, (eds N.J. Smelser and R. Swedberg), pp. 647–71. Princeton University Press, Princeton.

MacDonald, K. (1994). *A people that shall dwell alone: Judaism as a group evolutionary strategy*. Praeger, Westport, CT.

MacDonald, K.B. (1998a). *Separation and its discontents: Toward an evolutionary theory of anti-Semitism*. Praeger, Westport, CT.

MacDonald, K.B. (1998b). *The culture of critique: An evolutionary analysis of Jewish involvement in twentieth-century intellectual and political movements*. Praeger, Westport, CT.

Masters, R.D. (in preparation). Why welfare states rise – and fall: Ethnicity, belief systems, and environmental influences on the support for public goods. In *Welfare, ethnicity, and altruism. New data and evolutionary theory*, (ed. F.K. Salter), forthcoming.

Rose, S., Lewontin, R.C. and Kamin, L.J. (1984). *Not in our genes. Biology, ideology and human nature*. Pelican, Harmondsworth.

Salter, F.K. (1996). Sociology as alchemy. *Skeptic*, **4**(1), 50–59.

Salter, F.K. (2001). A defense and an extension of Pierre van den Berghe's theory of ethnic nepotism. In *Evolutionary theory and ethnic conflict* (eds. D. Goetze and P. James), pp. 39–70, Praeger, Westport, CT.

Sarkar, S. (1992). Science, philosophy, and politics in the work of J.B.S. Haldane, 1922–1937. *Biology and Philosophy*, **7**, 385–409.

Sherif, M. (1951). Experimental study of intergroup relations. In *Social psychology at the crossroads*, (eds. J.H. Rohrer and M. Sherif), Harper & Row, New York.

Sime, J.D. (1983). Affiliative behaviour during escape to building exits. *Journal of Environmental Psychology*, **3**, 21–41.

Simis, K.M. (1982). *USSR: The corrupt society. The secret world of Soviet capitalism*. (trans. J. Edwards and Mitchell Schneider). Simon & Schuster, New York.

Waddington, C.H. (1978/1975). Mindless societies [originally published in *The New York Review of Books*, 7 August 1975]. In *The sociobiology debate: Readings on the ethical and scientific issues concerning sociobiology*, (ed. A.L. Caplan), pp. 17–22. Harper & Row, New York.

Wiessner, P. (1982). Risk, reciprocity and social influences on !Kung San economics. In *Politics and history in band societies*, (eds E. Leacock and R. Lee), pp. 61–84. Cambridge University Press, Cambridge.

Williams, P. (1996). Introduction: How serious a threat is Russian organized crime? *Transnational Organized Crime*, **2**(2/3) [Special double issue: *Russian organized crime: the new threat?*], 1–27.

Wilson, E.O. (1975). *Sociobiology: The new synthesis*. Harvard University Press, Cambridge, MA.

# Notes

1. The fit between fact and evolutionary theory is so striking in the case of ethnic crime that it is fair to ask why the connection has not previously been remarked in the social sciences. The probable reason for this omission is that for much of the twentieth century social scientists have divorced themselves from biology. Reconciliation is, however, under way (Degler 1991). The insights offered by new discoveries about human biology, including human evolutionary history, are so compelling that more sociologists, anthropologists, and psychologists are taking a second (often a first) look at humans as an evolved species. After many decades a healthy reductionism is slowly replacing the sociological dogma that forbade using psychology or biology to explain social phenomena (van den Berghe 1978b, 1990; Fox 1989; Salter 1996). By reductionism I mean the basic analytic strategy, fundamental to the natural sciences, of describing and explaining complex phenomena in terms of simpler constituent parts. "Reductionism" is criticized in sociology for two reasons. Following

Durkheim, any attempt to explain social facts in terms of psychological, biological or other non-social causes is deemed to lie outside the purview of sociology. This objection is an expression of academic territoriality rather than philosophy, and so carries no epistemic weight. More seriously, reductionism is also defined as the attempt to explain complex social phenomena in terms of a single cause. This is often a good criticism, but of explanatory monism rather than of reductive analysis. The latter is a broader scientific strategy that is not committed to identifying single causes.

2.  This neo-Darwinian synthesis has by no means settled all disputes, and the field is alive with debates both theoretical and empirical. The field of human evolutionary research is at least as tumultuous, in part because our species' behaviour is complicated by culture and partly because beliefs about human origins and limitations touch on religious, ethical, and political issues.

3.  Considering the fervent Marxist criticism of neo-Darwinism (e.g. Rose et al. 1984), it is ironic that Haldane himself was a long-term Marxist (Sarkar 1992).

4.  "Insofar as it makes for the survival of one's descendants and near relations, altruistic behaviour is a kind of Darwinian fitness, and may be expected to spread as a result of natural selection" (J.B.S. Haldane, 1932, *The causes of evolution*, p. 131, quoted by Waddington 1978/1975, p. 254).

5.  Darwin's problem explaining sterile castes of social insects becomes evident in his chapter on the "Neuter Insects" in *Origins of the Species*, where he fails to fully comprehend the difficulty posed to his theory. "[I]f such insects had been social, and it had been profitable to the community that a number should have been annually born capable of work, but incapable of procreation, I can see no very great difficulty in this being effected by natural selection. But I must pass over this preliminary difficulty. The great difficulty lies [in radically different phenotypes]" (Darwin 1978/1859, pp. 17–18). Because he did not have a genetic theory, Darwin could not get beyond the vague notion that the sterile castes were "profitable to the community"; and was conceptually unprepared for the insight of inclusive fitness theory – that altruism is adaptive because it boosts the representation of altruistic genes in the next generation via the offspring of close relatives, in the case of insects, queens.

# ETHNOGRAPHY

## CHAPTER 2

# TAKING THE RISK OUT OF RISKY TRANSACTIONS

## A FORAGER'S DILEMMA

### *Polly Wiessner*

For the better part of our evolutionary history as foragers, the well-being of any individual rested heavily in the hands of others.[1] With no grain in the larder, no meat stored on the hoof, and no money in the bank, humans had little option other than to build savings in the form of social ties that could be drawn on to cover unforeseen losses caused by environmental or social hazards. Relationships bearing mutual obligations were well distributed over the population, so that in times of hardship losses could be absorbed by others. In other words risk, the probability of loss, was pooled within social networks.

Though ties of mutual obligation can be used effectively to reduce risks, they generate risks of their own – those of defection, debt, or dominance. In this paper, I address the issue of how risky transactions are handled within forager social security systems. First, I will very briefly review some of the archaeological evidence for the evolution of kinship systems and the social security networks they form, suggesting that such ties are deeply rooted in our past. Then I will focus on two questions regarding risky transactions: (1) What is done in foraging societies to define the terms of relationships of reciprocal altruism in such a way that if defection occurs, losses are relatively low? (2) Given that not all risks can be alleviated by carefully defining terms of relationships, how are partners chosen and relationships monitored to remove as much risk as possible from risky transactions? To address the former, I will draw on material from a number of modern foraging societies. For the latter, I will examine the effects of social and biological kinship, relationship history, social sanctions, and emotional bonds in securing partnerships of reciprocity amongst the Ju/'hoansi (!Kung San) foragers of southern Africa. Data from 1974–5, when hunting and gathering constituted the dominant mode of subsistence and environmental hazards were high, will be compared with those from the 1996–7, when the Ju/'hoansi were permanently settled at boreholes with insecurities in food and water supply alleviated by government and foreign aid programmes.

## Forager social networks: a glimpse into the past

The evolution of socially defined kinship networks that opened access to the resources of people outside the family and outside the residential group had an important impact on the ability of hominids to expand into and survive in niches with harsh environments and high variability in natural resources. Losses due to fluctuations in natural resources, inability to find mates, and conflict could then be absorbed by a broader population, as people redistributed themselves over social and natural resources according to availability and need (Cashdan 1985; Myers 1988; Smith 1988; Testart 1982; Wiessner 1977, 1982 ; Yengoyan 1968). With the advent of socially defined kinship, that is to say, the extension of kinship terms and nurturant behaviour from family members to more distant kin and to those related through marriage, support groups were no longer delimited by immediate family membership or physical cohabitation. Instead this wider definition of kinship allowed networks to be held "in the mind and heart", composed of kin of varying degrees of relatedness residing in different locations. Today all human societies have systems to classify kin by social means and the number of elementary systems of kinship classification systems is finite (Levi-Strauss 1969). In all human kinship systems, transactions bear risks; regulating these consumes much time and adds much spice to social relations.

Cognitive and behavioural prerequisites for systems of socially defined kinship that form and act to reduce risk include abilities to: (1) categorize and symbolize; (2) engage in relationships of delayed reciprocal altruism; and (3) treat less familiar individuals like family members even though their habits, behaviour, or ideas may seem foreign or even repellent. While kinship systems in and of themselves leave few traces in the archaeological record, there is some evidence regarding the evolution of the above capacities which might give some clues as to when socially defined kinship systems could have first entered the repertoire of human behaviour.

There is increasing evidence from the Lower and Middle Paleolithic indicating that hominids could long have had the capacity to symbolize (Marshack 1990; see also Bednarik 1995 for a good, though controversial, summary). This has led to a revision of the view that the Middle to the Upper Paleolithic transition (between *ca.* 30,000 and 40,000 B.P.) was abrupt with the sudden appearance of modern humans and their capacity for sophisticated manipulation of symbols and complex language (Klein 1973; Mellars 1973; White 1982) in favour of a much longer and more gradual transition from the Middle to Upper Paleolithic (McBrearty and Brooks 2000; Hayden 1993; Lindley and Clark 1990; Rigaud 1989). Nonetheless, examples of symbolic behavior in material remains that do exist from the Middle Paleolithic occur at low frequencies, and artefacts found exhibit little continuity or redundancy in form, suggesting that the social matrix in which they flourished had not yet congealed. Only in the early Upper Paleolithic (Aurignacian) is symbolic and stylistic expression in non-lithic artifacts and pierced pendants used for self-decoration found in larger quantities and on a regular basis (Taborin 1993; White 1989, 1993). Since expression of personal identity or worth via style and self-decoration would hardly be needed in small face-to-face residential groups where individuals knew one another well, the advent of self-decorative artefacts in volume may be an indication of increasing positive self-presentation to outsiders via symbolic means rather than physical display.

The extension of familial or "altruistic" behaviour directed towards more distant kin most likely evolved very gradually. In the Middle Paleolithic the widespread distribution of raw materials from a source may suggest importation by intergroup exchange. By the early upper Paleolithic a very substantial body of data from both western and eastern Europe concerning the long distance movement of goods and valuables indicates that intergroup ties of reciprocity were indeed active (see Gamble 1982; 1986, pp. 331–8, and 1999). Though results vary by area, the general trend is from a virtual absence of imported raw material in the Lower Paleolithic to the regular importation of raw materials and shells in significant proportions from sources 100–300 km. away during the upper Paleolithic, as kinship networks expanded to become a critical part of human adaptation.

Finally, the construction of socially defined kinship networks must overcome the formidable barrier of acting against immediate self-interest in anticipation of delayed returns and treating those with whom one is not so familiar as close kin. It is in this context that indoctrinability, the predisposition to be inculcated with loyalties that run contrary to immediate individual interest, may have entered the human behavioural repertoire. Certainly all relations of social kinship found today rely on some form of indoctrination to instil feelings of obligation or loyalty towards persons outside the immediate family, often through ritual. The flourishing of art in the Upper Paleolithic may have been a part of private or public ritual to standardize norms and values between people or groups and thereby facilitate the interaction and exchange that reproduce kinship relations (Wiessner 1998). Barton et al. (1994, p. 201) have argued persuasively that:

> Prior to the last glaciation, human populations appear to have displayed a very different response to environmental stress and loss of land area than is seen in the late Pleistocene. Europe, and presumably other middle latitude temperate regions of the Old World, were largely abandoned by human populations during glacial maxima in the Middle Pleistocene. In the Upper Palaeolithic, however, social mechanisms

evolved that permitted the maintenance of higher population densities that in turn resulted in the appearance of extra-familial corporate groups.

There is a vast amount of archaeological data relevant to the above topics, and current interpretations are by no means definitive. However, it seems reasonable to infer, based on strong evidence that first appears in the Middle to Upper Paleolithic transition, the evolution of socially defined kinship networks and their risky transactions that, when structured appropriately, served to reduce risk.

## The terms of forager ties

Designing the terms and obligations underlying social relationships to pool risk can do much to diminish investment, increase the probability of appropriate and timely reciprocation, and avoid incurring debt without compromising the effectiveness of such ties for covering serious losses. Certain common terms of relationships designed to do so characterize social systems of foraging groups throughout the world. The first is that the terms of exchange relationships within the population that pools risk approximate what Sahlins (1972) has called generalized reciprocity: that the one who *has* gives to the one who is in *need* (provided that the need is real). Returns occur when the donor is in need and when the recipient has the means to give; they are not stipulated by time, quality or quantity but by need and ability to fill it. Such loosely defined terms, though most suitable for covering unpredictable losses, are not without problems: establishing who has what, who is in need, and if the need is real are issues that fuel a good part of the daily social action in forager societies. The ramifications of these terms are enormous. For one, they do not permit sanctions to be levelled against a person who does not have anything to give for the moment. Second, they inhibit one person from putting another into debt, debt that may not be repayable for a long time if environmental or social conditions remain unfavourable. People have no obligation to reciprocate until they become haves, and so the only way for "haves" to avoid exploitation is to conceal what they do have or cease work, become have-nots, and as such claim reciprocation under the guise of need (Lee 1979; Myers 1988; Wiessner 1982). It does not take long before the free rider gets the message.

Second, it is generally not the obligation of the receiver to voluntarily reciprocate, but the obligation of the giver to make the receiver want to do so, or to demand that he or she do so. Generosity is not defined as unsolicited giving but as giving when legitimately requested. Peterson (1993), in an excellent discussion of terms of sharing relationships for foraging societies, describes forager sharing as "demand sharing". Social controls are built into demand sharing that nip stinginess or wilful non-reciprocation in the bud, as people pester those who have, particularly if return is due.

Third, and related, social ties to reduce risk are structured, whenever possible, so that the cost of giving assistance is small relative to its benefit to the receiver. For instance, if the resources in the area of one family fail totally and they take refuge with kinsmen for an extended period, the cost for the host family of open-ing their resources to temporary use by kin is small in relation to the value of the assistance given to the visitors. Or, a piece of meat given from a large animal is usually of far greater value to the meat-hungry recipient than to the meat-rich giver.

Fourth, relationships in all forager risk-reducing kinship networks operate within a matrix of egalitarian relations. On the one hand, forager societies encourage individual expression and individual difference – the greater the range of abilities fostered in a population, the greater its potential to absorb losses. On the other, egalitarian ethics define all people as having more or less equal rights to status and resources, regardless of individual ability. Egalitarianism, in turn, has powerful long-term implications for the costs of reciprocity, for giving takes place with the knowledge that the recipient cannot use assistance received to gain disproportionate social, economic, or reproductive advantage, to usurp the resources of others, or otherwise dominate them. Those who seek to do so are quickly levelled.

The above terms of reciprocity, held within populations that pool risk, make their characteristic marks on forager economies by inhibiting competition and capital accumulation. They are found with remarkable consistency in forager groups from the Arctic to Australia and guide internal relations, though a wide variety of different relationships may exist with outsiders (Altman and Peterson 1998; Bahuchet 1990, 1992; Bird-David 1990; von Bremen 1991; Clastres 1972; Endicott 1988; Gould 1981; Griffin 1984; Harako 1981; Heinz 1979; Ichikawa 1983 ; Kent 1993; Lee 1979; Marshall 1976; Myers 1988; Sharp 1977, 1981; Silberbauer 1981a, 1981b; van der Sluys 1993; Sugawara 1988; Tanaka 1980; Turnbull 1965; Williams 1974; Woodburn 1982). Though effective for pooling risk, such terms cannot eliminate all risks from relationships. Fortune may cause one partner to be a have and another a have-not for extended periods of time. Cost to the giver might not always be low in relation to benefit to the receiver – in times of great hunger, resource sharing is always costly. Though society sees that assistance given is not used to achieve disproportionate economic or reproductive advantage, it still serves to increase the recipient's welfare and relative success.

Despite the costs of risk-sharing, individuals cannot survive on their own as foragers, and the capable and incapable alike must remain in the system even if it is only to survive a few severe crises in their lives that would otherwise lead to death. How then are the unavoidable risks minimized?

Kin selection theory would predict that when risky relationships cannot be avoided, close kin would be favoured in direct proportion to their degree of relat-edness, because by helping kin one receives both economic and genetic "pay-offs". There are many statements in the forager literature that attest to the fact that kin are the ones most likely to engage in sharing and other forms of delayed reciproc-ity that serve to pool risk. However, it is difficult to infer from these to what extent biological relatedness plays a role, for human kinship systems permit familial terms to be extended to distant kin. Here I will address this issue and try to: (1) assess the effect of genetically based kinship on choice of partners; and (2) explore which factors, in the absence of close kin ties, help secure productive, long-term reciprocity between more distant kin.

## Risk reduction among the Ju/'hoansi in the 1970s

The Ju/'hoansi or !Kung San of N.W. Botswana and N.E. Namibia have been well documented in the work of Biesele (1990, 1993),Howell (1979), Lee (1979, 1986, 1993), Lee (1979,1986,1993), Lee and DeVore (1976), Marshall (1976), Shostak (1981), Wiessner (1977, 1982), and Yellen (1977) amongst many others. Since at least the nineteenth century and particularly since the 1950s, Ju/'hoansi life has been altered with every decade as they increasingly entered into interaction with surrounding populations (see Wilmsen 1989 and Gordon 1992 for excellent discussions of prehistoric and historic San contacts with surrounding populations).

In the mid-1970s, the Ju/'hoansi of the Dobe-/Kae/kae area of N.W. Botswana were primarily foragers (Map 2.1). Eighty five percent of subsistence was obtained from gathering, 12 percent from hunting, and 3 percent was acquired from neigh-bouring agro-pastoralists (Wilmsen 1989, p. 240). Both meat and vegetables were widely shared. Settlement patterns within a band's area of land rights (*n!ore*) con-sisted of dispersal into small scattered camps during the wet season and aggrega-tion at large camps during the dry season. While food was plentiful in the mid- and late wet season, Ju/'hoansi suffered shortages in the drier months, particularly as overgrazing by the herds of neighbouring agro-pastoralists destroyed bush foods. Environmental risks were high. Permanent waters were few and drought made many resources inaccessible for much of the year. Moreover, there were consider-able fluctuations in the yearly production of wild vegetable foods (Yellen and Lee 1976) as well as variation in game movement and hunting success (Wilmsen 1989). Plant foods such as nutritious mongongo nuts and morama beans were unevenly distributed, being abundant in some areas and totally absent 20–30 km. away. Other risks stemmed from demographic fluctuations in the small Bushman pop-ulation (Howell 1979) and from conflict which was usually settled by dispersal. In the 1970s the Ju/'hoansi constructed far-flung social networks which opened access to the resources of others, so that unpredictable losses could be absorbed by the broader population. They did so through kinship and a system of partnerships called *xaro* (*hxaro* in former publications).

The !Kung kinship system and its relation to *xaro* works as follows. Ju/'hoansi first define their kinship universe through conventional kin terms, an "Eskimo" system of classification which reflects some aspects of biological kinship in that nuclear family members are distinguished from collaterals and the majority of in-law terms are distinct from consanguineous kin, except for wife's sister and brother's wife. Standard !Kung kinship terms are structured by relative age and generation, and each term carries with it a relationship of joking or respect that delimits eligibility for marriage and a range of permitted behaviour (Lee 1986). Kin terms can then be extended to more distant relatives who share their name or names of family members via the name relationship (Marshall 1976). The name

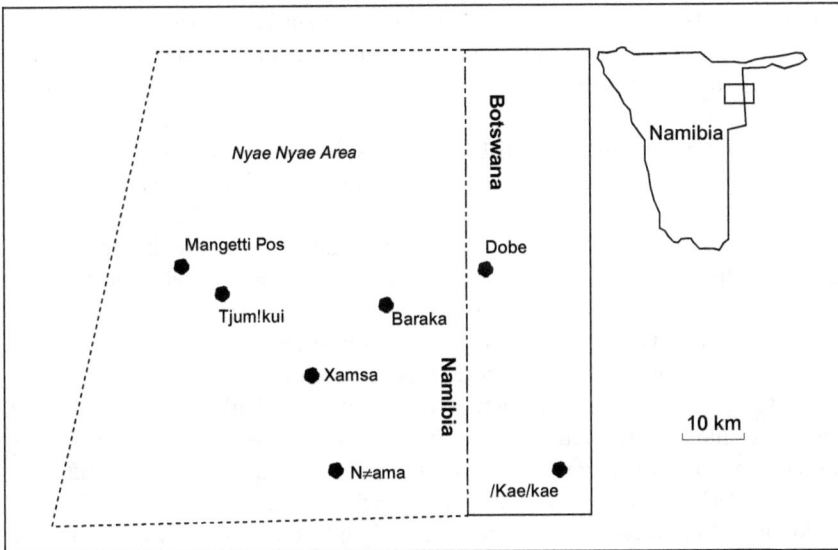

**Map 2.1** Location of places mentioned in text. In the 1974–5 study, people were interviewed at Dobe, /Kae/kae and Tjum!kui, and in the 1996–7 study, at Xamsa, N≠ama and Mangetti Pos. There were thirty-two villages in the Nyae Nyae area in 1997, of these only five are shown.

relationship thus destroys the logic of standard kinship, and continues to do so as demographic events add ever new names to a person's kinship repertoire. The discrepancy between conventional kinship terms and those applied via the name relationship is resolved by a principle called "*wi*" in which elders choose, amongst possibilities afforded by standard kinship and the name relationship, the terms that they wish to apply to juniors. Thus it is elders who have the potential to manipulate kinship. After these three principles of kinship, *xaro* comes into play (Wiessner 1994). Kinship terms and corresponding relations of joking or respect determine to a limited extent only who has obligations to whom; through *xaro* Ju/'hoansi further activate the responsibilities of kinship and specify with whom they want to have more binding commitments. For a *xaro* bond to be created, a consanguineous kinship link must be identified.

Xaro partners, as persons selected from the wide range of available kin, "hold each other in their hearts" and engage in a relationship with two components. The one is a roughly balanced, delayed, reciprocal exchange of non-food gifts – beads, arrows, tools, clothing – that gives information about the status of the relationship and reinforces emotional bonds. The second component of the *xaro* is an underlying relationship of mutual responsibility in many areas of life. A person has the right to call on a *xaro* partner in times of need, whether the need be precipitated by environmental failure, conflict, personal disability, or inability to find a suitable marriage partner. If the partner is able, he or she will assist. While *xaro* does serve to appease jealousies and reinforce sharing within a camp, its more important role is to open up alternate residences in neighbouring or distant groups that can be utilized for extended visiting in times of need. Ju/'hoansi reciprocity in general and *xaro* in particular, are constantly monitored and defection corrected before it leads to serious strife. For example, in conversations lasting more than fifteen minutes recorded in August 1974, 59 percent involved availability of food in other areas, food procurement or food redistribution – who had what and did or did not give it to whom. Complaining is a fine art mastered with age, but when bickering and pestering reach an intolerable level, social harmony is renewed during the trance dance, a metaphor of sharing. Men and women gather in the evening to sing and dance in support of healers who enter into a state of trance, travel to the world of the spirits, fend off misfortune and bring back preventative energy (*n/om*) to share with all community members (Katz 1982, Katz et al 1997).

As with kinship, Ju/'hoansi spheres of *xaro* develop with age (Wiessner 1982). A child is given *xaro* gifts by a maternal or paternal grandfather within the first six months of life to foster well-being. At the age of one to two, symbolic training for *xaro* begins when the parents periodically remove the child's beads, and put them in the child's hand to give to a relative, often inciting a tantrum. During childhood, children do *xaro* directly with parents, grandparents, or one or two maternal or paternal relatives with whom they have close bonds, while the parents may carry out *xaro* with others in the child's name. Maternal and paternal relatives invest equally in children, and there is concern with constructing *xaro* networks for boys and girls alike. During adolescence, young people expand their spheres of *xaro* within the camp and with relatives in other camps. By the time of first marriage most Ju/'hoansi have formed well-rounded sets of *xaro* partnerships. Should problems arise and the marriage shatter, each spouse has enough ties to stand on his or her own. Upon marriage, *xaro* ties are considered binding and a certain proportion of gifts received are expected to be passed on to the spouse who then gives them to his or her relatives, forming a link between the two families. If one spouse dies, the other may continue *xaro* directly with close affines of the deceased. As Ju/'hoansi approach middle age they enter a stage of great vitality, mobility, and social influence, seeking marriage partners for their children, assisting their children during the early years of marriage, and taking over responsibility from their ageing parents. At this time they almost double their set of *xaro* partners. In old age, as their mobility and energy decrease and their eyesight wanes, elders hand over some of their partnerships to their children. Still, as masters in knowledge of kinship and land rights, they continue to receive many gifts. Upon death a few possessions are buried with the deceased but most are taken and passed on to remaining partners with a request for return on the part of the children or grandchildren so that ties will not be broken.

During the 1970s, *xaro* networks distributed goods widely throughout the region, extending access to meat sharing to those outside a camp (Wiessner 1981), and most importantly, opening up access to the resources and assistance of partners over a broad region. *Xaro* partnerships were well distributed over people living within a radius of 200 km. of the study area and practising different ways of making a living – hunting and gathering, working for pastoralists, or residing in the settlement scheme of Tsumkwe set up by the South African administration which offered a store, school, clinic, possibilities for wage labour, and agricultural projects (Wiessner 1977, 1982). !Kung regularly made extended visits to *xaro* partners when food in their own areas was short, when seeking refuge after conflict, for arranging marriages, or while looking for jobs, amongst other reasons. A survey of the visits made by 20 !Kung adults in 1968[2] and 1974 of one week or longer in duration revealed that the average !Kung made 1.5 extended visits a year with a mean duration of 2.2 months per visit. Eighty out of the 86 visits recorded (93 percent) were made to a camp in which a person or his/her spouse had a *xaro* partner (Wiessner 1981, 1986). This means that for approximately three months a year, families lived from the resources of *xaro* partners, being hosted for the first few days and then hunting and gathering for their own living and participating in food sharing within the camp.

Reciprocity in *xaro* bears its own risks because individuals may be unable to be of assistance at any given time due to bouts of illness, absence from their own areas, shortages of resources, etc. Moreover, *xaro* relationships may be costly in terms of assistance given, resources shared, and time taken to maintain relationships and exchange gifts. For example, in the 1970s approximately five days per year per partner were spent making gifts for *xaro* or earning cash to buy gifts for *xaro* (Wiessner 1986). *Xaro* is also a relationship that opens people to exploitation, something which is constantly monitored by gossip, or when gossip fails, by efforts to become a "have not" by either concealing goods or limiting production. *Xaro* exchange also bears social risks – to give a gift may bring great pleasure to the recipient but incite jealousy in others. For all of these reasons, numerous options are secured by distributing partnerships widely – in the 1970s the average !Kung had 15–16 *xaro* partnerships which included people of both sexes, a variety of ages, living at different locations, and having different skills (Wiessner 1981, 1982). Within a person's lifetime, the process of forming new partnerships takes at least five years before the relationship is considered solid; conversely, existing ones may dwindle if both parties lose interest. Breaking of partnerships by intentional non-reciprocation is unusual, but when it does occur it causes serious social strife.

## *Xaro* and kin selection

Though hospitality of varying degrees, particularly the sharing of cooked food, may be extended to any kinsperson or even casual visitor, more binding relations and thus more risky ones fall within *xaro*. Following kin selection theory then, the probability of choosing partners should be proportionate to genetic relatedness. That is:

$$P_{1/2} > P_{1/4} > P_{1/8} > P_{1/16} > P_{1/32}+$$

where $P_{1/2}$ = the probability of doing *xaro* with an individual whose coefficient of relatedness, r, (Hamilton 1964) is ½ or 50 percent. $P_{1/4}$, $P_{1/8}$ and $P_{1/32}$ are defined similarly and $P_{1/32}+$ is the probability of doing *xaro* with an individual whose coefficient of relatedness to ego is $1/32$ or less.

The alternate hypothesis would be that the probability of doing *xaro* with people of all degrees of relatedness is equal:

$$P_{1/2} = P_{1/4} = P_{1/8} = P_{1/16} = P_{1/32}+$$

To test this hypothesis the number of *xaro* partners in each category of relatedness was counted and the number of individuals available for *xaro* in each category of r from $r=1/2$ to $r=1/16$ were calculated from ego's genealogy. Number of distant kin, $r=1/32+$, eligible for *xaro* had to be estimated. Since *xaro* required prior friendship and a putative consanguineous tie, it was not assumed that anybody in the surrounding population of some 2,000 was eligible. The average surrounding area contains 150–500 people, so it was estimated that a person knew at least 25 distant kin in his or her own area and 25 in each other surrounding area well enough to initiate *xaro*. Since knowledge of people in other areas increases with age and travel, an adolescent was assumed to know a minimum of 50 and maximum of 100 distant kin well enough to do *xaro*, adults with small children 50–150, and adults with mature children and older adults 50–200.

The data used to test this hypothesis come from a quantitative study of the *xaro* partners of 59 Ju/'hoansi carried out in 1974–5 from the communities of /Kae/kae and Dobe in N.W. Botswana and Tjum!kui in N.E. Namibia. The genealogy of each person in the sample was collected and then he or she was interviewed about the terms and rights of *xaro* relationships, and how they were regulated. Then ego was asked to list all *xaro* partners and give their age, sex, current location, area of land rights, and kinship relation to ego. These interviews provided data on 956 partnerships. Subsequently, each possession of ego was listed with information about how it was acquired (in *xaro*, purchased, made, etc.), from whom, and in the case of gifts, the age, sex, location and kin relation of the giver.

The results presented in Table 2.1 give strong support to the kin selection hypothesis. For all age categories, the probability of choosing a genetically close *xaro* partner was greater than that of choosing a more distant one: the alternatve

**Table 2.1** Average percent of individuals related to ego by $r=1/2$, $1/4$, $1/8$, $1/16$, and $1/32+$ who are *xaro* partners. (n=number of individuals in the sample for whom complete data on the number of kin in a given category are available.)

| Coefficient of relatedness | $r=1/2$ | $r=1/4$ | $r=1/8$ | $r=1/16$ | $r=1/32+$ |
|---|---|---|---|---|---|
| Adolescents | 93% | 45% | 26% | 8% | 5–10% |
| n= | 10 | 10 | 10 | 9 | 10 |
| Adults with small children | 92 % | 55% | 36% | 17% | 6–12% |
| n= | 27 | 27 | 26 | 13 | 27 |
| Adults with mature children | 98% | 59% | 43% | 24% | 7–27% |
| n= | 14 | 14 | 12 | 11 | 14 |
| Old, partially dependent adults | 90% | 39% | 24% | 9% | 2–10% |
| n= | 8 | 8 | 6 | 6 | 8 |
| Total | 93% | 52% | 34% | 15% | 5–15% |
| n= | 59 | 59 | 54 | 39 | 59 |

hypothesis was refuted (Page's L trend test, one-tailed, p<0.001). Kin with coefficients of relatedness up to r=¹⁄₁₆ made up 54 percent of a person's *xaro* partners. Nonetheless, despite a strong tendency to favour kin, 46 percent of a person's *xaro* partners were distant kin.

That the vast majority of a person's *xaro* partners were not closely related in genetic terms is not surprising given the role of *xaro* in reducing risk. First, many people have few kin and must seek partners among more distant relatives. Second, though kin may be the best investment in genetic terms, if they are not capable of helping a person to absorb losses, they are not of great economic value as partners. Third, as the Ju/'hoansi point out, it is close kin who are sometimes the poorest at reciprocation, for they know the strength of the family bond will allow for much leniency. Fourth, the success of *xaro* partnerships depends heavily on affective ties. Partners, kin or non-kin, who do not get along, can hardly live together for extended periods of time. This raises the questions of who were distantly related *xaro* partners and how were relations with them made more secure?

## *Xaro*, socially defined kin, and history

The next logical step in looking at choice of *xaro* partners is to turn to the second principle of kinship, the name relationship. To see if choice of partners was preferentially structured by the name relationship, the names of ego and family members, mother, father, and siblings were obtained from ego's genealogy. (Ego and siblings in turn are generally named after grandparents or parents' siblings.) Relative frequency of names in the population (P1) was calculated from census data for 700 Ju/'hoansi in the area and surrounding ones where most *xaro* partners were found. Expected frequencies were then calculated for each ego and each category of relationship and compared to actual frequency of these names in ego's set of *xaro* partners who are distant kin (r=¹⁄₃₂+).[3] The results, as given in Table 2.2, indicate that names of close relatives are found no more frequently in ego's set of *xaro* partners than in the population as a whole; Ju/'hoansi did not appear to do *xaro* preferentially with name relatives. This does not mean that the name rela-

**Table 2.2** Expected and observed frequencies for choice of *xaro* partners related to ego by r=¹⁄₃₂ or less according to predictions made from the name relationship for 59 Ju/'hoansi of the Dobe, /Kae/kae and Tjum!kui areas. (Total number of partnerships considered=431).

| | Number of partners sharing name | Number expected on null hypothesis | Number of partners not sharing name | Number expected on null hypothesis | Chi-square values |
|---|---|---|---|---|---|
| Ego's name | 15 | (10.6) | 416 | (420.4) | 1.87 p<.05 |
| Mother's name | 11 | (8.7) | 420 | (422.3) | 0.62 p<.05 |
| Father's name | 12 | (10.0) | 419 | (421.0) | 0.41 p<.05 |
| Sister's name | 9 | (6.5) | 422 | (424.5) | 0.98 p<.05 |
| Brother's name | 8 | (8.1) | 423 | (422.9) | 0.00 p<.05 |

tionship had no effect on Ju/'hoansi exchange relationships, for certainly it widened the sphere of potential kinship interaction, but that its impact on relationships with more binding obligations was not nearly as strong as genetic relatedness.

Who were distantly related partners? A closer analysis of this category reveals that 9 percent are with affinal kin. Though this appears to contradict the Ju/'hoansi claim that all *xaro* partners are consanguineous kin and that people do *xaro* only indirectly with affines via their spouses, in fact the contradiction is minor. Virtually all relationships in this category are between parents, siblings, or children in-law or between step relatives who continued to do *xaro* after the death of the spouse who linked them.

Ju/'hoansi claim that the remaining relationships with distant kin (37 percent of all relationships) are largely ties that have been handed down from parents to children. Because genealogical knowledge is shallow and complete information often does not extend beyond grandparent's descendents for both mother's and father's side of the family, they are unable to place them in their genealogies. However, for thirteen individuals in the sample for whom genealogies could be extended further, 16 percent of more distant partners could be identified on their genealogies as great-grandparents' descendants and another 9 percent as great-great grandparents' descendants. In other words, they were relationships that had been transmitted over three to four generations. Certainly inheritance is well developed in passing on land from generation to generation, and the same inheritance concerns might motivate attempts to secure long-term ties which open access to the land of others. Though one cannot argue that all *xaro* partnerships with distantly related partners are inherited, these figures suggest that history and inheritance are important factors in acquiring partners. There are at least two reasons for this. First, inheritance permits time-tested relationships to be continued – time-tested in terms of both the hospitality of the host group and the potential of the land owned by partners to have adequate complementary resources when those in ego's area are short. Second, ties with a long history of success cannot be easily replicated – Ju/'hoansi say that inherited relationships are therefore handled with the greatest care.

In summary, in the 1970s, *xaro* partners among the Ju/'hoansi were chosen to cover as wide a variety of losses as possible. The average person had 15–16 partners well distributed across ages, abilities, sex, and land. Risk of non-reciprocation due to inability on the part of specific partners was reduced by investing preferentially in more closely related genetic kin than in more distant ones. When close kin were few or could not satisfy the needs of risk reduction, more distant kin were chosen, often via inheritance. Inheritance of partnerships assured that time-tried relationships were continued. Emotional ties with both close and distant kin played a crucial role in assuring reciprocity and great efforts were made continually to monitor relationships through discussion and immediate complaint. When disharmony rose to intolerable levels, the community was repaired through communal ritual.

## *Xaro* in the 1990s

During the 1970s the Ju/'hoansi in the study population were entering a period of rapid change as the Government of Botswana stepped up programmes of rural development, amongst other initiatives. From 1976 onwards, people of the Dobe-/KaeKae area became recipients of food rations, greatly reducing dependence on hunting and gathering and corresponding mobility. Simultaneously, the growth of herds of pastoralists made hunting and gathering a less viable mode of subsistence. Across the border in the Nyae Nyae area, a Bushman homeland was proclaimed in 1970 and people voluntarily moved to the new centre at Tjum!kui where the South African Government established a settlement scheme that promised secure water, food rations, wage labour, agricultural projects, crafts marketing, a school, a clinic and a store. By 1975, as many as nine hundred Ju/'hoansi, largely from the Nyae Nyae area, were settled at Tjum!kui in government- built concrete bungalows and in more traditional "villages" surrounding Tjum!kui.

With such dense settlement and new economic opportunities, social inequalities began to develop. The pendulum at Tjum!kui swung between a tendency to show off new found wealth, in contravention of egalitarian social norms, and attempts to restore harmony and equalize wealth through giving. Tjum!kui became both a magnet for its wealth and action and the dreaded "place of death" marked by jealousy, conflict, alcohol, and sickness. *Xaro* flourished at Tjum!kui to activate a wide range of kinship ties and redistribute wealth to appease, and when these tactics failed, families went to live with partners in Botswana for months at a time until tensions dissipated. In 1978 and 1979, Ju/'hoansi of the Nyae Nyae area[4] (Tjum!kui) began joining the South African defence force when bases were established in west Bushmanland, a formerly waterless region. Only about 10 percent of the population was employed by the defence force, mostly males of suitable age and physical condition, but others flocked to the vicinity of the bases to reap benefits – cash from the employed, schooling, medicine, well-stocked stores, electronic entertainment, and so on. Pay was very high by Ju/'hoan standards, and previously unknown amounts of money poured into the area to be circulated in *xaro* networks and spent on alcohol, clothing, household goods, radios, phonographs, bicycles, and livestock. This situation was to last for the next ten years.[5]

In the early 1980s, small groups of Ju/'hoansi, repelled by the conditions at Tjum!kui, began to move back to their traditional lands. These initiatives received strong support from the anthropologists and film makers John Marshall and Claire Ritchie who together with the Ju/'hoansi founded the Nyae Nyae Development Foundation of Namibia. By 1992 over thirty groups had moved back to their traditional areas (Biesele 1990; Lee 1993, Marshall and Ritchie 1984). The Ju/'hoansi formed the Nyae Nyae Farmer's Cooperative in 1989, and drawing on funds raised by the foundation, were able to have bore holes drilled, provide their members with small herds of cattle at highly subsidized prices (Ritchie 1989), initiate agricultural programmes, promote Ju/'hoan literacy in their own language, and organize a crafts marketing programme. Wage labour, upon which many Ju/'hoan families had been dependent in the 1970s and 1980s, virtually ceased (except for a few government jobs at Tjum!kui) and programmes were aimed at self-sufficiency through a mixed economy of agriculture, hunting and gathering, and crafts production. An administrative and training centre was established for the cooperative at Baraka in the early 1990s. Decisions within the cooperative are made by a body of elected leaders representing each of the villages. In 1992 a further step to give Ju/'hoan rights over their resources came from an initiative by the LIFE Program (Living In a Finite Environment) to establish a community based natural resource management conservancy. Over a five-year period U.S.$1,500,000 were to be invested in the area (J. Marshall 1996) for establishing the conservancy and for planning resource utilization. The proceeds were to be returned to communities. The Namibian Government of the 1990s also made inputs into the area. During the better part of the period since independence, the government has provided communities with monthly "relief" rations of maize meal, oil, and beans via an effective distribution system. These rations are sufficient to support households throughout the year, though the Ju/'hoansi consider the diet tedious. Ju/'hoansi over 60 years of age receive monthly pensions.

Today, most Ju/'hoansi in the Nyae Nyae area are settled in permanent villages at boreholes providing secure water. People of the Nyae Nyae area still hunt and gather, but less effectively than in the 1970s since seasonal rounds are no longer made. Preliminary results from subsistence studies in three villages from July 1996 through August 1997 indicate that during the wet season, wild plant foods make up only 20–40 percent of calories consumed and in the dry season less than 10 percent. Meat from wild animals furnishes 15–25 percent of calories in most communities. That balance is made up by food rations of maize meal, beans and oil furnished by the government, tea, sugar, flour and maize meal purchased with cash from pensions or income from sale of crafts, and a minor contribution from local agricultural projects. Relatives across the border in the communities of Dobe and /Kae/kae have also undergone changes in lifestyle with a good part of their diets today coming from famine relief food provided by the government, small-scale agricultural initiatives, employment programs, and income from the sale of crafts. Most risks stemming from environmental fluctuations in water and food supply have thus been eliminated. With the dispersal of the people settled at Tjum!kui back to their former lands, risk of conflict was also alleviated, though the new sedentary lifestyle makes dispersal, the traditional means of conflict resolution, a less desirable option. Nonetheless, in an economy of dependency like that of today risks do remain. One is the occasional failure of programmes that provision Ju/'hoansi – famine relief rations or sale of crafts – which lead to periods of hunger. Despite these risks, conversations noted during evenings around the camp fire during field-work of 1996–8 indicate that for the Ju/'hoansi of the Nyae Nyae are optimistic about what the future will bring (Wiessner 1997). Unrealistic expectations were expressed by many regarding income to be received from conservancy, and perhaps the greatest perceived risk was that other individuals or communities would get more than their share of the wealth. In response, considerable efforts were made to keep up ties with those in other communities and maintain strict rights of equal access to proceeds from developments expected to take place within the population of the Nyae Nyae area.

The nature of risk, both real and perceived, has thus been greatly altered with no new means of risk reduction such as storage practised on a regular basis. With such changes in the profile of risks and permanent settlement, one would expect a decrease in costly *xaro* ties with distant kin in distant areas and increasing reliance on partnerships with close kin that yielded both genetic and economic benefits. To test his hypothesis, data on *xaro* partnerships comparable with those recorded in the 1970s were collected for 60 Ju/'hoansi residing in three villages in the Nyae Nyae area (Map 2.1).[6]

Tables 2.3 and 2.4 compare average number of *xaro* partners and their distribution for 1974–5 and 1996–7. The average number of *xaro* partners has decreased radically from 15.4 in 1974–5 to 6.8 in 1996–7 (Table 2.4), a change which is statistically significant (t-test, .01 level). The spatial extent of *xaro* networks linking individuals has also narrowed. While the average number of partners within a camp has increased very slightly, partnerships with those outside the camp have decreased radically and in proportion to distance (see Table 2.3). With more secure supplies of food and water, the high costs of maintaining ties at a distance are apparently greater than benefits received from such partnerships. To ascertain if reduction in *xaro* ties might be largely due to abandonment of *xaro* by the younger generation, participation in *xaro* by different age groups was compared for 1974–5 and 1996–7. Interestingly in 1974–5 adults with mature children had significantly more *xaro* partners than did adults with young children and old, partially dependent adults (ANOVA, p=.00), while in 1996–7 there were no statistically significant age differences in number of *xaro* partners by age category (ANOVA, p=.55). In

**Table 2.3** Distribution of *xaro* partners by distance from ego in 1975 and 1997.

|  | n | Own camp | 1–25 km. | 26–75 km. | 75 km.+ | Total |
|---|---|---|---|---|---|---|
| **1975** |  |  |  |  |  |  |
| Total number | 35 | 91 | 123 | 245 | 51 | 510 |
| Mean per person |  | 2.6 | 3.5 | 7.0 | 1.5 | 14.6 |
| Percent |  | 18 | 24 | 48 | 10 | 100 |
| **1997** |  |  |  |  |  |  |
| Total number | 60 | 168 | 104 | 120 | 5 | 397 |
| Mean per person |  | 2.9 | 1.8 | 2.1 | 0.1 | 6.9 |
| Percent |  | 43 | 26 | 30 | 1 | 100 |
| Change since 1975 |  | 110% | 51% | 30% | 6% | 47% |

n= number of Ju/'hoansi interviewed;
total number = total number of *xaro* partnerships in each category;
mean per person = mean number of *xaro* partnerships per person;
percent = percent of all *xaro* partnerships in each category;
change since 1975 = mean per person for 1997/mean per person for 1974.
(For 1975, only partners of 35 /Kae/kae Ju/'hoansi are considered as Nyae Nyae Ju/'hoansi were all settled at Tjum!kui as part of the South African development programme.)

**Table 2.4** Genetic relatedness and choice of *xaro* partners in 1975 and 1997.

**1975**

| Relatedness | n | r=½ | r=¼ | r=⅛ | r=¹⁄₁₆+ | Affines | Total |
|---|---|---|---|---|---|---|---|
| Total number | 49 | 149 | 75 | 107 | 357 | 82 | 756 |
| Mean per person | | 3.0 | 1.5 | 2.2 | 7.3 | 1.4 | 15.4 |
| Percent | | 20 | 10 | 14 | 47 | 9 | 100 |

**1997**

| | n | r=½ | r=¼ | r=⅛ | r=¹⁄₁₆+ | Affines | Total |
|---|---|---|---|---|---|---|---|
| Total number | 60 | 136 | 42 | 41 | 116 | 62 | 397 |
| Mean per person | | 2.3 | 0.7 | 0.7 | 2.0 | 1.1 | 6.8 |
| Percent | | 34 | 11 | 10 | 29 | 16 | 100 |

n= number of Ju/'hoansi interviewed;
total number = total number of *xaro* partnerships in each category;
mean per person = mean number of *xaro* partnerships per person;
percent = percent of all *xaro* partnerships in each category

1996–7 Ju/'hoansi of all age categories were maintaining relatively narrow spheres of *xaro*.

Turning to kinship, as would be predicted from kin selection theory, reduction of *xaro* ties was related to coefficient of relatedness (Table 2.4). Though reduction of the number of partners occurred in all categories of relatedness, the greatest occurred with more distant kin. In 1974–5, 20 percent of the average person's partners were related by r=½ and 47 percent by r=¹⁄₁₆+, while in 1996–7 34 percent were related by r=½ and only 29 percent by r=¹⁄₁₆+ (both differences are statistically significant; t-test, p=.00).

In 1996–7 *xaro* still played an important role in the circulation of material goods, through percent of a person's possessions received in *xaro* declined proportionately with number of *xaro* ties. While in 1974–5, 69 percent of possessions were received in *xaro*, 16 percent purchased, 5 percent made, 9 percent received from non-Ju/'hoansi, and 1 percent received as spontaneous gift, in 1996–7, 34 percent of possessions were received in *xaro*, 30 percent purchased, 6 percent made, 14 percent received from non- Ju/'hoansi and 16 percent received as spontaneous gifts. Food sharing like circulation of possessions indicates continuing widespread sharing and reciprocity. Of 297 meals recorded for eight families at Xamsa village between July 1996 and January 1997, 198 or 66 percent of meals were either furnished by others at their hearths or included food contributions from others (Wiessner 1997). Other core principles guiding social relations continue to structure interactions: that the one who *has* gives to the one *in need*; that kinship and history have strong impacts on relationships of sharing and exchange; and that equality and respect of all Ju/'hoansi is staunchly defended. It is these factors that have allowed Ju/'hoansi to pool risk within the broader population for decades and probably centuries. As long as this matrix of relationships, norms, rights, and obligations central to risk-pooling persists, configurations of *xaro* partnerships can be reduced, expanded, or restructured to give Ju/'hoansi access to the resources of others in the population in accord with the problems and possibilities that the future will bring.

## Concluding remarks

Risk pooling strategies similar to those described above are widely found within most forager societies known in the ethnographic record, though the system by which obligations are placed, *xaro*, is specific to the Ju/honasi and perhaps their neighbours the Nharo San (Barnard 1992). However, functional equivalents abound – meat-sharing, name-sharing, and wife-sharing partnerships among Inuit (Balikci 1970; Damas 1972, 1984; Robbe 1989), tribal section systems and prescribed marriage in Australia (Yengoyan 1968), band alliances in the !Xo San (Heinz 1979), or in many forager societies lineage systems or other kinship relations (Bahuchet 1992; Endicott 1988; Griffin 1984; Henry 1941; Meggitt 1962; von Bremen 1991; van der Sluys 1993). In all of these systems there is remarkable consistency in the following terms of relationships. (1) For all foragers internal relations depend on a matrix of egalitarianism and respect, so that assistance given cannot be turned to dominance or used to create indebtedness. (2) The terms of most relationships of mutual support for risk-sharing are that the one who has gives to the one who is in need, and that returns are not stipulated by time, quality, or quantity. (3) Giving is more often than not solicited by request; and requesting is a sign that one still cares (Marshall 1976). (4) Relationships are structured to make assistance given of little cost to the giver in relation to benefit to the receiver. (5) Control of defectors is exercised on a regular basis by the community and the metaphor of widespread reciprocity underwritten by religious ritual (Hayden 1987). (6) Genetically based kinship plays an important role in structuring reciprocity, and when kinship does not suffice, family relations and ethics are extended to more distant kin in the interest of social and economic security. The Ju/'hoansi data indicate that inheritance plays an important role in securing relationships through time, a factor that is rarely mentioned in forager ethnographies. Probably this is mostly due to the ideology of ethnographers, not foragers themselves. Foragers are seen as having "immediate return" economic systems (Barnard and Woodburn 1988; Woodburn 1982), and so questions concerning inheritance are rarely asked beyond those of land ownership. But it is likely that foragers, like all people of the world, are interested in passing on to their children that which has secured them throughout their lives, and that if the question is asked, foragers will be found to reproduce social ties over generations.

Foragers, who depended so heavily on social ties for their very existence over millennia, thus developed a complex social technology for pooling risk and for handling risky relationships. Throughout the course of history, with increasing population, inter-group competition and new techniques for harnessing energy and storing wealth, humans formed ever larger and more complex social groups. Membership in larger social groups confers many benefits, but the greater anonymity of such groups introduces ever more risk into transactions. In constructing larger social groups, some aspects of the forager repertoire of social technologies are expanded, for instance the bonding of larger groups by extending family terms and ethos to distant and non-kin (Eibl-Eibesfeldt 1989). Other aspects of forager relations are difficult to extend beyond small-scale face-to-face groups, for instance terms of relationships that structure giving on the basis of need and ability to provide, have and have not. Nonetheless, since developments build on what already exists, an understanding of forager tactics for dealing with risky transactions can provide a solid foundation for understanding subsequent developments – which aspects of these were abandoned, which preserved, and which expanded or transformed.

## Note on the orthography

Patrick Dickens has published a standard orthography for the Ju/'hoan language in his English-Ju/'hoan, Ju/'hoan-English Dictionary (Rüdiger Köppe Verlag, Cologne, 1994). This has been accepted by the Nyae Nyae Farmer's cooperative. Conforming to Dickens's orthography requires changing spellings so that they deviate from those used in my previous publications. Noteworthy changes are Tjum!kui for Tsumkwe, /Kae/kae for /Xai/xai, and *xaro* for h*xaro*. !Kung has been replaced by Ju/'hoansi which is the dialect group of !Kung speakers to which the central !Kung belong. "Ju/'hoan" is both the singular and adjectival form.

## References

Altman, J. and Peterson, N. (1988). Rights to game and rights to cash among contemporary Australian hunter-gatherers. In *Hunters and gatherers: Property, power and ideology*, (eds T. Ingold, D. Riches and J. Woodburn), pp. 75–94. Berg, Oxford.

Bahuchet, S. (1990). Food sharing among the pygmies of Central Africa. *African Study Monographs*, 11, 27–53.

Bahuchet, S. (1992). Spatial mobility and access to resources among the African Pygmies. In *Mobility and territorality*, (eds M. Casimir and A. Rao), pp. 205–57. Berg, Oxford.

Balikci, A. (1970). *The Netsilik Eskimos*. Natural History Press, Garden City, NJ.

Barnard, A. (1992). *Hunters and herders of Southern Africa: A comparative ethnography of the Khoisan peoples*. Cambridge University Press, Cambridge.

Barnard, A. and Woodburn, J. (1988). Property, power and ideology in hunting-gathering societies: An introduction. In *Hunters and gatherers: Property, power and ideology*, (eds T. Ingold, D. Riches and J. Woodburn), pp. 4–31. Berg, Oxford.

Barton, C.M., Clark, G. and Cohen, A. (1994). Art as information: Explaining Upper Paleolithic art in Western Europe. *World Archaeology*, 26, 185–207.

Bednarik, R. (1995). Concept-mediated marking in the Lower Paleolithic. *Current Anthropology*, 36, 605–34.

Biesele, M. (1990). *Shaken roots: The Bushmen of Namibia*. EDA Publications, Marshalltown, South Africa.

Biesele, M. (1993). *Women like meat. The folklore and foraging ideology of the Kalahari Ju/'hoan*. Indiana University Press, Bloomington Indiana.

Binford, L.R. (1980). Willow smoke and dogs' tails: Hunter-gatherer settlement systems and archaeological site information. *American Antiquity*, **45**, 4–20.

Bird-David, N. (1990). The giving environment: Another perspective on the economic system of hunter-gatherers. *Current Anthropology*, **13**, 189–95.

Bremen, V. von (1991). *Zwischen Anpassung und Aneignung: Zur Problematik von Wildbeuter-Gesellschaften im Modernen Weltsystem am Beispiel der Ayoreode*. Anacon, Munich.

Cashdan, E. (1985). Coping with risk: Reciprocity among the Basarwa of Northern Botswana. *Man*, **20**, 454–76.

Clastres, P. (1972). The Guayaki. In *Hunters and gatherers today*, (ed. M.G. Bicchieri), pp. 138–74. Holt, Rinehart &Winston, New York.

Damas, D. (1972). The Copper Eskimo. In *Hunters and gatherers today*, (ed. M.G. Bicchieri), Hold, Rinehart & Winston, New York.

Damas, D. (1984). Copper Eskimo. In *Handbook of North American Indians*, Vol. 5. (ed. D. Damas), pp. 387–414. Smithsonian Institution, Washington.

Dickens, P. (1994). *English–Ju/'hoan, Ju/'hoan–English Dictionary*. Rudiger Koppe Verlag, Cologne.

Eibl-Eibesfeldt, I. (1989). *Human ethology*. Aldine, New York.

Endicott, K. (1988). Property, power and conflict among the Batek of Malaysia. In *Hunters and gatherers: Property, power and ideology*, (eds T. Ingold, D. Riches and J. Woodburn), pp. 110–28. Berg, Oxford.

Gamble, C. (1982). Interaction and alliance in palaeolithic society. *Man*, **17**, 92–107.

Gamble, C. (1986). *The Paleolithic settlement of Europe*. Cambridge University Press, Cambridge.

Gamble, C. (1999). *The Paleolithic societies of Europe*. Cambridge University Press, Cambridge.

Gordon, R. (1992). *The Bushman myth: The making of a Namibian underclass*. Westview Press, Boulder, Colorado.

Gould, R.A. (1981). Comparative ecology of food-sharing in Australia and Northwest California. In *Omnivorous primates*, (eds R. Harding and G. Teleki), pp. 422–54. Columbia University Press, New York.

Griffin, P.B. (1984). All food is shared: Agta forager acquisition, distribution and consumption of meat and plant resources. Paper presented at conference on The Sharing of Food: From Phylogeny to History, Bad Homberg, Germany.

Hamilton, W.D. (1964). The genetical evolution of social behavior. *Journal or Theoretical Biology*, 7, 1–52.

Harako, R. (1981). The cultural ecology of hunting behavior among the Mbuti Pygmies of the Ituri Forest, Zaire. In *Omnivorous Primates*, (eds R. Harding and G. Teleki), pp. 499–555. Columbia University Press, New York.

Hayden, B. (1987). Alliances and ritual ecstacy: Human responses to resource stress. *Journal for the Scientific Study of Religion*, **26**, 81–91.

Hayden, B. (1990). Nimrods, piscators, pluckers and planters: The emergence of food production. *Journal of Anthropological Archaeology*, **9**, 31–69.

Hayden, B. (1993). The cultural capacities of Neanderthals: A review and re-evaluation. *Journal of Human Evolution*, **24**, 113–46.

Heinz, H. (1979). The nexus complex among the !Xo Bushmen of Botswana. *Anthropos*, **74**, 465–80.

Henry, J. (1941). *Jungle people: A Kaingáng tribe of the Highlands of Brazil*. J.J. Augustin, New York.

Howell, N. (1979). *Demography of the Dobe !Kung*. Academic Press, New York.

Ichikawa, M. (1983). An examination of the hunting-dependent life of the Mbuti Pygmies, Eastern Zaire. *African Study Monographs*, **4**, 55–76.

Katz, R. (1982). *Boiling energy: Community healing among the Kalahari !Kung*. Harvard University Press, Cambridge.

Katz, R., Biesele, M. and St. Denis, V. (1997). *Healing makes our hearts happy: Spirituality and cultural transformation among the Kalahari Ju/'hoansi*. Inner Traditions, Rochester, Vermont.

Kent, S. (1993). Sharing in an egalitarian community. *Man*, **28**, 479–519.

Klein, R. (1973). *Ice-age hunters of the Ukraine*. Chicago University Press, Chicago.

Lee, R. (1986). !Kung kin terms, the name relationship and the process of discovery. In *The past and future of !Kung ethnography*, (eds M. Biesele, R. Gordon and R. Lee), pp. 77–100. Buske, Hamburg.

Lee, R.B. (1979). *The !Kung San: Men, women and work in a foraging society*. Cambridge University Press, Cambridge, UK.

Lee, R.B. (1993). *The Dobe Ju'hoansi*. Holt, Rinehart and Winston, New York.

Lee, R.B. and DeVore, I., eds (1976). *Kalahari hunter-gatherers*. Harvard University Press. Cambridge, MA.

Levi-Strauss, C. (1969). *The elementary structures of kinship*. Eyre & Spottiswoode, London.

Lindley, J. and Clark, G. (1990). Symbolism and modern human origins. *Current Anthropology*, **31**, 233–61.

Marshack, A. (1990). Early hominid symbols and the evolution of the human capacity. In *The emergence of modern humans: An archaeological persepctive*, (ed. P. Mellars), Edinburgh University Press, Edinburgh.

Marshall, J. (1996). The need to be informed. *Anthropology Newsletter: American Anthropological Association*, May.

Marshall, J. and Ritchie, C. (1984). *Where are the Bushmen of Nyae Nyae? Changes in a Bushman society, 1958–1981*. Communication No. 9. University Centre for African Studies, Cape Town.

Marshall, L. (1976). *The !Kung of Nyae Nyae*. Harvard University Press, Cambridge, MA.

McBrearty, S. and Brooks, A. (2000). The revolution that wasn't: A new interpretation of the origin of modern human behaviour. *Journal of Human Evolution*, 39, 453–553.

Meggitt, M. (1962). *Desert people*. Angus & Robertson, Sydney.

Mellars, P. (1973). The character of the Middle-Upper Paleolithic transition in South-West France. In *The explanation of culture change: Models in prehistory*, (ed. C. Renfrew), Duckworth, London.

Myers, F. (1988). Burning the truck and holding the country: Property, time and the negotiation of identity among Pintupi Aborigines. In *Hunters and gatherers: Property, power and ideology*, (eds T. Ingold, J. Riches and J. Woodburn), pp. 52–74. Berg, Oxford.

Peterson, N. (1993). Demand sharing: Reciprocity and the pressure for generosity among foragers. *American Anthropologist*, **95**, 860–74.

Rigaud, J.-P. (1989). From the Middle to the Upper Paleolithic: Transition or convergence? In *The emergence of modern humans*, Vol. 142–53. (ed. E. Trinkhaus), Cambridge University Press, Cambridge.

Ritchie, C. (1989). The political economy of resource tenure in the Kalahari. Unpublished Master's thesis. Boston University.

Robbe, P. (1989). Le Chasseur Artique et son Milieu: Strategies individuelles et collectives des Inuit d'Ammassalik. Unpublished Doctorat D'État ès-sciences thesis. Université Pierre et Marie Curie, Paris.

Sahlins, M. (1972). *Stone age economics*. Aldine, Chicago.

Sharp, H.S. (1977). The Chipewyan hunting unit. *American Ethnologist*, **4**, 377–93.

Sharp, H.S. (1981). The null case: The Chipewyan. In *Woman the gatherer*, (ed. F. Dahlberg), pp. 221–4. Yale University Press, New Haven.

Shostak, M. (1981). *Nisa: The life and words of a !Kung woman*. Harvard University Press, Cambridge.

Silberbauer, G. (1981a). *Hunter and habitat in the Central Kalahari Desert*. Cambridge University Press, Cambridge.

Silberbauer, G. (1981b). Hunter/gatherers of the Central Kalahari. In *Omnivorous Primates*, (eds R. Harding and G. Teleki), pp. 455–98. Columbia University Press, New York.

Sluys, C. van der (1993). The dynamics of Jahai worldview. Seventh International Congress on Hunting and Gathering Societies, Moscow.

Smith, E.A. (1988). Risk and uncertainty in the 'original affluent society': evolutionary ecology of resource-sharing and land tenure. In *Hunters and gatherers: Property, power and ideology*, (eds T. Ingold, D. Riches and J. Woodburn), pp. 222–51. Berg, Oxford.

Sugawara, K. (1988). Visiting relations and social interaction between residential groups of the Central Kalahari San: Hunter-gatherer camp as a micro-territory. *African Studies Monographs*, **8**, 173–211.

Tanaka, J. (1980). *The San, Hunter-Gatherers of the Kalahari: A study in ecological anthropology*. (trans. David W. Hughes). University of Tokyo Press, Tokyo.

Tanborin, Y. (1993). Shells of the French Aurignacian and Perigordian. In *Before Lascaux: The complex record of the Upper Paleolithic*, (eds H. Knecht, A. Pike-Tay and R. White), CPR Press, Boca Raton, Florida.

Testart, A. (1982). The significance of food storage among hunter-gatherers: Residence patterns, population densities, and social inequalities. *Current Anthropology*, **23**, 253–530.

Turnbull, C. M. (1965). *Wayward servants: The two worlds of the African Pygmies.* Eyre & Spottiswoode, London.

White, R. (1982). Rethinking the Middle/Upper Paleolithic transition. *Current Anthropology*, **23**, 169–92.

White, R. (1989). A social and technological view of Aurignacian and Castelperronian personal ornaments in SW Europe. In *El Origen del Hombre Moderno en el Sudoeste de Europa*, (ed. V. Cabrera Valdés), Ministerio de Educacion y Ciencia, Madrid.

White, R. (1993). Technological and social dimensions of "Aurignacian-Age" body ornaments across Europe. In *Before Lascaux: The complex record of the Upper Paleolithic*, (eds H. Knecht, A. Pike-Tay and R. White), CPR Press, Boca Raton, Florida.

Wiessner, P. (1977). *Hxaro: A Regional System of Reciprocity for Reducing Risk among the !Kung San*. University Microfilms, Ann Arbor, Michigan.

Wiessner, P. (1981). Measuring the impact of social ties on nutritional status among the !Kung San. *Social Science Information*, **20**, 641–78.

Wiessner, P. (1982). Risk, reciprocity and social influences on !Kung San economics. In *Politics and history in band societies*, (eds E. Leacock and R.B. Lee), pp. 61–84. Cambridge University Press, Cambridge, UK.

Wiessner, P. (1986). !Kung San networks in a generational perspective. In *The Past and Future of !Kung Ethnography: Essays in honor of Lorna Marshall*, (eds M. Biesele, R. Gordon and R. Lee), pp. 103–36. Helmut Buske Verlag, Hamburg.

Wiessner, P. (1994). The pathways of the past: !Kung San hxaro exchange and history. In *Überlebensstrategien in Afrika*, (eds M. Bollig and F. Klees), Heinrich-Barth-Institut, Köln.

Wiessner, P. (1996). Leveling the hunter: Constraints on the status quest in foraging societies. In *Food and the status quest*, (eds P. Wiessner and W. Schiefenhövel), Berghahn Books, Providence.

Wiessner, P. (1997). Seeking guidelines through an evolutionary approach: Style revisited among the !Kung San (Ju/'hoansi) of the 1990s. In *Rediscovering Darwin: Evolutionary Theory and Archeological Explanation*, Vol. AP3A No. 7. (eds M. Barton and G. Clark), pp. 157–76. American Anthropological Association, Washington, DC.

Wiessner, P. (1998). Indoctrinability and the evolution of socially defined kinship. In *Warfare, ideology and indoctrinability*, (eds F. Salter and I. Eibl-Eibesfeldt), Berghahn Books, Oxford.

Williams, B.J. (1974). A model of band society. *American Antiquity*, **39**, 1–138.

Wilmsen, E. (1989). *Land Filled with Flies*. University of Chicago Press, Chicago.

Woodburn, J. (1982). Egalitarian Societies. *Man*, **17**, 431–51.

Yellen, J. (1977). *Archaeological approaches to the present: Models for reconstructing the past.* Academic Press, New York.

Yellen, J. and Lee, R. (1976). The Dobe-/Du/da environment: Background to a hunting and gathering way of life. In *Kalahari Hunter-Gatherers: Studies of the !Kung San and their Neighbors*, (ed. R. Lee and I. DeVore), Harvard University Press, Cambridge, MA.

Yengoyan, A. (1968). Demographic and ecological influences on Aboriginal Australian marriage sections. In *Man the hunter*, (eds R. B. Lee and I. DeVore), pp. 185–9. Aldine, Chicago.

# Notes

1. The term "forager" applies to hunter-gatherers who practise little storage, relying on social relationships to carry them through times of hardship. By contrast complex hunter-gatherers, such as those found on the coast of North America, produce and store large surpluses. For discussion of different types of hunter-gatherer societies, see Binford (1980), Hayden (1990), Wiessner (1996), and Woodburn (1982).
2. The data on visiting for 1968 were generously provided by Richard Lee.
3. I am grateful to Richard Sibly for assistance in formulating and testing these hypotheses.
4. This case study will be limited to the Nyae Nyae area of Namibia. Due to the current ban on anthropological research in Botswana, it has not been possible to follow developments at Dobe and /Kae/kae.
5. Scars remain from this time in the form of alcohol abuse and alienation, owing to the fact that the enemy whom they were hired to fight would soon become the builders of their new nation.
6. Comparable data were not collected for Dobe and /Kae/kae owing to a ban on San research in Botswana at the time of the study. However, the population is essentially one in respect of exchange. Some individuals in the 1996–7 sample were also subjects in the 1974–5 sample, and the majority of people in the 1996–7 sample were *xaro* partners of those interviewed in the 1974–5 sample.

# PSYCHOLOGICAL MECHANISMS

## CHAPTER 3

# KITH-AND-KIN RATIONALITY IN RISKY CHOICES

## THEORETICAL MODELLING AND CROSS-CULTURAL EMPIRICAL TESTING

## *X. T. Wang*

### Kinship, human group structure and decision rationality

Kinship is a central concept in both evolutionary analyses of social phenomena and anthropological and ecological models of social group dynamics. However, in contrast to its central position in evolutionary biology, anthropology, and ethology, kinship has been largely ignored in psychological studies of human decision making under risk.

In this chapter, I examine how dimensions of group living, particularly group size and kinship structure, affect human risk-taking. I am interested in situations where social cues are not explicitly given but implicit in the decision problem. I attempt to show that kinship and reciprocal relationships in small social groups not only determine the intimacy in social interactions among group members but also affect human reasoning and decision making in many specific and predictable ways. In particular, I hypothesize that the human species possesses a complex evolved "kith-and-kin rationality" adapted to the tasks of nepotistic decision making and risky choices in small groups. To test this hypothesis I ask subjects in China and the United States to solve fictional decision problems about the welfare of different groups. In these problems I vary group size and relatedness while leaving the overall pay-off the same. The results are intriguing because they indicate that the human mind is not the transparent, unitary, all-purpose computing device that it has been taken to be at least from the time of Descartes. Some problem solutions that humans find intuitive or plausible are irrational from the point of view of logic or game theory. The final and probably ultimate twist is that while human decision making about groups is not perfectly rational, it appears to be *adaptive*, or at least was so in our primordial past when the brain evolved.

The idea that human decision rationality can be captured by a small set of rational principles or heuristics independent of ecological and social context was long dominant in the decision-making literature. However, a growing body of empirical findings has shown that human reasoning and decision-making behaviours often violate the axioms of normative utility theories. As a result of the recognition of this inconsistency between normative decision-making principles and observed human decision-making behaviour, much effort has been spent exploring cognitive constraints on human mental processes. However, little attention has been paid to the ecological and social significance of decision mechanisms beyond information-processing efficiency. Yet such attention is critical if the adaptiveness of decision making, as distinct from its abstract logicality, is to be explored.

Over the last three decades, the recognition of the value of evolutionary and ecological approaches to understanding human behaviour has gone through several theoretical breakthroughs. For example, E.O. Wilson's landmark 1975 synthesis, *Sociobiology*, was an evolutionary approach to animal social behaviour. The general lesson appears to be that man, like other animals, is bound by many social and biological constraints that are best understood as the product of Darwinian evolution. Hamilton's (1964) inclusive fitness theory and Trivers (1971) theory of reciprocal altruism (see also Axelrod and Hamilton 1981; Williams 1966) have further enriched Darwinian theory and provided theoretical bases for interpreting and predicting a variety of human social behaviours. Most of these contributions have fallen within the broad fields of ethology, the biological study of behaviour (Eibl-Eibesfeldt 1989). Darwin's (1872) landmark study of emotions in humans is a classic of human ethology. However, the school of thought most relevant to the study of decision making is evolutionary psychology. Workers in this subdiscipline search for design features in human psychology that correspond to human-species-specific tasks and adaptations in primordial hunter-gatherer environments (see Alexander 1979, 1987; Buss 1991; Cosmides and Tooby 1992; Daly and Wilson 1988; Symons 1979, 1987, 1992; Tooby and Cosmides 1989, 1990, 1992).

Along with the exponential increase in complexity of the human brain during the last two million years or so, individual humans have been receiving and assessing more information than the members of any other species. Our unique brain allows us to form conceptual models of human-environment relationships and social interactions within and between groups. Based on these mental models, humans are then capable of symbolically anticipating possible outcomes of decisions and, for some types of problems, the probabilities of different outcomes. The selection pressures shaping these evolved information-processing capacities are enduring and recurrent adaptation problems – challenges to our ancestors' survival and reproduction.

The capacities to think, to imagine, to calculate, and to form symbolic representations of something would not evolve for the sole purpose of thinking, imaging, calculating, and forming symbolic representations. These could not have become ends in themselves, because individuals so preoccupied would have left fewer (if any) descendants. The genes coding for such (mental) behaviour would be weeded out of the gene pool. Rather, the evolutionary perspective leads to the expectation that these undoubted mental capacities are specialized to help in the performance of adaptive functions, including decision making.

## Human species-specific social structure as an organizing factor of human social cognition

Humans have always lived in groups – families, clans, tribes, villages, and communities. The persistence of groups in human history and prehistory might have been a major force for shaping the human mind. Evidence from several disciplines suggests that there is substantial reason to anticipate that humans' long group-living experience has helped shape social cognition. For over 95 percent of *Homo sapiens*' existence the species lived in hunter-scavenger/gatherer societies. The social structure in this enduring social environment consisted of small, nomadic bands with kinship, reciprocity, little wealth, adult status equality, and diffuse flexible intergroup alliances (see e.g. Knauft 1991). The size of primitive hunting groups rarely exceeded a hundred people, based on converging evidence from archeological findings, the anthropology of contemporary hunter-gatherer cultures, comparisons with nonhuman primates such as chimpanzees (man's closest relative) as well as theoretical predictions of ecological systems in equilibrium (see Dunbar 1993; Knauft 1991; Lee and DeVore 1968; Reynolds 1973). Generally speaking, evolutionary adaptation of human group living is geared to communities of multiple hunting-gathering groups, consisting of bands or households of around 25 members, linked by kinship (see Lee and DeVore 1968; Reynolds 1973).

The human evolutionary past was not considered in the development of formal decision-making theory. The concept of rationality in the decision-making literature has been normatively defined by a small set of formal rules, such as the von Neumann-Morgenstern axioms (von Neumann and Morgenstern 1947), or the Savage axioms (see Luce and Raiffa 1957; Savage 1954). This normative approach to decision making, represented by expected utility theory and its many modifications, appears to be a hybrid of utility axioms and statistical probability, as paraphrased by Laplace as "common sense reduced to calculus" (Laplace 1814/1951, p. 196). However, both theoretical and empirical attempts to describe actual decision rationality regardless of task, content or context of the decision itself have been unsuccessful. Since the advent of expected utility theory, persistent and systematic violations of utility axioms and various decision biases have been demonstrated time and again (see Luce 1992; Slovic, Lichtenstein and Fischhoff 1988; Tversky and Kahneman 1986). Advances in evolutionary thinking provide a basis for understanding these violations.

Both evolution and decision making are selection processes. As a conscious, intellectual population, humans must have been selected to match their mental models of the social world to the key features of small kith-and-kin groups. The kinship structure in human group living is then expected to be a fundamental part of human decision rationality.

In this chapter, I focus on two fundamental design features of human groups (group size and kinship structure) and examine how these design features influence human risk preference in decision making. Empirical findings reported in this chapter come from previous studies (Wang 1996a, 1996b, 1996c; Wang and Johnston 1995) as well as data collected for this chapter.

The basic assumption is that human decision makers possess a *kith-and-kin* rationality, a decision-making mechanism that takes into account group characteristics of friendship and kinship. The idea is that when making choices at risk, specialized risky-choice mechanisms are automatically (and probably subconsciously) triggered by simple and implicit cues. These cues include group size, relatedness, group composition and group characteristics that in our evolutionary past reliably signalled that an adaptive problem existed for all the members in the group.

## Search for empirical evidence: Activating choice mechanisms by social domain-specific cues

### *Group size effects*

Group size is the pivotal point of social structure at which civilizations made most significant changes. According to Reynolds (1973) the most significant social revolution is marked by the change from small agricultural or pastoral communities to large populations of many thousands of people whose economic, social and political centre is the city. This first happened around three or four thousand years B.C. and spread more widely, the process accelerating over the last few centuries. As a result, living in mass communities is novel for most human populations. It is especially novel when viewed on the evolutionary time-scale which stretches back tens of millennia for distinctly human characteristics, and millions of years for characteristics shared with earlier hominids and nonhuman primates. Put differently, the rapid demographic changes of the last few millennia have probably occurred too quickly for human genes to "catch up". Historical change may have opened a yawning gap between our current mass social environment and our evolved small-group social cognition.

The prolonged evolutionary experience in small face-to-face groups would have shaped the human mental mechanisms to be sensitive to variables characteristic of small group living in human evolution. For this reason, people may be sensitive to social cues about the size of a small group but indifferent when group size exceeds the primordial hunter-gatherer group size.

In the first two studies to be reported here, I focus on group size as a signal of adaptive significance in risky-choice situations. The hypothesis is that size is a powerful and parsimonious contextual cue for activating specific mechanisms that have been designed to solve important problems posed by human small-group living. Thus, when making choices at risk, a simple number, the size of a social group in which choice problems occur may become a reliable social cue for risk perception and risk management. The size of a social group serves as a comprehensive index about many important features of group-environment relationship, dominance and affiliation, and social interactions between groups as well as common social contracts endorsed in social transactions, reciprocity, and kinship within the group. For example, compared with large groups, members in small groups are more interdependent on each other. Therefore, in a small group situation, people may be more willing to share risks in order to pursue a fair and positive common outcome for every group member. In contrast, when a formally identical choice problem is stripped of information about its social context, or is presented in an evolutionarily naïve context, no specially designed mechanisms can be used to solve the problem. In such situations, we should expect the risk preferences of a decision makers to become ambiguous and inconsistent.

Our first two experiments (for details, see Wang and Johnston 1995) was designed to study (1) if human decision makers are, in fact, sensitive to cues about group size; and (2) if specific strategies of risk management can be activated by these cues in an automatic manner with little awareness.

The experiments deployed a well-known cognitive phenomenon, found in risky choices, called the *framing effect*. A classical demonstration of framing effects was provided by Tversky and Kahneman (1981) in a study using a hypothetical life-death decision problem. They found that the majority of their subjects preferred a sure outcome to a risky, probabilistic outcome when the two alternative outcomes were framed in terms of lives being saved. However, when the same outcomes, framed in terms of lives lost (i.e., number of deaths) were presented to another group of subjects, their risk preference reversed: The majority of the subjects preferred the probabilistic outcome over the sure outcome. In the decision-making literature, framing effects are often considered as a cognitive illusion that violates the invariance axiom of expected utility theory. The invariance axiom requires a rational decision maker to have a consistent preference order among choice prospects independent of the way the prospects are presented or framed (Tversky and Kahneman 1986).

The life-death decision problem provides a useful empirical paradigm to manipulate the social group context of the problem in an implicit manner. In our study (Wang and Johnston 1995), each subject was given only one version of the life-death problem. The cover story of the problem provided a hypothetical group context that differed only in the number of the people involved. All the subjects were asked to "Imagine that X people are infected by a fatal disease". The number X, however, was different for each group of subjects. Four numbers were used – six thousand, six hundred, sixty, and six. The underlying assumption was that the simple difference among these numbers may be perceived as qualitatively different cues for large group vs. small group conditions and as a result activate distinct risky choice mechanisms.

The second manipulation used in the study was the framing of the choice outcomes. The subjects were asked to evaluate two alternative medical plans in terms of their expected outcomes and then indicate which plan they would choose. In the *positive framing* condition, the choice outcomes were framed in terms of the number of lives to be saved. The subjects were told that if plan A was adopted one-third of the patients would be saved for certain; and if plan B was adopted, there would be a one-third probability that all the patients would be saved and a two-thirds probability that none of them would be saved. In contrast, in the *negative framing* condition, the same choice outcomes were framed in terms of the number of lives to be lost. The subjects were then told that if plan A was adopted, two thirds of the patients would die for certain; and if plan B was adopted, there would be a one-third probability that none of the patients would die and a two-thirds probability that all of them would die.

It was predicted that the effect of choice framing on risk preference would be a function of the perceived social group context. It was found, and replicated in other studies (e.g. Wang 1996c), that the framing effect (i.e., the irrational reversal in risk preference) was found only when the problem was presented in a large group context with either six thousand or six hundred people involved. However with smaller group sizes of six and sixty, the framing effect was absent, and the majority of the subjects favoured the risky probabilistic outcome under both framing conditions, suggesting a "live or die together" small group rationality (see Figure 3.1).

## Kinship effects

Campbell's (1986) view of rationality, which he called collective rationality, maintains that it is primarily a rationality of the means whereby individuals maximize inclusive fitness. Campbell pointed out that although in practice an individualistic self-centredness is often assumed, we should be open to expanding the nature of the utility being maximized. Campbell argues that "Human rationality is inevitably a theory about the rationality of the goals, interests, or utilities, as well as about the rationality of decision making in service of these interests. From the standpoint of evolutionary biology, our innate pleasures, hungers, lusts, fears, and pains are subgoals, selected by mediating inclusive fitness" (p. S357).

The theory of inclusive fitness was invented by Hamilton (1964). Traditional Darwinian fitness is measured by the number of offspring produced by an individual. Hamilton redefined fitness to include an individual's effects upon genes carried by genetic relatives. Hamilton's inclusive fitness, therefore, is measured by the number of offspring produced by an individual plus the number of offspring produced by the individual's relatives discounted by the relatedness, designated by $r$. Hamilton (1964, p. 19) claimed that: "The social behavior of a species evolves in such a way that in each distinct behavior-evoking situation the individual will seem to value his neighbor's fitness against his own according to the coefficients of relationship appropriate to that situation". If so, a subject would evaluate the choice outcomes only in terms of their differential effects on her/his own fitness rather than on someone else's fitness. Inclusive fitness is not a general, abstract concept; it has to be measured with reference to the decision maker herself/himself.

From the viewpoint of inclusive fitness maximization, each choice option should be evaluated in terms of its effects on a decision maker's inclusive fitness. The next two studies thus examine whether an evolved kin cognition is tuned to the relatedness in kinship between a decision maker and decision recipients.

In two studies (Wang and Johnston 1995, and Wang 1996c), we tested the hypothesis that the observed preference shift towards the risk-seeking direction in small group contexts would be further intensified in a kinship context. The results from both studies showed that whenever six hypothetical patients were described as their close relatives, subjects always unambiguously preferred the probabilistic outcome to the sure outcome, in order to give everybody an equal chance to survive. Interestingly, as a signature pattern of this risky choice in the kinship context, the subjects, although clearly being risk-seeking, became significantly more risk-seeking if the choice outcomes were framed negatively in terms of lives lost. The risk-seeking choice percentage increased from 72 percent under positive framing to 94 percent under negative framing in the first study and from 73 percent to 90 percent in the second study. The extreme risk-seeking in kinship context appears to have been elicited by the choice outcomes that were both objectively negative and negatively worded (see Figure 3.1).

The aim of the second kinship study was to further explore whether human risk preference is sensitive to the closeness in kinship. In this study, hypothetical

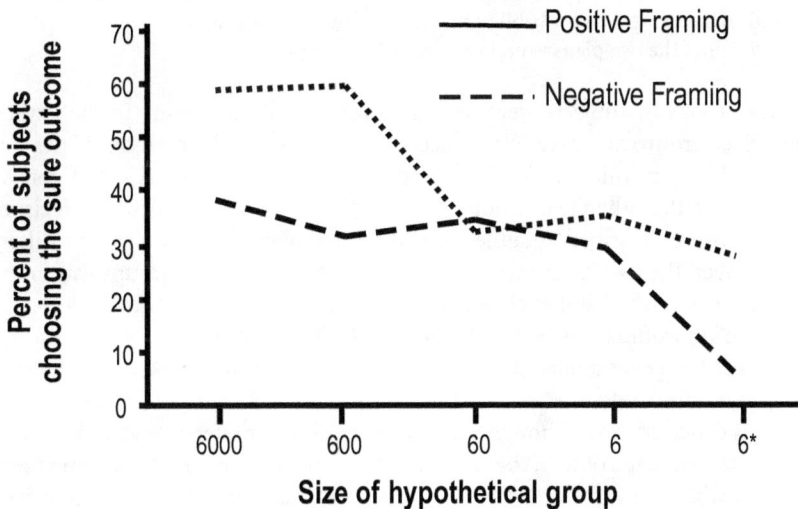

**Figure 3.1** Risk proneness as a function of the group size and kinship (adapted from Wang and Johnston, 1995).
* denotes that the six hypothetical patients were described as the close kin of the subject.

patients in the life-death problem were described as subjects' relatives or an anonymous person X's relatives. The expected value for both the sure outcome and the
probabilistic outcome was the same. That is, one third of hypothetical patients was
expected to be saved. All the choice outcomes were described in terms of lives
being saved. The sure outcome of the problem was different for subjects in different experimental groups in terms of who might be saved, close relatives (r=0.5) or
distant relatives (r=0.25), while the probabilistic alternative of equal expected value
remained the same. Hypothetical decision recipients were balanced in terms of
their gender and age. The following are examples of the questionnaire with the
sure outcome favouring remote relatives:

> Imagine that six people in your family, including *your mother, your daughter, your
> uncles and your nephews* are infected by a fatal disease. Two alternative medical plans
> to treat the disease have been proposed. Assume that the exact scientific estimates of
> the consequences of the plans are as follows:
>     If plan A is adopted, two males will be saved.
>     If plan B is adopted, there is a one-third probability that all six of them will be
> saved, and a two-thirds probability that none of them will be saved.
>     Which of the two plans would you favour?

---

> Imagine that six people in your family, including *your father, your son, your aunts, and
> your nieces*, are infected by a fatal disease. Two alternative medical plans to treat the
> disease have been proposed. Assume that the exact scientific estimates of the conse-
> quences of the plans are as follows:
>     If plan A is adopted, two females will be saved.
>     If plan B is adopted, there is a one-third probability that all six of them will be
> saved, and a two-thirds probability that none of them will be saved.
>     Which of the two plans would you favour?

Four groups of subjects were recruited from a state university in the United
States. Each group contained fifty subjects. Two groups of subjects received the life-
death problem in which the relatives were described as a person X's relatives (Xr
groups), and the other two groups received the problem in which the decision
recipients were described as subject's own kin members (Kr groups). The difference between the two Xr groups as well as between the two Kr groups was in the
sure outcome in which either close kin would be saved (Xr.5 group and Kr.5 group)
or remote kin would be saved (Xr.25 group and Kr.25 group). The labels of r.5 and
r.25 reflect the genetic relatedness (r) between the decision maker and the survivors in the sure outcome.

It was expected that although the dominant choice preference would be risk-
seeking in a kinship context, the unfavourable sure outcome might become more
attractive when the survivors of the outcome were meant to be close kin compared
to remote kin. The second prediction was that this predicted difference would disappear when the hypothetical decision recipients were described as person X's
family members.

Our two predictions based on Hamilton's inclusive fitness model are supported
by the results. More subjects chose the sure outcome when it implied that close rel-

atives would be saved at the cost of distant relatives than when it implied that distant relatives would be saved at the cost of close relatives. The choice percentage of the sure outcome significantly increased from 22 percent in the Kr.25 group to 40 percent in the Kr.5 group (see Figure 3.2). This finding suggests that decision rationality is kinship specific.

However, as illustrated in Figure 3.2, the difference in choice frequency disappeared when the decision recipients were described as person X's relatives. No significant choice difference was found between the Xr.5 and the Xr.25 groups; the choice percentage of the sure outcome was 30 percent and 34 percent respectively. The absence of a significant difference in risk preference between the Xr.5 and the Xr.25 groups argues against an all-purpose rationality viewpoint and indicates that human choice mechanisms automatically distinguish kinship from pseudo-kinship or quasi-kinship. As a result, a decision maker evaluates the options of the choice problem differently.

It is worth mentioning that even under the Kr.5 condition, the majority of the subjects (60 percent) chose the probabilistic outcome, suggesting that subjects were willing to risk their close relatives in order to save both close and distant relatives. This finding is open to interpretation. It might be evolutionarily rational to gamble to save the entire group if saving only close kin is not enough for the survival of the group.

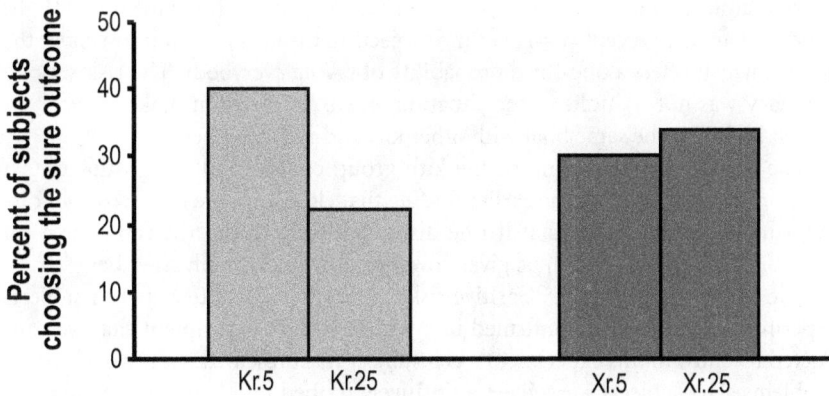

**Experimental**

**Figure 3.2** The choice of the sure outcome vs. the probabilistic outcome of equal expected value as a function of the closeness in kinship between a decision maker and the hypothetical survivors in the sure outcome.
Kr.5 vs. Kr.25 denote saving close kin vs. saving distant kin by choosing the sure outcome over the probabilistic outcome. XKr.5 vs. XKr.25 denote saving person X's close kin vs. saving person X's distant kin by choosing the sure outcome over the probabilistic outcome.

## Does kinship enhance risk-taking when the
## decision maker is also on the same boat?

Our data have shown that the willingness to take a joint risk to save the whole group was stronger in a kith-and-kin context. However, it is still not clear whether the same risk-seeking attitude would be held when a life-death decision would directly affect the survival of the decision maker as well as the decision recipients. We hypothesized that if kin selection had favoured a higher degree of cooperation among kin in small groups, it would have also favoured a risk preference for taking joint adventures together as a group. Therefore, in the case that the decision maker is part of the group at stake, the risk-seeking preference would not be reduced or reversed.

In a recent study, we randomly assigned one hundred and twenty-six subjects to each of the three experimental conditions. The subjects in each of the three experimental groups were asked to imagine that six hundred persons (or six persons, or six family members) including themselves were infected by a fatal disease. Similar to the previous experiments, each subject was then asked to make a binary decision between two alternatives: a sure outcome of saving one third of the group versus an "all or nothing" gamble of equal expected value.

The results from this experiment revealed a choice pattern that is consistent with the previous findings. A majority of the subjects (60 percent, n=42) in the large group condition (i.e., six hundred patients including the decision maker) favoured the sure thing. However, the subjects were clearly risk seeking in the kith-and-kin conditions (i.e., the lives at risk were "you and five of your friends" or "you and five of your family members". Seventy percent of the subjects (n=43) in the friend (kith) condition and 71 percent (n=41) of the subjects in the kinship condition chose the gamble which offers a one-third probability of saving everybody. The risk-seeking tendency was not reduced in the situation where the decision maker himself or herself is also on the same boat with other kin-and-kith members.

The choice patterns found in the kith group context and kin group context were similar. Considering the earlier finding that close kin were favoured over distant kin, it is conceivable that if fine distinctions are made between degrees of relatedness, then friends will be given lower priority than family members.

The kith-and-kin context sensitive risky choice found in our between-subjects experiments was further confirmed in a within-subject experiment that we conducted recently. In this experiment, each subject was presented with two life-death problems. The subjects were given a positively framed problem with six hundred lives at risk followed or proceeded by a negatively framed problem with six close kin at risk. Of the total of one hundred and twenty-three subjects, sixty-two of them chose the sure outcome for one problem and the gamble for the other. These sixty-two subjects who reversed their risk-preference showed a strong within-subject consistency; 94 percent of the risk-preference reversals were in the predicted direction from risk averse in the large group context to risk seeking in the kin context.

## When do you prefer a gamble to a sure thing even when the sure thing has a markedly higher expected value?

In this next study (see Wang 1996b, for details), I sought to examine how strong was the risk-seeking preference in the kith-and-kin contexts by decreasing the expected return of the favoured probabilistic outcome. Secondly, I tested how such a risk-seeking preference would vary as a function of the group context.

A total of one hundred and sixty subjects were randomly assigned to four experimental groups, each consisting of forty subjects. Subjects were asked to choose between a statistically dominant sure outcome that would save two thirds of the group members and a statistically inferior probabilistic outcome that had a one-third probability of saving all the group members. The subjects in the four experimental conditions were given the life-death problem presented in the group context with six hundred, six, and three persons, and six family members, respectively.

As predicted, the number of subjects choosing the sure outcome that had a higher expected value varied as a function of the size and the kinship of the social group (see Figure 3.3).

In the large group context, with six hundred anonymous persons, 90 percent of the subjects chose the statistically dominant sure outcome. As the group context was reduced from six hundred to six, to three, the choice percentage of the sure outcome also declined from 90 percent to 75 percent, to 67.5 percent, respectively. The subjects became even more biased when in the kinship context; the percent-

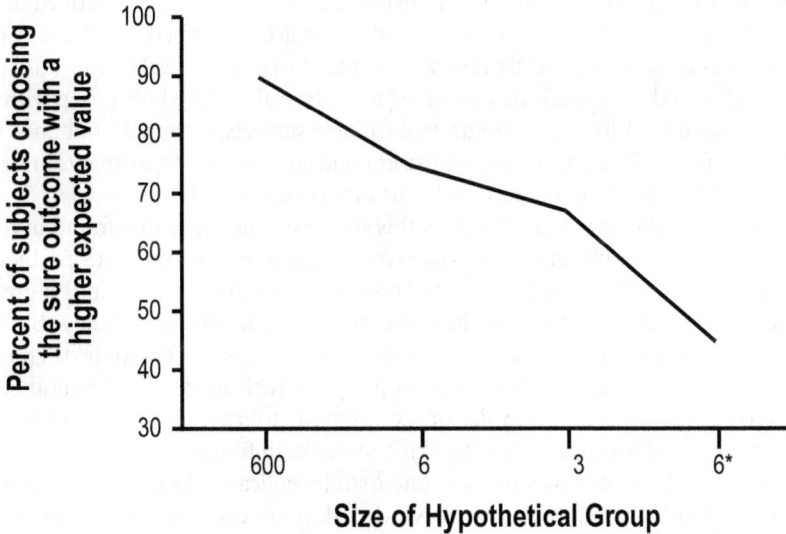

**Figure 3.3** The percentage of the subjects choosing the sure outcome to the inferior probabilistic outcome in different group contexts (adapted from Wang, 1996a).
\* denotes that the six hypothetical patients were described as the close kin of the subject.

age of the subjects choosing the sure outcome further declined to 45 percent. Presumably, for more than half of the subjects saving two-thirds of their kin was not enough so they resorted to the all-or-none probabilistic outcome even though it had only a one-third probability of saving all the family members and a two-thirds probability of losing everybody.

The percentage of the probabilistic choice in the large group context differed significantly from those in the two small group contexts (i.e., group sizes of six and three). In addition, the percentage of the probabilistic choice in the kinship context was significantly higher than those in the small group contexts. However, there was no significant difference in choice frequency between the two small group contexts. It is clear that the observed choice bias was not due to cognitive illusions but is a phenomenon sensitive to social group structure.

## Group size, kinship, and kin mimicry mechanisms: A cross-cultural examination

In order to test the robustness and universality of the observed kith-and-kin sensitive choice phenomenon, we conducted a cross-cultural study (reported in Wang 1996b). Five pairs of the life-death decision problems framed in terms of either lives to be saved or lives to be lost were translated into Chinese. These questions were identical to those used in the first experiment discussed earlier in this chapter. The first four pairs of the life-death problems differed in the size of hypothetical group (i.e., six thousand, six hundred, sixty, and six). The last pair of the problems was presented in a kin group context with six hypothetical patients being described as a decision maker's close kin. For all versions of the choice problem, the probability of survival was equal to one third: the sure option led to a sure survival of one-third of the group, and the probabilistic option led to a survival of the whole group with a one-third chance. A total of four hundred Chinese subjects, recruited from universities, research institutes, factories, companies, and government departments in Beijing (People's Republic of China), took part in this experiment.

The general choice pattern found in this study was similar to that found in the U.S. samples. First, subjects were more risk-seeking when the life-death problem was presented in kith-and-kin contexts. Second, no irrational reversal in risk preference was found when deciding the fate of a kith or kin group, and the subjects were even more risk-seeking under the negative framing in the kin context. Third, framing effect was found in the large group context with six thousand hypothetical patients. However, at group size of six hundred, no framing effect was found, and a majority of subjects were risk-taking under both frames.

In a nutshell, the results from the Chinese study replicated the U.S. data with the one exception that the group size at which risk preference switched from risk-averse to risk-taking was larger for Chinese subjects. This finding suggests that the subjective size of the we-group (kith-group) is larger for Chinese subjects (i.e., six hundred instead of sixty). This difference in the subjective scope of local kith group appears to be related to the finding that Asian people living in western societies tend to show stronger group loyalty than their western counterparts (e.g. Triandis 1991).

Human kith-and-kin perception appears to be adjusted to specific cultural features in group living through social experiences. In other words, human kin recognition and group identification are not an instant imprinted process; they involve culturally specific social learning. There is no known "green beard effect" (see Dawkins 1982) in humans that allows an instant recognition of kith or kin members by using a conspicuous and reliable physical feature, such as the imaginary green-coloured beard. Recognition of kinship and perception of group membership are acquired from social experiences.

The demographic features of Chinese population and social structure appear to be quite different from the counterparts of the U.S. These include a large overall population, extended family size, more complex kinship structure, larger reciprocal networks, enduring social interactions within a local society over generations, and low mobility of social groups. These differences in social group structure and networks may also manifest themselves in kith-and-kin cognition through some cultural means. One of the possible means of such cultural impact may be kin mimicry mechanisms (Balch 1986; Eibl-Eibesfeldt 1972; Salter 1995). Eibl-Eibesfeldt (1972) pointed out that many problems of modern societies started to occur when they grew to a size where small-group dynamics no longer applied, when familiarity between group members was replaced by anonymity among strangers. A common method to control these problems, according to Eibl-Eibesfeldt, has been kin mimicry for creating symbolic kinship that enables group members to perceive the group as an extended family.

Historically, nepotism and "brotherhood" have a long standing in an extended ethnic network in China. The conceptual members of a we-group could include kinsmen, fellow villagers, members of local kith groups, neighbours over many generations, offspring of the friends of one's ancestors, and people connected through marriage, factions, or gangs. In addition, collectivism rather than individualism has been a dominant social norm in China. This cultural atmosphere fosters the use of kin mimic devices and fits well with the demographic characteristics of Chinese social structure.

In sum, it appears that a larger conceptual scope of we-group for Chinese society members is a plausible result of culturally motivated adjustment to the specific features inherent in the social structures of Chinese society. The kith-and-kin decision rationality is also sensitive to the specific structures of social group living.

## A mean-variance model of risky choice

### Basic concepts

Recent discussions of domain-specific cognitive mechanisms for solving evolutionarily recurrent and adaptively important problems have drawn research attention to the design features of human information-processing (e.g. Cosmides 1989; Cosmides and Tooby 1992). In this light, the content and context of decision problems should not be considered as intervening or decorative variables but as the primary and defining factors of human judgment and decision making. Content and contextual variables thus can be used either for evaluating human judgement or as a research probe to uncover the underlying psychological mechanisms (e.g. Cosmides and Tooby 1992; Gigerenzer 1996; Gigerenzer and Hug 1992; Lopes and Oden 1991).

In the following section, a model of risk preference is presented, which takes into consideration both means and variances in the expected values of choice outcomes. The model is intended to be both normative and descriptive of context-dependent decision behaviour.

The kith-and-kinship dependent choices, although incompatible with the normative theory of rational choice, are consistent with the findings from modern studies on foraging behaviours. Theories of risk-sensitive foraging often address the interaction between the mean and variance of some important environmental variables, such as the food consumed or the time spent acquiring energy (e.g. Caraco 1981; Caraco, Martindale, and Whittam 1980; Houston, Kacelnik and McNamara 1982; Real 1991; Real and Caraco 1986; Stephens and Krebs 1986). The central idea embodied in these models is that risk preference of foraging animals is contingent on their concurrent survival requirement (e.g. energy budget) and the expected mean and variance of potential outcomes.

Suppose for example that a forager must consume M calories daily in order to survive, and has to decide where to forage between two places where the mean expected daily crop on both locations is equal, but their variances differ. In the low variance location, food resources are stable whereas in the high variance location, food resources are ephemeral and hard to find, but superabundant once located. If the mean value of the expected daily intake is less than the minimum requirement M, the adaptive choice is to take a risk and forage on the high variance location. As a result of this choice, the forager will have a better chance of getting more than the required M calories of daily intake. In contrast, if the mean expected daily crop is greater than M, the forager is better off foraging on the location with a lower variance, as this decreases the chance of death. That is, for gains above a specific minimum requirement, the choices should be risk averse; but to avoid potentially disastrous losses that fall below the minimum requirement, the choices should be risk-seeking.

The emphasis on environmental variance has also been a key feature of biological studies of behavioural strategies. Organisms evolve different survival strategies to fit different types of environments. Among theories that correlate behavioural strategies with environments, the theory of r- and K- selection developed by MacArthur and Wilson (1967) is a well-known example. In a high-variance, catastrophic environment everything is too unpredictable for a risk-averse strategy. Organisms in such a high variance situation would be better off if they make a rapid maximum investment in the "hope" that some offspring will survive the "expected" catastrophe. This evolutionary strategy of maximizing reproductive effort at the expense of delicate morphological adjustment is referred to as the r strategy. Species that live in stable environments, near the maximum population size that the environment can support, will gain nothing by producing a large number of poorly adjusted progeny. In such stable and low variance environments, the selection pressure would favour the organisms who invest in a few finely tuned offspring. This is called the *K* strategy. However, with a few exceptions (e.g. Allais 1979; Coombs 1975; Lopes 1987; Luce 1980) decision theories have largely ignored the role of variance in expected returns in determining risk-preference.

Borrowing relevant concepts from foraging theories, the present mean-variance model of risk preference assumes that decision makers are sensitive to outcome variance and risk distribution and have a minimum requirement determined by social and biological variables.

The model places a special emphasis on the three-way relationship between (1) the expected mean value of choice outcomes, (2) variances in the outcomes, and (3) a minimum requirement (MR) reference point, which may be psychologically translated into aspiration level. This three-way interaction obeys the mean-variance principle. The short-hand rule is: be risk/variance-seeking when the expected mean value of choice outcomes is below a task-relevant MR; but be risk/variance-averse when the expected mean value is above the MR.

It should be noted that in the present mean-variance model the concept of risk is correlated to but not tantamount to the concept of variance. For example, when the expected mean value of a choice outcome is just above its MR, a small variance in the outcome would be perceived as quite risky. However, when the mean value is much higher than the MR, the same or even larger amount of variance in the outcome would not be considered as risky as in the former case.

## *Empirical testing of predictions from the model: Effects of survival rate manipulation on risk preference*

Our previous empirical findings allow us to roughly locate the setting of the MR in each of the three distinct group contexts (i.e., large group, small group, and kin group). With regard to the life-death problem, the MR can be inferred by asking what is the minimum sure outcome that is preferable to the gamble outcome? The operational measure of the MR used here is the survival rate offered by the sure outcome that is favoured by at least 50 percent of subjects, called *MR50+*.

Considering the data obtained in large group contexts under positive framing, the MR50+ is no greater than one third of the total expected value (i.e., to save at least one third of the group members at stake). In the first study discussed in this chapter, about 60 percent of the subjects preferred the sure outcome when it resulted in the sure survival of one third of the members in a large group. However, the MR50+ for saving hypothetical family members is significantly higher. In another study discussed earlier, 55 percent of the subjects preferred the inferior probabilistic outcome to the sure survival of two thirds of the kin members, suggesting that saving two thirds of the kin group was not enough. Therefore, the MR50+, the minimum requirement for more than 50 percent of the subjects, in the kinship context is to save no less than two thirds of the family members at risk. The MR50+ for saving lives in a small group context then is expected to be in between: higher than one-third sure survival but lower than two thirds of sure survival. This analysis is illustrated in Figure 3.4.

According to the above analysis, if the expected survival rate in the life-death problem is increased from one third of the group members to two thirds of the

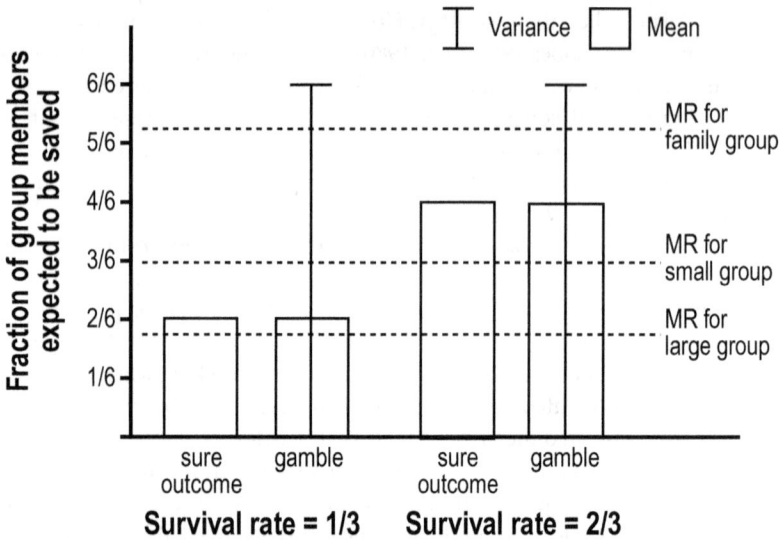

**Figure 3.4** Predicted minimum requirement (MR) for the sure saving of a fraction of the hypothetical group at stake in three social group situations.

group members, the likelihood that the expected sure outcome passes the MR of the decision maker would also increase. Thus, the decision maker would be more likely to choose the sure outcome. However, the effects of increasing the expected survival rate should depend on whether the increment is large enough to pass the MR of the decision maker. Depending on the group context in which the life-death problem is presented, the effect of the increased survival rate would vary. First, in a kinship context, increasing the survival rate from one third to two thirds would not significantly increase the percentage of the risk-averse choice because the sure survival of two-thirds of the family members is still below their MR50+. That is, saving two thirds of endangered kin for sure would not be enough for more than half of the subjects. Second, in a large group context, increasing the survival rate may only have a marginal effect on subjects' risk preference because the one-third survival rate would be already acceptable for more than half of the subjects. Thirdly, the survival rate manipulation, however, should be most effective when the problem is presented in a small group context where subjects' minimum requirement for the sure outcome is likely to be above one third but below two thirds of the entire group. Therefore, we predicted that by increasing the expected survival rate from one third to two thirds in small group contexts, more subjects would choose the sure option than its gamble equivalent.

These specific predictions were tested in a recent experiment. The results, as being presented in Figure 3.5, are in agreement with the predictions from the mean-variance model of risky choice. In the study, one hundred and ninety-one student volunteers from a mid-west state university were randomly assigned to

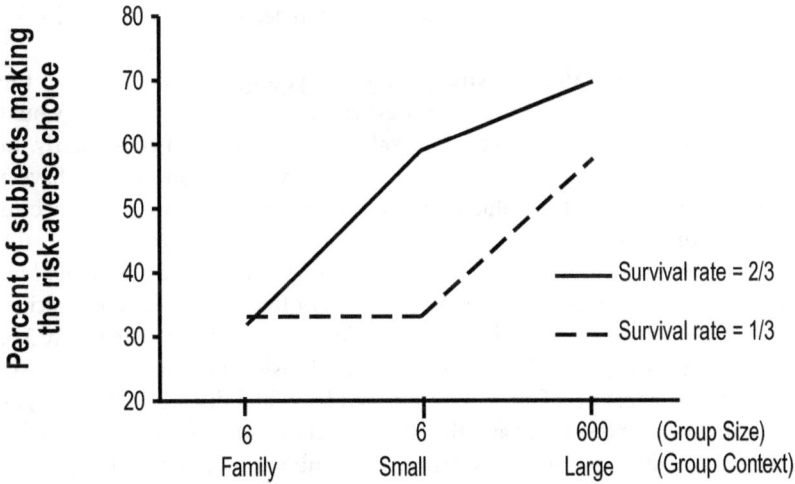

**Figure 3.5** The effects of increasing survival rate of hypothetical patients on subjects' risk preference across three social group contexts.

each of the six experimental conditions with thirty-one to thirty-four subjects in each condition. The six experimental conditions comprised a 2 x 3 design (2 survival rates x 3 social group contexts).

The only significant effect of increasing the survival rate from one third to two thirds was found between the two subject-groups receiving the life-death problem presented in the small group context with six anonymous lives. Under the one-third survival rate, only 33 percent of the subjects preferred the sure outcome to the probabilistic outcome of equal expected value whereas under the two-thirds survival rate, the percentage of the sure outcome over the all-or-none probabilistic equivalent increased to 59 percent. This finding suggests that the social domain-specific MR is a key determinant of risk preference.

### When my older kin is old: Effects of age and expected reproductive value on risk preference

From a kin-selection viewpoint, it is clear that the reproductive value of decision recipients should influence risk preference of the decision maker. In this final section of the chapter, I report a study (Wang 1996b) that further illustrates the implications of the mean-variance model. In this study, we manipulated the inclusive reproductive values of hypothetical decision recipients to the decision maker, using the standard life-death choice paradigm.

In making social decisions, a specific expected value of a choice option may be below or above the minimum requirement (MR) for a decision maker depending on the inclusive reproductive value of the decision recipients. The key hypothesis of the study was that a decision maker's own age, as a reference point, would affect the way the decision maker evaluates the so-called "older" or "younger" kin at stake. Compared with one's own age, the age cues of the hypothetical decision recipients (older versus younger kin) could be used to determine their inclusive fitness values to the decision maker.

It was hypothesized that for young subjects (young college students), the manipulation of saving-young (their siblings) vs. saving-old (their parents) would yield similar reproductive and fecundity values and thus weighted similarly. In contrast, for middle-aged subjects, their younger kin would, on average, have a higher expected reproductive value than their older kin. Therefore, the expected utility of the sure outcome would be up-weighted when the sure survivors were the subjects' younger kin but down-weighted when the survivors were their older kin.

The expected differences in reproductive values of hypothetical decision recipients with regard to young and middle-aged decision makers are shown in Figure 3.6.

The hypothesis was tested using a life-death decision problem in which six hypothetical members of a family were infected by a fatal disease. The six hypothetical patients were described as either the subject's or someone else's close relatives (parents, siblings, and offspring). The subject was asked to make a dichotomous choice between a sure outcome and a probabilistic outcome. The sure outcome led to a sure survival of one third of the kin (either two younger or two older family members) whereas the probabilistic outcome had a one-third probability of saving all of the six kin members.

As a between-subjects design each subject received only one version of the life-death problem. Therefore, the saving-young and saving-old manipulation was hidden to the subjects. A total of two hundred and nineteen student volunteers were assigned to one of the six experimental groups with thirty to forty-two subjects in each group. The six experimental conditions included two middle-aged subject groups receiving the life-death problem with either a saving-young or a saving-old

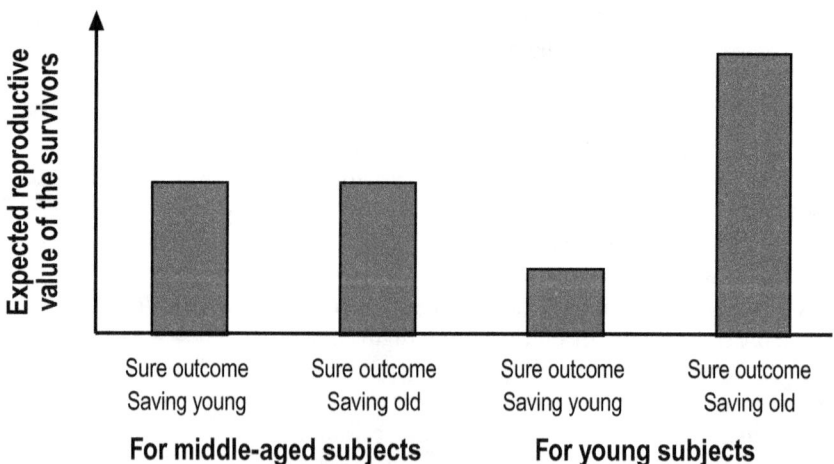

**Figure 3.6** Expected reproductive values of the hypothetical survivors in the sure outcome for the young and middle-aged subjects.

sure outcome. The subjects in two of the four young-subject groups were also given the life-death problem with either a saving-young or a saving-old sure outcome as did for the middle-aged subjects. The other two young-subject groups were given either a saving-young or a saving-old version of the life-death problem with the hypothetical patients being described as a person X's kin.

The age-window of 30–55 years was used to select the middle-aged subjects and the sampling process continued until there were at least thirty subjects in each of the two middle-aged subject groups. The mean age was 20.3 years for the young subjects and 41.4 years for the middle-aged subjects.

Consistent with the expected reproductive values illustrated in Figure 3.6, the young subjects equally valued their younger and older hypothetical kin and indistinguishably favoured the probabilistic outcome (77.5 percent in the "saving-old" group and 76.2 percent in the "saving-young" group). In contrast, for the middle-aged subjects, the saving-young vs. saving-old manipulation was expected to represent different fitness values to the subjects. As expected, the middle-aged subjects were much more prone to the sure outcome when it implied saving their younger family members but were extremely risk-seeking in favour of the probabilistic outcome when the sure outcome resulted in the survival of only older kin (see Figure 3.7).

These findings indicate that the increased utility to save two younger kin for middle-aged subjects was higher than for the young subjects and thus was more likely to pass the MR. Presumably, the saving-young sure outcome was particularly attractive to those of the middle-aged subjects whose MR was not too much above randomly saving one third of the family members. In contrast, the saving-old sure

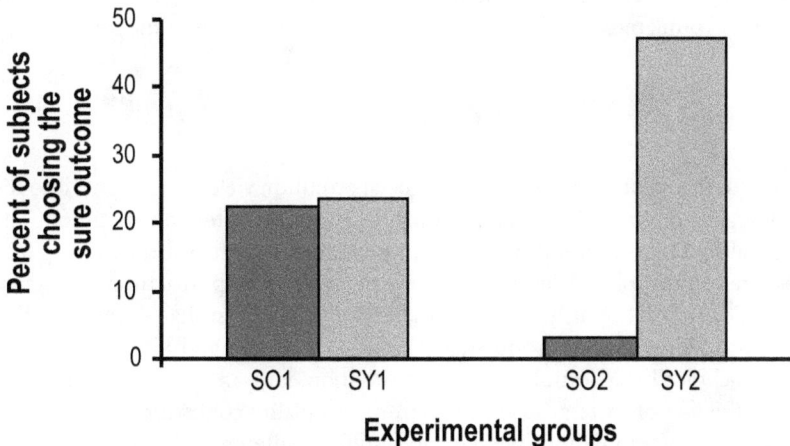

**Figure 3.7** The effects of age, perspective of decision makers, and reproductive cues about decision recipients on choice preference (adapted from Wang, 1996b). SO and SY denote saving-old and saving-young manipulations in the sure outcomes; x denotes perspective change from the subject's own family to a personx's family; 1 denotes young subject group; 2 denotes middle-aged subject group.

outcome would intensify the risk-seeking preference because it made the sure outcome less likely to pass subjects' MR.

Another experimental manipulation of the study concerned the effects of perspective change on subjects' risk preference. It was hypothesized that when the life-death problem was described in a context of an anonymous person's family, the subjects would not be inclined to use their own ages as a reference to measure the potential reproductive values of younger or older hypothetical survivors described in the sure outcomes. The subject would then be more likely to consider "younger" survivors as youth and "older" survivors as senile people and place higher values on the saving-young than the saving-old option. This is, in fact, the case. Although the overall choice preference was risk taking, more subjects favoured the saving-young sure outcome than saving-old sure outcome when compared with the same probabilistic outcome.

This result is consistent with the findings of a study by Burnstein, Crandall, and Kitayama (1994), in which the authors examined a key assumption of kin-selection that relatives who are helped must have sufficient fitness value (e.g. expected reproductive values) to benefit the altruist or the altruist's offspring. In this study, subjects had to decide how to use their resources to help others who vary in kinship. The study shows that the subjects' tendency to help in a live-or-die situation is affected by the hypothetical recipients' relatedness, age, health and wealth conditions, and fecundity status in directions which enhance the helpers' inclusive fitness. However, when the benefits of altruism are small, respondents, regardless of their age, conform to moral norms and help the older member. Similarly, the effects of perspective change discussed above suggest that kinship cognition is a self-referenced mechanism, which distinguishes real kinship decisions from pseudo kinship decisions. In the latter case, people tend to conform to social norms and generally value the lives of young members above the lives of elderly members of the society.

## Conclusion

Darwinian theory and details of human social evolution yield rich insights into the psychological mechanisms and functional organization of human cognition. The empirical findings discussed in this chapter demonstrate the value of taking into consideration the roles of species-specific group and kinship structures in shaping human decision rationality. These experiments have shown that simple, implicit information about social group structure (especially size and kinship) strongly regulates choice behaviour. In a decision situation, kith-and-kin rationality concerning the fate of local groups differs from rationality concerning the fate of a large number of anonymous people and results in different risk preferences. It is clear that the risk preference of a decision maker is determined not only by the formal structure (i.e., the expected values and probabilities) of a choice problem but also by the problem's social content and context.

These findings also have implications for understanding the kin and ethnic networking in risky transactions. Kin favouritism and kith group loyalty can be considered as built-in choice mechanisms that have been designed to minimize the probability of betrayal and to maximize inclusive fitness by conducting risky transactions with kith and kin. In addition, kith-and-kin rationality is also subject to cultural adaptation and social manipulations such as kin mimicry. The findings of our Chinese study provide a cognitive dimension with which to understand some ethnic phenomena involving kin mimicry in organizational and trading activities. For example, ethnic middleman groups often prioritize their trading relationship on the basis of kith-and-kin recognition and manage to expand the operational definition of kith-and-kin far beyond immediate family and friends, based on beliefs/myths about common ancestry (e.g. van den Berghe 1981; Landa 1981).

The kin- and social group-specific risk-preference patterns discussed in this chapter cannot be well explained by traditional models of rational choice. In contrast, the mean-variance model of risk preference has shown great potential for explaining and predicting human risky choices in a variety of social group contexts.

# References

Alexander, R.D. (1979). *Darwinism and human affairs.* University of Washington Press, Seattle, WA.

Alexander, R.D. (1987). *The biology of moral systems.* Aldine de Gruyter, New York.

Allais, M. (1979). The foundations of a positive theory of choice involving risk and a criticism of the postulates and axioms of the American School. In *Expected utility hypotheses and the Allais Paradox* (eds M. Allais and O. Hagen), Reidel, Dordrecht.

Axelrod, R., and Hamilton, W.D. (1981). The evolution of cooperation. *Science,* **2111,** 1390–6.

Balch, S. H. (1986). "The neutered civil servant": Eunuchs, celibates, abductees and the maintenance of organizational loyalty. In *Biology and bureaucracy* (eds E. White and J. Losco), pp. 271–303. University Press of America, Lanham, MD.

Berghe, P.L. van den (1981). The ethnic phenomenon. Elsevier, New York.

Burnstein, E., Crandall, C., and Kitayama, S. (1994). Some neo-Darwinian decision rules for altruism: Weighing cues for inclusive fitness as a function of the biological importance of the decision. *Journal of Personality and Social Psychology,* **67,** 773–89.

Buss, D.M. (1991). Evolutionary personality psychology. *Annual Review of Psychology,* **42,** 459–91.

Campbell, D.T. (1986). Rationality and utility from the standpoint of evolutionary biology. *Journal of Business,* **59,** S355–S364.

Caraco, T. (1981). Energy budgets, risk and foraging preferences in dark-eyed juncos. *Behavioral Ecology and Sociobiology,* **8,** 213–17.

Caraco, T., Martindale, S., and Whittam, T.S. (1980). An empirical demonstration of risk-sensitive foraging preferences. *Animal Behavior,* **28,** 820–30.

Coombs, C.H. (1975). Portfolio theory and the measurement of risk. In *Human judgement and decision processes*, (eds M. Kaplan and S. Schwartz). Academic Press, New York.

Cosmides, L. (1989). The logic of social exchange: Has natural selection shaped how humans reason? Studies with the Wason selection task. *Cognition*, **31**, 187–276.

Cosmides, L., and Tooby, J. (1992). Cognitive adaptations for social exchange. In *The adapted mind: Evolutionary psychology and the generation of culture* (eds J.H. Barkow, L. Cosmides, and J. Tooby), pp. 163–228. Oxford University Press, New York.

Daly, M., and Wilson, M. (1988). *Homicide*. Aldine, New York.

Darwin, C. (1872). *The expression of the emotions in man and animals*. Murray, London.

Dawkins, R. (1982). *The extended genotype*. Oxford University Press, New York.

Dunbar, R.I.M. (1988). *Primate social systems*. Chapman & Hall, London.

Dunbar, R.I.M. (1993). Coevolution of neocortical size, group size and language in humans. *Behavioral and Brain Sciences*, **16**, 681–735.

Eibl-Eibesfeldt, I. (1972). *Love and hate: The natural history of behavior patterns*, (trans. G. Strachan). Holt, Rinehart & Wilson, New York.

Eibl-Eibesfeldt, I. (1989). *Human ethology*. Aldine de Gruyter, New York.

Gigerenzer, G. (1996). Rationality: Why social context matters. In *Interactive minds: Life-span perspectives on the social foundation of cognition (eds P.B. Baltes and U. Staudinger)*, pp. 319–46. Cambridge University Press, Cambridge, UK.

Gigerenzer, G., and Hug, K. (1992). Domain-specific reasoning: Social contracts, cheating, and perspective change. *Cognition*, **43**, 127–71.

Hamilton, W.D. (1964). The genetical evolution of social behaviour. *Journal of Theoretical Biology*, **7**, 1–52.

Houston, A., Kacelnik, A., and McNamara, J. (1982). Some learning rules for acquiring information. In *Functional ontogeny (ed. D. McFarland)*. Pitman, London.

Knauft, B.M. (1991). Violence and sociality in human evolution. *Current Anthropology*, **32**, 391–428.

Landa, J.T. (1981). A theory of the ethnically homogeneous middleman group: An institutional alternative to contract law. *Journal of Legal Studies*, **10**, 349–62.

Laplace, P.S. (1814/1951). *A philosophical essay on probabilities*, (trans. F.W. Truscott and F.L. Emory). Dover, New York.

Lee, R.B., and DeVore, I (eds) (1968). *Man the hunter*. Aldine, Chicago.

Lopes, L.L. (1987). Between hope and fear: The psychology of risk. *Advances in Experimental Social Psychology*, **20**, 255–95.

Lopes, L.L., and Oden, G.C. (1991). The rationality of intelligence. In *Rationality and reasoning: Essays in honor of L.J. Cohen* (eds E. Eells and T. Maruszewski). Rodopi, Amsterdam.

Luce, R.D. (1980). Several possible measures of risk. *Theory and Decision*, **12**, 217–228.

Luce, R.D. (1992). Where does subjective expected utility fail descriptively? *Journal of Risk and Uncertainty,* **5,** 5–27.

Luce, R.D., and Raiffa, H. (1957). *Games and Decisions.* Wiley, New York.

MacArthur, R., and Wilson, E.O. (1967). *The theory of island biogeography.* Princeton University Press, Princeton.

Neumann, J. von, and Morgenstern, O. (1947). *Theory of games and economic behavior.* Princeton University Press, Princeton, NJ.

Real, L. (1991). Animal choice behavior and the evolution of cognitive architecture. *Science,* **253,** 980–86.

Real, L., and Caraco, T. (1986). Risk and foraging in stochastic environments. *Annual Review of Ecology and Systematics,* **17,** 371–90.

Reynolds, V. (1973). Ethology of social change. In *The explanation of culture change: Models in prehistory* (ed. C. Renfrew), pp. 467–80. University of Pittsburgh Press, Pittsburgh.

Salter, F.K. (1995). *Emotions in command: A naturalistic study of institutional dominance.* Oxford University Press, New York.

Savage, L.J. (1954). *The foundations of statistics.* Wiley, New York.

Slovic, P., Lichtenstein, S., and Fischhoff, B. (1988). Decision making. In *Stevens' handbook of experimental psychology* (eds R.C. Atkinson, R.J. Herrnstein, G. Lindzey, and R.D. Luce), pp. 673–738. Wiley, New York.

Stephens, D.W., and Krebs, J.R. (1986). *Foraging theory.* Princeton University Press, Princeton,NJ.

Symons, D. (1979). *The evolution of human sexuality.* Oxford University Press, New York.

Symons, D. (1987). If we're all Darwinians, what's the fuss about? In *Sociobiology and psychology: Ideas, issues, and applications* (eds C.B. Crawford, M.F. Smith, and D.L. Krebs), pp. 121–46. Lawrence Erlbaum Associates, Hillsdale, NJ.

Symons, D. (1992). On the use and misuse of Darwinism in the study of human behavior. In *The adapted mind: Evolutionary psychology and the generation of culture* (eds J.H. Barkow, L. Cosmides, and J. Tooby), pp. 137–59. Oxford University Press, New York.

Tooby, J., and Cosmides, L. (1989). Evolutionary psychology and the generation of culture, Part I. Theoretical considerations. *Ethology and Sociobiology,* **10,** 29–49.

Tooby, J., and Cosmides, L. (1990). The past explains the present: Emotional adaptations and the structure of ancestral environments. *Ethology and Sociobiology,* **11,** 375–424.

Tooby, J., and Cosmides, L. (1992). Cognitive adaptations for social exchange. In *The adapted mind: Evolutionary psychology and the generation of culture* (eds J.H. Barkow, L. Cosmides, and J. Tooby), pp. 19–136. Oxford University Press, New York.

Triandis, H.C. (1991). Cross-cultural differences in assertiveness/competition vs. group loyalty/cohesiveness. In *Cooperation and prosocial behaviour* (eds R.A. Hinde and J. Groebel). Cambridge University Press, Cambridge, UK.

Trivers, R.L. (1971). The evolution of reciprocal altruism. *Quarterly Review of Biology,* **46,** 35–57.

Tversky, A., and Kahneman, D. (1981). The framing of decisions and the psychology of choice. *Science*, **211**, 453–58.

Tversky, A., and Kahneman, D. (1986). Rational Choice and the framing of decisions. *Journal of Business*, **59**, S251–S278.

Wang, X.T. (1996a). Domain-specific rationality in human choices: Violations of utility axioms and social contexts. *Cognition*, **60**, 31–63.

Wang, X.T. (1996b). Evolutionary hypotheses of risk-sensitive choice: Age differences and perspective change. *Ethology and Sociobiology*, **17**, 1–15.

Wang, X.T. (1996c). Framing effects: Dynamics and task domains. *Organizational Behavior and Human Decision Processes*, **68**, 145–57.

Wang, X.T., and Johnston, V.S. (1995). Perceived social context and risk preference: A re-examination of framing effects in a life-death decision problem. *Journal of Behavioral Decision Making*, **8**, 279–93.

Williams, G.C. (1966). *Adaptation and natural selection: A critique of some current evolutionary thought.* Princeton University Press, Princeton, NJ.

Wilson, E.O. (1975) *Sociobiology: The new synthesis.* Harvard University Press, Cambridge, MA.

# Acknowledgements

The author thanks Victor Johnston, Frank Schieber, and Frank Salter for their helpful comments and suggestions on this chapter. This project was supported in part by Grant SBR-9876527 from the National Science Foundation. Correspondence concerning this article should be addressed to X.T. Wang, Psychology Department, University of South Dakota, Vermillion, SD, 57069, U.S.A (e-mail:xtwang@usd.edu).

## CHAPTER 4

# ALTRUISM BEGINS AT HOME

## EVIDENCE FOR A KIN SELECTION HEURISTIC SENSITIVE TO THE COSTS AND BENEFITS OF HELPING

*Eugene Burnstein, Christine Branigan, and Grazyna Wieczorkowska-Nejtardt*

Arguably the most important psychological corollary of the neo-Darwinian analysis of *inclusive fitness* is that we are designed to care more deeply about close kin than about distant kin or unrelated individuals (Hamilton 1964; Maynard Smith 1964; also see Fisher 1930; Haldane 1932). According to classical Darwinian theory, fitness is measured by a person's reproductive success because it this success that determines his or her *genetic continuation*. However, if what counts is the likelihood of someone's genes being replicated over succeeding generations, then individual reproductive success is not the sole or may not even be the most important determinant of fitness. Since we share genes identical by descent with relatives, their fecundity could easily contribute as much or more to genetic continuation than our own fecundity. Therefore, according to Hamilton, an estimate of fitness that is "inclusive" and takes into account the reproductive contributions of kin is more valid than the classic Darwinian procedure. Hamilton's analysis has been persuasive giving rise to numerous arguments, widely known by now, to the effect that selection occurs not at the level of the individual or group but at the level of the gene; that the individual is merely a gene's vehicle for making another gene, a machine for replicating and transmitting itself to future generations, etc. (e.g. Dawkins 1976, 1982; Williams 1966; but see Boehm 1997; Wilson 1989; Wilson and Sober 1994).

Social psychological analyses need to take inclusive fitness theory into account because it describes the circumstances under which behavioural strategies and the social transactions they cause become widespread (or disappear). Suppose that an actor does something to help a recipient and the action costs the former $C$ while benefiting the latter $B$, costs and benefits referring to decreases and increases, respectively, in individual reproductive success, and that there is a genetically influenced structure mediating the action. According to traditional Darwinian fitness, a tendency causing its possessor reproductive harm will be selected *against*. Hamilton's insight is that, as the traditional Darwinian model predicts, if the genes underlying such a tendency experience no reproductive benefits, only costs, then they must decrease in frequency. However, if the actor and recipient are related, there is a likelihood that they share the genes in question, so there is no decrease. Hence, a genetic structure in the actor can experience a net benefit; that is, its chances of replication are improved if the cost of helping to the actor is less than the benefit to the recipient weighted by the degree of relatedness, $r$, that is, if

$$Br > C.$$

So in order for an action, whose recipient is a sibling ($r = 0.5$), to produce a genetic profit for the altruist and to be favoured by natural selection, it must benefit the recipient by more than twice the cost to the altruist. And an action whose recipient is an aunt ($r = 0.25$) must benefit her more than four times the amount of the cost to the altruist, etc.

Many have argued that inclusive fitness is useful in understanding the adaptive function of social norms, cooperation and competition, and interpersonal attraction (e.g. Alexander 1987; Axelrod and Hamilton 1981; Caporeal, Dawes, Orbell and van de Kragt 1989; Kenrick and Trost, 1988). In this chapter we discuss several simple experimental demonstrations that are concerned with the broader issue of constraints imposed by the model on the encoding of social information. The nature of these constraints may be outlined in terms of two processing principles that follow from the assumption of inclusive fitness. The more general principle concerns a capacity that can be labelled *social acuity*. It asserts that natural selection favours a tendency in actors to distinguish between potential partners according to the cost and benefits of a transaction. Are the others rich or poor, benevolent or selfish? Can they figure out my resources and intentions? The more specific principle has to do with what is usually called *kin selection*. It implies that when a transaction is altruistic (i.e., $C > B$), natural selection favours those who discriminate between potential recipients according to their degree of relatedness.

## Recognizing the cost and benefits of a social transaction

Inclusive fitness assumes that any group-living species has evolved mechanisms to detect the costs and benefits of a social transaction. The upshot, roughly speaking, is that as they are about to begin their dealings the participants know their own interests and seek to understand those of the other by searching for cues to his or her costs and benefits. In effect, they ask themselves (i) what they will have to expend relative to what they might gain; and (ii) what the other person will expend and gain, a more problematic question. The evidence in the standard social psychological literature for a social acuity mechanism is appreciable but far from overwhelming. For example, group members are adept at recognizing individual differences in who has what resources and how likely he or she is to expend them for the good of others; they readily categorize members according to their capacity to contribute to the general welfare (e.g. those with many good ideas vs. those with few good ideas, intelligent members vs. unintelligent members, active members vs. passive members, etc.) and their benevolence, the likelihood that these resources will be used to help others (e.g. cooperative members vs. competitive members, friendly members vs. hostile members, warm members vs. cold members, etc.). Moreover, behaviours signalling actors' resources and benevolence as well as observers' sensitivity to such cues appear early in an interaction, probably within the first minute (Fisek and Ofshe 1970; Lee and Ofshe 1981; Willard and Strodtbeck 1972). These phenomena have been demonstrated using a variety of methods ranging from the members themselves or trained observers rating ongoing interaction in *ad hoc* laboratory groups, groups of friends, work teams, or psychotherapeutic groups (e.g. Bales 1970; Borgatta 1962; Leary 1957; Schutz 1958) to individuals analysing the behaviour in written descriptions of everyday social episodes (e.g. Benjamin 1974; Foa 1961; Triandis 1972; Wish, Deutsch, and Kaplan 1976). Virtually every study in this literature has found that the capacity to benefit others in the group and the likelihood of a person doing so are by far the two most important dimensions used by members in differentiating or ranking each other (Hare 1976; McGrath 1984). Furthermore, the differentiation seems automatic in that it occurs universally and quickly; and even in tasks where actual social transactions are out of the question or where differences in resources or benevolence are irrelevant (DeSoto and Albrecht 1968; DeSoto and Bosley 1962). Based on observations in more natural settings Cheney and Seyfarth (1985) argue that children and young primates can infer the ranking in a group merely by watching a small number of transactions: If *A*, say, is friendly to, cooperates with, or dominates *B* and *B* is friendly to, cooperates with, or dominates *C*, they sense that *A* is probably friendly to, cooperates with, or dominates *C*. Indeed, these researchers find that monkeys are adept at inferring causality, transitivity, and reciprocity in social relations early in life, before they are skilled in recognizing comparable relationships between physical events of more obvious biological significance (e.g. that a particular pattern of tracks is produced by the python, a common predator of the monkey).

Research on mixed-motive games is another source of evidence for an adaptive mechanism dedicated to encoding the costs and benefits of social transactions. Of particular interest are the studies that compare transactions in which such a mechanism is likely to be activated with transactions in which it remains dormant. For instance, if students playing a prisoner's dilemma game believe their unseen partner is another student, they adopt a cooperative strategy whereby they try to understand the other's intentions and to use such knowledge to persuade the partner to cooperate also. If they believe the partner is a computer, however, they use a minimax (competitive) strategy, not attempting to understand or to persuade – there is no point, of course, when the "other" is a program – but simply to protect themselves against the most costly outcome that the computer could inflict on them. The tendency to minimax persists even when the computer plays a flexible, forgiving, and nice strategy like TIT-FOR-TAT which, when played by a human, usually elicits cooperation (Abric, Faucheux, Moscovici, and Plon 1967).

Similar effects are found in pure coordination games (see the minimal social situation in Sidowoski, Wyckoff, and Tabory 1956). Kelley and his colleagues (Kelley, Thibaut, Radloff, and Mundy 1962; Rabinowitz, Kelley, and Rosenblatt 1966) had individuals engage in a long series of transactions with a partner who, again, was said to be either another student or a machine. To benefit, participants first needed to ascertain how their own actions affected the partner. Once this was known, coordination could be achieved and from then on both individuals would gain; otherwise, both would continue to experience losses. The results were comparable to those obtained in the mixed-motive studies: Individuals who believed they were interacting with a person, but not those who believed it was a machine, try to figure out the consequences of their actions more readily, how they affect the other's costs and benefits. Interestingly enough, they seemed to do so by assuming that the partner would adopt a heuristic resembling TIT-FOR-TAT. As a result, they solved the coordination problem with greater frequency than those who believed they were interacting with a machine.

Occasionally social psychologists observe social transactions in which a person cannot understand others' costs and benefits. The best known research along these lines follows from Asch's classic experiments on conformity (Asch 1956). Asch instructed a unanimous majority to make a judgement that, from a naïve member's point of view, seemed clearly wrong and to do so for no apparent reason – the naïve member could not see what individuals in the majority had to gain from their judgement. What Asch observed is that the naïve member tended to go along with the majority publicly while rejecting its position privately. According to Ross, Bierbrauer, and Hoffman (1976), these findings reflect a default strategy used by members who are puzzled and dismayed because they cannot understand the incentives the group has for making a judgement that ordinarily is recognized to be incorrect. Put differently, the inability to grasp others' costs and benefits encourages wariness, distrust, and even deception in the sense of pretending to agree while actually disagreeing. On game theoretic grounds a wariness-distrust-deception state of mind elicits a minimax or competitive strategy which is likely to produce costly conflicts in the group. Hence it is reasonable to assume an adaptation whereby people (or any group living animal) search for information about others' costs and benefits in order to understand their intentions. Once this information is obtained the default response to differences of opinion, public agreement and private disagreement, is suppressed. Which is precisely what Ross et al. demonstrated: After learning that the majority had an atypical incentive structure promising large benefits should this dubious judgement turn out to be correct (and imposing minimal costs should it be in error), the member undertands the majority's motivation, namely, they have much to gain and nothing to lose by taking this position. As a result, he or she no longer conforms but instead tells the others, in effect, that they are engaging in wishful thinking and leading the group into error.

Other important findings suggesting that humans by nature are prepared to encode the costs and benefits of social transactions is found in research by developmental psychologists on children's "theory of mind" (Wellman 1990). Their results indicate that we have the capacity very early in life to represent the subjective state of others and do in fact take their feelings and intentions into account when responding to them. More direct evidence on social acuity is presented by Cosmides (1989; Cosmides and Tooby 1989; but see Cheng and Holyoak 1989; Politzer and Nguyen-Xuan 1992; Pollard 1990) who observed that formally identical problems of logical reasoning are easily solved when presented in the form of a social transaction, where cost-benefit thinking is helpful, but are difficult to solve otherwise. On the basis of these findings Cosmides argues that humans have specialized mental capacities for recognizing and elaborating upon the costs and benefits of social relationships and that these capacities reflect built-in encoding mechanisms "… or [are] the product of experience structured by innate algorithms that are specialized for reasoning about social exchange." Other researchers have focused on sex-specific costs and benefits of a social transaction, especially those involving reproduction, to predict differences between males and females in mating heuristics (Buss 1988, 1989; Buss and Barnes 1986; Daly and Wilson 1988; Daly, Wilson, and Weghorst 1982; Kenrick and Trost 1988; Symons 1979, 1987). For example, one widely recognized implication of this analysis is that females should be most sensitive to a potential mate's ability to invest resources in the family whereas males should focus on a potential mate's reproductive potential as well as her ability to allay concerns about paternity. In a cross-cultural study Buss (1989) found considerable support for these hypotheses in that females put relatively high value on their mate's earning capacity, ambitiousness, industriousness, and intelligence; and males, on their mate's youth, physical attractiveness, and chastity.

## Kinship psychophysics

Hamilton's model does not require kinship cues to be a perfectly reliable indicator of actual kinship. The correspondence between biological and perceived relatedness merely has to be reliable enough. Since the cues to kinship probably vary in diagnosticity depending on the kin category (e.g. if contact with relatives drops precipitously beyond the nuclear family and declines more slowly as relatedness further decreases, then familiarity would be a more useful cue for distinguishing, say, sibs from nieces than nieces from cousins), our capacity to differentiate between a very close and a moderately close relative may be different from our capacity to discriminate between a moderately close and distant relative. In fact, from the point of view of inclusive fitness the difference between a parent, sib, or offspring and an aunt, uncle, niece, or nephew *is* more significant than the difference between any of the latter set and a cousin. Hence, theory as well as intuition (plus our knowledge of psychophysics and social judgement) suggest that Weber's law is also likely to hold for kinship: Differences between close relatives appear greater than differences between distant relatives. If so, then effects involving close relatives may be more robust than those involving distant relatives.

To demonstrate the relationship between perceived and actual kinship a small study was carried out by my colleague, Warren Holmes, in which respondents rated how closely related they perceived themselves to be to a large number of kin ranging from an identical twin, parents and siblings, to cousins and great-grand-parents; also included were fictive kin (e.g. step-parents) and acquaintances. Holmes's results are shown in Figure 4.1. The decline in perceived relatedness between each pair of adjacent points is quite similar to our findings (Burnstein, Crandall, and Kitayama 1994). The most precipitous declines occur between very close kin ($r = 0.5$) and moderately close kin ($r = 0.25$).

Suppose, as is the case in the studies that follow, we have to decide which of two recipients to help and the latter differ in how closely related they are to us. To the extent that our decision depends on perceived relatedness, kinship should have the greatest impact when one of the two potential recipients is a very close relative ($r = 0.5$) and the other a more distant relative ($r < 0.25$), or someone unrelated to us. Interestingly, both in Holmes's and our own data, respondents regardless of sex perceived themselves to be more closely related to their mother than to their father. Paternal uncertainty at work, perhaps. Finally, the difference in perceived related-

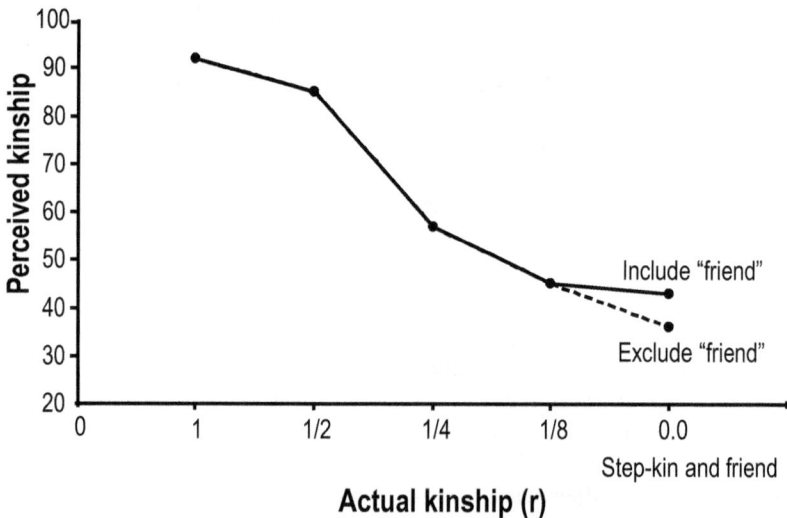

**Figure 4.1** Relationship between perceived and actual kinship

ness between fictive kin, friends, and acquaintances suggests that kin categories which aggregate biological relatives with non-biological relatives and primary group alliances have considerable influence on our sense of relatedness. In any event, based on these results, if you want to cut kin selection at its joints do it between $r = 0.5$ relatives and $r = 0.25$ relatives. It is at these points, where the perceived difference between adjacent values of relatedness are greatest, that we should observe the strongest effects of a kin selection heuristic.

## The kin selection heuristic

Inclusive fitness increases not only with a person's own reproductive success but also with the reproductive success of kin, which is why those who do costly things to benefit a relative also benefit themselves, genetically speaking. It takes no great leap of imagination to see how this notion could become the theoretical foundation for the evolution of cooperation (Axelrod and Hamilton 1981): In a population of cooperators and competitors, if the benefits of a transaction between pairs of cooperators is greater than that between any other pairing, then the genetic structures underlying cooperation are replicated more frequently in future generations than those underlying competition, particularly when, as is likely to happen, individuals are capable of distinguishing potential cooperators from potential competitors and can choose with whom they will have dealings. Hamilton, to illustrate the point in respect to kin selection, argued that our most common form of help, parental care, is a case of a family ministering to those who are most likely to have the genetic structures conducive to "ministering-to" (for proximal psychological mechanisms that may produce helping, see Batson [1987], and Lanzetta and Englis [1989]).

In the case of altruism, a decision informed by inclusive fitness concerns should reflect the following rule of thumb: Help those most closely related to you, especially when the cost and benefits are large. Among other things, such a heuristic is important because it allows the person to distinguish those social transactions in which inclusive fitness plays a major role from those in which it does not. To take the most obvious case, one that will preoccupy us throughout the chapter, it implies that help as a matter of life-or-death is significantly different from help as an everyday favour. Chagnon and Bugos (1979) describing an ax fight in a Yanomamo village in southern Venezuela, make the point that it is when individuals are in peril that "... some of the essential and rock-bottom characteristics of kinship ... reveal themselves ... Here ... the axiomatic qualities of human kinship as prescriptive altruism take on form and substance ... If we are interested in examining individual human behavior with an eye toward understanding the extent to which that behavior is 'tracking' biologically relevant dimensions of kinship relationships, it seems that crisis or conflict situations involving potential hazards to the actors are a reasonable place to begin" (p. 215).

From this perspective it is useful to distinguish between two versions of the kin selection heuristic, an everyday version that is primed by social transactions with no *immediate* or *direct* significance for inclusive fitness, and, we hypothesize, is driven by reputational concerns, a desire to do what is socially approved and, hence, to appear benevolent and fair to third parties who are potential partners for future transactions (see below), versus a life-or-death version that comes into play when social transactions do have important *immediate* and *direct* consequences for inclusive fitness. We assume that under everyday favour conditions the potential recipient's vulnerability, need, or worthiness is the default value for deciding whom to help. Other things being equal, a reputation for benevolence is best served by helping persons who are most deserving or least able to help themselves. In the case of the life-or-death heuristic what is important is their capacity to contribute to the altruist's inclusive fitness.

The cues used in altruistic decisions are no doubt only partially reliable and correlate imperfectly with fitness maximization as specified in a normative theory of selection. Kinship, however signalled, is of necessity such a feature and a critical one. In addition, there are various others that affect the recipient's capacity to produce and nurture offspring (or to contribute to the well-being of the altruist's offspring). Our studies examine some of the most obvious: The recipient's age, state of health, wealth, sex, and environment. Someone who is old, impoverished, in poor health, or lives in a malignant environment is less likely to produce viable offspring (or to be able to help others and their offspring) than a person who is young, rich, in good health, or lives in a benign environment. At the same time, however, many of these features also are cues to vulnerability and need. Typically the very young and very old are perceived as less able to help themselves than those of intermediate age; similarly, individuals who are in poor health, impoverished or, in all likelihood still, female are seen as more vulnerable than those who are in good health, rich, or male.

## How the kinship heuristic takes into account other's age, sex, and relatedness

This analysis has several implications for decisions to help. First, an altruist who is obliged to choose among potential recipients decides according to their degree of relatedness and the benefit-to-cost ratio. Hence, altruists prefer to help close over distant kin and this preference strengthens as costs and benefits increase, say, when helping is a matter of life-or-death rather than an everyday favour. Similarly, they prefer to help the young over the old, except when it is a matter of an everyday favour where costs and benefits are minimal and reputational concerns arise. Then altruism and recipient's age are curvilinearly related so that the very young or the very old are favoured over those of intermediate age. Finally, female recipients are favoured over male recipients but the differences attenuate in late middle age, especially when the costs and benefits of helping them are large. Our second study examined these predictions using Japanese as well as American respondents who were given a questionnaire describing triads of potential recipients and asked to choose which member of each triad they would most likely help and which they would least likely help. They did this under two conditions. In one, they imagined the potential recipients were in separate parts of a burning house and would not survive unless the respondent came to their rescue even though it was dangerous to do so; in the other they imagined that each potential recipient needed an item for a party and would be unable to get it in time unless the respondent went to the store for them even though doing so might make the respondent late for an appointment. In both cases the respondent was to assume that there was only enough time to help one member of the triad – the others, depending on the condition, would either perish or have to do without the item. The triad members varied in age, sex, and degree of kinship to the respondent. Some typical results are shown in Figure 4.2.

Surprisingly, neither the sex of respondent nor the country makes a difference. The patterns of altruism as we measure it are the same for men and women and for Japanese and American undergraduates. Kinship, age, and sex of recipient do make a difference, however. The weight given to kinship when help is a matter of life or death is greater than when it is a matter of an everyday favour as demonstrated by the finding that altruism decreases with relatedness more rapidly in the former than in the latter circumstances (see Figure 4.2). Moreover, in line with Study 1, this effect is more robust between $r$-values of 0.5 (parents, sibs, and offspring) and 0.25 (aunts, uncles, nieces, and nephews) than between the latter and 0.125 (cousins).

Furthermore, the relationship between help and age when costs and benefits are large is different than when costs and benefits are small. Under high cost-benefit conditions (i.e., life-or-death) we argue that the heuristic reflects kin selection; hence, help is allocated according to the recipient's fitness-value. Under low cost-benefit conditions (i.e., everyday favour) the heuristic is hypothesized to reflect reputational concerns met by allocating help according to the recipient's vulnerability

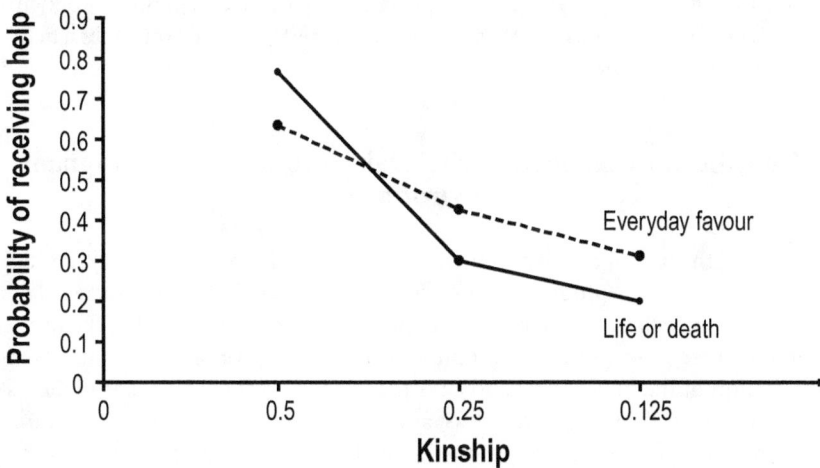

**Figure 4.2** Probability of receiving help under life-or-death vs. everyday favour conditions.

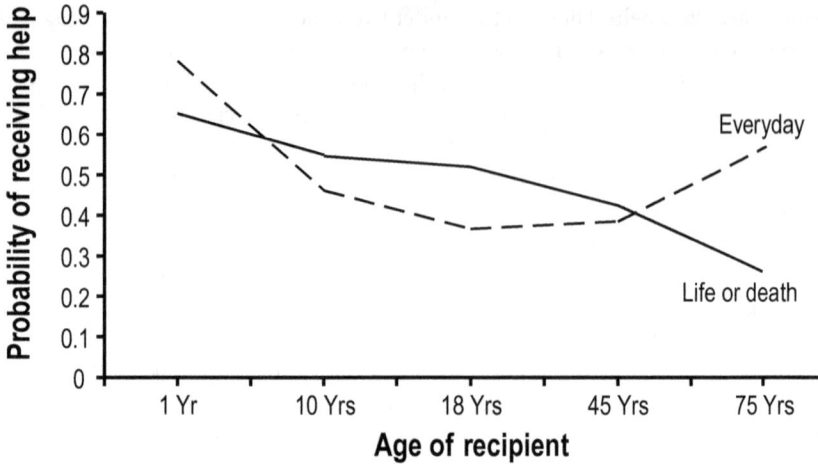

**Figure 4.3** Probability of receiving help as a function of the recipient's age under life-or-death vs. everyday conditions.

or need. Fitness value, of course, decreases linearly with age from puberty on. Vulnerability or need, however, probably varies in a curvilinear fashion with age. Both the very young and the very old are perceived as more vulnerable than individuals of intermediate age (and females as more vulnerable than males). Our findings are quite consistent with this analysis (see Figure 4.3): Under high cost-high benefit conditions altruism decreases linearly with recipient's age; however, under low cost-low benefit conditions altruism is curvilinear with recipient's age, the young and the old getting the most help and those in between the least. Finally, there is a menopause effect: altruists of either sex consistently prefer to help females rather than males until late middle age, the point at which female reproductive value begins to diminish rapidly. Equally important is that concern about reproductive value, which presumably underlies the menopause effect, occurs only when help is dear, not when it is cheap.

## How the kin selection heuristic take into account a malignant environment

Recouping the cost of altruism is increasingly uncertain the longer it takes recipients to realize their reproductive value. To help an infant is riskier than to help an adolescent since there are many more opportunities for harm to befall the former than the latter prior to them beginning their reproductive career. An interesting implication of the findings in Study 2 is that respondents seem to ignore the risk and to assume that infants have at least as much likelihood of a reproductive career as do ten-year-olds even though one is much closer to puberty than the other. Probably in benign environments, healthy, well-off young adults, which describes the vast majority of our Japanese and American respondents, do not readily think of infant mortality, childhood diseases, accidents of the nursery, and the like. As a consequence, when deciding between young and old recipients, they give little or no weight to the possibility that an infant or pre-adolescent may not survive to reproduce. Otherwise they would have chosen to aid a ten-year-old over an infant and the relationship between altruism and age of recipient under high cost-high benefit conditions would tend toward curvilinearity in the form of an inverted-U (opposite in direction to that obtained when the costs and benefits of altruism are small), which it does not (see Figure 4.3). However, if this line of reasoning is correct, curvilinearity ought to be observed when respondents are primed to think about the dangers to infants of baleful living conditions and to take into account infant mortality.

We asked several dozen undergraduates to picture themselves as citizens of a sub-Saharan country that for many years has suffered severe famine and disease so that infant mortality is very high and a large proportion of the newly born died during the first six months of life. Next they were given the life-or-death scenario with pairs of potential recipients varying in age as in the preceding study, namely, less than three months old, ten years old, eighteen years old, forty-five years old, and seventy-five years old. Respondents then decided which member of each pair they would save. In contrast with the high cost-high benefit condition in the preceding study where infant mortality was not primed and altruism decreased regularly with the age of the recipient, we find that here altruism is curvilinear with age starting out relatively low for infants, increasing for children beyond infancy, and then declining with age (see Figure 4.4). It seems, therefore, that if altruists are made to recognize that the younger the potential recipient, the more uncertain reproduction and, thus, the more his or her fitness value should be discounted, they do discriminate in favour of older over younger pre-pubertal kin.

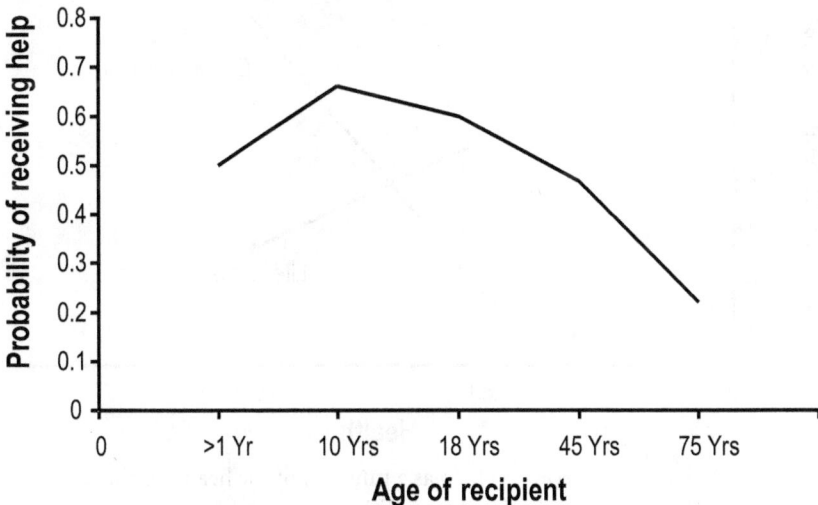

**Figure 4.4** Probability of receiving help under famine conditions.

# How the kin selection heuristic
## takes into account the other's health

Besides age, health is one of the more reliable cues to a recipient's capacity to increase the altruist's inclusive fitness. Of course, it is also a fairly unequivocal indication of the recipient's vulnerability. The healthier the relatives, the greater their fitness-value; the sicker the relatives, the greater their need. The state of health, therefore, is a particularly good feature to demonstrate the difference between allocating help under conditions of high costs and high benefits, where the recipient's fitness-value should receive the greatest weight, versus allocating help under conditions of low costs and low benefits, where vulnerability or need (and, thus, the reputation enhancing value of help) should receive the greatest weight.

Using the same procedure described in the earlier studies, we presented over two hundred undergraduates either the life-or-death or the everyday favour scenario and asked them to decide which member of a pair of potential recipients they would help. The members of a pair differed in their relatedness to the respondent and in their state of health. For example, the choice might be between a niece who is in excellent health and a sister who is in very poor health. As shown in Figure 4.5, we found good support for the inclusive fitness hypothesis, namely, under high cost-high benefit conditions altruists discriminate in favour of the recipient in good health; whereas under low cost-low benefit conditions they do the reverse, discriminating in favour of those in poor health.

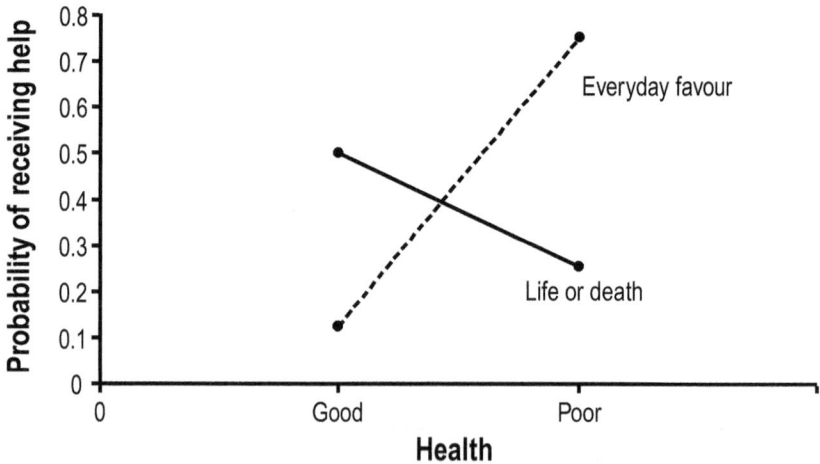

**Figure 4.5** Probability of receiving help as a function of the health of the recipient under life-or-death vs. everyday favour conditions

## The kin selection heuristic in young and old altruist

The degree to which an altruist is related to recipients, like their age and health, are cues to the return for altruism. The diagnosticity of these cues, however, changes over a lifetime because the gains to the altruist's fitness do not vary monotonically as recipients get older or sicker. Hence, a kin selection heuristic should be designed to be flexible in computing a cue's significance and to modify the weight assigned to a cue as its relationship to fitness waxes and wanes. This is most obvious in the case of age whose significance for fitness goes up from birth to a maximum at some point where individuals are well launched in their reproductive careers and then decreases continuously until they retire from reproduction and eventually die. An especially interesting challenge to computational flexibility arises from the correlation between age and kinship. Altruists in their twenties or thirties, for example, are likely to have sibs who are in their twenties or thirties rather than in their sixties and seventies; while altruists in their sixties or seventies are likely to have sibs who are in their sixties or seventies rather than in twenties and thirties. Hence, a truly adaptive kin selection heuristic would produce regular reversals of preference over the life history, causing the altruist to discount kinship as its fitness value decreases relative to other features such as age or health. For instance, a twenty-five-year-old should choose to help his thirty-year-old sister instead of her three-month- old son (his nephew); whereas forty years later at sixty-five he should choose to help his forty-year-old year old nephew or the nephew's fifteen-year-old daughter (his grandniece) instead of his seventy-year-old sister.

We examined these ideas by presenting pairs of potential recipients to a sample of over one hundred and twenty-five Ann Arbor residents and asking them to choose which member of the pair they would help. The pairs consisted of different relatives. In some pairs one member was more closely related to the respondent (e.g. sister vs. niece); in other pairs they were equally related to the respondent (e.g. father vs. son). One member in every pair was older than the other member; and when they also differed in relatedness to the altruist, the older member was always the closer relative. Each respondent received either the life-or-death scenario or the everyday favour scenario. For purposes of analysis the sample was divided approximately into thirds according to respondents' age: those under twenty-nine were considered young; from twenty-nine to fifty-six, middle aged; and over fifty-six, old.

We reason that kinship is more diagnostic of fitness value than age for younger altruists; and age is more diagnostic of fitness value than kinship for older altruists. Accordingly, the hypothesis of an adaptively flexible kin selection heuristic implies younger altruists discount the age of potential recipients relative to their kinship because for them degree of kinship has greater consequences for fitness than differences in age; whereas older altruists discount the kinship of potential recipients relative to their age because for them differences in age have greater consequences for fitness than degree of kinship. This suggests that when costs and benefits are large, young respondents prefer to help the more closely related member of a pair and ignore differences in age while older respondents prefer to help the younger member of a pair and ignore differences in degree of kinship. These effects should disappear, however, when the cost and benefits of altruism are small and concerns about reputation dominate the decision. In the earlier studies the recipient's age was specified (see above; also Burnstein, Crandall, and Kitayama, 1994). In this study recipient's age is not specified and must be inferred from the altruist's age and the logic of relatedness (e.g. if altruists are in their teens, then parents as potential recipients are likely to be in their thirties or forties; if altruists are in their forties, then parents as potential recipients are likely to be in their sixties or seventies; etc.). Hence, we might expect that when the cost and benefits of altruism are small, young altruists will not discriminate between sibs and parents since in terms of age neither are particularly vulnerable; however, middle-aged or old altruists will discriminate in favour of parents over sibs since parents have reached an age at which they are vulnerable.

The percentage of young, middle-aged, and old respondents who decide to help the younger over the older relative is shown in Tables 1 and 2. Table 1 describes the result when the two potential recipients have the same degree of kinship to the altruist. In this case, when costs and benefits are large, the preference to help the younger increases appreciably with the age of the altruist. However, when costs and benefits are small, young altruists are indifferent to the age of the recipient, whereas older altruists discriminate in favour of the older recipient. If the older potential recipient is also more closely related to the altruist (see Table 2), then when costs and benefits are large, young people do not discriminate on the basis of the recip-

**Table 4.1** Percentage of altruists who discriminate in favour of the younger over the older recipient when both are equally related to the altruist.

| | Costs and benefits of altruism (in %) | |
|---|---|---|
| Age of altruist Type of favour | High (Life or death) | Low (Everyday favour) |
| Young | 69% | 55% |
| Middle Age | 78% | 38% |
| Old | 83% | 24% |

**Table 4.2** Percentage of altruists who discriminate in favour of the younger over the older recipient when the older recipient is more closely related to the altruist.

| | Costs and benefits of altruism (in %) | |
|---|---|---|
| Age of altruist Type of favour | High (Life or death) | Low (Everyday favour) |
| Young | 47% | 32% |
| Middle Age | 71% | 33% |
| Old | 68% | 30% |

ient's age while older people do, again to the advantage of younger recipients; and when costs and benefits of altruism are small, altruists, regardless of age, prefer to help the old over the young.

Once more we find that the kin selection heuristic is quite flexible. When help is a matter of an everyday favour it leads altruists regardless of their age to discriminate in favour of old recipients before teenage and middle-aged recipients (pre-pubertal recipients, as reasoned above, were probably rare in this sample). However, when the costs and benefits of altruism are large their preferences change rather drastically. Then young altruists tend to ignore differences in age and prefer to risk their life to save close relatives rather than distant relatives. However, from middle age onwards, altruists tend to ignore difference in relatedness and chose to risk their life to save young relatives over old relatives.

## How the kin selection heuristic takes into account another's wealth

For fitness purposes altruists may not perceive a recipient's wealth in the same way as they do age or health. Unlike age or health, wealth can be transferred to others at the owner's whim. Moreover, in most societies people assume that wealth is shared by individuals as a function of their relatedness; or at least that close kin have a stronger legitimate claim on each others' wealth than distant kin do. That this assumption may reflect reality is nicely suggested in the Smith, Kish, and Crawford (1987) study of inheritance in Vancouver where (excluding spouse) 84 percent of kin's share of the estate belonged to offspring and siblings, 15 percent to nephews, nieces, and grandchildren, and 1 percent to cousins. Hence, as relatedness decreases, we perceive that people's return from another's wealth depends increasingly on the owners' feelings of goodwill or indebtedness toward them. If $x$ is rich, one is confident that $y$, her brother, is rich or ought to be, but less sure about $z$, her cousin. Moreover, wealth can be used by its owners to benefit others immediately and directly while nontransferable resources such as youth and good health affect others' fitness only in the long term and indirectly, to the extent that their "owners" themselves benefit from them and are related to the others (i.e., via the enhancement of inclusive fitness).

This implies that people expect as a matter of course to share in a close relative's riches. But when it comes to a distant relative, they expect that a claim on wealth depends on the obligation or gratitude their actions cause the relative to feel toward them. Consequently, individuals believe that in order to participate in the prosperity of close kin, they do not have to make an effort to ingratiate themselves but they do have to with distant kin. Generally speaking, altruism ingratiates to the extent that it is beneficial to the recipient and costly to the actor. Therefore, a kin selection heuristic should lead to discrimination in favour of the richer recipient when they are distant kin and costs and benefits are large. If the costs and benefits of altruism are small, reputational concerns once again come into play. In order to appear benevolent, altruists are likely under these conditions to discriminate in favour of poorer relatives regardless of whether they are close or distant. A bit of supporting evidence comes from a study of natural disasters which reported that upper class acquaintances receive more help than lower class acquaintances, but upper class relatives do not receive more help than do lower class relatives (Kaniasty, Norris, and Murrel 1990).

As in the previous studies we examined the relationship between altruism and wealth by presenting several dozen undergraduates with pairs of relatives and asking which member of the pair they would help when costs and benefits were either large (i.e., the life-or-death scenario) or small (i.e., the everyday favour scenario). Members of each pair differed in their relatedness to the respondent and in their wealth (e.g. your nephew who is rich vs. your brother who is poor). In line with our hypothesis, when costs and benefits are large, altruists do not discriminate between close relatives based on differences in their wealth, but they do between distant relatives. Hence, if it is a matter of life or death, a rich brother is no more likely to receive help than a poor brother; whereas a rich cousin is more likely to be helped than a poor cousin. However, when the costs and benefits of altruism are small, rich kin are markedly less likely to receive help than are poor kin regardless of the degree relatedness (see Figures 4.6 and 4.7). Again there is good support for a kin selection heuristic flexible enough to take into account differences in wealth while calculating the costs and benefits of altruism. That is to say, when altruism has direct and immediate impact on fitness, altruists count wealth more as relatedness decreases and, thereby, discriminate in favour of richer recipients if they are distant kin but not if they are close kin. When altruism can affect reputation but is cheap, having no immediate or direct impact on fitness, altruist reverse themselves and discount wealth to the point of discriminating in favour of poorer recipients regardless of whether they are close or distant kin.

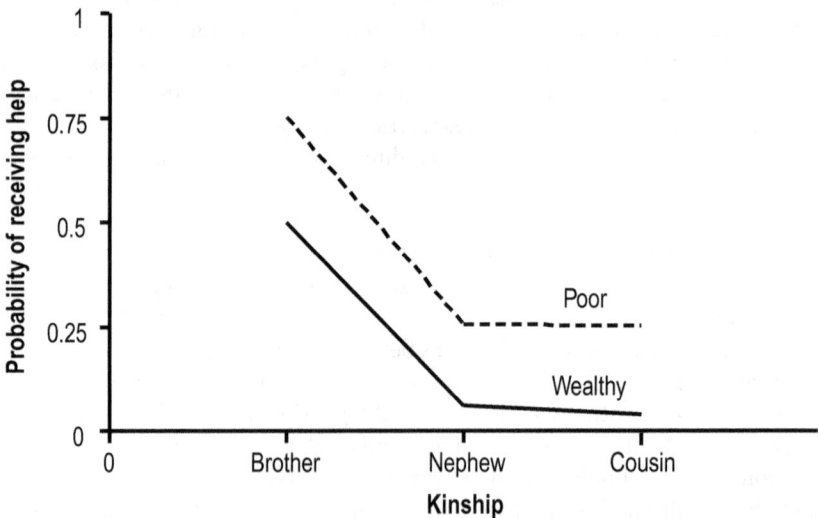

**Figure 4.6** Probability of receiving help as a function of kinship and wealth under everyday conditions

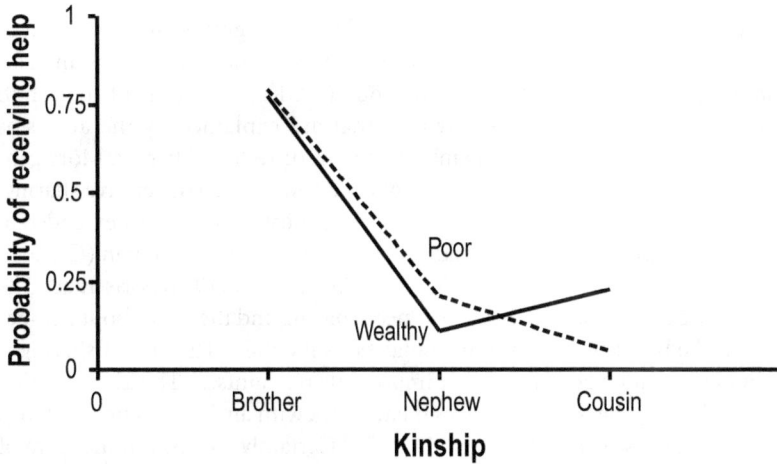

**Figure 4.7** Probability of receiving help as a function of kinship and wealth under life-or-death conditions

## General implications of a kin selection heuristic

Like any group-living species, humans must have evolved rules for encoding social transactions. To understand these rules we can, among other things, try to analyse the adaptive problems that a social transaction presented to individuals in their environment of evolutionary adaptedness. For humans, this environment was primarily low-intensity hunting-gathering in small, nomadic bands with decentralized authority, generalized reciprocity, little wealth, adult male status equality, and diffuse, flexible interband alliances (Knauft 1991). Not until the advent of agriculture and the domestication of animals, a mere 10,000 years ago, was hunting-gathering replaced by sedentism, food- storage, centralization of political power, individual ownership of property, ranked societies, and status competition. An essential feature of a low-intensity hunting-gathering system is intraband and, to some extent, interband cooperation (Boehm 1993, 1997). The !Kung, to take a case in point, have over the years been pushed by more warlike tribes ever further into the barrens where food, game, and water are scarce. An important reason for their successful adaptation has been the development of norms prescribing altruism in the form of generalized reciprocity: Valuable resources are readily shared within the band with only a vague expectation of repayment at some indefinite point in the future and not necessarily to the original donor (Silberbauer 1972). Ethnographers report that it seems unthinkable to the !Kung to do otherwise and that the custom of sharing is perceived as intrinsic to human nature. Some remarkable observations by Thomas (1959) even suggests that altruism of this kind occasionally occurs between non-allied bands. During a long hungry time, a hunter in a band that she was studying made a successful kill. While the meat was being prepared, another group of Bushmen whom they did not know arrived at the edge of the camp and watched in silence. After some discussion Thomas's band decided to give most of the meat to the other group in order, they said, that the strangers did not feel envious and also to establish good relations with them. Turnbull (1961) in his study of the Mbuti reports comparable examples of altruism that are explained by the actors as attempts at helping others to avoid embarrassment or feeling different. More generally, in all simple societies that ethnographers know about, cooperative sharing, especially in respect to prized commodities such as meat, is commonly extended to all others within the band and is considered as a symbol of being human (Cashdan 1980, 1985; Knauft 1991; Testart 1985, 1987). Marshall (1979) reports that "The !Kung are quite conscious of the value of meat-sharing and they talk about it, especially about the benefits of the mutual obligations it entails. The idea of sharing is deeply implanted and very successfully imposes its restraints…. The idea of eating alone is shocking to the !Kung. It makes them shriek with an uneasy laughter. Lions could do that, they say, not men (pp. 363, 357)." Certainly altruism in the form of food-sharing is peculiarly human in that its frequency and pervasiveness among hunter-gatherers contrasts sharply with the pattern of sharing typical of our nearest primate relatives (Fossey 1979; Goodall 1986; Kuroda 1980).

Some theorists have argued that in simple societies subsistence constitutes a less common problem than defense against hostile outgroups. Alexander (1974, 1979), for instance, compared the benefits to individual reproduction of group living under different adaptive problems such as scarcity or disease and concluded that the pressures towards mutual help and cooperation among low-intensity hunter-gatherers must have been generated primarily by the need for alliances with other bands as a means of protection against dangerous neighbours. In support of this line of reasoning, Wrangham's (1987; Wrangham and Peterson, 1996) comparative analysis of primate sociality indicates that intergroup hostility is common not only in humans but also in closely related species, namely, gorilla, bonobo, and chimpanzee, suggesting to him that animosity toward outgroups, whether motivated by fear or greed, is likely to be a conservative feature, reflecting a propensity of the common ancestor; as a result, Wrangham argues, it served to generate strong selection pressures for cooperative and protective relationships within human groups (also see Ember, 1978; Rodseth, Wrangham, Harrigan, and Smuts 1991). For our purposes, however, it makes no difference if the primary adaptive problem has to do with meagre resources or hostile outgroups. The essential points are, first, that the environment typical of low-intensity hunting-gathering puts a premium on ingroup cooperation and also satisfies the theoretical preconditions for its evolution (e.g. low dispersal rate, long lifespan, living in small, interdependent, stable groups, and a long period of parental care leading to extensive non-competitive contact with close relatives over many years [Axelrod 1984; Axelrod and Hamilton 1981; Trivers 1985]). And, second, that cooperation requires an understanding of the costs and benefits of our own and of other's actions, plus the ability to remember this information in the appropriate circumstances. In short, we are designed to cooperate, and cooperation is profitable only if the participants are also designed to take into account the interdependence between their outcomes (Abric et al. 1967; Axelrod 1984; Axelrod and Hamilton 1981; Kelley et al. 1962; Rabinowitz et al. 1966).

However, to go beyond merely asserting that individuals capable of calculating costs and benefits in a social relationship are positively selected, we have attempted to sketch the underlying mechanisms. Hamilton's model implies a heuristic that sensitizes altruists to the recipients' fitness value. Needless to say, the proximal (or conscious) decision to help rarely represents features explicitly signalling a recipient's relatedness, age, health, or wealth. Typically the subjective experience depends on the costs and benefits of altruism, or rather the ideation and emotions evoked by the unconscious calculation of these costs and benefits, and might range from a frightened, impulsive reaction when the other is loved and in dire peril to a cool, self-interested analysis when he or she is an acquaintance who needs a favour. Our ongoing research suggests that when altruists report why they decided to help a relative, their reasons have to do with impulsivity, affection, empathy, and familiarity; and that these feelings seem specific to kin altruism since they are not used by altruists to explain their decision to help non-kin. Whatever the nature of the experience, the encoding process must take into account fitness-relevant cues since the decision it produces has critical consequences for genetic continuation.

At the same time inclusive fitness theory says relatively little about the decision to grant an everyday favour, except that when the costs and benefits of altruism are neither immediate nor large, kinship and fecundity are unimportant cues in deciding whom to help. So we are left to reasonable speculation. If not according to the recipient's relatedness and reproductive potential, how then is help allocated? Our hypothesis is that in these circumstances altruists distribute help so as to gain social approval. In fitness terms, when the immediate consequences of altruism are insignificant, appearing benevolent, generous, or moral in the eyes of third parties eventually rebounds to one's credit by increasing the chances of being chosen by them for future transaction. In short, we argue that granting an everyday favour is adaptive to the extent that it is perceived by others as a benevolent act; and we further argue that it is perceived as a benevolent act when it cannot be explained by the potential return, that is, when the recipient is vulnerable or needy. Hence, if it is a matter of life or death, a kin selection heuristic would tell the altruist to benefit close rather than distant relatives, young rather than old relatives (when the environment is benign), healthy rather than sick relatives, wealthy rather than poor relatives (when recipients are distant kin), and the pre-menopausal over the post-menopausal female relatives. However, if it is an everyday favour then fitness is best served by presenting the self as concerned with the welfare of others, not with their resources. Accordingly, altruists prefer to do a favour for very young or very old relatives rather than those of intermediate age, sick rather than healthy relatives, poor rather than wealthy relatives, and female rather than male relatives.

While our results support the hypothesis that there is a psychological mechanism for encoding fitness cues in altruistic transactions that is consistent with kin selection theory, they say little directly about its origins; except, of course, the heuristic does reflect the type of social reasoning that ought to be positively selected for in group-living animals. Given a few reasonable assumptions about the perception of fitness value and kinship, it does follow directly from Hamilton's model, whereas none of the purely psychological analyses of altruism seem able to predict such effects. Actually, they are not obliged to do so. Although it is some-times overlooked, psychological and evolutionary models of altruism provide complementary explanations. A psychological theory of altruism is less concerned with why a particular mechanism (e.g. empathy, self-presentation, etc.) was favoured by natural selection but rather with how it works under present condi-tions to produce altruistic behaviour; an evolutionary theory of altruism, on the other hand, is less concerned with how a mechanism actually operates but why this particular design was positively selected. Nonetheless, psychologists might get some helpful leads from evolutionary theory about the adaptive constraints on mental processes. Certainly, the hypothesis of an evolved encoding mechanism for detecting potential "cheaters" in a social transaction (e.g. Cosmides and Tooby, 1992) would alert psychologists to the possibility that humans make at least as much effort to imagine and understand the intentions and feeling of foes as they do the intentions and feeling of friends; but to different ends and with different affective consequences – the success of a foe makes us sad while the success of a friend makes us happy (Lanzetta and Englis 1989). There does not seem to be a lot of enthusiasm for this approach, however. So, for instance, the most thorough psy-chological analyses of empathy (e.g. Batson 1991) pay little attention to kinship or to kin-like roles linking altruist and recipient, concentrating instead on factors such as similarity in social beliefs without recognizing that these are the psycho-logical correlates of relatedness. As a result, some of the most intriguing questions about empathy do not get asked. For example, why does belief-similarity, even in domains unrelated to the empathic state, influence empathy; why is it that two individuals who have the same opinions about something like capital punishment better understand how the other feels when succeeding or failing on a difficult mathematics problem than do two individuals who have different opinions?

However, if you ask for evidence that kin-selection reasoning informs real as opposed to hypothetical decisions, one can only surmise and cite interesting case histories. There is not a great deal of systematic evidence (but see Cosmides 1989; Segal 1984; Wang 1996). For instance, we think that Milgram's (1974) studies of obedience would have turned out differently had the "learner" and the "teacher" been related; we would even venture that proximity and physical contact with the "learner" served to drastically reduce the punishment the "teacher" inflicted on him because in the ancestral environment they are ecologically valid correlates of kinship. Research comparing altruism with non-altruistic forms of help such as reciprocity indicate that in primary group or communal relationships altruism arouses pleasant emotions and is considered appropriate while reciprocity arouses unpleasant emotions and is considered inappropriate; on the other hand in more formal transactions, altruism is unpleasant and inappropriate while reciprocity is pleasant and appropriate (Clark and Mills 1993; Litwak and Nesseri 1989; Mills and Clark 1982). In the environment of evolutionary adaptedness the primary group, of course, was in good part kindred. Yet even in modern urban societies unrelated males who have a close long-term friendship are found to be genetically more similar to each other than randomly paired individuals (Rushton 1989); and in field studies (Drabek et al. 1975; Kaniasty et al. 1990) if non-blood relatives are observed to be as altruistic as blood relatives, it is primarily in cases where the help is cheap and more in the nature of an everyday favour (e.g. visiting individuals or shopping for them when they are sick).

There are also reports of behaviour under extreme conditions that may have some relevance. Cohen (1989) cites testimony by concentration camp inmates suggesting that related individuals allowed to remain together, even though housed near crematoria, were more successful than groups of unrelated individuals in convincing themselves that they and their family would survive. Similarly, while most concentration camp inmates did not have a great deal of hope for the future and, thus, did not make elaborate plans, Cohen (1953, p. 129) notes that the most important feature distinguishing those who did maintain hope and attempted to plan was that they thought their close relatives were still alive, either in the concentration camp or else in hiding: "(the) view ... that (life in the camp makes the person) unable to live toward an aim ... (to) make plans for the future ... holds ... for those ... prisoners whose entire family had been exterminated ... however, plans for the future were not entirely ruled out; I remember having made a 'date' with a woman prisoner in Auschwitz, for after the liberation." Cohen then goes on to say that the death of one's entire family was such a common experience for Jewish prisoners and produced such prolonged mourning that in his opinion it is one of the main reasons for failures on their part to adapt to the concentration camp (p. 157).

One of the most interesting analyses of kin-altruism in catastrophic circumstances is due to Sime (1983). It examines reactions to a massive fire at a large seaside vacation complex on the Isle of Man during the summer of 1973 in which fifty people died. According to Sime's theory of escape behaviour "... when faced by ... an impending physical threat to people's lives and access to an escape route diminishing rapidly ... individuals will not be concerned solely with self-preservation. They will be even more concerned than usual to retain contact or make contact with other group members with whom they have close psychological ties and who are also threatened" (p. 21). Operationally, by "close psychological ties" Sime means kinship. Hence, his hypothesis, in fact, pits Darwinian fitness (i.e., self-preservation) against inclusive fitness (i.e., helping kin to escape): In what circumstances do individuals in a life-or-death situation simply flee to safety as quickly as possible without waiting for anyone else and in what circumstances do they risk waiting in order to help others escape with them? Of the one hundred and forty-eight individuals studied, one hundred and twenty-eight went to the central section of the vacation complex with a group, eighty-seven with immediate family and forty-one with friends or a mixture of friends and relations. Among other things, Sime distinguishes groups in which all the members exited from the burning structure together from those in which all the members did not exit together. At the moment they recognized their danger, about 66 percent of the families and 54 percent of the non-families were together in the central section. Of the initially "together" groups, over two thirds of the families and only about a quarter of the non-families emerged together as a group. Moreover, there also were thirty families and nineteen non-families that had been separated at the time members perceived themselves in peril. Of the initially "separated" groups, 50 percent of the families risked waiting to find each other and emerge from the building together, whereas none of the non-family groups did so (for other studies of kinship and help in disasters, see Cunningham 1986; Drabek, Key, Erickson, and Crowe 1975; Killian 1952; Quarantelli 1960).

Most researchers who are interested in testing kin selection theory in human groups follow a somewhat different course. In general, they observe how people behave in roles that *permit* or *oblige* them to help others. In socially stratified communities do the people with wealth and power use their status for nepotistic ends? And if their social position demands that they use it to benefit non-kin, are they inclined to evade the demands? Numerous ethnographic studies demonstrate that high status confers fitness advantages. Among the more recent examples, on Ifaluk, an atoll in the Western Carolines, Betzig (1988) found that clan chiefs spend about half the time of an ordinary citizen in the physical work associated with a communal catch and take home twice as much fish. In addition, they receive a variety of foodstuffs from virtually every family on the island irrespective of its kinship to them but dole out these commodities selectively to benefit close kin. Perhaps most significantly, these privileged individuals father appreciably more children than the average Ifaluk male (also see Turke and Betzig 1985). Similarly among the Ache, a low-intensity hunter-gatherer population in eastern Paraguay, the better hunters acquire more matings and produce offspring with higher survivorship than the poorer hunters. This is particularly interesting because it suggests that individuals can gain significant fitness benefits through their ability to acquire food even when the food is shared cooperatively among band members, as is the case in most simple societies (Hill and Kaplan 1988). Not very far away from the Ache, the more sedentary Yanomamo value fierceness in combat over prowess in hunting because they believe groups that show ferocity gain a reputation that deters violent neighbours – it is common for a Yanomamo to observe that villages whose inhabitants take revenge swiftly not only are attacked less often and suffer fewer casualties but are also spared other types of predation such as the abduction of their women. Hence, they appreciate and reward the more bloody-minded members: The Yanomamo village performs an elaborate public ceremony of ritual purification that confers high status, called *unokai*, on villagers who have killed an enemy during a revenge raid. That the effort to achieve *unokai*hood is widespread is suggested by the Chagnon's (1988) finding that, since 1965, 44 percent of Yanomamo males of twenty-five years of age or older have participated in the killing of someone, that about 30 percent of male deaths are due to violence, and that almost 70 percent of all adults over forty have lost a close relative due to violence, primarily intergroup battles. What is noteworthy from the point of view of Hamilton's model is that on the average *unokai*s have over 2.5 times more wives and over 3.0 times more offspring than non-*unokai*s (Chagnon 1988). In short, a fair summary of the ethnographic research is that individuals whose social role allows them to benefit another do so in a manner that enhances their fitness as measured by the number, fecundity, survivorship, social rank and wealth of their offspring (also see Betzig 1988; Borgerhoff Mulder 1988; Daly and Wilson 1983; Hrdy 1981; Irons 1979; Turke and Betzig 1985); similar effects are observed in Western societies ranging from fifteenth-century Tuscany to nineteenth-century Canada, United States, and

Germany (Becker 1991; for cases in eighteenth- and nineteenth-century Germany, where female offspring benefit more as a result of their parents' status than do male offspring, see Voland, Siegelkow, and Engel 1991). How do individuals behave in statuses that oblige them to be altruists when altruism reduces inclusive fitness? The most straightforward prediction is that such statuses are stressful and people avoid them or else they suffer. Hence, they should be infrequently occupied and those who do occupy them should be subject to the sundry disorders associated with stress. We know of no direct evidence on the relationship between the fitness-enhancing properties of a status and the frequency with which the status is occupied. However, it has been shown that the suicide rate of individuals in infrequently occupied statuses is considerably higher than the suicide rate of those in frequently occupied statuses. And the explanation given for these findings is that infrequent occupancy means the statuses are highly stressful (Gibbs 1982; Gibbs and Martin 1964).

The classic case of status obligations detracting from fitness has to do with paternal uncertainty. Husbands who invest in their wives' children benefit from doing so unless, of course, they are not the father. Confidence of paternity is a sufficiently pervasive adaptive problem that Daly and Wilson (1982) had little trouble discovering in North American maternity wards one clear proximal mechanism, among what must be many, for reducing paternal uncertainty: When describing the new-born, speakers tend to remark that his or her features are similar to those of the father rather than to those of the mother or other relatives. The alternative explanation is that rather than being a reassuring conversational ploy, similarity to the father is mentioned most often because on average an infant *is* more similar to the father than to the mother – an even more intriguing possibility that makes much evolutionary sense implying as it does that there is positive selection for paternal similarity (Salter 1996).

The naming of the new-born is equally interesting as a mechanism for influencing parental investment and paternal uncertainty. Let us assume that namesaking is a signal of forthcoming parental investment or a strategy to elicit such investment by establishing in the mind of the parents as well as third parties a new-born's claim on kin resources. Namesaking, accordingly, is increasingly likely when investment becomes problematic, as when the child is adopted or the mother and father are not married. It is no surprise, therefore, that a study of unmarried teenage mothers found that if the infant was named after a relative, it was nearly always the presumed father, with almost half of the infants also taking the father's last name even though the parents never married; nor that a extensive study of naming patterns in Higham, Massachusetts observed that in the seventeenth century nearly two thirds of the first sons and three quarters of the first daughters shared a first name with their parent. And since wealth was typically transferred through the father's lineage, special efforts were made to assuage the concerns of the patriline and establish the infant's claim to its resources as evidenced in first children being twice as likely to be named after paternal grandparents than after maternal grandparents (see review in Johnson, McAndrew, and Harris 1991). It has been argued by Johnson et al. (1991) that the more parenthood was certain, the less the need to establish a claim to family resources and, hence, the less the likelihood of naming an infant after relatives. In their sample of biological and adoptive parents, slightly less than 50 percent of the biological parents and slightly more than 75 percent of the adoptive parents named their child for a relative; in addition, since paternal uncertainty is irrelevant to adoptive parents but not to biological parents, adoptive parents were not biased towards patrilineal namesakes whereas biological parents decidedly were.

As males reduce inclusive fitness if obliged to help their wives' children when the probability of paternity is low, many cultures with high paternal uncertainty sanction male investment in sisters' offspring instead of wives' offspring. The Nayar, a group of castes in the southern India region of Kerala, are especially interesting since their history is approximately a "before-after" experimental design for testing the relationship between paternal uncertainty and investment in child rearing (Gough 1961). Prior to colonial rule, Kerala was divided into a number of petty kingdoms that were continually at war with one another. To carry out the fighting the rulers of these mini-states had armies that by tradition consisted of Nayar men recruited along lines of vassalage. In fact, Kerala society was organized so that military service to the sovereign was not just a caste obligation but virtually the only respectable career open to a Nayar male. Most importantly, the demands of military service required him to be absent from home frequently and for prolonged periods during his wife's most fertile years. It is no accident, therefore, that pre-colonial Nayar society developed a quite loose marriage system, loose enough that there was little social pressure on either partner to behave in a manner that was incompatible with their fitness. That is to say, the marital or *sambandham* relationship demanded no more than the participants take the role of lovers. Each was able to terminate the arrangement at will and was free to enter a number of similar relationships at the same time. Moreover, although one of the men with *sambandham* ties to the woman had to acknowledge paternity publicly when she became pregnant, this was a formality since he had no obligation to invest in her offspring. Rather the child was seen as belonging to the mother's lineage and its only prescribed relationship with a male of the mother's generation was with the mother's brother. In Nayar society he is the person perceived to be responsible for the rearing and education of the child. The investment demanded of the mother's brother was quite compatible with the latter's fitness because, from his point of view, a sister's child's $r$-value was certain and appreciable, namely, at least 0.125, since the mother was often really a half-sister, or at most 0.25, whereas the $r$-value of his own children was unknown and probably zero. To be more precise, Greene (1978) demonstrates that males are on average more closely related to their sister's children than to their wives' when the probability of paternity falls below about 0.27. This means that when a husband can accurately identify paternity in slightly more than a quarter of the cases, he will on average be more closely related to his wife's children than to his sister's children. However, the Nayar pattern of mating suggests that paternal certainty could easily be below this level (Irons 1979).

If we compare the situation in Central Kerala before and after British colonization, then in the "before" condition when military vassalage pushed paternal uncertainty to a level that males were more closely related to their sister's than to their wives' children, the roles of husband and mother's brother were defined in a manner consistent with fitness maximization, that is, males had no obligation to help their wives' children whereas they did have an obligation to help their sister's children. In the "after" condition, however, the situation changed markedly. Now that the armies of the petty kingdoms were disbanded and the benefits of a military career nil, monogamy became the rule. The result was, obviously, a marked decrease in paternal uncertainty and, not so obviously, a switch in the role of husband and mother's brother in respect to paternal investment. So within thirty years after the arrival of the British, an amazingly short period for a change of this magnitude, Nayar husbands assumed responsibility for rearing their own children and abandoned responsibility for the rearing their sisters' children. In Western society there are comparable co-variations between parental uncertainty and institutions regulating child rearing investment. Divorce, for example, increases in likelihood with the number of extra-marital partners a wife has and abortion increases in likelihood with the certainty that her husband was not the father (Essock-Vitale and McGuire 1988). Finally, were we to speculate about Nayar males' default heuristic for allocating help, there is an interesting observation in Fuller (1976) indicating a pent-up desire for stronger, more monogamous *sambandham* ties and, presumably, a predisposition towards paternal investment that applied before the arrival of the British, and was held in check by traditional norms.

The Nayar case illustrates the way in which the expectations associated with a role such as husband and mother's brother track paternal uncertainty and thereby enhance fitness. The tracking, however, is inherently imperfect. Changes in expectations in one domain occur at a different rate from those in another domain and there is often appreciable inertia. At some point in our lives, therefore, we are bound to occupy a role whose demands are incompatible with fitness. When parents migrate, for instance, the religious obligations to their children for arranging their marriage may remain relatively unchanged; but under the system of law in their new homeland, parents' legal duties towards their children may become so inconsistent with their religious duties, that the children's marriages become problematic. A sizeable body of research exists on a comparable inconsistency between social obligations and fitness, namely, parental investment by step-parents. Fathers and mothers everywhere have been prematurely widowed, and females with dependent children are often forsaken. Should the surviving parent attempt to forge a new marital relationship, the fate of the children becomes problematic. From the point of view of inclusive fitness, the step-parent's dilemma is similar to that of the Nayar husband: While helping stepchildren increases the spouse's fitness, it decreases the fitness of the step-parent. However, if the parents' commitment to a new spouse is strong, then absent institutions like the *avunculate*, where the responsibilities for investing in offspring fall to the mother's brother, the *levirate*, where a widow and her children become part of the family of the dead man's brother, or simply the leaving of children with postmenopausal matrilineal kin (e.g. maternal grandparents), a world-wide custom, step-parents in protecting fitness interests often imperil the well-being of the children.

Both in Duberman's (1975) U.S. urban sample as well as in Flinn's (1988) Trinidadian village sample only a minority of step-parents admit to "parental feeling" toward their stepchildren and even fewer say they feel "love" toward them. This suggests that in almost any society tensions occur in families where the spousal role obliges helping unrelated children (also see Hill and Kaplan 1988). That husbands in Tikopia and Yanomamo can demand the death of their new spouses' earlier children or that after their fathers' death, Ache children who are raised by other men have much higher mortality than those who are raised by their biological father and mother, also suggest that the consequences of these tensions can be devastating. However, the clearest evidence that this is the case comes primarily from studies of modern societies. In North America the likelihood of a child being abused is many times greater when there is a step-parent rather than two natural parents, even when socio-economic factors are controlled. In Ontario, Canada during 1983 the rate of per capita child abuse for children between nought to four years living with one natural and one step-parent is over 1.3 percent whereas the comparable rate for similar aged children living with two natural parents is much less than 0.1 percent (Daly and Wilson 1988). To avoid reporting biases, let us focus on the most unequivocally abused: In the over 87,000 instances of maltreatment of children identified by the American Humane Association in 1976, there were 279 fatalities. Of these, 43 percent lived with step-parents. According to Daly and Wilson (1988) this means that an American child – they report similar data for Canadian children – living with at least one step-parent in 1976 was about 100 times as likely to be fatally abused as a child residing with natural parents only. Needless to say, therefore, the kin selection heuristic also has dire consequences: If a social role demands that we behave altruistically to an unrelated person, we are inclined to renege and occasionally may do so viciously.

What is disconcerting is that these actions are usually impulsive and difficult to explicate by the actors who seem unable to comprehend what they gain from abusing stepchildren while vividly aware of what it costs them. The unconsciousness and inexplicability of intentions is striking and suggests an affective mechanism, overridden in stepchild abuse, that allows unrelated individuals to develop emotional attachments and identifications similar to those they have with kin by disassociating or discounting knowledge of their unrelatedness. The fact that prescriptive egalitarianism and sharing almost without regard to kinship is characteristic of human communities in the ancestral environment and remains deeply ingrained among modern hunter-gatherers (e.g. Boehm 1993, 1997) makes an adaptation designed to treat unrelated people as kin highly likely. For an as-if-kin mechanism to work, however, emotions antithetical to altruism, say, feeling that the other is a burden, may have to be disassociated to such an extent that they remain unconscious even when the person is driven to extraordinary actions to terminate the relationship. In short, when there are long-term benefits obtained from a social transaction, it is adaptive, for purposes of cognitive economy as well as self-deception, to feel and think about the other in a kin-like fashion. Accordingly, the cognitive system is predisposed to assimilate benevolent individuals, those with whom we cooperate or whose group is in alliance with our group, to the category of family or clan. And in so doing it is often abetted by a culture that encourages the use of categories like brother, sister, father, mother, etc. as a metaphor for affection, trust, or shared fate, a linguistic signal to consciousness that the other person is affectively a family member.

An as-if-kin mechanism assumes social categorization which is a process whereby individuals are cognitively grouped based on common features in *contraposition* to those not possessing these features. Cognitive grouping, therefore, has an important corollary: In assimilating benevolent individuals into the category of family-like people, the cognitive system automatically contrasts them with those that do not belong in this category. By default, then, those whom we or our fictive family dislike, compete with or even those whom we simply do not interact with (e.g. foreigners) are located in some subcategory under anti-family, anti-clan, or a quasi-foe (Sherif and Hovland 1961). The most obvious candidate to illustrate the process is the social category of ethnicity. Not just because it seems to evoke greater emotion, identification, and self-sacrifice than other social categories such as class or gender; but also, and perhaps more significantly, because its members may have unconsciously absorbed and some even consciously believe a myth that is peculiar to *ethnie* and no other social category, namely, that common ethnicity implies common ancestry (Connor 1990; van den Berghe 1981). Once knowledge of this kind has insinuated itself the member is likely to feel that whereas relations in other collectivities are instrumental with reciprocity the rule, relations within the *ethnie* are communal and altruistic. Our conjecture is that unless they are subject to deliberate conscious control, the emotions stirred by the myth of common ancestry, like other once-adaptive affective signals, still inform behaviour towards the other even in developed societies. This is most likely to happen if the notion of common ancestry is collectively endorsed, inculcated early in life, and spared critical analysis; and also if much is at stake for the *ethnie*. Informal observation suggests that when the *ethnie* is at risk, those who consciously dismiss common ancestry as poppycock, though safe themselves, experience a sense of shared fate with the endangered members, feel as if they are kindred, and want to help despite the cost.

A sense of shared fate in the face of threat not only serves to motivate altruism; it is also useful in controlling attention and dominating the content of consciousness since it would not do for members of the *ethnie* to be aware of the connection between a dubious narrative about group origins and their urgent need to come to the aid of the group. Such a dissociative mechanism might also explain why simply knowing that group differences are illusory or irrelevant is insufficient to prevent wariness or fear of other *ethnie*. In any event, as a result of dissociation, the benefits of ethnic conflict tend to be framed in rather abstract, pallid terms, for example, a struggle against subordination ("... if we [Malay] don't beat the Chinese, we will remain under them forever ...") or extinction ("... if the Georgians control the state, our [Ossetian] community will vanish ..."). However, the costs that ensue as the conflict escalates are tangible and often quite vivid. Even ethnic élites, who tend not to suffer the consequences of their leadership, can dissociate to the point that it is easier for them to grasp what they are losing as a result of the conflict than what they intended to gain. Several years ago the *New York Times* (2 June 1992) printed an interview with the Serbian commander of the army that at the very moment was laying siege to Sarajevo, in which he despaired that "After living so well in Yugoslavia, and creating this disaster, we should get a Nobel Prize for stupidity."

Suppose the costs of ethnic conflict in fact tend to be more tangible and available to consciousness than its benefits. Then what motivates *ethnies* to fight? Consider that people everywhere throughout history have categorized themselves according to culture, religion, language, phenotype (i.e., race), and proximity (i.e., territory) and have made the peculiar inference of shared descent (*cum* shared destiny) from common category membership. This myth then becomes the cognitive and affective foundation for the members' implicit theory of *the* social unit, an evolved mental model describing boundaries between those similar and dissimilar to the self, and offering rules that locate individuals in respect to these boundaries. The rules work automatically since it seems impossible to see, hear, or think of a person without immediately coding for age, sex, skin colour, speech, dress and various other features that make for grouping and categorization. The affective component of this adaptation comes to the fore when there is some prospect of a transaction with the other under mixed-motive conditions. As cooperation would leave the person vulnerable to defection, it is a strategy that elicits wariness or even anxiety to the extent that the other is unfamiliar or dissimilar, hence, unpredictable, and the temptation to defect, appreciable. Without evidence to the contrary, the person doubts the other's trustworthiness enough to play it safe and to shun the transaction. Or, if a transaction is unavoidable, to adopt a minimax strategy in which competition is not for gain but for protection. In fact, there is considerable experimental evidence (Diehl 1990; Tajfel 1981; Turner 1987) that when the environment is inhospitable to cooperation, groups behave competitively toward each other even though the benefits (or costs) of membership are nil. The groups are typically very short-lived, have little purpose, and belonging is on the face of it virtually meaningless, being either arbitrary or based on trivial characteristics of the individual. This is probably the clearest demonstration that if the setting offers no incentives for intergroup alliances – an atypical circumstance, we think, as far as the environment of evolutionary adaptedness goes – then members are predisposed to be wary and to follow a minimax strategy in dealing with another group. Nonetheless, people can make a conscious effort to control predispositions of this kind and override them. We know, therefore, that group differences do not necessarily imply intergroup conflict. For instance, individuals belonging to different groups may cooperate in a prisoners' dilemma game, especially if they believe they will not be deceived by a player from the other group, *unless* they are pressured to compete by their own group (Insko and Schopler 1987; Insko, Schopler, Hoyle, Dardis, and Graetz 1990). This suggests to us that ingroup-outgroup categorization is overridden when the possibility of useful alliances between groups is salient, which implies that overriding may have to be accomplished after or in parallel with a more deliberative decision process whereby members consciously calculate the degree of common interest with the other group and the relevance of group differences to realizing this interest. However, this should not be news. After all, it was fifty years ago when Sherif (1951) carried out his celebrated research on intergroup conflict that demonstrated, contrary to what still seems to be the conventional wisdom, that past antagonisms of a rather severe sort do not prevent groups from appreciating that they have important common interests, or what Sherif called a "superordinate goal", and from recognizing that the achievement of these interests would not be in the least facilitated by them sharing culture, language, religion, race, or territory nor need it be in the least hindered by them not sharing these features.

# References

Abric, J.C., Faucheux, C., Moscovici, S., and Plon, M. (1967). Role de l'image du partenaire sur la cooperation en situation de jeu. *Psychologogie Francaise*, **12**, 267–75.

Alexander, R.D. (1974). The evolution of social behavior. *Annual Review of Ecology and Systematics*, **5**, 325–83.

Alexander, R.D. (1979). *Darwinism and human affairs*, (pp. 43–65, 219–233). University of Washington Press, Seattle.

Alexander, R.D. (1987). *The biology of moral systems*. Aldine De Gruyter, Hawthorne, NY.

Asch, S.E. (1956). Studies of independence and conformity: 1. A minority of one against a unanimous majority. *Psychological Monographs*, **70**, (Whole No. 416).

Axelrod, R. (1984). *The evolution of cooperation*. Basic Books, New York.

Axelrod, R., and Hamilton, W.D. (1981). The evolution of cooperation. *Science*, **211**, 1390–6.

Bales, R.F. (1970). *Personality and interpersonal behavior*. Rinehart & Winston, New York.

Batson, C.D. (1987). Prosocial motivation: Is it ever truly altruistic? In *Advances in experimental social psychology, Vol. 20*, (ed. L. Berkowitz), pp. 65–122). Academic Press, New York.

Batson, C.D. (1990). How social an animal: The human capacity for caring. *American Psychologist*, **45**, 336–46.

Batson, C.D. (1991) *The question of altruism*. Erlbaum, Hillsdale, NJ.

Becker, G. (1991). *A treatise on the family* (enlarged edn). Harvard University Press, Cambridge, MA..

Benjamin, L.S. (1974). Structural analysis of social behavior. *Psychological Review*, **81**, 392–425.

Berghe, P.L. van den (1981). *The ethnic phenomenon*. Elsevier, New York.

Betzig, L. (1988). Redistribution: Equity or exploitation? In *Human reproductive behaviour* (eds L. Betzig, M.B. Mulder and P. Turke), pp.49–64. University of Cambridge Press, Cambridge, UK.

Boehm, C. (1993). Egalitarian society and reverse dominance hierarchy. *Current Anthropology*, **34**, 227–54.

Boehm, C. (1997). Impact of the human egalitarian syndrome on darwinian selection mechanics. *The American Naturalist*, **150**, (supplement), 100–21.

Borgerhoff Mulder, M. (1988). Reproductive success in three Kipsigis cohorts. In *Reproductive success: Studies of individual variation in contrasting breeding systems* (ed. T.H. Clutton-Brock), pp. 419–35. University of Chicago Press, Chicago.

Borgatta, E.F. (1962). A systematic study of interaction process scores, peer and self-assessments, personality and other variables. *Genetic Psychology Monographs*, **65**, 219–91.

Burnstein, E., Crandall, C., and Kitayama, S. (1994). Some neo-Darwinian decision rules for altruism: Weighing cues for inclusive fitness as a function of the biological importance of the decision. *Journal of Personality and Social Psychology*, **67**, 773–89.

Buss, D.M. (1988). The evolution of human intrasexual competition: Tactics of mate attraction. *Journal of Personality and Social Psychology*, **54**, 616–28.

Buss, D.M. (1989). Sex differences in human mate preferences: Evolutionary hypotheses tested in 37 cultures. *Behavioral & Brain Sciences*, **12**, 1–49.

Buss, D.M., and Barnes, M.F. (1986). Preferences in human mate selection. *Journal of Personality and Social Psychology*, **50**, 559–70.

Caporeal, L.R., Dawes, R.M., Orbell, J.M., and van de Kragt, A.J.C. (1989). Selfishness examined: Cooperation in the absence of egoistic incentives. *Behavioral and Brain Science*, **12**, 683–739.

Cashdan, E.A. (1980). Egalitarianism among hunters and gatherers. *American Anthropologist*, **82**, 116–120.

Cashdan, E.A. (1985). Coping with risk: Reciprocity among the Basarwa of northern Botswana. *Man*, **20**, 454–74.

Chagnon, N.A. (1979). Mate competition, favoring close kin, and village fissioning among the Yanomamo Indians. In *Evolutionary biology and human social behavior* (eds N.N. Chagnon and W. Irons). Duxbury Press, North Scituate, MA.

Chagnon, N.A. (1988). Life histories, blood revenge, and warfare in a tribal population. *Science*, **239**, 985–92.

Chagnon, N.A., and Bugos, P.E., Jr. (1979). Kin selection and conflict: An analysis of a Yanomamo ax fight. In *Evolutionary biology and human social behavior: An anthropological perspective* (eds N.A. Chagnon and W. Irons). Duxbury Press, North Scituate, MA.

Cheney, D.L., and Seyfarth, R.M. (1985). Social and non-social knowledge in vervet monkeys. *Philosophical Transactions of the Royal Society of London*, **308**, 187–201.

Cheng, P., and Holyoak, K.J. (1989). On the natural selection of reasoning theories. *Cognition*, **33**, 285–313.

Clark, M.S., and Mills, J. (1993). The difference between communal and exchange relationships: What it is and is not. *Personality and Social Psychology Bulletin*, **19**, 684–91.

Cohen, E.A. (1989). *Human behavior in the concentration camp*. W.W. Norton, New York.

Connor, W. (1990) When is a nation? *Ethnic and Racial Studies*, **13**, 92–103.

Cosmides, L. (1989). The logic of social exchange: Has natural selection shaped how humans reason? Studies with the Wason selection task. *Cognition*, **31**, 187–276.

Cosmides, L., and Tooby, J. (1989). Evolutionary psychology and the generation of culture, Part II. Case study: A computational theory of social exchange. *Ethology and Sociobiology*, **10**, 51–91.

Cosmides, L., and Toobey, J. (1992). Cognitive adaptations for social exchange. In *The adapted mind: Evolutionary psychology and the generation of culture* (eds J. Barkow, L. Cosmides, and J. Toobey). Oxford University Press, New York.

Cunningham, M.R. (1986). Levites and brother's keepers: A sociobiological perspective on prosocial behavior. *Humboldt Journal of Social Relations*, **13**, 35–67.

Daly, M., and Wilson, M. (1982). Whom are newborn babies said to resemble? *Ethology and Sociobiology*, **3**, 69–78.

Daly, M., and Wilson, M. (1983). *Sex, evolution and behavior* (2nd edn). Willard Grant Press, Boston, MA.

Daly, M., and Wilson, M. (1988). *Homicide*. Aldine de Gruyter, Hawthorne, NY.

Daly, M., Wilson, M., & Weghorst, S. J. (1982). Male sexual jealousy. *Ethology and Sociobiology*, **3**, 11–27.

Dawkins, R. (1976). *The selfish gene*. Oxford University Press, Oxford.

Dawkins, R. (1982). *The extended phenotype: The gene as the unit of selection.* Oxford: University Press, Oxford.

DeSoto, C.B., and Albrecht, F. (1968). Cognition and social orderings. In *Theories of cognitive consistency: A sourcebook.* (eds R.P. Abelson, M.J. Rosenberg, and R.H. Taunenbaum). Rand McNally, Chicago.

DeSoto, C.B., and Bosley, J.J. (1962). The cognitive structure of a social structure. *Journal of Abnormal and Social Psychology*, **64**, 303–7.

Dickemann, M. (1979). Female infanticide, reproductive strategies, and social stratification: A preliminary model. In *Evolutionary biology and human social behavior: An anthropological perspective* (eds N.A. Chagnon and W.G. Irons), pp. 321–67). Duxbury Press, North Scituate, MA.

Dickemann, M. (1981). Paternal confidence and dowry competition: A bicultural analysis of purdah. In *Natural selection and social behavior* (eds R.D. Alexander and D.W. Tinkle). Chiron Press, New York.

Diehl, M. (1990). The minimal group paradigm: Theoretical explanations and empirical findings. In *European review of social psychology*. Vol. 1. (eds W. Strobe and M. Hewstone). John Wiley, New York.

Drabek, T.E., Key, W.H., Erickson, P.E., and Crowe, J.L. (1975). The impact of disaster on kin relationship. *Journal of Marriage and the Family*, **34**, 481–94.

Duberman, L. (1975). *The reconstituted family: A study of remarried couples and their children*. Nelson-Hall, Chicago, IL.

Ember, C.R. (1978). Myths about hunter-gatherers. *Ethnology*, **17**, 439–48.

Essock-Vitale, S. (1984). The reproductive success of wealthy Americans. *Ethology and Sociobiology*, **5**, 45–9.

Essock-Vitale, S.M., and McGuire, M.T. (1988). What 70 million years hath wrought: Sexual histories and reproductive success of a random sample of American women. In *Human reproductive behaviour* (eds L. Betzig, M.B. Mulder, and P. Turke), pp. 221–36. Cambridge University Press, Cambridge, UK.

Essock-Vitale, S.M., and McGuire, M.T. (1985). Women's lives viewed from an evolutionary perspective. II. Patterns of helping. *Ethology and Sociobiology*, **6**, 155–73.

Fisek, M.H., and Ofshe, R. (1970). The process of status evolution. *Sociometry*, **33**, 327–46.

Fisher, R.A. (1958/1930). *The genetical theory of natural selection.* Dover Press, New York.

Flinn, M.V. (1981). Uterine vs. agnatic kinship variability and associated cousin marriage preferences. In *Natural selection and social behavior: Recent research and new theory* (eds R.D. Alexander and D.W. Tinkle), pp. 439–75. Chiron Press, New York.

Flinn, M.V. (1988). Parent-offspring interactions in a Caribbean village: Daughter guarding. In *Human reproductive behavior: A Darwinian perspective* (eds L.Betzig, M.B. Mulder, and P. Turke), pp. 189–200). Cambridge University Press, Cambridge, UK.

Foa, U.G. (1961). Convergences in the analysis of the structure of interpersonal behavior. *Psychological Review*, **68**, 341–53.

Fossey, D. (1979). Development of the mountain gorilla (Gorilla *gorilla beringei*): The first thirty-six months. In *The great apes* (eds D.A. Hamburg and E.R. McCown), pp. 139–84). Cummings, Menlo Park, CA.

Fuller, C.J. (1976). *The Nayars today.* Cambridge University Press, London..

Gibbs, J.P. (1982). Testing the theory of status integration and suicide rates. *American Sociological Review*, **47**, 227–37.

Gibbs, J.P., and Martin, W.T. (1964). *Status Integration and Suicide: A Sociological Study.* University of Oregon Press, Eugene, OR.

Goodall, J. (1986). *The chimpanzees of Gombe: Patterns of behavior.* Belknap/Harvard University Press, Cambridge, MA.

Gough, K. (1961). Nayar: Central Kerala. In *Matrilineal kinship* (eds D.M. Schneider and K. Gough). Berkeley: University of California, Berkeley.

Greene, P. J. (1978). Promiscuity, paternity, and culture. *American Ethnologist*, **5**, 151–59.

Haldane, J.B.S. (1932). *The causes of evolution.* Longmans, Green & Co., New York.

Haldane, J.B.S. (1955). Population genetics. *New Biology*, **18**, 34–51.

Hames, R.B. (1979). Relatedness and interaction among the Ye'kwana: A preliminary analysis. In *Evolutionary biology and human social behavior: An anthropology perspective* (eds N. Chagnon and W. Irons). Duxbury Press, North Scituate, MA.

Hamilton, W.D. (1964). The genetical evolution of social behavior, Parts I and II. *Journal of Theoretical Biology*, **7**, 1–52.

Hare, A.P. (1976). *Handbook of small group research* (2nd edn). Free Press, New York.

Hartung, J. (1976). On natural selection and the inheritance of wealth. *Current Anthropology*, **17**, 607–22.

Hartung, J. (1982). Polygyny and inheritance of wealth. *Current Anthropology*, **17**, 607–22.

Hill, K., and Kaplan, H. (1988). Tradeoffs in male and female reproductive strategies among the Ache. In *Human reproductive behaviour* (eds L. Betzig, M.B. Mulder, and P. Turke), pp 277–306. Cambridge University Press, Cambridge, UK.

Hinde, R.A. (1987). *Individuals, relationships and culture: Links between ethology and the social sciences.* Cambridge University Press, Cambridge, UK.

Holmes, W.G., and Sherman, P.W. (1983). Kin recognition in animals. *American Scientist*, **71**, 46–55.

Hrdy, S.B. (1981). *The woman that never evolved*. Harvard University Press, Cambridge, MA.

Insko, C.A., and Schopler, J. (1987) Categorization, competition and collectivity. In *Group processes* (ed. C. Hendrick), pp. 213–51. Sage, New York.

Insko, C.A., Schopler, J., Hoyle, R.H., Dardis, G.J., and Graetz, K.A. (1990) Individual-group discontinuity as a function of fear and greed. *Journal of Personality and Social Psychology*, **58**, 68–79.

Irons, W. (1979). Investment and primary social dyads. In *Evolutionary biology and human social behavior: An anthropological perspective* (eds N.A. Chagnon and W. Irons). Duxbury Press, North Scituate, MA.

Johnson, J.L., McAndrew, F.T., and Harris, P.B. (1991). Sociobiology and the naming of adopted and natural children. *Ethology and Sociobiology*, **12**, 365–75.

Kaniasty, K.Z., Norris, F.H., and Murrell, S.A. (1990). Received and perceived social support following natural disaster. *Journal of Applied Social Psychology*, **20**, 85–114.

Kelley, H.H., Thibaut, J.W., Radloff, R., and Mundy, D. (1962). The development of cooperation in the "minimal social situation." *Psychological Monographs*, **76**(19).

Kenrick, D.T., and Trost, M.R. (1988). A reproductive exchange model of heterosexual relationships: Putting proximate economics in ultimate perspective. In *Review of personality and social psychology*, Vol. 10 (ed. C. Hendrick). Sage, New York.

Keuthe, J.L., and DeSoto, C.B. (1964). Grouping and ordering schemata in competition. *Psychonomic Science*, **1**, 115–16.

Killian, L.M. (1952). The significance of multiple-group membership in disaster. *American Journal of Sociology*, **57**, 309–14.

Kirk, R.E. (1968). *Experimental design: Procedures for the Behavior Sciences.* Brooks/Cole, Monterey, CA.

Knauft, B. M. (1991). Violence and sociality in human evolution. *Current Anthropology*, **32**(4), 391–428.

Kuroda, S. (1980). Social behavior of the pygmy chimpanzees. In *The pygmy chimpanzee: Evolutionary biology and behavior* (ed. R.L. Susman), pp. 301–24. Plenum Press, New York.

Lanzetta, J.T., and Englis, B.G. (1989). Expectations of cooperation and competition and their effects on observers' vicarious emotional responses. *Journal of Personality and Social Psychology*, **56**, 543–54.

Latané, B., and Nida, S. (1981). Ten years of research on group size and helping. *Psychological Bulletin*, **89**, 308–24.

Leary, T. (1957). *Interpersonal diagnosis of personality*. Ronald, New York.

Lee, M.T., and Ofshe, R. (1981). The impact of behavioral style and status characteristics on social influence: A test of two competing theories. *Social Psychology Quarterly*, **44**, 77–82.

Litwak, E., and Nesseri, P. (1989). Organizational theory, social support, and mortality rates: A theoretical convergence. *American Sociological Review*, **54**, 49–66.

Marshall, L. (1979). Sharing, talking, and giving: Relief of social tensions among !Kung Bushmen. In *Kalahari hunter-gatherers: Studies of the !Kung San and their neighbors* (eds R.B. Lee and Irven DeVore), pp. 349–72. Cambridge University Press, Cambridge, UK.

Maynard Smith, J. (1964). Group selection and kin selection. *Nature*, **201**, 1145–7.

McGrath, J.E. (1984). *Groups: interaction and performance*. Prentice-Hall, Englewood Cliffs, NJ.

Milgram, S. (1974). *Obedience to authority*. Harper & Row, New York.

Mills, J., and Clark, M.S. (1982). Communal and exchange relationships. In *Review of Personality and Social Psychology* (ed. L. Wheeler), **3**, 121–44.

Murdock, G.P. (1945). The common denominator of cultures. In *The science of man in the world crisis* (ed. R. Linton). Columbia University, New York.

Politzer, G., and Nguyen-Xuan, A. (1992). Reasoning about conditional promises and warnings: Darwinian algorithms, mental models, relevance judgements or pragmatic schemas? *The Quarterly Journal of Experimental Psychology*, **44A**(3), 401–21.

Pollard, P. (1990). Natural selection for the selection task: Limits to the social exchange
theory. *Cognition*, **36**, 195–204.

Quarantelli, E.L. (1960). A note on the protective function of the family in disasters. *Marriage and Family Living*, **22**, 263–64.

Rabinowitz, L., Kelley, H.L., and Rosenblatt, R.M. (1966). Effects of different types of interdependence and response conditions in the minimal social situation. *Journal of Experimental Social Psychology*, **2**, 169–97.

Rodseth, L., Wrangham, R.W., Harrigan, A.M., and Smuts, B.B. (1991). The human community as a primate society. *Current Anthropology*, **32**, 221–54.

Rosenblatt, P.C., Walsh, R.P., and Jackson, D.A. (1976). *Grief and mourning in cross-cultural perspective*. Human Relations Area File, New Haven, CT.

Ross, L., Bierbrauer, G., and Hoffman, S. (1976). The role of attribution processes in conformity and dissent. *American Psychologist*, **31**, 148–57.

Rushton, J.P. (1989). Genetic similarity, human altruism, and group selection. *Behavioral and Brain Sciences*, **12**, 503–9.

Salter, F. (1996). Carrier females and sender males: An evolutionary hypothesis linking female attractiveness, family resemblance, and paternity confidence. *Ethology and Sociobiology*, **17**, 211–20.

Schutz, W.C. (1958). *FIRO: A three-dimensional theory of interpersonal behavior.* Holt, Rinehart, New York.

Segal, N.L. (1984). Cooperation, competition, and altruism within twin sets: a reappraisal. *Ethology and Sociobiology*, **5**, 163–77.

Sentis, K.P and Burnstein, E. (1979). Remembering schema-consistent information: Effects of a balance schema on recognition memory. *Journal of Personality and Social Psychology*, **37**, 2000–211.

Sherif, M. (1951). Experimental study of intergroup relations. In *Social psychology at the crossroads.* (eds J.H. Rohrer and M. Sherif), pp. 388–426. Harper & Row, New York.

Sherif, M. (1966). *In common predicament: Social psychology of intergroup conflict and cooperation.* Houghton Mifflin, Boston.

Sherif, M., and Hovland, C.I. (1961). *Social judgment: Assimilation and contrast effects in communication and attitude change.* University Press, New Haven, CT.

Sherman, P.W. (1977). Nepotism and the evolution of alarm calls. *Science*, **197**, 1246–53.

Sidowski, J.B., Wyckoff, L.B., and Tabory, L. (1956). The influence of reinforcement and punishment in a minimal social situation. *Journal of Abnormal and Social Psychology*, **52**, 115–19.

Silberbauer, G. (1972). The G/wi Bushmen. In *Hunters and gatherers today* (ed. M. Bicchieri). Holt, New York

Sime, J.D. (1983). Affiliative behaviour during escape to building exits. *Journal of Environmental Psychology*, **3**, 21–41.

Smith, M.S., Kish, B.J., and Crawford, C.B. (1987). Inheritance of wealth as human kin investment. *Ethology and Sociobiology*, **8**, 171–82.

Symons, D. (1979). *The evolution of human sexuality.* Oxford University Press, Oxford.

Symons, D.(1981). *Human groups and social categories: Studies in social psychology.* Cambridge University Press, London.

Symons, D. (1987). Can Darwin's view of life shed light on human sexuality? In *Approaches and paradigms in human sexuality* (eds J.H. Geer and W.T. O'Donohue). Plenum Press, New York..

Tajfel, H. (1981*). Human groups and social categories.* Cambridge University Press, Cambridge, UK.

Testart, A. (1985). *Le communisme primitif: Economie et ideologie.* Maison des Sciences de l'Homme, Paris.

Testart, A. (1987). Game sharing systems and kinship systems among hunter-gatherers. *Man*, **22**, 287–304.

Thomas, E.M. (1959). *The harmless people.* Knopf, New York.

Triandis, H.C. (1972). *The analysis of subjective culture.* Wiley-Interscience, New York.

Trivers, R.L. (1971). The evolution of reciprocal altruism. *Quarterly Review of Biology*, **46**, 35–57.

Trivers, R.L. (1985). *Social evolution*. Benjamin/Cumming, Menlo Park, CA.

Trivers, R.L., and Willard, D.E. (1973). Natural selection of parental ability to vary the sex ratio of offspring. *Science*, **179**, 90–2.

Turke, P., and Betzig, L.L. (1985). Those who can do: Wealth, status, and reproductive success on Ifaluk. *Ethology and Sociobiology*, **6**, 79–87.

Turnbull, C.M. (1961). *The forest people*. Simon & Schuster, New York.

Turner, J.C. (1987). *Rediscovering the social group: A self-categorization theory*. Basil Blackwell, New York.

Voland, E., Siegelkow, E., and Engel, C. (1991). Cost/benefit oriented parental investment by high status families. *Ethology and Sociobiology*, **12,** 105–18.

Wang, X.T. (1996). Evolutionary hypotheses of risk-sensitive choice: Age differences and perspective change. *Ethology and Sociobiology*, **17**, 1–15.

Wellman, H.M. (1990). *The child's theory of mind*. Bradford Books/MIT Press, Cambridge, MA.

Willard, D., and Strodtbeck, F. L. (1972). Latency of verbal response and participation in small groups. *Sociometry*, **35**, 161–75.

Williams, G.C. (1966). *Adaptation and natural selection*. Princeton University Press, Princeton.

Wilson, D.S. (1989). Levels of selection: An alternative to individualism in biology and the human sciences. *Social Networks*, **11**, 257–72.

Wilson, D.S., and Sober, E. (1994) Reintroducing group selection to the human behavioral sciences. *Behavioral and Brain Sciences*, **17**, 585–654.

Wish, M., Deutsch, M., and Kaplan, S.J. (1976). Perceived dimensions of interpersonal relations. *Journal of Personality and Social Psychology*, **33**, 409–20.

Wrangham, R.W. (1987). The significance of African apes for reconstructing human social evolution. In *The evolution of human behavior: Primate models* (ed. W.G. Kinzey), pp. 51–71. State University of New York, Albany.

Wrangham, R., and Peterson, D. (1996). *Demonic males*. Houghton Mifflin, New York.

# RISKY BUSINESS,
# ILLICIT AND LICIT

## Chapter 5

# Mafia and blood symbolism[1]

## Anton Blok

~~~

### I

This essay considers the nature of social ties between people who conduct risky transactions. As the example of the Sicilian mafia suggests, socially defined kinship and other institutions that draw on the metaphor of blood, structure salient coalitions involved in extra-legal practices called "organized crime". Since members of these sodalities cannot – for obvious reasons – turn for protection to institutions of the state, trust and retaliation have to be generated within their own ranks-a point already recognized by Simmel in his treatise on secret societies.[2]

We shall see that the relationships through which mafiosi in Sicily operate, evoke blood imagery, and that blood metaphors are used to mark and foster reciprocity. These relationships include agnatic kinship (consanguinity), affinal kinship, ritual kinship (godparenthood, co-parenthood), and ritual friendship (blood brotherhood). Moreover, violence and death mark sanctions and retaliation (vendetta). This essay explores how these relationships are socially and culturally defined, how loyalty and trust are built up, betrayed, and sanctioned, and how organizational flexibility and structural fluidity are quintessential to extra-legal coalitions in modern nation-states.[3] From this perspective, I hope to shed some light on the question why blood as a symbolic device dominates the discourse and practices of mafiosi.

# II

At the local level, bonds of kinship and friendship make up coalitions of mafiosi called "families" or *famiglie* (singular *famiglia*). The idiom of kinship and blood is significant because not all members are authentic kinsmen.

Each family controls its own territory – a rural village or town, an urban street or neighbourhood. Incursions are considered slights and invite a violent response. The territory is closely identified with the family as seen from the prevailing naming practices and sensitivity to even minor forms of trespassing. Overwhelming evidence suggests that the power base of mafiosi is always local.[4]

The size of these local groups ranges between half a dozen and well over fifty members. Families include a boss or *capo*, an underboss or *sottocapo*, one or more *consiglieri* or counsellors, and other "men of honour". They all have a reputation for violence and are able to "mind their own business", that is, keep secrets and cultivate *omertà*. At higher levels of integration, these local groups were represented in the so-called *Commissione* or *Cupola*, which makes rules and serves as a coordinating board. Since the early 1980s, following the confessions of several mafiosi who started cooperating with the authorities, much has been made of the alleged hierarchical and unified structure of the Sicilian mafia or Cosa Nostra. As the two notorious mafia wars of the early 1960s and the early 1980s demonstrate, however, centralizing tendencies have always been offset by segmentation. From the very moment the Commission (meant to control internal fights) was set up in the late 1950s, local groups and their allies tried to control the Commission and use it for their own ends.[5] The best known example is the rise of the "Corleonesi," originally a local group of mafiosi from Corleone (a rural town of about 14,000 inhabitants in Sicily's western interior) and their allies, who carefully planned and established their hegemony after the cruel civil war of 1981 to 1982 in which more than a thousand mafiosi lost their lives.[6]

As is well known, mafia enterprise involves control over the local economy (including real estate, building contracts, and markets), canvassing votes for politicians-protectors, and (since the 1970s) international drug trafficking. There were well over a hundred of these families in Sicily as a whole and about twenty-five in Palermo alone. They included several thousand mafiosi.[7] What is known about the composition and structure of these families?

First, they include agnatic kinsmen, that is, blood relatives who are exclusively related through males or, differently phrased, related on the father's side. Often, the core of these families consists of a father and his sons, a set of brothers, sometimes including one or more agnatic uncles and cousins.[8] In particular, sets of brothers have always been very common in mafia families, both in the city and in the countryside.

All these people are related by blood, that is, both biologically and culturally. Here obtains what David M. Schneider wrote about American kinship: "The facts of biological relatedness and sexual relations play a fundamental role, for they are symbols, culturally formulated symbols in terms of which a system of social relationships is defined and differentiated" (1977, p. 66).[9] Given its pre-eminence in mafia coalitions, agnatic kinship in Sicily, as in other Indo-European kinship systems, provides for relationships of "diffuse, enduring solidarity" (ibid.).[10] If in the absence of effective state control trust can be found anywhere, it is primarily in the bonds between agnatic kinsmen, that is, "blood" relatives.

Succession to positions of leadership usually follows the same agnatic lines. The oldest son often takes the place of his father, or, sometimes, his father's brother or, less commonly, his mother's brother. For example, in San Giuseppe Jato, Giovanni Brusca succeeded his father, Bernardo; in Palermo, Stefano Bontate succeeded his father, Paolino; in Alcamo, Filippo Rimi succeeded his father, Vincenzo; and in Riesi, Giuseppe Di Cristina also succeeded his father.

# III

Bonds within and between mafia families are reinforced by intermarriage. Along with agnatic kinsmen, therefore, these families include in-laws or affines. Also defined as kinsmen (*parenti*) they are relatives by marriage and as a rule not people to whom one is related by blood, although marriage between cousins does occur. Bonds with in-laws figure prominently in coalitions of mafiosi. Next to sets of agnatic kinsmen, one often finds sets of brothers-in-law as the core of these local groups of mafia families.

Among the Corleonesi,[11] for instance, Salvatore ("Toto") Riina maintained strong bonds with his brother-in-law Leoluca Bagarella, a brother of his wife. Riina was also on intimate terms with Giuseppe Marchese, whose sister married Leoluca Bagarella (see Figure 5.1). Moreover, to emphasize the organizational flexibility and structural fluidity of the Sicilian Mafia, matrilineal relations are also used to build powerful alliances. Of particular importance are the bonds between a mother's brother and sister's son since the position of leadership may be transferred also

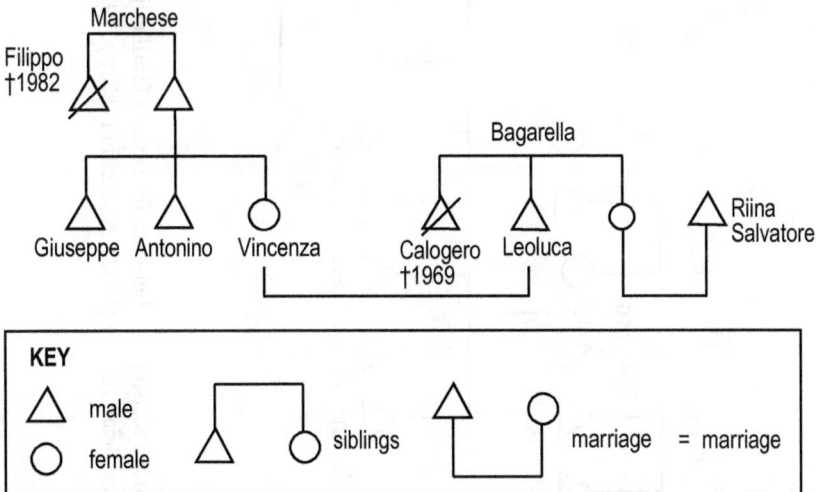

**Figure 5.1** Kinship ties between mafiosi: brothers-in-law

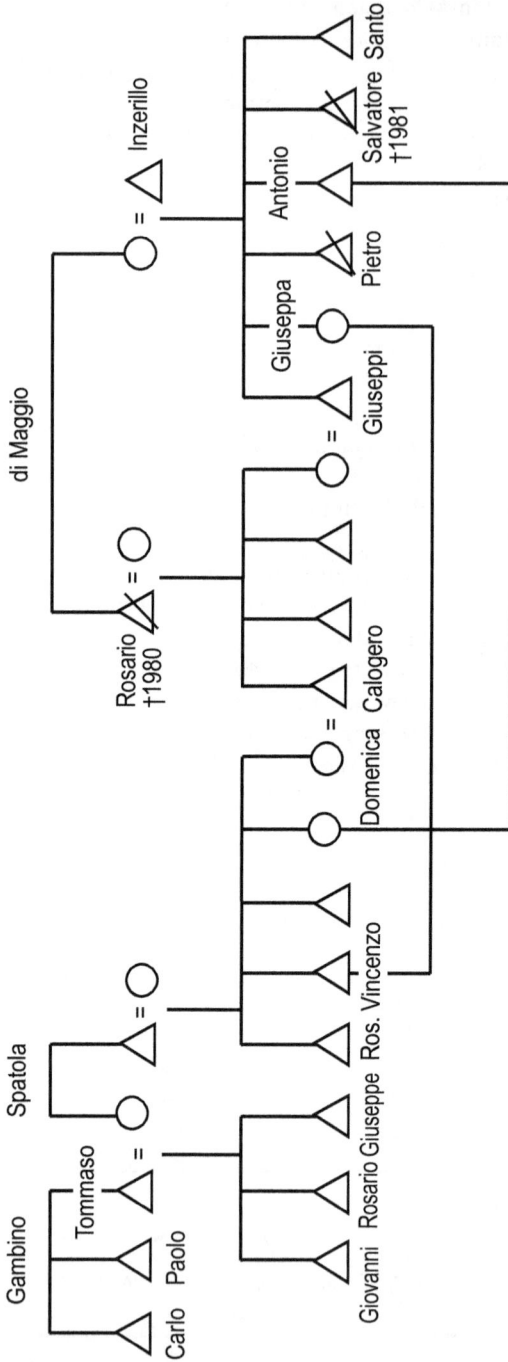

**Figure 5.2** Kinship ties between four mafia families in the U.S.A. and Sicily.
Sources: Sciacchitano (1982); Arlacchi (1987, pp. 193–202); Sterling (1990, pp. 199–206), Stille (1995, *passim*).

matrilineally. This happened when Salvatore Inzerillo was chosen to head the inter-continental superclan by his retiring mother's brother, Rosario Di Maggio.[12]

The composition of these families, who were all involved in the international heroin traffic, is instructive for our purposes because it illustrates the structural principles operating in groups that conduct risky transactions: kinship, marriage, and ethnicity, each of which animates global networks as much as local groups.

In his discussion of the entrepreneurial mafia and the heroin economy, Arlac-chi (1987, pp. 196–200) quotes from a 1982 indictment of the Palermo Public Prosecutor's Office, which provides further details on these mafiosi related through marriage, including intermarriage with American mafia families (see Figure 5.2):

> [T]hat the Gambino brothers are cousins of the Spatola brothers Rosario, Vincenzo and Antonio, their father, Salvatore, being brother to the Gambino's mother; that Giuseppe Inzerillo married Giuseppa Di Maggio-sister of Calogero, Giuseppe and Salvatore Di Maggio-while Calogero Di Maggio married Domenica Spatola, thus strengthening the kinship links between these families (1987, p. 200).

Although Arlacchi recognizes the implications of these alliances for the internal cohesion of these groups, he strangely but not untypically categorizes intermar-riage, adoption, and sponsorship as "apparently irrational practices", and dismisses them as "artificial" (1987, p. 199). Drawing on the same report from the Palermo public prosecutor, Sterling (1990, pp. 199–200) is more specific about these alliances and also more sensitive to their importance:

> The Spatolas were found to be one of the four Mafia Families forming a transatlantic colossus. The Cherry Hill Gambinos were another. The Inzerillos, closest of all clans to Stefano Bontate, were a third. The fourth, related to the other three by blood and marriage, were the Di Maggios of Palermo and southern New Jersey. Their intercon-tinental family ties resembled the Hapsburgs' or Hohenzollerns', the marriages arranged to strengthen dynasties and preserve the blood royal. There were six Spato-las involved, five Gambinos (three brothers and two cousins), four Di Maggios, and fifteen Inzerillos. The Gambinos mother's brother was a Spatola. The Inzerillos' father has married a Di Maggio, whose brother had married a Spatola.
>
> Salvatore Inzerillo, the biggest heroin broker of all, had been chosen to head the Family's clan by his retiring uncle, Rosario Di Maggio.... . Inzerillo was married to a Spatola. His sister was married to a Spatola. His uncle in New Jersey was married to a Gambino. His cousin and namesake in New Jersey was married to a Gambino. His cousin Tommaso was a brother-in-law of John Gambino, who was married to a dif-ferent Gambino. His cousin Maria Concetta was the wife of John Gambino's younger brother, Giuseppe. All the American-side members of these families were made Men of Honor from Sicily; and all had homes in or around Cherry Hill.

As Sterling's source, the Sicilian prosecutor Sciacchitano, concludes:

> These four families, living partly in Sicily and partly in New York, form a single clan unlike anything in Italy or the United States-the most potent Family in Cosa Nostra. John Gambino is the converging point in the United States for all of the group's activ-ities in Italy, and the final destination for its drug shipments. Salvatore Inzerillo has

emerged as the Gambino brothers' principal interlocutor, the central personage in Sicily, with myriad interests and heavy capital investments.

Like most of their fellow mafiosi in America, writes Sterling, the Gambino brothers were sending their heroin money back to Sicily. It was going to Inzerillo and Spatola, to be invested in legitimate business such as the construction industry and real estate. By 1982, the Gambino-Inzerillo-Spatola holdings in Palermo alone were found to be worth about one billion dollars.[13]

Next to agnatic bonds, affinal ties, i.e., relations between in-laws, especially relations between brothers-in-law, are salient options for mafiosi. These relations help build and strengthen the basic units of the Sicilian mafia, both within and between local groups or families. Recall that before Rosario Di Maggio retired (and died), he had left the leadership of these interrelated families to Salvatore Inzerillo, who was his sister's son (Sterling 1990, p. 200).

The once powerful Rimi – father and sons Vincenzo and Filippo – of Alcamo in the province of Trapani solidified their ties through intermarriage with Gaetano Badalamenti, the boss of Cinisi who controlled the Palermo airport in Punta Ráisi: Filippo and Gaetano were brothers-in-law.[14]

Discussing the relations between mafiosi from both sides of the Atlantic who were involved in the drug trade, Gambetta (on the basis of a 1985 report from the Italian parliament) touches on the structural principle of ethnicity underlying transnational Mafia networks:

> Mafiosi were attractive intermediaries because of their strong connections with the Sicilian Americans running the market in the United States. These ties allowed greater flexibility and safety. In the relationships between mafioso organizers and the Italo-American gangs receiving the merchandise, where there is mutual trust over time, it is possible for one courier to arrive from America with the money while the merchandise itself is entrusted to another courier. Since no such privileged bonds existed between Sicilians and Middle Eastern suppliers, importing was a more cumbersome operation (1993, p. 236).

Three organizations are capable of handling drugs on a wholesale, intercontinental scale: the Chinese Triads for heroin, the Colombian cartels for cocaine, and the Sicilian Mafia for both (Sterling 1990, p. 311). It would be rewarding to explore how these transnational operations are masterminded and orchestrated in remote hinterlands (precisely the kind of places anthropologists used to select for their fieldwork); to investigate how these operations hinge on kinship, marriage, and ethnicity (precisely the kind of subjects anthropologists used to study in such remote places), and how they sustain a form of reverse globalization that no government can stop or control – the transport of unlicensed cultural goods from the world's peripheries and the impact of the product on its main centres in North America and Europe.

# IV

Although in-laws are related by marriage rather than blood, the concept of blood is not entirely lacking from the bonds between affines. First, affinity involves relationships with people who are related by blood among themselves. Second, in Sicily as elsewhere in the Mediterranean, people place a strong emphasis on virginity and female chastity.[15] Ideally (at least in the Christian tradition) brides should come from outside the agnatic group and should be virgins.[16] The consummation of marriage involves breaking the hymen and is followed by birth. Both involve the spilling of blood. (Tellingly, one's children are called one's "blood".) It has been argued that in this context, too, blood has a symbolic significance in that it marks culturally and helps build a relationship – also a relationship between groups. In the Indo-European conception of blood, this blood comes from the outside into the group of agnates, and shedding it helps incorporate the bride into the agnatic kingroup of her husband.[17]

Writing on feuding in nineteenth-century Corsica and other Mediterranean societies, Wilson points out a connection between the blood shed in feuds and the blood of virginity that the bride yields to her husband (and by extension also to his agnates) at marriage:

> Also of relevance, among the Bedouin, too, the shedding of blood of a virgin given in marriage to settle a feud was seen as a kind of symbolic vengeance, blood for blood (Wilson 1988, p. 529, note 222).

Peacemaking in feuds was similar among pastoral families in the Barbagia. About these "symbolic" resolutions of the vendetta in contemporary Sardinia, Cagnetta notes:

> Le mode de conciliation le plus typique du pays est le mariage d'un homme du clan du victime et d'une femme du clan de l'assassin. Le sang virginal répandu présente en effet un caractère symbolique de rachat du sang versé au cours de l'homicide qui a précédé (1963, p. 89).

We will come back to this point when discussing the concept of blood in feuding and peacemaking. Remember that the practice "blood for blood" has distinctly homeopathic implications. Writing on ancient Rome, Barton argues that:

> the Romans, unlike ourselves, were deeply accustomed to thinking in terms of homeopathic systems. Like things are cured by like (similia similibus curantur). This was true not only in sorcery and medicine but also in religion and law ... (1993, p. 180).

In a note she refers to "Plato"s Pharmacy" (the *pharmakon* as poison and antidote, both sickness and cure), and recalls that Roman justice operated on the *lex talionis*, the principle of equivalent vengeance (*par vindicta*).

These connotations of the concept of blood may help explain why in Mafia networks, next to the bonds between brothers, relations between brothers-in-law are so important. Mafiosi draw on the idiom of kinship (with its implications of con-sanguinity) to constitute the units that make up the Sicilian mafia. Loyalty to supe-riors in the families of the men of honour takes priority over commitments to one's own agnates if they fail to follow the rules prevailing among "men of hon-our." As a case in 1994 in Bronte (a town in the western foothills of Etna) illustrates, a mafioso may kill his mafioso-brother who "talks," that is, reveals information about the organization to outsiders.[18]

This brings us to the imagery of blood in recruitment rituals. Since the mid-1980s and as a consequence of the Mafia war in which the Corleonesi wiped out many established Mafiosi in Palermo and its hinterland, hundreds of *pentiti* (pen-itents)[19] provided the investigating magistrates with information about the orga-nization of Cosa Nostra. As a consequence, today much more is known about the mafia than before. One of the first and most famous *pentiti*, Tommaso Buscetta, mentioned that recruitment into a mafia family – initiation into the brotherhood or to be made a man of honour – involved a rite of passage the high point of which was a simple act and formula, as in many other secret societies.[20] Blood from his pricked finger was rubbed on a paper saint's image, which was set on fire in his hand. As it burned, he repeated the following vow: "May my flesh burn like this holy picture if I am unfaithful to this oath."[21] Through these rituals of incorpora-tion, blood assumes magical properties of mediation and social cohesion. But blood is also associated with impurity and can impede rather than promote social bonding. The polluting potential of blood is probably at least partly responsible for the often noted exclusion of women from these sodalities – and from secret soci-eties in general.[22]

# V

The blood symbolism is no less striking in the settlement of feuds and the impo-sition of sanctions. Vengeance and feuding are trademarks of mafiosi. We have already referred to retaliation and the principle of the *lex talionis* in the settling of accounts between mafiosi. As a form of negative reciprocity, retribution means the culprit is to suffer what he has done.[23]

Mafiosi are guided by sayings such as "blood washes blood", "offences have to be washed with blood", and "vendetta is the best forgiveness". As in the case of shed-ding blood in the initiation ritual of mafiosi ("May my blood be spilled just as these drops are spilled," etc.), there is an element of what Frazer calls homeopathic magic in retaliation or negative reciprocity: "Blood washes blood", "Like produces or kills like."

As elsewhere in the Mediterranean (e.g. Sardinia, Corsica, Montenegro, Albania, the Moroccan Rif, and among Bedouins), retaliation between mafiosi includes vendettas against an entire family in revenge for offences by single members.[24] In these feuds, the concept of blood assumes critical importance. Retaliation occurred on a large scale during the mafia war of the early 1980s when the Corleonesi deci-mated the Palermo mafia establishment by killing leaders and their kinsmen, including twenty-one Inzerillos and eleven relatives of Gaetano Badalamenti (Sterling 1990, pp. 209–10).[25] The way the Corleonesi waged this deadly (it has been said "terroristic") campaign shows the flexibility and fluidity of mafia coalitions, the relative ease with which alliances change according to circumstances. As Claire Sterling puts it:

> The Corleonesi had worked in from the outermost provinces, courting the envious, the voracious, the upwardly mobile. Now they had secret allies from Trapani to Agrigento to Catania to the heart of Palermo (1990, p. 206).

Commenting on the murder of the mafioso Vincenzo Puccio in prison in 1989 on Riina's orders, Stille summarizes the strategy of the Corleonesi as follows:

> The murder of Vincenzo Puccio [and the killing of his brother on the same day] in a sense closed the circle on the gruesome killings among the "winners" of the great mafia war. Examined as a whole, the events that Marino Mannoia recounted looked like a "food chain" in the grisly Darwinian struggle of Cosa Nostra, with each fish eating the other until the big fish, Totò Riina, finally swallowed them all. Filippo Marchese had been killed by Pina "the Shoe" Greco, Greco had been killed by Vincenzo Puccio, and now Puccio had been eliminated by Marchese's nephews [Giuseppe and Antonino Marchese]. Then Riina had killed four birds with one stone, eliminating the Puccios, while making sure that their assassins, the Marchese brothers, were out of the way (1995, p. 308; cf. 305 ff. and 382).[26]

Already several years before his arrest in January 1993, however, Riina had become a victim of his own success:

> As the mafia wars have demonstrated, those most successful at destroying the "honoured Society" have been its own members; first through the shoot-outs of the 1960s, and later through the vicious tactics of the Corleonesi. In challenging the Italian state by murdering its representatives, they forced the government to retaliate; in attacking their enemies with relentless terror, they generated a powerful resentment which would find its apotheosis in the declarations of Tommaso Buscetta (Shawcross and Young 1987, p. 306).

One backlash of this war was the *pentito* or penitent. Mafiosi who had survived the war started (under a protection programme) to cooperate with investigating magistrates. Turning state's evidence contravened the most sacred rules of Cosa Nostra and triggered a violent response. Many *pentiti* lost close kinsmen after they testified. The culture of blood feuds – the launching of vendettas against entire families in revenge for offences by single members – seems to fit the Indo-European notion that blood symbolizes the strongest and most enduring of human bonds.[27]

Blood is a powerful symbol: through its metaphorical and metonymical qualities it can stand for life and death, for defilement and purification, for mediation and social cohesion. This is obvious in the ethnography of blood revenge. The concept of blood helps define and reinforce relationships between close kinsmen: the ties between fathers and sons, the bonds between brothers, and by extension the bonds between bloodbrothers. Blood symbolizes the life of an individual and that of a group.[28] Moreover, as a symbolic device, blood mediates between individuals and between groups, between insiders, and between insiders and outsiders, shoring up relationships that are inherently unstable, flexible, and subject to change. In the context of retaliation, shedding blood is a powerful way to "wash the stains of dishonour" and thus supersede the state of pollution and social exclusion.

Blood revenge, then, involves more than retaliation and deterrence. In her book on tribal origins and customs in the Balkans, Mary Durham suggests that revenge was taken on behalf of the soul of the victim, rather than to punish the actual killer (1928, p. 170). As Montenegrins viewed it, vengeance "replaced" to the victim's clan the blood that had been lost (1928, p. 170).

An echo of this sense of loss (and the magical way to make up for it) also reaches us from older sources. As Burkert reminds us, at the funeral pyre of Patrocles, Achilles slaughtered several animals but also twelve captured Trojans:

> This can be understood as an outburst of helpless fury: "If you are dead the others should not live." Nevertheless, when it is related that "about the dead man flowed blood such as could be drawn in cups," it is clear that the intention was for blood to reach the dead man in some way, to give him back life and colour... (1985, p. 60; cf. Burkert 1983, p. 53).

Very similar forms of retribution and "replacement" occur today. Recall the remark by the Serbian General Mladic after his troops conquered the Muslim enclave of Srebrenica on 11 July 1995. Addressing his soldiers and referring to Serbian civilians killed by the Muslim military in the area, Mladic is reported to have said: "It is going to be a *meza* [a long, luscious feast]. We will kill so many of them that we will wade through their blood up to our knees."[29]

Other aspects of blood revenge deserve mention. We have already referred to the liminal position of those who have been dishonoured and who are therefore expected, even socially obliged, to take revenge. Plunged into mourning, these victims have all the features of people out of place. They are avoided, excluded, ostracized – until they have taken revenge. Only after they have "taken blood" (and thus removed their defilement), is their mourning over and can they be reincorporated into everyday social life. This often happens in a festive way and they feel, as they say, reborn and sanctified, having moved from shame to honour, from defilement to purity – a symbolic equivalent of the transition from social death to life. Depending on context, the bloodshed can have either a polluting or a purifying effect.

Vengeance in Calabria, we are told, works as a social regulator: by taking blood revenge, a man finds again his status as a man and, as a consequence, the group recovers its fullness:

> Tant que la vengeance n'a pas eu lieu, on porte, d'une façon ou d'une autre, le deuil, et l'on vit dans la honte. Par la vengeance, le groupe retrouve la vie: elle est saluée par une véritable fête (Breteau and Zagnoli 1980, p. 49).

Blood vengeance implies far-reaching forms of reciprocity. Revenge aims at repairing the stained reputation of both the dishonoured person and his group. It seeks to reach this goal by killing a member of the opposing group in order to make the shed blood "flow back" to the victim according to the principle of homeopathic magic, "like cures (or kills) like."

In these cases of blood vengeance more is involved than metaphorical relations in practices that Frazer called "homeopathic" or "imitative" magic. This first branch of sympathetic magic is based on the principle of similarity. However, the beliefs and practices concerning blood vengeance may also be understood in terms of metonymical relations, that is, in terms of contact and contiguity, as part-whole relationships. For this second branch of sympathetic magic, based on the principle of contact, Frazer used the term "contagious" magic. When people say they are "in blood" and "take blood" to make it "flow back" to the victim and his group to compensate for the lost blood, the relations are also conceived in terms of contact and are therefore clearly metonymical.[31]

Frazer's notion of sympathetic magic-especially its "contagious" or metonymical variety – dovetails with what Lévy-Bruhl called "participation": an ordering of reality that is not causal but mystical. As a recent commentator puts it:

> Participation can be represented as occurring when persons, groups, animals, places, and natural phenomena are in a relation of contiguity, and translate that relation into one of existential immediacy and contact and shared affinity. (In the language of semiotics, humans on the one hand and places, objects, and natural phenomena on the other, are represented as mutually representing one another "iconically", and as transferring energies and attributes as "indexically"). (Tambiah 1990, p. 107)

Among other things, Tambiah refers to a south Italian village where grandparents speak of their ancient rootedness in farms and villages of orgin. He also mentions national monuments like Arlington Cemetery and battlefields like Gettysburg that "are believed to enshrine a people's history or radiate their national glories." In all these instances, writes Tambiah, we have manifestions of "participation" among people, places, nature and objects. Moreover,

> people participate in each other as well: the bonding and the relation between parents and children, between kinsmen by the ties of blood and amity, [and] the transmission of charisma (…) are intimations of participation (1990, pp. 107–8).

Discussing kinship among Sarakatsani shepherds in Greece, Campbell downplays the metaphorical aspect of blood and refers to "participation":

> The solidarity of the corporate family is symbolized in the idea of blood. In marriage a man and a woman mix their different blood to produce "one blood" which is the blood of their children. One says of a child, "he is my blood". Relationships in the family are a participation in this common blood (1964, p. 185).

Reciprocal vengeance killings may be understood in terms of "participation" as well. As mentioned before, by shedding blood of an opponent one believes to compensate for the loss of a kinsman, make the blood "flow back" to the victim's group. Campbell notes that Sarakatsani:

believe that in some way a killer absorbs the strength from the blood of the man he slays. "I shall drink your blood", is a phrase that threatens murder... . One avenger bathed his hands in the blood of the original killer and returned to show his mother "the blood of her son" (1964, p. 193).[32]

We have seen that similar customs prevailed in Montenegro. The people with whom Durham first and later Boehm lived had no term for what we call "blood feud", i.e., "a protracted state of homicidal aggression between two individuals or two groups that are consumed by bitterness and hatred" (Boehm 1983, p. 51). But they possessed a rich vocabulary for speaking of different aspects of blood vengeance. Most significantly, the words *u krvi* mean "in blood," and designate a "state of hostility where the purpose was to take blood revenge" (Boehm 1987, pp. 51–2). According to Boehm the words describe a state of being, not a feud as a total event of a certain size, shape, and duration.

With the state of being "in blood" (*u krvi* or *krvna osveta*) we have a manifestation of participation – the bonding between enemies who reciprocally take "blood for blood". Durham argues that *osveta*, the act of "taking blood," goes beyond the punishment for a crime: one kills to replace the blood lost by the house or the group. *Osveta* has a religious quality, and Durham recalls that in "Serbian the word *osvetiti* refers both to hallow or consecrate [p. 162, and] to take blood in a feud [p. 170]."[33]

This type of bonding also surfaces in the interviews with Buscetta. For example, he compares the "mentality" of mafiosi in the United States with his own attitudes finding the younger generation more Americanized:

> They always talked about the rights and obligations of the individual. It was almost an obsession. At home in Sicily this "individual" did not exist. The "family" came first before everything else. Also before the real family, that of blood.[34]

These considerations leave us with the question if we can actually speak of "metaphorical" relations when people accept a sacred identity between things of different orders. It seems rewarding to understand these relations in terms of participation or performance.[35] This way one avoids seeing either too much or too little in other peoples' forms of ordering reality by simply imposing one's own categories – as happens when one mistakes the discourse of magic for science or pseudo-science.

# VI

Finally, we should briefly look at the type of social structure that sustains the beliefs and practices connected with blood. The representations of blood and the corresponding ritual practices are especially prevalent in remote, mountainous regions of former empires and present-day nation-states: Sicily, Calabria, Corsica, Sardinia, the Moroccan Rif, Montenegro, and other parts of the Balkans. In the absence of effective central control over the means of violence or by simply evading the law, people could for trust, loyalty, and protection only turn to kin and quasi-kinsmen, however culturally constructed.[36]

These arrangements worked both ways in Sicily. Because forms of self-help[37] became – right after the unification of Italy – a force in their own right, the very existence of mafia coalitions made effective central control in these territories even more difficult. Parallel structures consisting of kinship, friendship, and patron-client ties developed in the interstices of the state.[38] These ties involved politicians from the highest echelons in local sociability and collusion – from being guests of honour at weddings and other parties at the home of their canvassers and henchmen to membership in Masonic lodges.[39] Under these conditions a culture of blood feuds and atrocities prevailed at the local level. Peripheral and out of the way, the villages and towns in Sicily's western interior resembled remote communities in the mountainous border zones of large, declining empires (Ottoman, Habsburg, Russian, and former Communist).[40]

The pre-eminence of kinship bonds in Mafia also reflects the origin of mafiosi: many come from small rural towns and villages of Sicily's interior, in what may be called the periphery of the periphery.[41] In these remote rural areas lives were lived among kinsmen. Since the beginning of this century, several important mafia leaders, whose influence transcended the limits of their hometowns (for which reason they erroneously acquired the epithet of *capo di tutti capi*), came from and often remained all their lives in relatively small, out of the way communities.[42] Located in Sicily's western interior, these agrotowns rarely exceeded 12,000 inhabitants. Vito Cascio Ferro lived in Bisaquino, Calogero Vizzini in Villalba, and Giuseppe Genco Russo had his residence in Mussomeli; Salvatore Riina came from Corleone, and his close friends Bernardo and Giovanni Brusca lived in the nearby town of San Giuseppe Jato.[43]

To summarize, blood symbolizes solidarity between agnates and affines as well as between friends and "brothers" who are ritually (and through the medium of blood) turned into quasi-kinsmen. These practices prove especially important among people who conduct risky transactions and who cannot for protection rely on the institutions of centralized states.

Under these conditions, the vocabulary of blood and kinship is pervasive.[44] We find the term "families" used for the most salient of mafia sodalities – the local groups that make up the network of Sicilian mafiosi. Members of the "brotherhood" are often called *fratelli*, or "brothers".[45] A politician who protects his mafioso clients is referred to as *zio* ("uncle").[46] The term *padrino* ("godfather") for powerful mafia leaders is too familiar to require further comment. There is nothing artificial or irrational about these relationships. They attest to a holistic world-view and forms of interconnectedness that can perhaps be best understood in terms of "participation".

Blood is culturally associated with virginity and procreation, and therefore also imbues the bonds between in-laws. Finally, the imagery of blood governs relations between enemies and former friends since it is intimately related with conflict and the settlement of scores between mafiosi. Depending on context, bloodshed can mean defilement or purification. Blood feuds show how kin groups are decimated in vengeance for offences committed by single members. There is no getting away from the ubiquity of blood as a symbolic device.

# References

Arlacchi, P. (1987). *Mafia business.* Verso, London.

Arlacchi, P. (1992). *Gli uomini del disonore. La mafia siciliana nella vita del grande pentito Antonino Calderone.* Mondadori, Milan.

Arlacchi, P. (1994). *Addio Cosa Nostra. La vita di Tommaso Buscetta.* Rizzoli, Milan.

Barton, C.A. (1993). *The sorrows of the ancients Romans. The gladiator and the monster.* Princeton University Press, Princeton.

Benveniste, E. (1973). The vocabulary of kinship. In Benveniste, *Indo-European language and society* (transl. Elizabeth Palmer). Faber, London.

Berland, J.C. (1982). *No five fingers are alike. Cognitive amplifiers in social context.* Harvard University Press, Cambridge, MA.

Black-Michaud, J. (1975). *Cohesive force. Feud in the Mediterranean and the Middle East.* Basil Blackwell, Oxford.

Blok, A. (1974). *The Mafia of a Sicilian Village, 1860–1960.* Basil Blackwell, Oxford. (*Die Mafia in einem sizilianischen Dorf 1860–1960* [transl. Holger Fliessbach]. Suhrkamp, Frankfurt, 1981.)

Blok, A. (1983). On negative reciprocity among Sicilian pastoralists. In *Production pastorale et société. Bulletin de l'équipe écologie et anthropologie des sociétés pastorales* (ed. Maria Pia di Bella), **13**, 43–6.

Blok, A. (1999). Les ambiguités de l'amitié. À propos de quelques proverbes siciliens. In *Amitiés. Anthropologie et histoire* (ed. Georges Ravis-Giordani). Publications de l'Université de Provence, Aix-en-Provence, pp. 305–10.

Boehm, C. (1987). *Blood revenge. The enactment and management of conflict in Montenegro and other tribal societies.* 2nd edn. University of Pennsylvania Press, Philadelphia.

Breteau, C.H., and Zagnoli, N. (1980). Le système de gestion de la violence dans deux communautés rurales méditerranéennes: La Calabre méridionale et le N.E. Constantinois. In *La vengeance* (ed. Raymond Verdier). 4 vols. **I**, pp. 42–73. Editions Cujas/CNRS, Paris.

Buckley, T., and Gottlieb, A. (eds) (1988). *Blood magic. The anthropology of menstruation.* University of California Press, Berkeley.

Burkert, W. (1983). *Homo necans. The anthropology of ancient Greek sacrificial ritual and myth* (transl. Peter Bing). University of California Press, Berkeley.

Burkert, W. (1985). *Greek religion* (transl. John Raffan). Harvard University Press, Cambridge, MA.

Burkert, W. (1996). *Creation of the sacred. Tracks of biology in early religions.* Harvard University Press, Cambridge, MA.

Cagnetta, F. (1963). *Bandits d'Orgosolo* (Inchiesta su Orgosolo. *Nuovi Argomenti,*1954). Buchet/Chastel, Paris.

Campbell, J.K. (1964). *Honour, family and patronage. A study of institutions and moral values in a Greek mountain community.* Clarendon Press, Oxford.

Camporesi, P. (1984). *Il sugo della vita. Simbolismo e magia del sangue.* Edizioni di Comunità, Milan.

Danner, M. (1998). The killing fields of Bosnia. *New York Review of Books* (24 September), **45**(14), 63–77.

De Seta, V. (1962). *Banditi ad Orgosolo*. Film. Scenario: Vittorio de Seta.

Dossier, Andreotti. (1993). *Il testo completo delle accuse dei giudici di Palermo*. Mondadori, Milan.

Durham, M.E. (1928). *Some tribal origins, laws, and customs of the Balkans*. Allen & Unwin, London.

Follain, J. (1995). *A dishonoured society*. Warner Books, London.

Frazer, J.G. (1957). Sympathetic magic. In Frazer, *The golden bough* (1922). 2 vols. I, pp. 14–63. Macmillan, London.

Friedrich, P. (1979). Proto-Indo-European kinship. In Friedrich, *Language, context, and the imagination*. Stanford University Press, Stanford.

Gambetta, D. (1993). *The Sicilian Mafia*. Harvard University Press, Cambridge, MA.

Goody, J. (1983). *The development of the family and marriage in Europe*. Cambridge University Press, Cambridge.

Gouldner, A. (1960). The norm of reciprocity. *American Sociological Review* **25**,161–78.

Herzfeld, M. (1993). *The social production of indifference. Exploring the symbolic roots of western bureaucracy*. University of Chicago Press, Chicago.

Huizinga, J. (1955). *Homo ludens. A study of the play-element in culture* (1938). Beacon Press, Boston, MA.

Jamous, R. (1981). *Honneur et baraka: Les structures sociales traditionelles dans le Rif*. Cambridge University Press, Cambridge, UK.

Koliopoulos, J.S. (1987). *Brigands with a cause. Brigandage and irredentism in modern Greece 1821–1912*. Clarendon Press, Oxford.

La Fontaine, J. (1985). *Initiation. Ritual drama and secret knowledge accross the world*. Penguin Books, Harmondsworth.

Linke, U. (1985). Blood as metaphor in Proto-Indo-European. *Journal of Indo-European Studies* **13**, 333–76.

Maxwell, G. (1957). *God protect me from my friends*. Longmans, London.

Meeker, M.E. (1976). Meaning and society in the Near East: Examples from the Black Sea Turks and the Levantine Arabs. *International Journal of Middle Eastern Studies* **7**, 243–70 and 383–422.

Peters, E.L. (1990). Aspects of the feud [1967]. In Emrys L. Peters, *The Bedouin of Cyrenaica. Studies in personal and corporate power* (eds J. Goody and E. Marx). Cambridge University Press, Cambridge, UK.

Pigliaru, A. (1975). *Il banditismo in Sardenga. La vendetta barbaricina come ordinamento giuridico* (1959). Giuffrè, Varese.

Rhode, D. (1997). *End game. The betrayal and fall of Srebrenica: Europe's worst massacre since world war II*. Farrar, Straus & Giroux, New York.

Ruffini, Julio L. (1978). Disputing over livestock in Sardinia. In *The disputing process – Law in ten societies*. (eds L. Nader and H.F. Todd Jr). Columbia University Press, New York.

Sahlins, M. (1974). On the sociology of primitive exchange. In M. Sahlins, *Stone age economics*. Tavistock, London.

Schneider, D.M. (1968). *American kinship: A cultural account*. Prentice- Hall, Englewood Cliffs, NJ.

Schneider, D.M. (1977). Kinship, nationality, and religion in American culture. Toward a definition of kinship. In *Symbolic anthropology* (eds J.L. Dolgin et al.). Columbia University Press, New York.

Schneider, D.M. (1984). *A critique of the study of kinship*. The University of Michigan Press, Ann Arbor, MI.

Schneider, J. (1971). Of vigilance and virgins. *Ethnology* **10**, 1–24.

Sciacchitano, G. (1982). *Requisitoria del PM Sciacchitano nel processo contro Rosario Spatola più 119*. Public Prosecutor's Office, Palermo.

Shawcross, T., and Young, M. (1987). *Men of honour. The confessions of Tommaso Buscetta*. Collins, London.

Siebert, R. (1997). *Le donne, la mafia*. 2nd edn. EST, Milan.

Simmel, G. (1983/1908). Das Geheimnis und die geheime Gesellschaft. In G. Simmel, *Soziologie. Untersuchungen über die Formen der vergesellschaftung. Gesammelte Werke* **II**, pp. 256–304 (1908). Duncker & Humblot, Berlin. (*The secret and the secret society*. In *The sociology of Georg Simmel* [transl. K.H. Wolff]. The Free Press, Glencoe, IL, 1950.)

Stajano, C. (ed.) (1986). *Mafia. L'atto d'accusa dei giudici di Palermo*. Editori Riuniti, Roma.

Steinmetz, S.R. (1931). Selbsthilfe. In *Handwörterbuch der Soziologie* (ed. A. Vierkandt). Ferdinand Enke Verlag, Stuttgart, pp. 518–22.

Sterling, C. (1990). *Octopus. The long reach of the international Sicilian mafia*. Simon & Schuster, New York.

Stille, A. (1995). *Excellent cadavers. The mafia and the death of the first Italian Republic*. Jonathan Cape, London.

Sudetic, C. (1998). *Blood and vengeance. One family's story of the war in Bosnia*. W.W. Norton, New York and London.

Tambiah, S.J. (1990). *Magic, science, religion, and the scope of rationality*. Cambridge University Press, Cambridge, UK.

Wilson, S. (1988). *Feuding, conflict and banditry in nineteenth-century Corsica*. Cambridge University Press, Cambridge, UK.

Wolf, E.R. (1966). Kinship, friendship, and patron-client relationships in complex societies. In *The social anthropology of complex societies* (ed. M. Banton). Tavistock, London.

# Notes

1. An earlier version of this paper was presented at the conference "Risky Transactions: Kinship, ethnicity, and trust", organized by Frank Salter and Wulf Schiefenhövel of the Max Planck Institute for Human Ethology, 23–25 September 1996, at the Werner Reimers Foundation in Bad Homburg, Germany. Subsequently published in Anton Blok, *Honour and Violence*, Polity Press, Cambridge, 2001. I owe a special debt to Rod Aya for his commentary on and editing of this text.

2. See also Arlacchi (1987, pp. 196 ff., 221).

3. For the terms "organizational flexibility" and "structural fluidity", I have drawn on Berland (1982, pp. 84–93 and *passim*), who explores the social structure of the peripatetic Qualandar (service nomads in western Pakistan) and stresses the importance of the sibling group: "of all interpersonal relationships, the most valued, loved, and respected are those between brothers and sisters within a tent" (1982, p. 92).

4. Mafia families take their name from the territories they "protect" and control, e.g. the "family of Santa Maria del Gesù" in Palermo once headed by Stefano Bontate, "the family of Passo di Rigano" led by Salvatore Inzerillo, the "family of Corso dei Mille" led by Filippo Marchese, etc. In the hinterland of Palermo, almost every town has its eponymous family. For maps of the territories of Sicilian mafia families, see Sterling (1990); Stille (1995); and the sketch of Buscetta in Arlacchi (1994, pp. 106–10).

5. There are good reasons to argue against the "monolithic theorem" that, according to some, has served as a useful instrument in judicial politics. In a recent review article entitled "How organized is organized crime?", Martin Clark points out that anthropologists and sociologists traditionally had a different view of the Sicilian Mafia: "Far from being a unitary organization, to them 'The Mafia' is a fluid network of competing 'families', each loosely organized and subject to constant conflicts and reversals of fortune and alliance." (*Times Literary Supplement*, 1 September 1995, p. 7.) See also Stajano (1986, pp. 24, 41–9); Gambetta (1993, pp. 153–5); and Stille (1995, p. 364). Insider Buscetta also takes issue with the notion of a centralized leadership: "Cosa Nostra non ha una vera e propria testa, ma un centro di gravità collocato tra Palermo e Trapani" (quoted in Arlacchi 1994, pp. 106–7). After the arrest of Salvatore Riina in January 1993, hierarchical tendencies gave way to a cellular model, i.e., a segmentary system. This is the view of the chief public prosecutor in Palermo, Giancarlo Casella, professed in June 1997 after the arrest of Pietro Aglieri, the alleged number two of Cosa Nostra and considered one of the people to have been entrusted with this reorganization. See *La Repubblica*, 7 June 1997; and *NRC-Handelsblad*, 10 June 1997.

6. For a sketch of this war, see Stajano (1986, pp. 17–37); Sterling (1990, pp. 203–35); and Stille (1995). Buscetta conveyed his premonitions in his talks with Arlacchi: "that many of these killings [in 1979 and 1980 of prominent people] were carried out by the Corleonesi without warning and without the authorization of the Commission" (1994, pp. 222–3).

7. Sicily has a total population of about 5 million people.

8. Some early examples are discussed in Blok (1974, pp. 103 ff.). Sterling recognizes the importance of sets of brothers in the network of mafiosi running the international drug trade (1990, p. 287).

9. Cf. Schneider (1968, pp. 49–54; 1984, pp. 165–201).

10. See also Benveniste (1973); and Friedrich (1979, pp. 201–52).

11. Corleonesi: mafiosi from Corleone, a rural town in the hinterland of Palermo, but also including their allies from the neighbouring town of San Giuseppe Jato and some families from Palermo and Catania. From the late 1970s until their demise in the early 1990s (following the arrest of Salvatore Riina in January 1993 and the death of Luciano Leggio in November that year), the Corleonesi dominated the Sicilian mafia. As mentioned before, in the second Mafia war (1981–82), they decimated the ranks of their more traditional rivals in Palermo and some neighbouring towns. For details, see Stajano (1986, pp. 16–37); Shawcross and Young (1987); Sterling (1990, pp. 54–66, 203–35); Follain (1995, pp. 95–175); and Stille (1995).

12. See Sterling (1990, p. 200). Another example of matrilineally transferred leadership among mafiosi concerns the brothers Calderone from Catania. It seems that the older brother, Giuseppe, followed in the steps of one of his mother's brothers, a man called Luigi Saitta. See Arlacchi's biography of Antonino Calderone (1992, pp. 10–20).

13. Sterling (1990, pp. 199–200). Her source, which I could not consult, is Giusto Sciacchitano (1982). See also Shawcross and Young, who note that "In the mid-1970s the Sicilian branch of the Gambino family was up to its neck in heroin trafficking mainly through the clan headed by Salvatore Inzerillo and Rosario Spatola, both relatives of the Gambinos [i.e., the cousins Rosario and Carlo Gambino]. It has been estimated that by the late seventies the Inzerillo-Gambino-Spatola network was smuggling $600 million worth of heroin into America each year (1987, pp. 77–8).

14. In January 1996, Tommaso Buscetta was interviewed by the lawyers of Giulio Andreotti who is accused of having protected mafiosi. One of the lawyers, Franco Coppi, asked Buscetta why Gaetano Badalamenti would have met Andreotti. Buscetta answered: "Per interressamente nella

soluzione del processo del cognato Filippo Rimi." *La Repubblica*, 11 January 1996, p. 7. For more examples of intermarriage between mafiosi, see Stajano (1986, p.33).

15. Cf. J. Schneider (1971); and Meeker (1976).

16. Cf. Goody (1983, pp. 6–33).

17. See Linke (1985, pp. 357–61). See also Herzfeld (1993, pp. 28–34), who drew my attention to Linke's work.

18. We also know of fraternal rivalry coming close to fratricide: a resentful brother may have had a hand in the murder, in the spring of 1981, of Stefano Bontate, one of Palermo's most important mafia bosses. See also Buscetta's observations on loyalty to the "family" in Arlacchi (1994, pp. 157–8).

19. The term *pentito* (plural: *pentiti*) can perhaps be best translated as "crown witness" or a person who, under a protection programme, has turned state's evidence.

20. See La Fontaine (1985, pp. 58–80). Buscetta did not consider himself a *pentito*: "Non sono un pentito". See Arlacchi (1994, p. 3).

21. Quoted in Shawcross and Young (1987, pp. 34–5). See also Stajano (1986, p. 43) and Arlacchi's interviews with Buscetta (1994, pp. 35–8). For more examples of how men of honour are "made" (including the mixing of blood between old and new members, which implies notions of strong solidarity), see Gambetta (1993, pp. 262–70); the testimony of Vincenzo Marsala from Vicari in Stajano (1986, pp. 63–6); and the description of Antonino Calderone from Catania in Arlacchi (1992, pp. 52–61). Discussing the organization of bandit gangs in nineteenth-century Greece, Koliopoulos points to the close relationship between banditry and foster-brotherhood (1987, pp. 263–5). He refers to the tradition of the mixing of blood of foster-brothers and argues that the "foster-brotherhood created bonds that transcended those of kinship, and like kinship rendered the band an instrument in the quest for security" (1987, pp. 264–5). For ancient examples of oath rituals that enact irreversibility, see Burkert who mentions an oath ceremony in *The Iliad*: "as Agamemnon cuts the [sheeps'] throats, the other participants pour wine to the ground from their goblets and pray: 'Whoever does wrong against the oath, his brain shall flow to the ground as does this wine, his and his children's, and their wives shall be given to others.' Flowing blood, flowing wine, flowing brain are brought together; as the one is enacted, the other is conjured to follow suit" (1996, p. 173).

22. See Buscetta's observations on gender relations among mafiosi in Arlacchi (1994, p. 159 and *passim*); cf. Shawcross and Young (1987, pp. 76–7). On menstrual taboos, see the collection edited by Buckley and Gottlieb (1988, pp. 28–9). Following Douglas, they argue that menstrual blood is seen as polluting only "when it symbolically encodes an underlying social-structural ambiguity regarding women". On the conspicuous absence of women from nineteenth-century Greek bandit gangs and the world of bandits in general, see Koliopoulos (1987, pp. 283–4). The monosexual character of mafia organizations is the subject of a recent book (Siebert 1997).

23. On negative reciprocity, see Gouldner (1960); Sahlins (1974, pp. 191–5); Blok (1983); and Burkert (1996, p. 133).

24. See Durham (1928, pp. 63–92, 147–84); Cagnetta (1963); Black-Michaud (1975); Jamous (1981, pp. 75, 78–87); Boehm (1987, p. 191 ff.); Wilson (1988); Peters (1990, pp. 59–83). See also De Seta (1962); Pigliaru (1975, pp. 131 ff.); and Ruffini (1978) on the *ius talionis* among Sardinian shepherds in the Barbagia.

25. Intra-mafia violence is by no means exceptional. For Calabria, Arlacchi mentions that "of the 244 mafia-type murders committed in [this region] between 1970 and 1979, some 176 (over 70 percent) arose from conflicts among mafia groups; and of these 176, at least 141 can be traced back to clashes between mafia family/enterprises struggling for economic and territorial supremacy" (1987, p. 157).

26. Several popular expressions attest to the common practice of betrayal and betrayals within betrayals. Cf. Maxwell (1957). In the biography of Tommaso Buscetta, the protagonist observes: "L'uomo che ti sta accanto ti può portare a una festa come alla tua tomba. L'amico più caro può essere il tuo assassino" (Arlacchi 1994, p. 155). For a discussion of Sicilian proverbs conveying the ambiguities of friendship, see Blok (1998).

27. When Tommaso Buscetta had become *persona non grata* and had moved to Brazil in January 1981, within two years several close kinsmen, including two sons and one brother-in-law, disappeared and were not heard of again. Another brother-in-law, a son-in-law, two grandchildren, and a

brother and his son, were also killed. As Buscetta pointed out, none of these nine people was a mafioso; their only fault was that they had his name or were related to him through kinship. See Arlacchi's biography (1994, pp. 236–43).

28. For a brief documentation of the close relationship between blood and life, see Camporesi (1984).

29. Roy Gutman, "Dutch Reveal Horrors of Mission Impossible." *Newsday*, 25 July 1995. Quoted in Danner (1998, p. 67), who refers to the massacre of Serb civilians near Bratunac in December 1992, for which the young Muslim commander in Srebrenica, Naser Oric, was held responsible. For detailed accounts of the fall of Srebrenica and the preceding fighting between Muslims and Serbs in this area, see Rohde (1997, pp. 215–6 and *passim*); and Sudetic (1998, pp. 147 ff. and *passim*).

30. Frazer (1957, I, pp. 16 ff. and 49 ff.).

31. Involving a system of messages and signs, mafia violence can be understood in terms of culture and communication. This is not always recognized by Italian sociologists and historians. See, for example, the discussion in Siebert (1997, pp. 35–9 and *passim*). She shows little patience with "folk-loristic explanations" and seems completely unaware of the anthropological discussion on ritual and the ethnography of feuding in the Mediterranean area.

32. See also Durham (1928, p. 164); Boehm (1987, pp. 51 ff.); and Wilson's ethnographic sketch of the idiom of blood in Corsican feuding (1988, pp.408–10). His observations on the real and figurative meaning of "taking blood" in reciprocal fashion, e.g. "in Corsica as in Albania, it was felt necessary to literally replace the blood which the kindred had lost through a murder of one of its members by making offerings of blood in a variety of ways, of which vengeance killing was only one", easily fit the metonymic paradigm of "participation". Sicilian examples are mentioned by Siebert (1997, pp. 37–8, 247 and passim), who dismisses them as "folklore".

33. Durham (1928, pp. 162, 170). Durham suggests that the swearing of blood brotherhood when set-tling a blood feud also denotes a replacement of lost blood (1928, p. 170).

34. Quoted in Arlacchi (1994, pp. 157–8).

35. See Huizinga (1955, p. 25), who discusses this issue in his book on play: "When a certain form of religion accepts a sacred identity between two things of a different order, say a human being and an animal, this relationship is not adequately expressed by calling it a 'symbolical correspondence' as *we* conceive this. The identity, the essential oneness of the two goes far deeper than the corre-spondence between a substance and its symbolic image. It is a mystic unity. The one has *become* the other....We must always be on our guard against the deficiencies and differences of our means of expression."

36. The case of the transhumant Sarakatsani shepherds in the Zagori mountains of north-western Greece confirms this. Although the idea of feuding is very real and the Sarakatsani have a taste for violence, they have a notably low incidence of vengeance. Their ethnographer Campbell relates this pattern to the well-organized and omnipresent Greek police (1964, pp. 194–5).

37. Steinmetz's definition of *Selbsthilfe* (self-help): "Wo und wann der Einzelne aber von ihm [dem Staat] und seinen Organen entweder im Stich gelassen oder umgekehrt erstickt zu werden droht, tritt die Selbsthilfe als Rettungsmöglichkeit wieder auf" (1931, p. 22). See Boehm (1987, pp. 65–6, 173) for a more recent view of self-help.

38. See Wolf (1966).

39. See, for example, *Dossier Andreotti* (1993); Buscetta's view in Arlacchi (1994, pp. 206–9); and Stille (1995, pp. 390–412). On the "faccia pulita" of the Mafia, see also Stajano (1986, p. 43).

40. I draw here on a passage in Misha Glenny's article "Why the Balkans Are So Violent" in the *New York Review of Books*, **43**(14), 19 September 1996, pp. 34–9, esp. p. 36.

41. The *pentito* Vincenzo Marsala (from the "family" of Vicari near Termini Imerese) emphasized in his testimony that the mafia has its strongholds and main recruitment areas in the little towns of Sicily's agrarian *retroterra*. See Stajano (1986, p. 69).

42. The expression "capo di tutti capi", which is often uncritically used in the popular press whenever an important mafioso is arrested, unwittingly underscores the distinctly segmentary character of Cosa Nostra. For critical comments on the expression "capo di tutti capi", see also Buscetta's obser-vations in Arlacchi's biography (1994, pp. 106–7).

43. About the modest living quarters of the famous Genco Russo in Mussomeli, see Buscetta's descrip-tion of his visit in the 1950s. He emphasizes stereotypical representations including "sleeping with

the mule at home" and the lack of privacy with respect to defecation. See Arlacchi (1994, pp. 16–17).

44. The concepts of blood and kinship overlap in the colloquial *meo sangue* ("my blood"), a term of endearment used by mothers when they hug their young children. Cf. Campbell (1964, p. 185).

45. See, for example, Buscetta's references in Arlacchi (1994, pp. 153, 219, 228, and *passim*).

46. See Buscetta's comments on the denomination of "uncle" in Arlacchi (1994, pp. 209, 225). On the use of kinship terms outside the realm of kinship, Goody notes that in "Christianity, kin terms were used not only for addressing the gods and the priesthood, but also for addressing all the fellow-members of the sect, and later those specially chosen as spiritual kin or godkin. God the Father is served by priests and helpers who are 'fathers' and 'brothers', 'mothers' and 'sisters'. The Head of the Church is *il Papa*, the Pope, the head of the monastery is called the Abbot, again a 'father', derived from the Aramaic *abba*" (1983, p. 194).

## CHAPTER 6

# COGNITIVE AND CLASSIFICATORY FOUNDATIONS OF TRUST AND INFORMAL INSTITUTIONS

## A NEW AND EXPANDED THEORY OF ETHNIC TRADING NETWORKS[1]

### *Janet T. Landa*

܅ܚ ܚܙ

Take Belfast. Two strangers meet and a guessing game starts immediately. The first thing you think is, "Is this person a Catholic or a Protestant?" … It's a kind of self-preservation technique. If it fails, and if your luck is really out, you could end up being killed.[2]

[T]hinking depends upon institutions… . Classifications, logical operations, and guiding metaphors are given to the individual by society.[3]

In the beginning, however, there were no words. Language seems to have appeared in evolution only after humans and species before them had become adept at generating and categorizing actions and at creating and categorizing mental representations of objects, events, and relations.[4]

## Introduction

All rational action is preceded by cognitive processes in the individual's mind in which classification pays a fundamental role. The opening quote in this paper dramatically reveals the cognitive and classificatory foundations of human mental processes as they interact with living things. Consider the hero in Bernard MacLaverty's (1995) title story in his collection of stories entitled *Walking the dog, and other stories*. The hero is kidnapped by gunmen in Northern Ireland; the gunmen identified themselves to him as members of the IRA, but the hero knew that they could really be Loyalists passing as IRA members in order to trap potential Catholics. He therefore tries to identify his kidnappers. Similarly, his kidnappers wanted to know his religious identity as well: Is he a Catholic or a Protestant? To identify him and put him in the correct category, they asked him a series of questions: What is his surname? If his surname is MacLaverty then any Belfast native will instantly know that he is a Catholic. Does he have a tattoo on his arm? How does he pronounce the letter *h* (since Protestants pronounce it as "aitch" and Catholics as "haitch")?

Despite the importance of classification in human sociality rational choice approaches underlying the New Institutional Economics (NIE) and the "New Institutionalism" (NI) have ignored the cognitive and classificatory foundations of social institutions. In this chapter, I develop a new approach to institutions, with special reference to informal institutions (e.g. codes of conduct) embedded in ethnically homogeneous middleman groups/networks (EHMG) that promote mutual trust and reciprocity among trading partners. EHMGs coordinate the activities of various interdependent traders linked in complex networks of exchange. This new approach to informal institutions combines my NIE approach to EHMG (Landa 1981, reprinted in Landa 1994, chapter 5) with anthropologist Mary Douglas's (1986) cognitive and classificatory approach to institutions. The result is a new NIE-cognitive and classificatory approach to trust and informal institutions, an approach which also falls into the new subdiscipline of "bioeconomics" (the integration of economics with biology).

The paper is organized into four parts. Part I will review some of the definitions of the concept of institution by scholars of NIE and NI, and will describe in some detail anthropologist Mary Douglas's (1986) conception of institutions. Part II will revisit and re-examine my NIE theory of the EHMG (Landa 1981) and place it explicitly on cognitive and classificatory foundations. Part III will discuss some wider theoretical implications of working with an NIE-cognitive theory of trust and informal institutions. Part IV will discuss some wider implications of our theory for understanding the performance of economies in different contexts.

## I. Some definitions of social institutions

The study of institutions is at the heart of NIE and of NI: "Institutions matter" because they economize on transaction costs by reducing uncertainty.[5] But what exactly is a "social institution"? James Buchanan (1975, p. 6) sees institutions –

Adam Smith's "laws and institutions" – simply as rules. But what are institutions-as-rules? Political scientist Elinor Ostrom (1986, p. 5) provides one definition:

> Rules ... refer to prescriptions commonly known and used by a set of participants to order repetitive, interdependent relationships. Prescriptions refer to which actions (or states of the world) are *required, prohibited, or permitted*. Rules are the result of implicit or explicit efforts by a set of individuals to achieve order and predictability within defined situations by (1) creating positions (e.g. member, convenor, agent, etc.); (2) stating how participants enter or leave positions; (3) stating which actions participants are required, permitted, or forbidden to take; and (4) stating which outcome participants are required, permitted, or forbidden to affect.

To illustrate this definition of institutions-as-rules consider the formal institution of contract law. A breaching party is legally permitted to breach a contract for a fungible good provided that the defendant pays monetary damages to the plaintiff if the plaintiff sues the defendant in court. Thus parties to a contract are subject to a legal constraint enforced by the courts. The existence of contract law reduces contract uncertainty by constraining a trader's breach of contract and hence helping to coordinate the activities of interdependent actors (Landa 1976, reprinted in Landa 1994, chapter 2). Economist Douglas North (1990, pp. 3–4) provides another definition of social institutions:

> Institutions are the rules of the game in a society, or more formally, are the humanly devised constraints that shape human interaction.... Institutional constraints include both what individuals are prohibited from doing and, sometimes, under what conditions some individuals are permitted to undertake certain activities.

North's definition of institutions includes both formal institutions such as written rules as well as informal institutions such as conventions and codes of conduct. A convention, according to philosopher David Lewis (1969, p. 42), is a regularity in behaviour of members of a population when they are in a recurrent situation in which every one conforms to the convention, and expects everyone else to conform, and prefers to conform to the convention on condition that the others also conform. Lewis (1969, p. 44) provided an example of a convention: In the United States (and Canada) drivers drive in the right lane on roads; in Britain the left lane is used. Convention thus may be considered to be equivalent to tradition or custom. More recently, Susan Crawford and Elinor Ostrom (1994) classified definitions of institutions by a group of rational choice scholars into three categories: (a) insitutions-as-rules; (b) institutions-as-shared norms; and (c) institutions as "shared strategies."

Unlike the analysis of institutions by rational choice economists, political scientists, and sociologists cited by Crawford (1994), anthropologist Mary Douglas (1986, p. 8) has a very different approach to the analysis of institutions. She criticizes the rational choice approach to institutions for relying too heavily on individualist foundations and as a result having great difficulties with the idea of group solidarity. According to Douglas (1986, p. 1):

Writing about cooperation and solidarity means writing at the same time about rejection and mistrust. Solidarity involves individuals being ready to suffer on behalf of the larger group and their expecting other individual members to do as much for them.

To bridge the gap between the individual and society, Douglas (1986, p. 19), drawing on the sociological theory of Max Weber and Emile Durkhiem, as well as the work of Ludwik Fleck, Ian Hacking and Nelson Goodman in the philosophy of science, proposes to develop

> ... a double stranded view of social behavior. One strand is cognitive: the individual demand for order and coherence and control of uncertainty. The other strand is transactional: the individual utility maximizing activity described in a cost-benefit calculus.

This she would do by supplementing the "unsociological" weakness of rational choice approaches to institutional analysis with a cognitive and classificatory theory of institutions that bridges the concept of the individual and society. Institutions promoting cooperation and social solidarity need to be grounded by a cognitive device in order for individuals to be certain about each other's strategies, thus generating the necessary trust in other individuals' behaviour (Douglas 1986, p. 55). For human discourse and cooperation to be possible, individuals have to agree on basic categories of thought. And that, according to Douglas (1986, pp. 55, 91), is provided by institutions which "define sameness", "confer identity", and "do the classifying". In which ways do "institutions do the classifying" for us? Douglas (p. 91) argues that:

> Our social interaction consists very much in telling one another what right thinking is and passing blame on wrong thinking. This is indeed how we build the institutions, squeezing each other's ideas into a common shape so that we can prove rightness by sheer numbers of independent assent.

Classification of different kinds of people begins with the distinction between Ego and other individuals (Douglas 1986, p. 62). Classification also guide peoples' choice of "their allies, and opponents and the pattern of their future relations" (Douglas 1986, p. 63). For Douglas, classification is a fundamental cognitive process based on institutions that define standard expectations of his society. Institutions do the classifying for individuals by providing "labels": "People have always been labeling each other, with the same consequence – labels stick (p. 100)"; "persons realize their own identities and classify each other through community affiliation (p. 102)." Douglas (p. 103) illustrates the importance of social identities in conveying information about a person, by quoting from the work of anthropologist Lawrence Rosen (1984):

> Thus where an American may wish first to place another by asking what he *does* (i.e., what occupation he practices) because such information conveys a host of implications for economic, social and political attitudes, in Morocco, the central question is "where are your origins," since it is this information which, initially, conveys a degree of predictability about the sort of ties that are possible with such a man.

The importance of knowing a person's identity in predicting behaviour has also been emphasized by anthropologist Elizabeth Colson (1974, p. 25):

> [I]f you know a person's clan, you have a good chance of being able to find out an appropriate kinship term to signal the etiquette to be used between the two of you and to define the moral imperative that ought to govern your relationships.

More recently, Douglas (1992, pp. 244–5) has restated her theory of the cognitive and classificatory foundations of institutions by linking the cognitive nature of "collective beliefs" with institutions-as-rules:

> Collective beliefs are embodied in rules of behaviour ... A version of the world depends on the rules, and is guaranteed by the social system in which mutual claims are honoured. Categories are right if they fit well with the relevant rules and claims, and wrong if they do not.

## II. Cognitive and classificatory foundations of trust, informal institutions, and ethnic trading networks

Until recently, I was unaware that my theory of the EHMG was built on cognitive and classificatory foundations. My theory of the EHMG (Landa 1981) is a theory of how traders protect themselves from breach of contract in economies in which the legal framework for enforcing contracts is not well developed. Under conditions of contract uncertainty, a rational trader will have the incentive to reduce uncertainty, hence reducing transaction costs of enforcing contracts, by particularizing exchange relations on the basis of kinship or ethnicity. A Chinese middleman in South-east Asia, for example, uses an informal institution, the Confucian code of ethics, embedded in the EHMG, to reduce contract uncertainty. Under conditions of contract uncertainty, Ego (e.g. a Hokkien-Chinese trader) must identify his potential trading partner because to enforce contracts Ego must rely on the Confucian code of ethics shared with his trading partner rather than on formal contract law. Ego will arm himself with a subjective "calculus of relations" (Fortes 1969) which establishes a system of classifying all traders in a market into seven categories corresponding to different "grades" of traders in descending order of trustworthiness: (1) kinsmen from the nuclear family; (2) distant kinsmen from extended family and lineage; (3) clansmen; (4) fellow villagers; (5) people speaking the same dialect from the same province in China, for example, Hokkiens from Fukien province in China; (6) Chinese speaking a different dialect; and (7) non-Chinese.

It may be inferred from Ego's subjective discriminatory system of ranking of traders that Ego uses four basic structural principles to classify all traders into seven categories of traders: kinship, clanship, territory, and ethnicity; the general classificatory principle being based on the degree of social distance between Ego and his trading partner. But this general classificatory principle based on social distance by itself does not naturally mark off the boundaries separating different grades of traders into *seven* categories. What then is the principle of classification of traders into *seven* groupings/grades of traders? For Chinese merchants in Southeast Asia, the principle of classification is based on the informal institution of *Confucian ethics* (of reciprocity). Confucian ethics, in overseas Chinese society, prescribes differences in the patterns of mutual aid obligations between people with *varying degrees of social distance within a well-defined social structure* – near kinsmen (e.g. family members), distant kinsmen in extended family and lineage, clansmen, fellow villagers, and people speaking the same dialect. Kinship relations within the family in which social distance is at a minimum, are strong ties that involve the severest degree of constraint in dealings among kinsmen. Thus near kinsmen are the most trustworthy people with whom to trade. On account of the differences in institutional constraint, each of the five categories of members occupies a special place within the overall social structure of a specific Chinese ethnic community (e.g. Hokkien-Chinese-speaking community). This implies that different behavioural patterns can be predicted for each of the five categories of traders: close kinsmen will be predicted to be the most reliable traders, while Hokkien-Chinese will be predicted to be the least reliable traders. This, then, forms the cognitive basis for Ego's classification of all traders within the Hokkien community into *five* different categories/grades of traders. The *limits* of Confucian ethics form the basis for Ego's classification of all traders into two major categories: the insiders (category 1 to 6) and outsiders (category seven). Thus Ego's discriminatory system of classification of all trading partners into *seven* categories reflects the *content* and the *limits* of the Confucian code of ethics.

Having established his subjective classification system for ranking traders into seven grades of trustworthiness, it remains for Ego to *identify* a potential trading partner in order to place him in the correct category. To do so efficiently, Ego looks for highly visible ethnic or biological markers, such as facial features, in order to identify correctly a potential trader's ethnicity/race. Ego can also acquire information directly from his potential partner at low cost in order to slot him into one of the categories simply by asking his name, where he comes from, and the dialect/language he speaks. By this process of identification of all potential traders, and sorting them into their respective categories, Ego can *predict* the reliability of a trading partner in honouring his contracts with a high degree of accuracy. Ego thus economizes on the costs of directly acquiring information of the reputation of the traders that he actually chooses to become his trading partners.

Trading partners linked by kinship or ethnic ties in an EHMG have an incentive to honour contracts not only because of the existence of the Confucian code of ethics, but also because economic sanctions are imposed upon the trading partner who violates the ethics of the group (see also Carr and Landa 1983, reprinted in Landa 1994, chapter 6). The economic sanctions imposed by the victim of breach and other traders in the ethnic trading network on the breaching party include: (a) withdrawal of credit so that the offending party has to deal on a cash basis; (b) exclusion from future dealings; and (c) expulsion from the group via bankruptcy proceedings. The Confucian code of ethics, enforced by members of the EHMG, functions to deter trading partners from breach of contract and hence may be regarded as the functional equivalent of modern contract law.

In light of my recent research into the bioeconomics of folk and scientific classification (Ghiselin and Landa 1995), and into the sociology of traditional Chinese social structure, I wish to make some comments about my 1981 analysis of ethnic trading networks. First, while Ego's classification of different categories of traders in terms of trustworthiness is "socially constructed",[6] the social construction of social categories of members with shared identities – members in each category sharing the same social identity – itself rest on *biological* foundations in the kin relations embedded in the family, extended family, and the lineage. Second, while it is true that humans use institutions to help them classify and label themselves and other humans, nonhumans (e.g. animals) also have the cognitive ability to classify nonhuman kinds into different categories (example, conspecifics, mother, offspring, predator, prey, etc.), and this ability is fundamental to the very survival of nonhuman species (Landa 1998a; Ghiselin and Landa 1995).[7] Third, I recently came across the work of Chinese sociologist Fei Xiaotong (1992, translated by Hamilton and Zheng) who describes the basic characteristic of Chinese traditional society in terms of the concept of "*chaxugeju*" ("differential mode of association"): each individual is at the centre of a series of widening concentric circles or networks of overlapping kin and social relationships. Chinese social structure, unlike Western social structure which is individualistic in nature, consists of a careful ranking of people who are classified according to distinct categories of social relationships. Confucian ethics facilitate social categorization. To explain the emergence of ethnic trading networks under conditions of contract uncertainty, it is necessary to combine the NIE/NI "institutions-as-rules" transaction costs approach with Mary Douglas's "institutions-as-classification" cognitive approach.

## III. Some theoretical implications of a cognitive theory of trust and informal institutions

### *Classification matters: Introducing "Homo classificus"*

One of the limitations of rational choice theory that underlies the economics of institutions is that it abstracts from the fundamental cognitive, mental processes that occur in the mind. The theory implicitly assumes that all the mental processes involved in arriving at a rational choice have already been performed in the human brain; subjective mental processes are thus ignored. Rational choice theory of institutions is thus an objective and not a subjective theory dealing with mental models, cognitive processes and the like. By ignoring how the mind economizes on information costs by classifying information, rational choice theory loses sight of some important aspects of economizing behaviour that takes place in the brain of rational economic agents. This is especially true if economists are doing the economics of trust and informal institutions.[8] The analysis of trust involves not only a person's actual rational choice of trading partners, along benefit-cost lines, but also an analysis of the person's mental process of classifying who is trustworthy and who is not, and making finer discriminations of categories of trading partners in terms of the degree of trustworthiness. A NIE approach to the analysis of trust/commercial morality embedded in ethnic trading networks must therefore rest on cognitive and classificatory foundations. "Classification matters" because of its cognitive role in economizing on information costs. A fuller analysis of the behaviour of *Homo eonomicus* (Economic man) must therefore be supplemented by his cognitive counterpart, whom I shall call, *Homo classificus*.[ix]

Nowhere is the role of *Homo classificus* more important than *Homo sapiens'* use of language for communication with others. The origin of language, according to Antonio Damasio and Hanna Damasio (1992, p. 89), neurologists renowned for their research on the neurology of vision, memory, and language, has to do with the way the mind efficiently categorizes the world:[x]

> Language arose and persisted because it serves as a supremely efficient means of communication, especially for abstract concepts.... . But language also performs what Patricia S. Churchland of the University of California at San Diego aptly calls 'cognitive compression.' It helps to categorize the world and to reduce the complexity of conceptual structures to a manageable scale.... . The cognitive economies of language ... make it possible for people to establish ever more complex concepts and use them to think at levels that would otherwise be impossible. In the beginning, however, there were no words. Language seems to have appeared in evolution only after humans and species before them had become adept at generating and categorizing actions and at creating and categorizing mental representations of objects, events and relations.... . Language exists both as an artifact in the external world ... and as the embodiment in the brain of those symbols and the principles that determine their combination.

And institutions, communicated and transmitted to others via language, facilitate human beings to categorize things, events, and human relations, and thus economize on the limitations of human memory.

## Classificatory rationality

Herbert Simon (1957) rejected the maximizing postulate of economic man and substituted instead the concept of satisficing as the relevant behavioural concept. This is based upon his concept that man's rationality is "bounded." As a consequence, models of man based upon the assumption of "bounded rationality" take into account the individual's limited mental computational abilities. My cognitive theory of trust and informal institutions embedded in the EHMG sees rationality of *Homo classificus* in terms of the concept of what I call "classificatory rationality", i.e., the rational person classifies and categorizes because of the cognitive limitations of the human agent's brain/memory. My concept of "classificatory rationality" is consistent with Simon's bounded rationality concept, but provides some details of how cognitive limitation of the brain is circumvented.

## North's cognitive science approach to institutions

In a co-authored paper with Arthur Denzau (Denzau and North 1994), Nobel Laureate in Economics Douglas North in his recent work on institutions, has taken a new route – a cognitive science approach to the analysis of the role of ideologies and institutions. According to Denzau and North (1994, p. 4), "mental models are the internal representations that individual cognitive systems create to interpret the environment; the institutions are the external (to the mind) mechanisms individuals create to structure and order the environment." The individual categorizes and classifies in order to learn and interpret the environment. Unfortunately, by treating institutions as external to the mind of the economic agent, Denzau and North fail to build an important bridge between the individual's mental processes and the institutions of the group in which he is embedded. Only by explicitly treating institutions-as-rules and institutions-as-classification, as set out in this paper, can the bridge be built between the individual and his group, and the institutional environment in which the individual is embedded.

It is at this point in the development of an NIE-cognitive theory of trust and informal institutions that the frontiers in law-and-economics of informal institutions, forming a part of the NIE, cross over into the cognitive sciences covering such disciplines as neuroscience, cognitive psychology, cognitive anthropology (as exemplified by the work of Mary Douglas), and bioeconomics.[xi]

But Denzau and North (1994, p. 27) are certainly right in pointing to the importance of developing a cognitive science approach to institutions for understanding the performance of different economies:

> [O]nce we open up the black box of 'rationality', we encounter the complex and still very incomplete world of cognitive science. This essay is a preliminary exploration of some of the implications of the way in which humans attempt to order and structure their environment and communicate with each other. Does the argument have relevance for social science theory? Certainly it does. Ideas matter and the way by which ideas evolve and are communicated is the key to developing useful theory which will expand our understanding of the performance of societies both at a moment of time and over time.

In this paper, I have looked at informal institutions from the point of view of a NIE-cognitive theory of trust and informal institutions. Such an approach to the analysis of trust and informal institutions has great relevance for social science theory. Understanding the cognitive and classificatory processes of choice of trading partners under conditions of uncertainty provide us with useful theoretical insights for explaining the successful performance of certain economies, such as the East Asian economies, China's economy in transition, and the Mafia-dominated underground economy of Russia in transition to a market economy.

## IV. Wider Implications

Important insights are yielded by a cognitive theory of trust and informal institutions directed to understanding the performance of different economies. The theory uses the NIE-cognitive theory of trust and informal institutions.

### *The "East Asian Miracle"*

According to Root and Campos (1995), the rapid and sustained economic growth in East Asia after the Second World War was due to the ability of regime leaders in these economies to provide the "institutional foundations" necessary for high economic performance. Political institutions fostered business confidence in leaders' ability to make commitments for long-term growth. Their analysis is, however, incomplete because the writers fail to take account of the cognitive and cultural foundations of Confucian ideology in which entrepreneurs in many of the high-performance East Asian economies are embedded. Chinese firms in East Asian economies are predominantly family firms, and Asian regional and international trading networks are predominately organized as kin and ethnic-based exchange networks (see Hamilton 1996). These ethnic networks are self-governing economic organizations that function to mobilize capital and information, and to enforce contracts, thus providing for themselves the essential public/club goods for themselves in an environment characterized by underdeveloped infrastructure. Landa (1978) argued, using a Property Rights-Public Choice approach (part of NIE), that it is this ability of Chinese middleman-entrepreneurs in South-east Asia to perform "gap-filling"/"input-completing" (Leibenstein 1968) functions that gave them a differential transaction cost advantage over the indigenous population to appropriate middleman roles in the first place; Landa thus rejects the traditional Marxian exploitation thesis of Chinese middleman success in South-east Asia. The very success of Chinese middleman-entrepreneurs in South-east Asia historically had generated a great deal of ethnic/racial conflict between Malays and Chinese in South-east Asia, especially in the late 1960s. Pointing only to the state's economic role in the development of these high-performance economies, therefore, greatly underestimates the economic significance of cultural and cognitive embeddedness of entrepreneurs in Confucian ethics/ideology, i.e., the capacity of entrepreneurs for creating self-governing ethnic communities in providing for themselves the ethnic-club infrastructure for entrepreneurship in less-developed economies, hence contributing to the "East Asian Miracle."

## *Entrepreneurship in the informal sectors of economies in transition*

Beginning in 1978, China's leaders embarked on a series of economic reforms designed to transform China's socialist economy into a more market-oriented economy. The major economic reform took place in rural China with the introduction of the Household Responsibility System (HRS) in 1979. As part of China's programme of economic reforms, leaders of the Communist Party recognized that the success of the HRS depends on the existence of legal institutions for the protection of property rights arising from contracts. Thus almost contemporaneous with the introduction of the HRS in 1978, the domestic contract law was established in 1982. Under the HRS, individual household farms replaced the commune system. Peasants, after fulfilling government quotas, are now allowed to sell their surplus agricultural products in markets where prices are higher and for appropriate profits for themselves; under the HRS, peasants were transformed into peasant-entrepreneurs. The HRS greatly increased the volume of trade and facilitated the growth of markets. The growth of markets led to the emergence of a class of specialized profit-seeking traders engaged in long-distance trade. The Chinese leaders also legalized their activities by allowing them to transport goods over long distances and sell their goods in newly freed-up wholesale markets. Since 1983, the private merchants have helped to generate a national network of wholesale markets. The emergence of a class of profit-seeking private merchants and transport operators also saw the "resurgence of cultural and social ties" (Watson 1988, p. 2) linking merchants together. These cultural and social ties linking merchants together is a manifestation of the same phenomenon which occurred in its most developed form as the Chinese EHMG in South-east Asia, discussed earlier. These cultural and social ties between merchants supplemented mediation, arbitration, and the role of formal contract law in enforcing contracts and contributed greatly to China's success during the transition period (see Landa 1998b).

China's relative success in transition to a market economy is in great contrast to the experience of Russia and Eastern Europe in transition where private profit-making entrepreneurship flourished predominately in the *underground* economy dominated by Mafia-type "black and informal marketeers" and "speculators" who use trust as well as extra-legal mechanisms for enforcing contracts (Brenner 1990).[xii] Brenner (1990) sees the underground economy as a fertile source for the emergence of legitimate entrepreneurship once that sector of the economy is legalized and a new contract law adopted. But, instead,

> ... legalizing much that was illegal, and letting the black market's customary law to serve as the seed of the new system, one of the first laws of the *perestroika* was the May 1986 law against "non-labor" (Brenner 1990, p. 3).

Outside Russia's underground economy there is little entrepreneurship, not only because of the absence of a well-developed contract law, but also because all the institutions that foster bonds of trust and social solidarity were systematically destroyed during Russia's transition to a market economy (Brenner 1990). Like Russia in transition, powerful informal and Mafia-like networks, which had been entrenched in Communist Poland and Eastern Europe, continued to be a source of private illegal entrepreneurship in Poland and Eastern Europe in transition to market economies. Under communism, informal barter networks, based on kinship, friendship, ethnic, and patronage ties generate mutual trust and mutual obligations. These informal networks, substituting for missing social structures, such as family, Church, religious orders or private societies, had been effectively destroyed in the name of Communist ideology (Los 1992b, pp. 360–1). In addition to the informal barter networks, entrepreneurship also flourished in the illegal organized crime economy where stolen goods are sold through Mafia networks. In these Mafia networks, personal ties among participants ensure mutual assistance and enforcement of contracts through swift and cruel punishment (Los 1992a, pp. 117, 121).

# References

Berger, P.L. and Luckmann, T. (1966). *The social construction of reality: A treatise in the sociology of knowledge.* Doubleday, New York.

Buchanan, J.M. (1975). *The limits of liberty: Between anarchy and leviathan.* The University of Chicago Press, Chicago.

Brenner, R. (1990). The long road from serfdom and how to shorten it. *Canadian Business Law Journal,* **17**, 195–225.

Carr, J.L. and Landa, J.T. (1983). The economics of symbols, clan names, and religion. *Journal of Legal Studies* **12**(1), 135–6.

Colson, E. (1974). *Tradition and contract: The problem of order.* Aldine, Chicago.

Crawford, S. and Ostrom, E. (1994). A grammar of institutions. Paper presented at the workshop on political theory and policy analysis, Indiana University, Bloomington, 16–18 June.

Damasio, A.R. and Damasio, H. (1992). Brain and language. *Scientific American.* **267**(3), 89–95.

Denzau, A.T. and North, D.C. (1994). Shared mental models: ideologies and institutions. *Kyklos* **47**, 3–31.

Douglas, M. (1986). *How institutions think.* Syracuse University Press, New York.

Douglas, M. (1992). Rightness of categories. In *How classification works: Nelson Goodman among the social sciences* (eds M. Douglas and D. Hull). Edinburgh University Press, Edinburgh, pp. 239–71.

Eggertsson, T. (1990). *Economic behaviour and institutions.* Cambridge University Press, Cambridge, UK..

Fei X. (1992). *From the soil: The foundations of Chinese society* (transl. G.G. Hamilton and W. Zheng). University of California Press, Berkeley.

Fortes, M. (1969). *Kinship and the social order: The legacy of Lewis Henry Morgan.* Aldine, Chicago.

Ghiselin, M.T. and Landa, J.T. (1995). The bioeconomics of folk and scientific classification. Paper presented at the Western Economic Association International Conference, 5–9 July 1995, San Diego.

Hamilton, G.G. (ed.) (1996). *Asian business networks.* Walter de Gruyter, New York.

Landa, J.T. (1976). An exchange theory with legally binding contract: A public choice approach. *Journal of Economic Issues* **10**(4), 905–22.

Landa, J.T. (1978). The economics of the ethnically homogeneous Chinese middleman group: A property rights-public choice approach. PhD Dissertation, Virginia Polytechnic Institute and State University.

Landa, J.T. (1981). A theory of the ethnically homogeneous middleman group: An institutional alternative to contract law. *Journal of Legal Studies* **10**(2), 349–62.

Landa, J.T. (1988). Underground economies: Generic or *sui generis?* In *Beyond the informal sector: Including the excluded in developing countries* (ed. J. Jenkins). ICS Press, San Francisco, pp. 75–103, 237–41.

Landa, J.T. (1994). Exchange and the problem of order in the social sciences: An introduction to this book. In *Trust, ethnicity, and identity: Beyond the new institutional economics of ethnic trading networks, contract law, and gift-exchange* (J.T. Landa). University of Michigan Press, Ann Arbor.

Landa, J.T. (1996). Doing the economics of trust and informal institutions. In *Foundations of research in economics: How do economists do economics?* (eds S.G. Medema and W.J. Samuels). Edward Elgar, Cheltenham, UK, pp. 142–62.

Landa, J.T. (1998a). The co-evolution of markets, entrepreneurship, laws and institutions in China's economy in transition: A new institutional economics perspective. *University of British Columbia Law Review* **32**(2), 391–421.

Landa, J.T. (1998b). The bioeconomics of schooling fish: Selfish fish, quasi free-riders, and other fishy tales. *Environmental Biology of Fishes* **53**(4), 353–64.

Landa, J. T. and Ghiselin, M. (1999). The emerging discipline of bioeconomics: Aims and scope of the journal of bioeconomics, *Journal of Bioeconomics* **1**(1), 5–12.

Leibenstein, H. (1968). Entrepreneurship and development. *American Economic Review* **58**(May), 72–83.

Lewis, D. (1969). *Convention: A philosophical study.* Harvard University Press, Cambridge, MA.

Los, M. (1992a). From undergound to legitimacy: The normative dilemmas of post-communist marketization. In *Privatization and entrepreneurship in post-socialist countries: Economy, law and society.* (eds B. Dallago, G. Ajani, and B. Grancelli). St. Martin's Press, New York, pp. 111–42.

Los, M. (1992b). Legislating the post-totalitarian transition, *The Polish Sociological Bulletin* **99/100**(3/4), 345–64.

MacLaverty, B. (1995).*Walking the dog, and other stories.* W.W. Norton & Co., New York.

North, D.C. (1990). *Institutions, institutional change and economic performance.* Cambridge University Press, Cambridge, UK.

Ostrom, E. (1986). An agenda for the study of institutions. *Public Choice* **48**, 3–25.

Rosen, L. (1984). *Bargaining for reality: The construction of social relations in a Muslim community.* The University of Chicago Press, Chicago.

Root, H. and Campos, E. (1995). The institutional foundations of East Asia high-performance economies. Paper presented at the Western Economic Association International Conference in San Diego, 5–9 July.

Searle, J.R. (1995). *The construction of social reality.* Free Press, New York.

Simon, H.A. (1957). *Models of man.* Wiley, New York.

Watson, A. (1988). The reform of agricultural marketing in China since 1978. *The China Quarterly* **113**(March), 1–28.

Williamson, O.E. (1985). *The economic institutions of capitalism: Firm, markets, relational contracting.* The Free Press, New York.

## Notes

1. This is a revised version of a paper presented at the Werner Reimers Foundation Symposium on "Risky Transactions: Kinship, ethnicity, and trust", Bad Homburg, Germany, 23–25 September 1996; and at the Canadian Law and Economics Association Eighth John M. Olin Annual Conference on Law and Economics, Faculty of Law, University of Toronto, 27–28 September 1996. I would like to thank Dr Frank Salter and Dr Stefan Voigt for comments that were helpful in revising this paper.
2. Review of Maclaverty (1995) by Philip Marchand, *The Toronto Star,* 25 April 1995, p. B8.

3. Mary Douglas (1986, p. 10).
4. Antonio Damasio and Hanna Damasio (1992, p. 89).
5. For the various subdisciplines that make up transaction cost economics or "New Institutional Economics", see Williamson (1985, pp. 1–14, and chapter 1), Eggertsson (1990, chapter 1) and Landa (1994, chapter 1). The NI is broader than NIE, and includes the work of economists, political scientists, and rational choice sociologists.
6. I am using the concept "social construction" in the sense of sociologist Berger (1966), where reality has a subjective and an objective dimension. Berger (pp. 135–6) provides an explanation with an example: "In primary socialization, then, the individual's first world is constructed. Its peculiar quality of firmness is to be accounted for, at least in part, by the inevitability of the individual's relationship to his very significant others." See also philosopher John Searle's (1995) view of the "construction of social reality" which also consists of an objective and a subjective/cognitive component.
7. It must be emphasized here, however, that animals do not depend on institutions for their ability to make social classifications. As Frank Salter pointed out to me (personal communication, December 1996), "social classification is pre-human and certainly pre-institutional."
8. For a discussion of the evolution of my work on the economics of trust and informal institutions, see Landa (1996).
9. Wulf Schiefenhövel suggested to me at the Reimers Foundation Conference, 25 September 1996, that *Homo classificans* is a better terminology than the one I am proposing. According to Faisal Bari (e-mail correspondence, 19 October 1996) "To term humans as *Homo classificus* is perfect and support for it would come not only from scoiology and anthropology, but you could get wonderful arguments from philosophy as well as evolutionary biology. The debate between British empiricism especially David Hume and Kantian idealism was surely centred around that, and I think there is general agreement that Kant was right against Hume when he said that categories are indispensable for humans. In fact he went further and said that no thinking is possible without that, and our world is thus and so because of our thinking being in certain categories."
10. I thank my brother, neurologist Dr Tai Chao, for giving me the citation to the Damasio and Damasio (1992) article.
11. For a brief survey of the new subdiscipline of bioeconomics, see Landa (1994, chapter 1, pp. 18–20. Bioeconomics has its own journal, *Journal of Bioeconomics*;the inaugural issue was published on 2 July 1999. For an editorial on the nature of bioeconomics as a discipline, and the aims and scope of the *Journal*, see Landa and Ghiselin (1999).
12. For a discussion of entrepreneurship operating in the informal sectors of less developed economies, see Landa (1988).

# OPPRESSED FAMILIES
# AND MINORITIES

## Chapter 7

# Risky Transactions under a Totalitarian Regime

## The Romanian case

### *Carmen Strungaru*

Dissidents, those who disagree with an officially imposed doctrine, do forbidden things. Unlike members of Mafia-type groups they do not have at their disposal weapons and other martial equipment, nor economic nor, usually, much political power. To oppose a totalitarian regime means risk, ranging from loss of professional position to imprisonment and death. Members of criminal organizations do not, at least under Western-type juridical conditions, usually have to reckon with punishment as severe as that meted out in totalitarian societies, except those executed by their own peers. Hence one prediction, inspired by the theme of this symposium, is that because of the high risk attending their joint activities, members of dissident groups benefit from being socially bonded. Quasi-kinship ties between them might serve as protection against mutual betrayal under duress.

This chapter will examine: (a) social control mechanisms used by the former Romanian Communist government and its institutions; (b) the risks run by individuals who opposed this government; (c) whether there was more loyalty within families than outside them; and (d) whether it was true for Romania under

Communist rule that dissidents formed the kind of tightly knit groups that often conduct other kinds of risky transactions.

In his introductory paper Frank Salter stated that "once the Soviet Union ceased to exist as a political power, Mafia-type organizations flourished." This statement is central to my argument because it refers to the very powerful and dynamic dyad existing between power and risk, not only in the former Soviet Union but all over the world. Political power makes and administers the rules and norms, but a common attitude towards these rules is that they "are made to be broken". In traditional as well as in the modern cultures, long before the Bible was written, there have been fundamental rules that many individuals have failed to respect. Rule breaking is perhaps genetically determined, since it is found in all social species. For some, it seems quite natural to try to grab advantages, to trick when possible while obeying when there is no alternative, when very strict and powerful controls are exerted. Ultimately, it is very difficult to find a rule forbidding a nonexistent tendency.

To break the rules means exposing oneself to some risk of being discovered and admonished. There are individual risks and sometimes risks to one's group. As argued by Salter in the introductory chapter, from a theoretical point of view when a relationship is risky people tend to choose partners they can trust the most, such as family, friends, or fellow ethnics. In reality, in a totalitarian, oppressive regime such as former Communist Romania, which exposed its people to diabolical, subtle control and indoctrination, the notions of kin, family, and friends were distorted so that they lost traditional meanings and functions.

The Communist Government made constant efforts to induce in the public's mind, and especially in the minds of children, new meanings for terms like parents, brotherhood, and friendship. A successful way of compromising family meanings was the well-known "transfer of paternity". I am reminded of the "personal tragedy" felt and demonstrated in public during the days of "Father Stalin" and later of "Father Dej" (the predecessor of Ceausescu), at the time of these dictators' funerals. All the tragicomedy was directed by the Romanian Communist Party and played by adults but mainly by their children whose sensibilities and tears were exploited in order to express the fidelity and sorrow of the holy family. When we were teenagers, we were amazed to learn that Chinese and Cubans felt so much love for their "Father Mao" or their "Brother Fidel". The leitmotiv of the universal parental "love disease" overwhelmed us once more, and this time we gained not only a "Father" but also a "Mother", together with a lot of Security "relatives." Children had to learn unending poems and songs about their glorious "parents", to reproduce these verses in school shows, in sports parades, in daily talks, while parents had to applaud them and to be proud that their child was carefully selected to offer flowers to the "Conductor" on 30 December (Republic Day), in the street, wearing only a popular blouse and skirt, while the temperature was several degrees below zero.

The Communist Party tried to replace normal family relationships using a number of methods, an effort in which they partly succeeded. Firstly, they separated new-born babies from their mothers after only one to three months. A new mother had the right to stay at home for only three months, after which she had to return to work, or she would not receive any financial support and would lose her job. The new-born baby had to be brought up in special institutions with daily or weekly programmes, where one assistant alone took care of about thirty children. This stress affected not only the children who developed more slowly, both physically and psychologically, and whose periodic separations from their mothers was of course very traumatic, but also the parents who could not watch their children grow up, and who had to struggle with all the kinds of accidents and illnesses that befell the children in that collective. It was very difficult and costly to obtain medical permission to stay at home with a sick child.

A second method was to substitute the parental authority partly with that of the teachers in various kinds of institutions, including schoolteachers, Pioneer and Young Communist organizational instructors, and university professors, all of whom were obliged to shape children to become the "golden future of the Communist state". Any commands coming from these officials responsible for the child's education had to be obeyed for fear of creating suspicions about the political beliefs of the parents.

A third Communist method was to involve children and parents in obligatory activities on special religious holidays such as Christmas or Easter, which were not recognized nor permitted, so that they could not celebrate together as a family. A fourth method was spying. A particularly intrusive spying tactic was to report to the authorities comments made by children at school about their families' activities, meetings, friends, discussions, etc. This had the result of reducing trust between family members. Another effect was to subvert traditional morality, since it was the authority figures of the teachers who were required to demonstrate the greatest duplicity.

A fifth method that also tended to destroy families worked by stigmatizing the families of class enemies. One's own merits were not enough for living a decent life, for reaching a good position. It was the famous Personal File Dossier Era in full action. One autobiography appeared each year with special emphasis on "origins", meaning much information about parents, grandparents, brothers, and uncles as well as parents and grandparents-in-law. Occupations, private property, political orientation, and so on were also revealed. The only way to be seen as a normal individual was to have "healthy origins", i.e., poor ancestors and in-laws (the best relations to have were workers or very poor villagers who never owned anything of value). The ones who lacked this "fortune" had to invent as healthy an origin as possible, usually by omitting details or denying personal relationships with their families' "black sheep" (i.e., the well-off). Otherwise there would be no access to universities or to important jobs for members of the offending family. Much true information as well as rumours about the consequences of having "wrong relatives" meant that families became less and less bonded, less and less confident of their own kin.

At the same time, we had to treat all acquaintances as brothers and sisters, whatever our true feelings. The ideal of universal brotherhood might sound humanistic as a principle, but in practice it does not function well because indiscriminate love and affection are so very far from what we are naturally programmed to feel and do. Like any imposed rule, this one also developed counterreactions. Too many "relatives" are hard to accept and harder still to trust; better to be alone and "not trust even your shadow", as a Romanian proverb says.

Under these conditions of very strong sociopolitical control, whose effects were reinforced by a "surveillance psychosis" fed by government disinformation, was it possible to form a successful dissident group, and were kin relationships functioning better than other kinds of relationships? The first wave of dissidents fighting against the communists was the partisan groups hidden in the mountains. In the early 1950s, all of them were captured and killed or sent into prisons and work-camps for long periods of time. However, they did not go there alone. All the adults from their families were punished in the same way, as were friends and supporters and even individuals who failed to inform on the partisans. To disappear forever from one's home during the night was a very common occurrence in the first decade of the Romanian Communist regime.

This exemplary punishment for being "counter-revolutionary" or having the smallest connection with a "people's enemy" was very efficient in diminishing any drive to look and fight for a different freedom or justice than that offered and granted by the Party. As Mircea Dinescu, one of our famous dissidents wrote on 11 November 1988 in the *Frankfurter Algemeine Zeitung*, "Fear of death (meaning here a very strong fear, but I don't know how to express it), fear became the national product offered without special ticket and *ad libitum* at every Romanian street corner."

To explain better the mechanisms used by the security police to intimidate and control people, I will just select some fragments from a collection of notes and reports from their archive, published in Romania in 1996, under the title *The White Book of Security*. Even the summary of this book is very eloquent. Its constituent 505 files refer to the "nonconformist attitudes" of incriminated people, Romanian writers, poets, artists; to their private and public conversations; and to their comments concerning different political and social events such as conferences, speeches, theatre productions and film shows, etc. This information was collected by informants, interrogators, hidden listening devices, intercepted mail, and other techniques (*Special Report*, April 1970, pp. 19–25). The comments by a security general, spoken to Dumitru Tepeneag, a Romanian writer, are also very revealing:

> Who gave you the right to meet there, four to five persons … ? The authorities do not allow meetings whatever name you give them, or to discuss freedom of writers and other things… . Freedom is meant to serve socialism. There is no other kind of freedom… . All group discussions conducted outside of an organized framework (i.e., officially approved) are illegal according to our laws… . You must know that I can take you (to jail) for ten years… . It is not permitted to do anything, to do something against the regime… We crush anybody who raises his head. That is why the Party formed these organs (security).

This comes from a report dated 27 September 1977, p. 131, on the activity of Paul Goma, a Romanian writer who tried to promote ideas among the Romanian intellectuals favoured by the Czechoslovak movement named "Charter 77". After being strongly interrogated and imprisoned for some time, he denied his actions and begged for clemency:

[F]or around two months he (Paul Goma) has avoided contacts with people from his old entourage, despite the fact that in front of members of his family and of some close friends, under the influence of the "Free Europe" radio station transmissions to which he is listening each day, he continues to accuse the so-called lack of rights and freedom in our country… . Together with his family he discussed the possibility of emigrating to the west. In order to block the departure of Paul Goma outside the country, together with the Presidium for Socialist Culture and Education we (Security) are taking steps to influence several personalities from the French Pen-Club so that they will cancel their invitation … [We are misinforming them that] he is an informant of the Romanian security services …

This example illustrates that dissidents tended to trust their families more than colleagues, though, as noted above, the regime did succeed in eroding family bonds to some extent. It is my impression that under pressure from the authorities loyalty between husband and wife may have been lower than between blood relatives. Evidence of surveillance of family life comes up repeatedly in the files:

He had subversive discussions in his house, in the presence of his wife and mother- in-law… There are some animosities in his family (Report on the hostile activity of Manolescu Apolzan Nicolae, writer and literary critic, p. 45).

The security services knew that interpersonal trust was vital for the operation of dissident groups. Here is a report of a successful disinformation operation that managed to sow distrust in a group.

At Security headquarters Boeru Adrian, Radu Constantin, Cioata Irinel, Gondi Eugen, Tautu Dumitru, Grisa Gherghei, and Negoescu Valeriu were warned, with the result that a normal working climate was established. The named elements have no more tendentious discussions, either inside their institution or outside of it, suspecting one another reciprocally… . In the process of issuing the warning we intensified the suspicion that our involvement was determined by the fact that Mihailescu Razvan and Vulcan Maria, colleagues of this group, had informed Security organs about the activity of the group… . These actions (of Security) led to the dissipation of the group whose members suspect one another reciprocally. We will continue to act so as to compromise this group and completely dissipate it.

The documents (pp. 72–5) contain a list of Romanian writers who were imprisoned from the beginning of the Communist regime until 1975. Below I will select some of the reasons given for their imprisonment in order to illustrate better the strength of control the security services had over people's lives and everyday activities:

- Writing and reproducing manifestos – seven years imprisonment plus house arrest for twenty-four months.
- Antirevolutionary discussions with other people, reciting antirevolutionary poems in the house of a friend – five years.
- Attempting to cross the border – six years plus ninety-six months of house arrest.

- Crime against peace and humanity (writing a book against communists in 1942!) – seven years.
- Failing to denounce an antirevolutionary group to the security services – one year plus confiscation of private property.

Other reports refer to such punishments as books being confiscated in the Otopeni Airport, and manuscripts being confiscated from their authors' homes or from the people who tried to smuggle them across the border. Punishments were meted out to individuals who had illegal contacts with Romanian emigrants and with foreigners, and those who had demonstrated unfavourable verbal and nonverbal reactions in every variety of situation, including during the funerals of some antirevolutionary personalities, while watching theatre productions, and so on.

One of the objectives of the security services in 1978 concerning Romanian intellectuals was "to select all talented young writers who have demonstrated that in the near future they will become 'personalities', to contact them immediately, even if they are still students or are working in different domains. By this measure we can achieve a positive influence, bringing them closer to the security organs, and those who reach our criteria can be recruited early. It is better to recruit them young rather than when they have become successful."

Many of the reports and notes contained in the reports end with comments such as "… we (Security) act for tempering and positively influencing (the problematic subject) through the intermediaries of his relatives and his connections in the country, as well as other measures" (p. 453).

The foregoing examples show that it was very easy to become a target of the security services for any kind of nonconformist attitude or activity. Citizens were correct to assume that they were surrounded by actual or potential informers, in their own homes, in their workplaces, and in public places. It was extremely risky to form a group, not only to plan dissident acts but even for the limited purpose of discussing events and complaining to one another about the system, because almost always the group contained a traitor. One of the most efficient ways to discredit a person or a group was to spread a rumour alleging his or the group's cooperation with Security. Finally, details of a dissident's personal life – relations, friendships, and animosities – were used in order to isolate him or her by sowing mistrust.

To conclude, organized dissident groups were rendered impracticable, or at least very short-lived, under the totalitarian social controls in place during the era of Romanian communism. Personal experiences and archival records indicate that the bonds of kinship are indeed strong and a last refuge for interpersonal trust between dissidents. Nevertheless, even this human bond can be compromised when subjected to intense surveillance and punishment.

## CHAPTER 8

# STRATEGIES FOR MITIGATING RISK AMONG JEWISH GROUPS

## *Kevin MacDonald*

### Introduction: Judaism as a group evolutionary strategy

Mainstream Darwinism has emphasized natural selection at the level of the gene or the individual, not the group. As a natural corollary of this model of individual selection, applications of evolutionary theory to human behaviour have tended to focus on the individual. Individuals are viewed as free agents whose self-interested behaviour has been shaped by evolutionary forces acting on psychological mechanisms. Human social relationships are viewed as permeated by conflicts of interest, but research has tended to focus on the individual actor confronting an infinitely fractionated social space. Within that social space, individual strategy is viewed as depending crucially on biological relatedness to other individuals (the result of kin selection theory [Hamilton 1964]), as well as on several other individual difference variables such as sex, age, and resource control. Within this individualist perspective the group is nothing more than a concatenation of self-interested individuals. Cooperation among individuals is understood as depending on perceived benefits to each individual.

The result is that we have paid scant attention to groups and how they are able to structure themselves in order to become an important force so that it is meaningful and important to talk about the group as the vehicle of selection (Wilson and Sober

1994). Within this conceptualization there is no requirement that human group evolutionary strategies have evolved as the result of natural selection favouring altruistic groups. The idea is that humans are able to create and maintain groups that minimize the differences between group and individual interests. I argue that in some of the more interesting examples, the fundamental mechanisms involved rely ultimately on human abilities to monitor and enforce group goals and to create ideological structures that rationalize group aims both to group members and to outsiders.

This perspective is consistent with the idea that natural selection has been most powerful at the individual level. The difficulty confronting those attempting to develop theories of groups is that there would always be natural selection within groups for selfish individuals. However, humans, presumably unlike other animals, are able to monitor the behaviour of other members of the group and enforce sanctions against those who fail to adopt behaviours agreed to by other members of the group. In fact, traditional Jewish groups developed a wide range of sanctions against behaviours viewed as inimical to group goals (MacDonald 1994).

Within this perspective, the evolved goals of humans, such as achieving social status, were determined by our evolutionary past. But there are few, if any, constraints on how humans can *attempt* to achieve these goals. Of critical importance for understanding human adaptation in uncertain and novel environments is the evolution of domain-general cognitive abilities (MacDonald 1991; MacDonald and Geary 2000). There is little doubt that humans have evolved a set of domain-specific psychological mechanisms designed to solve recurrent problems in the Environment of Evolutionary Adaptedness (EEA) – the environment humans evolved in and presented the set of problems designed by the set of human psychological adaptations. However, the human EEA also consisted of novel, unpredictable problems best solved with domain-general mechanisms. These mechanisms, including especially the $g$-factor of intelligence tests, are not restricted to solving, and enable the attainment of evolutionary goals in unfamiliar and novel conditions characterized by a minimal amount of prior knowledge.

In the case of Judaism, the clearly articulated evolutionary goals of Judaism are enshrined in the Old Testament: obtain wealth, have large numbers of children, and marry only other Jews (MacDonald 1994). The means by which particular Jewish groups have attempted to achieve these goals have varied widely over historical time; in general, Jewish groups have been very flexible in responding to novel environments, such as the post-Enlightenment decline of more traditional forms of Judaism with their overtly separatist ways. However, in all historical periods, at least until very recently, the structure of the group has been critical to its success or failure. Jews who did not comply with the rules and standards of the community by, for example marrying non-Jews or informing on Jews, were excluded from the community.

I have developed the view that Judaism in traditional societies was characterized by efforts to resist genetic and cultural assimilation with surrounding populations; these efforts have been substantially successful, resulting in closer genetic relatedness among widely dispersed contemporary groups of Jews than between Jewish groups and the gentile populations they have lived among for centuries (see also, Hammer et al. 2000); (2) Jews have typically engaged in resource and reproductive competition with at least some sectors of gentile societies, often successfully; (3) there is a significant (but limited) degree of within-group altruism, traditionally enforced by powerful social controls and enshrined in religious ideology; and (4) there is a significant degree of role specialization, specifically specialization for a role in society above the level of primary producer that is facilitated by cultural and eugenic practices centred around intelligence, the personality trait of conscientiousness, high-investment parenting, and group allegiance (MacDonald 1994).

At a fundamental level, a genetically closed group evolutionary strategy for behavior within a larger human society, as proposed here for traditional Judaism, may be viewed as pseudospeciation: Creation of a closed group evolutionary strategy results in a gene pool that becomes significantly segregated from the gene pool of the surrounding society. Within the strategizing group, there is increasing specialization so that the group becomes highly adept at occupying a specific type of niche that is commonly available in human societies. If the strategizing group has undergone a Diaspora and therefore lives among a wide range of human societies, members of the strategizing group, like conspecifics in the natural world, will have greater genetic ties with the dispersed members of their ingroup than with the other members of the society in which they live. Moreover, the within-group genetic commonality predisposes strategizing group members to relatively high levels of within-group altruism and cooperation, while the genetic gradient between the strategizing group and the surrounding society facilitates instrumental behaviour directed toward the latter.

Nevertheless, while the population genetic and historical data indicate that traditional Judaism actively maintained genetic barriers with surrounding populations, these barriers have been significantly breached in recent years, at least in Western societies, although opposition to intermarriage remains strong within all levels of the official Jewish community (Kosmin et al. 1991; Winer 1991). The result is that it is conceivable that in the future Judaism would denote a non-genetic, cultural strategy significantly divorced from genetic implications. However, because evolved mechanisms typically work at the phenotypic level, it is expected that genetic assimilation may not affect the "riskiness" of Judaism. To the extent that the riskiness of Judaism comes from attributions of group membership, it is expected that there will continue to be significant risk even if genetic barriers are lowered. This is because at least some evolved mechanisms of ingroup-outgroup conflict are sensitive to group membership – a phenotypic property – rather than genetic distance.

Social controls on the behaviour of group members are critical for the development of successful group strategies. For example, traditional Jewish groups were characterized by high levels of within-group charity maintained at least partly by social controls on individuals. Penalties for avoiding Jewish charity were severe. The following passage from the Frankfort Synod of 1603 is an excellent example of social controls which resulted in high levels of within-group charity among Jews: Individuals were assessed a certain sum of money and threatened with expulsion from the community if they did not comply:

> Whatever sum is decided on by us as necessary shall be collected each year, and each person shall pay the sum assessed against him. If any Jew fail to give their share and

disobey the agent of the General Community, their names shall be announced in every community of Germany. The announcement shall take the following form: "The following men, who are mentioned by name, have been separated from the remainder of the Dispersion, they may not mingle or intermarry with us, neither they nor their children, and no person may recite from them the benediction of marriage. If anyone transgresses this order and does marry them, whether he act willingly or under compulsion, the marriage is declared void. (In Finkelstein, 1924, p. 260).

Interestingly, the penalty described in the regulations of the Frankfort Synod is phrased as applying to all members of the violator's family, not just the violator. Thus an individual could not flaunt this regulation by simply accepting his own expulsion while assuming that his children could remain Jews. Such a person had essentially forfeited any future membership in the community for himself and his entire family – clearly a recognition by the authorities that (as expected by an evolutionary theory) penalties to relatives would be a potent source of motivation for individuals.

The extension of penalties for violating group norms to the violator's extended family appears to be a general aspect of social controls within traditional Jewish society: For example, marriage to a gentile or conversion to another religion was a blot on the entire family which would have a profound effect on the marriage prospects of the remaining members of the extended family and their descendants (see MacDonald 1994, p. 88). Such a policy would doubtless have very powerful emotional consequences, and at a level of evolutionary theory, the policy clearly raises the cost of individual defection from the group to a very high level indeed, since it effectively penalizes one's relatives.

## Judaism as a risky strategy: The pervasiveness of anti-Semitism

Whenever the quantity of Jews in any country reaches the saturation point, that country reacts against them… . [This] reaction … cannot be looked upon as anti-Semitism in the ordinary or vulgar sense of that word; it is a universal social and economic concomitant of Jewish immigration and we cannot shake it off. (Weizmann 1949, p.90)

[Anti-Semitism] has demonstrated a remarkable ability to persist, to revive time and again through the ages … . (Lindemann 1991, p. 280)

The roots of anti-Semitism are universal in character and as incomprehensible as they are deeply ingrained. (Kamen 1965, p. 15)

Ultimately … the suffering of no other nation can compare with the uniqueness of the Jewish experience, and not just in the Nazi period. This is true not simply because of the amount of suffering entailed, but also because of its frightening recurrence over time, which lends it the character of utter inescapability. (Katz 1983, p. 44)

In 1936 Chaim Weizman observed that "The world seems to be divided into two parts – those places where the Jew cannot live, and those where they cannot enter" (in Abella and Troper 1981, p. 51). Weizman's comments illustrate a remarkable aspect of the Holocaust and the years leading up to it: The pervasiveness of anti-Semitism throughout Europe, North America, North Africa, the Middle East and Latin America was an important contributing factor in condemning Jews to Nazi genocide (e.g. Breitman and Kraut 1987).

These are remarkable examples of the pervasiveness of anti-Semitism. While I will not attempt to develop a theory of anti-Semitism here, elsewhere I have concluded that anti-Semitism will be a common characteristic of human societies for the following reasons deriving from contemporary research in social psychology (MacDonald 1998a). (1) Jewish cultural separatism results in both Jews and gentiles developing stereotypically negative attitudes toward outgroup members and the culture of the outgroup; (2) resource and reproductive competition between groups has been a common component of Jewish/gentile relationships; (3) because of Jewish within-group cooperation and altruism, as well as eugenic and cultural practices tending to result in high levels of intelligence and resource acquisition abilities, Jews are highly adept in resource competition with gentiles (MacDonald 1994).

A more general formulation is that anti-Semitism arises when there are perceived conflicts of interest between the Jewish community (or segments of the Jewish community) and the gentile community (or segments of the gentile community). On account of Jewish within-group cooperation as well as eugenic and cultural practices that have resulted in an intelligence quotient of at least one standard deviation above the Caucasian mean (see MacDonald 1994), Jews are highly adept in achieving their goals, whether the goals involve establishing a homeland in the Middle East, developing business and financial networks, competing for positions in prestigious graduate and professional schools, leading political, intellectual, and cultural movements, or influencing the political process. The success of these pursuits and the fact that these pursuits inevitably conflict with the interests of groups of gentiles (or, at least are perceived to conflict with them) is, in the broadest sense, the most important source of anti-Semitism.

There is evidence for anti-Semitism in a wide range of Western and non-Western societies, in Christian and non-Christian societies, and in pre-capitalist, capitalist, and socialist societies (see MacDonald 1998a). Indeed, there is considerable evidence that Jews themselves were aware that their group strategy entailed a great deal of risk:

> And the LORD shall scatter thee among all peoples, from the one end of the earth even unto the other end of the earth … . And among these nations shalt thou have no repose, and there shall be no rest for the sole of thy foot; but the LORD shall give thee there a trembling heart, and failing of eyes, and languishing of soul. And thy life shall hang in doubt before thee; and thou shalt fear night and day, and shalt have no assurance of thy life. In the morning thou shalt say: "Would it were even!" and at even thou shalt say: "Would it were morning!" (Deut. 28, vv. 64–67).

Indeed, Jews generally perceived anti-Semitism to be more or less normal and expected. Jewish writers "treat Judeophobia as an inevitable reality that Jews have to learn to live with without giving up in despair on the one hand, or trying in vain to 'correct' its causes on the other" (Peli 1991, p. 110).

## Jewish strategies for mitigating risk

Richard Alexander (1979) argues convincingly that humans are "flexible strategizers" in pursuit of evolutionary goals. Within this framework, one expects that strategies for combating anti-Semitism will be highly variable and able to respond adaptively to novel situations in contrast to genetically determined responses to a few evolved cues. Domain-general cognitive processes – prototypically the *g*-factor of IQ tests – can be utilized to develop a wide array of survival strategies in response to specific situations that could not have been recurrent features of the human environment of evolutionary adaptedness.

There is, of course, no guarantee that any given strategy will be successful. Rather, it is expected that unsuccessful strategies will be replaced in a trial-and-error process or insightful manner, and there will be a continual search for new strategies to encounter new, perhaps unforeseen difficulties. A group strategy that tends to result in intra-societal hostility is like a widely dispersed fleet of ships attempting to navigate a hostile environment while keeping in touch. Different ships in the fleet encounter different local problems and must develop their own solutions.

Moreover, different members of a ship's crew may advocate different solutions to the same problem, and, in the absence of a strong centralized authority, the crew of one ship may fractionate and pursue their own solutions by, in effect, constructing their own ships (e.g. Reform, Conservative, Neo-Orthodox, secular, and Zionist solutions to the assimilatory pressures resulting from the Enlightenment). And, as will be apparent in the following, different subgroups of Jews may develop different and incompatible strategies for confronting anti-Semitism, leading to conflicts among groups of Jews.

### *The role of economic cooperation and within-group charity in mitigating risk in traditional Jewish society*

Traditional Judaism was characterized by high levels of within-group charity and economic cooperation. From an evolutionary perspective, high levels of within-group cooperation and charity are critical components in developing highly cohesive groups able to overcome the powerful centrifugal forces of individualism assumed by many evolutionists to be a critical component of the evolved psychology of humans (see MacDonald 1994, chapter 7).

It is noteworthy that this charity mitigated not only risks resulting from anti-Semitism, but from general economic uncertainty as well. Hundert (1992) notes the perception among Jews in Poland that wealth was ephemeral, and Katz (1961) notes that Jewish capital in traditional Poland was always precarious, since it was liable to expropriation by the authorities. Jews often specialized in obtaining forms of wealth that could be concealed and that "could be quickly switched from a point of danger to a point of resettlement" (Johnson 1988, p. 246).

Moreover, in traditional societies the economic basis of wealth among gentiles has often been the control of large areas of land – a relatively stable source of wealth. But, among Jews, the economic basis of wealth has been much more likely to depend on trade and commerce – occupations which are more prone to economic fluctuations, and Jews were often prohibited from owning land. Economic success in trade and commerce would also be facilitated by a safety net, which would encourage Jews to take economic risks. Engaging in economically risky behaviour has been noted by many writers as being characteristic of Jewish economic activity throughout history (e.g. Johnson 1988; Mosse 1987, pp. 314ff).

Within-group economic cooperation mitigated general economic risks among Jews. Several writers have noted the high degree of commonality of interest and lack of class conflict in traditional Jewish Diaspora societies. In traditional Poland, Jewish "communications and interests were similar, as were their fears and hopes, despite increasing socioeconomic stratification" (Weinryb 1972, p. 96). In the seventeenth and eighteenth centuries in Europe, "Generally speaking, [Jewish society] conformed hardly at all to the Marxist notion of class differentiation and struggle. Almost always, the vertical ties which lent Jewish society its inner cohesion – commercial collaboration and the patronage network implicit in Jewry's institutions, charities, and welfare system – were of much greater significance than any occasional friction between rich and poor" (Israel 1985, p. 171). The Court Jews of seventeenth-century Europe overwhelmingly employed their relatives and other Jews in their operations on behalf of various governments. Jewish economic activity during the period is described as a complex interdependent pyramid in which all classes benefited from each other's activities: "From Court Jew to peddler these divergent groupings penetrated and depended on each other economically" (Israel 1985, p. 171).

Economic success can be short-lived for all groups, but the ephemeral nature of economic success is likely to be particularly salient to Jews since they have often been subject to capricious seizures of property, expulsions, and confiscatory taxation. A medieval German synod enacted a law that required the entire Jewish community to pay when the king required a Jew to pay a capricious contribution, the only exception being in cases where the Jew was at fault (Finkelstein 1924, p. 60). In other words, if a Jew was penalized capriciously because of his group membership, the entire group was expected to pay. Regulations such as this could be an important concomitant of a group strategy, since the risks of group membership were spread throughout the entire group and individuals who were subject to such capricious acts were less likely to defect because their individual losses were minimized.

There are also many examples of general within-group charity in widely dispersed Jewish groups. "A Jewish wayfarer was assured of protection and welcome among his brethren in any part of the world. The essential unity of Jewish life in the Middle Ages transcended geographical boundaries and rendered Jews one sympathetic community in which the Oriental, African, Spanish, Italian and German brethren were perfectly at home with one another" (Neuman 1969, Vol. I, p. 171). There are numerous examples of Jews supporting the poor in distant Jewish communities in the medieval Arab world. "Gifts were sent to localities in which the need was greatest" (Goitein 1971, p. 95), so that, for example, Jews in Cairo contributed to ransoming Jews in Byzantium, Spain, and other parts of Europe.

At times, charity between widely dispersed Jewish groups mitigated not only economic risks, but also the risks of anti-Semitism. During the anti-Semitic uprisings of the seventeenth century in Poland, Jews were welcomed as refugees in other Jewish communities in Poland and were ransomed by other Jewish communities from Italy, Constantinople, Amsterdam, and Hamburg (Weinryb 1972). Taxes imposed on the communities of central Europe during the seventeenth century intended to free captives in the Mediterranean area (Israel 1985); Jewish communities in the Ottoman Empire "taxed themselves very heavily" in order to ransom Jewish slaves in the entire period from 1300 to the nineteenth century (Shaw 1991, p. 74).

### *Abandoning phenotypic characteristics that provoke gentile hostility*

Jews have tended to use distinctive languages, clothing and personal appearance to separate themselves from the peoples they live among (MacDonald 1994, chapter 4). These Jewish characteristics tend to emphasize the foreignness and separateness of Jewish populations, and, as expected on the basis of social identity theory (e.g. Hogg and Abrams 1987), the salience of group separatism has been linked with anti-Semitism – a result that is highly compatible with an evolutionary interpretation of group conflict (MacDonald 1998a). The result has been a powerful trend since the Enlightenment to minimize those phenotypic features which have sharply distinguished Jews from gentiles in traditional societies in order to minimize the risk of anti-Semitism (MacDonald 1998a). There was a "dynamic – albeit contradictory – process in modern Jewish life between efforts to decrease visibility in order to reduce hostility to the group and the need for public perpetuation and legitimization of the Jewish religion and community, pressure on the powerful to aid Jewish interests, and the desire for a good image of Jews.... Much of the content of American Jewish culture can be seen as an outcome of different strategies of image management" (Zenner 1991, p. 141).

I propose that this attempt to maintain separatism and group cohesiveness while nevertheless making the barriers less visible is the crux of the problem for post-Enlightenment Judaism, at least during periods of anti-Semitism. While never abandoning the ideology of genetic separatism and group continuity, the Reform movement in Judaism beginning in the nineteenth century has been characterized by an attempt to eradicate civil disabilities and defamation directed at Jews while simultaneously de-emphasizing the appearance of differences between Judaism and other religions in order to change negative images of Jews held by gentiles (Endelman 1991, p. 195). Reform Jews hoped to retain traditional genetic and cultural separatism but "as to outward appearances, [they would] differ from any Christian church to no greater degree than did the various Christian denominations among themselves" (Patai 1971, pp. 37–8).

Reform Judaism in contemporary societies may thus be viewed as a "semi-cryptic" Jewish strategy, which like other religious forms of Judaism acts as what Daniel Elazar terms a "protective coloring" (Elazar 1980, p. 9) adopted because "it is a legitimate way to maintain differences when organic ways [i.e., kinship and ethnic group affiliation] are suspect" (Elazar 1980, p. 23). While Judaism in other parts of the world was and remains openly ethnic, Judaism in the West developed a religious veneer because of its usefulness in facilitating perceptions of surface similarity with other, nonethnic religions. In Israel, where there is no need for semi-crypsis, Reform Judaism is virtually nonexistent.

Jews have also responded to anti-Semitism by abandoning overt behaviour that would give rise to charges of dual loyalty. In the mid- to late-1920s an upsurge in anti-Semitism resulted in American Jews abandoning Zionism because of a heightened concern with charges of dual loyalty: "Anti-Semitism obliged all Jews to adopt a lower profile ... [and avoid] a movement that might cast doubt on their Americanism" (Sachar 1992, p. 505). "Even the Jews closest to President Roosevelt often went to excessive lengths to avoid identification with 'parochial' interests" (Sachar 1992, p. 552).

Indeed, avowals of religious belief were often made in order to escape the charges of Jewish nationalism – another example of the role of religion as a "protective coloring" for Jewish ethnic/national interests. In the era of the First World War in Germany, "liberal laymen ... were in the mass irreversibly secularized Jews, who called themselves religious principally to escape suspicion that their Judaism might be national" (Meyer 1988, p. 212).

## Political strategies for minimizing anti-Semitism

In a statement that would apply to Jewish responses to anti-Semitism throughout history, Lindemann (1991) portrays Jews "individually and collectively, as active agents, as modern, responsible, and flawed human beings, not merely as passive martyrs or as uncomprehending objects of impersonal forces" (p. 279). A very wide array of political strategies have been pursued with varying success. Jews in traditional Poland responded to anti-Semitism with strategies such as physical defence, attempts to fill indispensable functions for the king, cultivating friendly personal relationships with the powerful, and paying bribes and protection (Weinryb 1972). This led to the perception of Jews among Polish writers as controlling the nobility and the political process (see also Goldberg 1986, pp. 49–51) – charges that have been common in other times and places as well (Ginsberg 1993).

Jews engaged in a wide range of activities to combat anti-Semitism in Germany in the period from 1870–1914, including the formation of self-defence committees (e.g. the *Zentralverein deutscher Staatsbürger jüdischen Glaubens*), lobbying the government, utilizing and influencing the legal system (e.g. taking advantage of the laws on libel and slander to force anti-Semitic organizations into bankruptcy), writing apologias and tracts for distribution to the masses of gentile Germans, and funding organizations opposed to anti-Semitism which were not overtly Jewish (Ragins 1980, pp. 23ff).

Similarly, in the early twentieth century, the American Jewish Committee (AJCommittee) engaged in a wide range of activities to minimize anti-Semitism and pursue Jewish interests:

> The distribution of articles on czarist Russia, the exposure of the *Protocols of the Elders of Zion*, and the analysis of the economic effects of immigration were all directed to mobilize mass sympathy for immediate and concrete problems. Studies like *Jewish Disabilities in the Balkan States* and *Jews in the Eastern War Zone* were circulated among government officials as a prelude to Committee requests for diplomatic intercession. The Committee even had ready a scholarly rebuttal when criticism of the ritual method of animal slaughter arose. Less immediate but more ambitious was Joseph

Jacob's study *Jewish Contributions to Civilization*, answering the "higher anti-Semi-tism" propagated by Werner Sombart, Houston Stewart Chamberlain, and their ilk. (Cohen 1972, p. 34)

## The uses of universalism

Jews attempting to appeal to gentiles have often framed their interests in universal-ist terms and/or recruited prominent gentiles to back the cause publicly. From an evolutionary perspective, the intent is to make the Jewish cause appear to be in the interests of others as well. When goals are cast in ethnic or national terms they are not likely to appeal to those outside the group. Indeed, such obviously self-inter-ested goals would be likely to alert outsiders to conflicts of interest between the group and outsiders, and could well be a source of animosity between the groups.

The attempt to cast particularistic interests in universalist terms has appeared periodically beginning in the ancient world (MacDonald 1998a, chapter 7). A typ-ical strategy has been to portray Judaism as "a light unto the nations". For example, a major aspect of Reform ideology, especially during the nineteenth century, was to recast the traditional messianic hope of Judaism into universalist terms and to de-emphasize the ethnic/national character of Judaism while nevertheless maintain-ing traditional Jewish cultural separatism. The traditional hopes for the restoration of Jewish political power were replaced by the hope of a world of peace and justice for all of humanity.

This use of a universalist ideology has also been apparent in the statements of Jewish political organizations. There are many instances in which Jewish organi-zations have attempted to include statements which explicitly advocate universal-ist aims for human rights and de-emphasize the ethnic character of Judaism (Patai 1971). A good example is the series title "Studies in Prejudice" for the books on anti-Semitism commissioned by the AJCommittee. The title was chosen (rather than the more descriptive "Studies in Anti-Semitism") "in the hope that democrats would be more likely to respond to a call to fight prejudice and social discrimina-tion in general than they would be to a call to fight anti-Semitism" (Wiggershaus 1994 409). In the words of Max Horkheimer, the editor of the series, the purpose of the studies was to provide experimental proof of the threat that anti-Semitism poses to democratic civilization" (in Wiggershaus 1994, p. 418).

Within this perspective, opposition to anti-Semitism is conceptualized as in the interests of all. For example, Jewish organizations in Germany in the period 1870–1914 argued that anti-Semitism was a threat to all of Germany (Ragins 1980, p. 55). Anti-Semitism was argued to be a form of anarchy and fundamen-tally "un-German".

> It followed that those Jews who now banded together to oppose anti-Semitism did so out of concern for their nation and in order to make a contribution to the welfare of their fatherland. In their dedication to defense, Jewish citizens gave proof of their patriotism and deep devotion to the national interests of Germany.

Another use of universalism has been to recruit gentile leaders to endorse Jew-ish causes. From an evolutionary perspective, this technique takes advantage of the importance of similarity in inducing positive attitudes and altruism (Rushton 1989). An individual is more likely to agree with and have positive attitudes toward similar others than dissimilar others, so it is expected that gentiles would be more likely to be persuaded to go along with Jewish political causes by gentile political leaders than by Jews whose actions would be more likely to be viewed as self-interestedly ethnocentric.

This type of activity can involve deception, as occurred in the ancient world where there developed an entire apologetic literature written by Jews adopting gentile *noms de plume* (Schürer 1986, pp. 617ff). By adopting a gentile pseudonym the author hoped to make gentiles more sympathetic to Jewish ideas, particularly the superiority of Jewish religious beliefs (e.g. Jewish ethics and monotheism), as well as to defend Jewish honour against gentile criticisms. For example, the famous Letter of Aristeas defends the Jewish law of purity and "tends to glorify the Jewish people with its excellent institutions and its sumptuous prosperity" (Schürer 1986, p. 678).

Jewish organizations opposed to anti-Semitism had an active role in establishing and maintaining predominantly gentile organizations opposed to anti-Semitism in Germany in the period from 1870–1933 (Niewyk 1980, p. 88; Ragins 1980, pp. 53–54; Schorsch 1972, pp. 79ff), leading to accusations among anti-Semites that such organizations were "no more than a front for 'moneyed Jewry'" (Levy 1975, p. 147). Much earlier Moses Mendelsohn obtained the services of Christian Wilhelm von Dohm, a prominent gentile historian and diplomat, to argue the cause of emancipation of the Alsatian Jews (Schorsch 1972, p. 79). One reason why gentiles were attractive spokesmen for Judaism was that for Jews to fight openly against anti-Semitism was in effect "a repudiation of concealment as the price for equality" (Schorsch 1972, p. 12) – a comment which shows the importance of adopting a semi-cryptic profile during this period in which emancipation was viewed as a *quid pro quo* for assimilation. Similar strategies were common in the U.S. during this period: "Jews offered to provide the professional staffs and most of the financing if prominent Gentiles would grace the organizational letterheads" (Dinnerstein 1994, p. 147).

## *Strategies for combating anti-Semitism focusing on controlling behaviour within the Jewish community*

Jews have often taken actions within their own community designed to limit anti-Semitism. Such measures are theoretically important because a successful group strategy must be protected from invasion by deceivers, exploiters and those who endanger the community (MacDonald 1994, chapter 7). This type of activity is important because psychological research on social identity processes has indicated that the negative behavior of a few outgroup members tends to be uncritically generalized to all of the outgroup (e.g., Hogg and Abrams 1987). As a result, a strategizing group is well advised to have mechanisms which control the behaviour of individual members likely to draw general hostility.

One of the most important roles of Jewish self-government was to regulate the personal behaviour of Jews so as not to needlessly offend gentile sensibilities. In the communal reorganizations of fifteenth-century Spain there were laws that prohibited extravagant dress and entertainment, the purpose of which was partly "to prevent householders ... from arousing Christian envy and hatred 'on account of which new edicts are enacted against us'" (Baer 1961, Vol. II, p. 269). A commentary on the Jews of Cairo in the nineteenth century noted that wealthy Jews dressed well at home, but put on "plain or shabby dress" when they went out. Similarly, "though their houses have a mean and dirty appearance from without, many of them contain fine and well-furnished rooms.... . They are careful, by every means in their power, to avoid the suspicion of being possessed of much wealth" (in Stillman 1979, p. 327). Another nineteenth-century commentator on Jews in the Ottoman Empire noted that "at weddings they make a dangerous display of their wealth" (in Stillman 1979, p. 339) – dangerous because the Turks were always looking for an excuse to extort money from them.

Besides the flaunting of wealth, Jewish writers in Spain prior to the Inquisition often directed their hostility against the wealthy Jewish courtier class because their activities, such as money-lending and tax farming, were potent sources of anti-Semitism (Baer (1961, Vol. I, pp. 257ff.). A regulation of the Synod of Frankfort of 1603 stated that "No member of our community whether young or old, shall be permitted to lie to Gentiles or deceive them, whether in regard to what Jews buy from them or in regard to what the Jews sell them. Those who deceive Gentiles profane the name of the Lord among the Gentiles" (from Finkelstein 1924, p. 280). Resolutions also prohibited large groups of Jews from congregating in public. "In general, any action that might arouse the notice, the envy, or the anger of the Gentile population was deprecated" (Finkelstein 1924, p. 88).

Despite the decline of the *Kehilla* system, there have been continuing attempts to restrain other Jews in the interests of lowering anti-Semitism. The "extraordinarily large representation of Jews among traffickers and their victims" (Niewyk 1980, p. 118) in international prostitution from 1870–1939 was a major source of negative stereotypes by gentiles (Bristow 1983), and in the early twentieth-century America, Jews were active in attempts to eradicate Jewish prostitution and Jewish control of prostitution, Jewish street crime, and gangster activities (see Sachar 1992). In New York in 1912, the Bureau of Social Morals was established by Jewish philanthropists to provide information to the district attorney regarding Jewish criminal activities.

Attempts to moderate Jewish economic behaviour have also continued in the modern world. In the 1930s in England, Neville Laski, President of the Board of Deputies, set up a subcommittee to "to deal with such social conditions as sweatshops, bad employers, landlords and price-cutting in the East End." The committee attempted to raise the public image of Jews by making Jews more aware of the effect their "individual malpractices" had on fomenting anti-Semitism and pressuring them to change their behaviour.

> I submit that the time has passed for us to pretend that we are a perfect community and to ignore the fact that not a day goes by without anti-Semitism being created by Jews themselves ... a new generation of unethical Jewish traders are by bankruptcy, due to complete irresponsibility and lack of principle, causing hardship over a wide

field and manufacturing anti-Semitism at high pressure. (M.G. Liverman, Chairman of the Defence Committee of the Board of Deputies, November 1938; in Alderman 1992, p. 294)

Another source of conflict has been over the external signs of Jewish group separateness. In the period from 1870–1914, Ragins (1980, p. 49) notes the effort on the part of liberal German Jews to actively dissociate themselves from Jews, especially Orthodox Jews, who refused to adopt the outward appearances of assimilation and thus justify the charge that Jews were foreigners. Active attempts were made to get other Jews to abandon typical Jewish gestures and social behaviour because it was offensive to Germans: "(O)ne was required to be ever watchful and take great care to avoid all provocative behavior" (Ragins 1980, p. 88). Indeed, "as late as 1890 [Jews] were still consciously suppressing every conspicuous and distinctive Jewish trait" (Schorsch 1972, p. 66).

Concerns about the potential for anti-Semitism resulting from the external signs of group separateness were also behind the attempts by some of the more established German-American Jews to decrease immigration of their Eastern European co-religionists. Thus in the 1880s a Jewish spokesman tried to prevent European Jewish organizations from sending Eastern European Jews to America by noting that "the Jewish position in America was not yet secure.... American Jews could not 'afford to incur the ill will of their compatriots'" (Sachar 1992, 124; see also Neuringer 1980, pp. 15ff). A Jewish publication warned about the "uncouth Asiatics" from Russia, and there were concerns that the new immigrants would ultimately lower the social class of the established Jewish community.

A particularly potent source of conflict within the Jewish community occurred over the issue of Zionism. In 1914 at the outbreak of the First World War I, the German Zionist Federation (the main German Zionist organization) resolved that Jews had no roots whatsoever in Germany. Such declarations of Jewish nationalism and lack of commitment to Germany were perceived as fanning the flames of anti-Semitism due to charges of Jewish disloyalty, and a major goal of the Reform movement was therefore to suppress public expressions of Zionism. Meyer (1988, p. 339) notes that two prominent German reform rabbis declared during this period that a Zionist newspaper was a "calamity" to German Jews: "As long as the Zionists wrote in Hebrew, they were not dangerous, now that they write in German it is necessary to oppose them" (in Meyer 1988, p. 209). A low-profile Zionism was perceived as harmless, but these Jews perceived danger if gentiles become aware of strident assertions of Jewish nationalism.

The conflict between Zionists and anti-Zionists in America can be seen from the following quotations from *The American Hebrew*, a periodical that reflected the views of the older Jewish establishment represented by the AJCommittee that had become numerically overwhelmed by the recent immigration of Eastern European Jews inclined toward Zionism and political radicalism:

[The vast majority of American Jews] feel that they cannot participate in an undertaking predicated on what, in effect, would be an acknowledgment that they are a people apart from the rest of the population of the countries of which they are citizens and to which they owe their allegiance. (*American Hebrew*, 15 June 1923, p. 93)

Also related to charges of disloyalty, there was great concern within the Jewish community that the disproportionate representation of Jews within the American Communist Party (CPUSA) would lead to anti-Semitism from the 1920s through the Cold War period: "The fight against the stereotype of Communist-Jew became a virtual obsession with Jewish leaders and opinion makers throughout America (Liebman 1979, p. 515), and indeed, the association of Jews with the CPUSA was a focus of anti-Semitic literature at this time (e.g. Beaty 1951). Jewish organizations were well aware of that a majority of communists were Jews, that an even greater majority of Communist leaders were Jews, that the great majority of those called up by investigative bodies of Congress were Jews, and that the great majority of those prosecuted for spying for the Soviet Union were Jews (Novick 1999). As a result, the AJCommittee engaged in intensive efforts to change opinion within the Jewish community by showing that Jewish interests were more compatible with advocating American democracy than Soviet communism (e.g. emphasizing Soviet anti-Semitism and Soviet support of nations opposed to Israel in the period after the Second World). (Cohen 1972, pp. 347ff.)

## *Offensive strategies for combating anti-Semitism: Cultural critique and pathologizing Anti-Semitism*

While the foregoing are fundamentally defensive strategies aimed at deflecting recurrent bouts of anti-Semitism, Jewish groups have also gone on the offensive in an effort to create social, political, and intellectual environments conducive to Jewish interests, particularly combating anti-Semitism (MacDonald 1998b). For example, Jews have figured prominently in movements of political radicalism beginning in the late nineteenth century (Rothman and Lichter 1996). While aimed at developing societies devoid of anti-Semitism, as indicated above, Jewish radicalism has been a potent source of anti-Semitism in the twentieth century and has resulted in a variety of defensive strategies aimed at dissociating Jews from radicalism, at least among non-Jews. Similarly, Jewish organizations have aggressively pursued immigration policies aimed at diminishing the power of European-derived groups and thereby preventing the recurrent bouts of anti-Semitism that have characterized European cultures (MacDonald 1998b).

In the intellectual arena, individuals who strongly identified as Jews have been the main force behind several highly influential intellectual movements that have simultaneously subjected gentile culture to radical criticism and allowed for the continuity of Jewish identification, including Boasian anthropology, psychoanalysis, radical political ideology, the New York Intellectuals, and the Frankfurt School of Social Research (MacDonald 1998b). (I am not implying that these movements involve most Jews, only that strongly identified Jews pursuing Jewish agendas were the prime moving force. The influence of these movements is independent of the number or percentage of Jews involved in these movements.) For example, the Frankfurt School centred around Max Horkheimer and T.W. Adorno developed the highly influential view that gentile ethnocentrism was a sign of psychopathology. They viewed the end of anti-Semitism as a precondition for the development of a Utopian society and the liberation of humanity. Their Utopian society was one in which Judaism would continue as a cohesive group but in which cohesive, nationalistic, corporate gentile groups based on conformity to group norms would be eradicated as manifestations of psychopathology. Through works such as *The Authoritarian Personality*, these intellectuals have had a vast and continuing influence on American social science and the humanities, and on popular attitudes regarding racial and ethnic conflict.

Finally, Novick (1999) shows that since the 1970s the Jewish community has promoted the Holocaust as part of the effort to combat to anti-Semitism. This includes a large-scale educational effort (including mandated courses in the public schools of several states) spearheaded by Jewish organizations aimed at conveying the lesson that "tolerance and diversity [are] good; hate [is] bad, the overall rubric [is] 'man's inhumanity to man' " (pp. 258–9). The Holocaust has thus become an instrument of Jewish ethnic interests as a symbol intended to create moral revulsion at violence directed at minority ethnic groups – prototypically the Jews.

## Conclusion: An evolutionary perspective on the psychological mechanisms underlying group conflict

I conclude that Jews have used a variety of strategies to minimize risks resulting from their group strategy. Jews have often been able to respond effectively to anti-Semitism arising in vastly different environments and for a variety of different reasons. Nevertheless, these strategies have not always achieved their aims. Strategizing groups must continually search for effective methods for preventing hostility or the effects of hostility, and there is no guarantee of long-term success.

I have tried to highlight the ways in which Jewish strategies to minimize risk have relied upon mechanisms revealed by contemporary psychological research as important to understanding group dynamics, particularly social identity theory and the importance of similarity in eliciting affiliation and trust. Both of these phenomena may be viewed within an evolutionary perspective. As noted above, Rushton (1989) has developed an evolutionary theory of the importance of similarity in human relationships. The empirical results of social identity research are also highly compatible with an evolutionary basis for group behaviour. Current evidence indicates that the central findings of positive ingroup bias and negative outgroup bias can be generalized across subjects of different ages, nationalities, social classes, and a wide range of dependent variables (Bourhis 1994), and anthropological evidence indicates the universality of the tendency to view one's own group as superior (Vine 1987). Moreover, social identity processes occur very early in life, prior to explicit knowledge about the outgroup. An evolutionary interpretation of these findings is also supported by results indicating that social identity processes occur among primate species closely related to humans, such as chimpanzees. Van der Dennen (1991, p. 237) proposes, on the basis of his review of the literature on human and animal conflict, that advanced species have "extra-strong group delimitations" based on affective mechanisms. I would agree and suggest that in humans one affective mechanism is the self-esteem mechanism proposed by social identity theorists. Other affective mechanisms which may be involved are the social conscientiousness/guilt mechanism and the experience of psychological relief obtained by individuals who join highly collectivist, authoritarian groups (see Galanter 1989). These latter mechanisms, although not considered by social identity theorists, would result in strong positive feelings associated with group membership and feelings of guilt and distress at the prospect of defecting from the group.

Research supporting the importance of self-esteem as underlying the motivation for social identification processes has not been entirely supportive (e.g. Hogg and Abrams 1993). An evolutionary approach would emphasize the importance of evolved affective motivational systems as central to motivation generally (MacDonald 1991), but there are a variety of possible affective motivations which could be involved, including those mentioned by Hogg and Abrams. Evolved motivational systems often include both positive and negative components (e.g. anxiety in the presence of danger and relief consequent to deliverance [MacDonald 1995]). I suspect that studies of real-life groups with a high degree of group commitment (such as Judaism) would reveal not only strong positive affective motivations concomitant with group membership, but a strong role also for negative emotions such as guilt for motivating non-defection from the group and compliance with group goals. Indeed, Trivers (1971) and Baumeister and Leary (1995) emphasize the importance of guilt and empathy for cementing ingroup relationships.

The powerful affective components of social identity processes are difficult to explain except as aspects of the evolved machinery of the human mind. We have noted that the tendency to seek self-esteem via social identity processes is a theoretical primitive in the system. As Hogg and Abrams (1987, p. 73) note, this result cannot be explained in terms of purely cognitive processes, and a learning theory seems hopelessly *ad hoc* and gratuitous. The tendencies for humans to place themselves in social categories and for these categories to assume immense affective and evaluative overtones involving the emotions of guilt, empathy, self-esteem, relief at securing a group identity, and distress at losing it are the best candidates for the biological underpinnings of participation in highly cohesive collectivist groups.

An evolutionary perspective is also highly compatible with the falsity and contradictory nature of many anti-Semitic beliefs. As Krebs, Denton, and Higgins (1988) note, evolution is concerned only with ensuring accuracy of beliefs and attitudes when the truth is in the interests of those having those beliefs and attitudes. In the case of anti-Semitism there is no expectation that specific anti-Semitic beliefs will be accurate, but from the standpoint of evolutionary theory, these beliefs may be eminently adaptive in group competition.

Finally, the fact that social identity processes and tendencies toward collectivism increase during times of resource competition and threat to the group (see Hogg and Abrams 1987; Triandis 1990, 1991) is highly compatible with supposing that these processes involve facultative mechanisms that emerged as a result of selection at the level of the group in the sense that the group becomes the vehicle of selection (Wilson and Sober 1994). In other words, social identity processes show evidence of adaptive design as a mechanism underlying group conflict. Social identity processes are intensified during times of perceived danger. At such times, individuals more willingly submerge themselves in groups, develop a powerful sense of membership in a cohesive, morally superior group, and gird themselves to fight the morally depraved enemy.

Within this perspective, there is no conflict between selection at the level of the individual and the level of the group, because under conditions of external threat, individual self-interest increasingly coincides with the survival interests of the group. As emphasized by evolutionists such as Alexander (1979) and Johnson (1995), external threat tends to reduce internal divisions and maximize perceptions of common interest among group members. Under conditions of external threat, human societies expand government and there is an increase in cooperative and even altruistic behaviour. Such changes presumably reflect a species-wide facultative strategy of accepting increasing levels of leadership under conditions of external threat and/or opportunities for territorial expansion.

Similarly, students of anti-Semitism have often noted that anti-Semitism tends to increase during periods of political and economic instability. This suggests that during periods of perceived external threat, gentiles are more prone to forming cohesive, cooperative groups directed against outgroups, and especially against groups perceived as having a disproportionate influence on the economic circumstances of ingroup members. The result is an escalation of between-group conflict and a search among Jews for mechanisms that might mitigate the rising threat of anti-Semitism.

# References

Abella, I., and Troper, H.E. (1981). "The line must be drawn somewhere": Canada and Jewish refugees, 1933–1939. In M. Weinfeld, W. Shaffir, and I. Cotler, *The Canadian Jewish mosaic*. Wiley, Toronto.

Alderman, G. (1983). *The Jewish community in British politics*. The Clarendon Press, Oxford.

Alderman, G. (1992). *Modern British Jewry*. The Clarendon Press, Oxford.

Alexander, R. D. (1979). *Darwinism and human affairs*. University of Washington Press, Seattle.

Baer, Y. (1961). *A History of the Jews in Christian Spain*, Vols. I & II, Trans. L. Schoffman. The Jewish Publication Society of America, Philadelphia.

Baumeister, R. F., & Leary,. M. R. (1995). The need to belong: Desire for interpersonal attachments as a fundamental human motivation. *Psychological Bulletin*, **117**, 497–529.

Beaty, J. (1951). *The Iron Curtain Over America*. Wilkinson Publishing Co, Dallas, TX.

Bourhis, R. Y. (1994). Power, gender, and intergroup discrimination: Some minimal group experiments. In M. P. Zanna & J. M. Olson (Eds.), *The psychology of prejudice: The Ontario symposium, Volume 7*. Erlbaum, Hillsdale, NJ.

Breitman, R., & Kraut, A. M. (1987). *American refugee policy and European Jewry, 1933–1945.* Indiana University Press, Bloomington.

Bristow, E. J. (1983). *Prostitution and prejudice: The Jewish fight against white slavery, 1870–1939.* Oxford University Press, Oxford.

Cohen, N. W. (1972). *Not free to desist: The American Jewish committee 1906–1966.* The Jewish Publication Society of America, Philadelphia.

Dawidowicz, L. S. (1952). "Anti-Semitism" and the Rosenberg case. *Commentary,* **14** (July), 41–45.

Dennen, J.M.G. van der (1991) Studies of conflict. In *The sociobiological imagination* (ed. M. Maxwell). State University of New York Press, Albany.

Dinnerstein, L. (1994). *Antisemitism in America.* Oxford University Press, New York.

Elazar, D. J. (1980). *Community and polity: Organizational dynamics of American Jewry,* first published in 1976. The Jewish Publication Society of America, Philadelphia.

Endelman, T. M. (1991). The legitimization of the Diaspora experience in recent Jewish historiography. *Modern Judaism,* **11**, 195–209.

Frommer, M. (1978). The American Jewish Congress: A History 1914–1950 (2 vols.). Ph. D. Dissertation, Ohio State University.

Finkelstein, L. (1924). *Jewish self-government in the Middle Ages.* Greenwood Press, Westport, CT.

Galanter, M. (1989). *Cults: Faith, healing, and coercion.* Oxford University Press, New York.

Ginsberg, B. (1993). *The fatal embrace: Jews and the state.* University of Chicago Press, Chicago.

Goitein, S. D. (1971). *A Mediterranean society, Vol. II: The community.* The University of California Press. Berkeley.

Goldberg, J. (1986). The privileges granted to Jewish communities of the Polish Commonwealth as a stabilizing factor in Jewish support. In C. Abramsky, M., Jachimczyk, & A. Polonsky, (Eds.), *The Jews in Poland.* Basil Blackwell, London.

Goldstein, J. (1990). *The Politics of ethnic pressure: The American Jewish committee fight against immigration restriction, 1906–1917.* Garland Publishing, New York.

Hamilton, W. D. (1964). The genetical theory of social behaviour, I, II. *Journal of Theoretical Biology* **7**, 1–52.

Hammer, M. F., Redd. A. J., Wood, E. T., Bonner, M. R., Jarjanazi, H., Karafet, T., Santachiara-Benerecetti, S., Oppenheim, A., Jobling, M. A., Jenkins, T., Ostrer, H., & Bonné-Tamir, B. (2000). Jewish and Middle Eastern non-Jewish populations share a common pool of Y-chromosome biallelic haplotypes. *Proceedings of the National Academy of Science,* May 9.

Hogg, M. A. & Abrams, D. (1987). *Social identifications.* Routledge, New York.

Hogg, M. A., & Abrams, D. (1993). Toward a single-process uncertainty-reduction model of social motivation in groups. In M. A. Hogg & D. Abrams (Eds.). *Group motivation: Social psychological perspectives.* Harvester Wheatsheaf, London.

Hundert, G. D. (1992). *The Jews in a Polish private town: The case of Opatow in the Eighteenth Century.* Johns Hopkins University Press, Baltimore.

Israel, J. I. (1985). *European Jewry in the age of mercantilism.* The Clarendon Press, Oxford.

Johnson, G. (1995). The evolutionary origins of government and politics. In J. Losco & A. Somit (eds.), *Human nature and politics*, 243–305. JAI Press, Greenwich, CT.

Johnson, P. (1988). *A history of the Jews.* Perennial Library, New York. (Originally published by Harper & Row, 1987).

Kamen, H. (1985). *Inquisition and society in Spain in the sixteenth and seventeenth centuries.* Indiana University Press, Bloomington.

Katz, J. (1961). *Tradition and crisis: Jewish society at the end of the middle ages.* The Free Press of Glencoe, Inc, New York.

Katz, J. (1983). Misreadings of Anti-Semitism. *Commentary,* **76** (1), 39–44.

Kosmin, B. A., Goldstein, S., Waksberg, J., Lerer, N., Keysar, A., & Scheckner, J. (1991). *Highlights of the CJF 1990 national Jewish population survey.* Council of Jewish Federations, New York.

Krebs, D. L. Denton, K., & Higgins, N. C. (1988). On the evolution of self-knowledge and self-deception. In K. B. MacDonald (ed.), *Sociobiological perspectives on human development.* Springer-Verlag, New York.

Levy, R. S.*(1975). *The downfall of the anti-semitic political parties in imperial Germany.* Yale University Press, New Haven.

Liebman, A. (1979). *Jews and the left.* John Wiley & Sons, New York.

Lindemann, A. S. (1991). *The Jew Accused: Three anti-semitic affairs (Dreyfus, Beilis, Frank) 1894–1915.* Cambridge University Press, New York.

MacDonald, K. B. (1991). A perspective on Darwinian psychology: Domain-general mechanisms, plasticity, and individual differences. *Ethology and Sociobiology,* **12**, 449–480.

MacDonald, K. (1994) *A people that shall dwell alone: Judaism as a group evolutionary strategy.* Praeger, Westport, CT.

MacDonald, K. B. (1995a). Evolution, the five factor model, and levels of personality. *Journal of Personality,* **63**, 525–567.

MacDonald, K. B. (1998a). *Separation and its discontents: Toward an evolutionary theory of anti-semitism.* Praeger, Westport, CT.

MacDonald, K. B. (1998b). *The culture of critique: An evolutionary analysis of Jewish involvement in twentieth-century intellectual and political movements.* Praeger, Westport, CT.

MacDonald, K. B. & Geary, D. C. The evolution of general intelligence: Domain-general cognitive mechanisms and human adaptation. Paper presented at the meetings of the Human Behavior and Evolution Society, Amherst, MA, June 8, 2000.

Meyer, M. A. (1988). *Response to modernity: A history of the reform movement in Judaism.* Oxford University Press, New York.

Neuman, A. A. (1969). *The Jews in Spain: Their political and cultural life during the middle ages;* Vols. I & II. Octagon Books, New York. (Originally published in 1942.)

Niewyk, D. L. (1980). *The Jews in Weimar Germany.* Louisiana State University Press, Baton Rouge.

Novick, P. (1999). *The holocaust in American life.* Houghton Mifflin, Boston.

Patai, R. (1971). *Tents of Jacob: The diaspora yesterday and today.* Prentice-Hall, Englewood Cliffs, NJ.

Peli, P. H. (1991). Response to anti-semitism in Midrashic literature. In S. L. Gilman & S. T. Katz (Eds.), *Anti-semitism in times of crisis.* New York University Press, New York.

Ragins, S. (1980). *Jewish responses to anti-semitism in Germany, 1870–1914.* Hebrew Union College Press, Cincinnati: .

Rothman, S., & Lichter, S. R. (1996). *Roots of radicalism: Jews, christians, and the new left.* Transaction, New Brunswick, NJ. (Reprinted from the 1982 version with a new introduction.)

Rushton, J. P. (1989). Genetic similarity, human altruism, and group selection. *Behavioral and Brain Sciences, 12,* 503–559.

Sachar, H. M. (1992). *A history of Jews in America.* Alfred A. Knopf, New York.

Schorsch, I. (1972). *Jewish reactions to German anti-semitism, 1870–1914.* Columbia University Press, New York.

Schürer, E. (1986). *The history of the Jewish people in the age of Jesus Christ (175 B. C.-A. D. 135),* Vol. III; revised and edited by G. Vermes, F. Millar, & M. Goodman; originally published in 1885. T. & T. Clark Ltd, Edinburgh.

Shaw, S. J. (1991). *The Jews of the Ottoman empire and the Turkish republic.* New York University Press, New York.

Stillman, N. A. (1979). *The Jews of Arab lands: A history and source book.* The Jewish Publication Society of America, Philadelphia.

Triandis, H. C. (1990). Cross-cultural studies of individualism and collectivism. *Nebraska symposium on motivation 1989: Cross cultural perspectives.* University of Nebraska Press, Lincoln, NE.

Triandis, H. C. (1991). Cross-cultural differences in assertiveness/competition vs. group loyalty/cohesiveness. In R. A. Hinde & J. Groebel (eds.), *Cooperation and prosocial behavior.* Cambridge University Press, Cambridge, UK.

Trivers, R. (1971). The evolution of reciprocal altruism. *Quarterly Review of Biology, 46,* 35–57.

Vine, I. (1987). Inclusive fitness and the self-system. The roles of human nature and sociocultural processes in intergroup discrimination. In V. Reynolds, V. Falger, & I. Vine (eds.), *The sociobiology of ethnocentrism.* The University of Georgia Press, Athens, GA.

Weinryb, B. D. (1972). *The Jews of Poland: A social and economic history of the Jewish community in Poland from 1100 to 1800.* The Jewish Publication Society of America, Philadelphia.

Weizmann, C. (1949). *Trial and error: The autobiography of Chaim Weizmann.* Harper and Brothers, New York.

Wiggershaus, R. (1994). *The Frankfurt School: Its history, theories, and political significance*, trans., M. Robertson. MIT Press, Cambridge.

Wilson, D. S., & Sober, E. (1994). Re-introducing group selection to the human behavioral sciences. *Behavioral and Brain Sciences*, **17**, 585–684.

Winer, M. (1991). Will success spoil Reform? *Reform Judaism* (Spring), **26**.

Zenner, W. P. (1991). *Minorities in the middle: A cross-cultural analysis*. State University of New York Press, Albany, NY.

# AIDS,
## THE U.S. SUPREME COURT, AND TOURISM

## CHAPTER 9

# ETHNICITY, TRANSACTIONAL RISK OF HIV, AND MALE HOMOSEXUAL PARTNERING BEHAVIOUR

## James N. Schubert and Margaret Ann Curran

❧ ❧

## Introduction

This is a political era in which issues of race and biology are returning to the policy discussion agenda in the form of books, such as *The bell curve* (Herrnstein and Murray 1996), where claims are advanced regarding racial differences in the biology of social behaviour (Rushton 1995), and in which such governmental bodies as the Centers for Disease Control (CDC) in the U.S.A emphasize racial/ethnic parameters of the AIDS pandemic (1996, *HIV Surveillance Report*). As AIDS has become a leading cause of mortality and morbidity in the Hispanic and African-American communities in the United States, scholarly attention to the relationship between race/ethnicity and transactional risk behaviour is timely.

One hypothesis examined in this book is that people show increased preference for physiognomic similarity under conditions of heightened transactional risk. Risk is used in this chapter to refer to the risk of negative personal consequences resulting from an interpersonal transaction. Increased transactional risk is hypothesized to be associated with greater racial/ethnic ingroup preference in the selection of transaction partners. It is assumed that physiognomic similarity is weighted more heavily by decision makers under risk conditions because of its association with trust in others as partners and the association of trust with genetic relatedness.

Risk of HIV exposure in sexual transactions sets the stage for a rigorous test of our hypothesis because HIV infection for most people, roughly 99 percent, resulted in death prior to the treatment advances of the mid-1990s. In the AIDS epidemic, there was a brief period in the early 1980s during which the risk of HIV infection for male homosexuals was known – during this period AIDS was known as GRID, an acronym for Gay-Related Immunological Depression – but the mechanisms of transmission – exchange of bodily fluids and tissue – were not yet known. Although by mid-1985 gays might have known that preventing fluid exchange would prevent exposure to HIV, such knowledge allowing safety without modification of partnering behaviour was not available between 1981 and 1985. Therefore, if a tendency toward racial/ethnic exclusivity in partner preference under conditions of transactional risk exists, it may have been at work in the behaviour of gays from mid-1981 until the end of 1984 in the United States.

Figure 9.1 plots the monthly frequency of new cases diagnosed for each racial/ethnic group. These data show that the epidemic among gays was in fact overwhelmingly concentrated within the White population during the critical early period in the epidemic. There were so few cases among Blacks and Hispanics that the underlying base of HIV+ minorities was also quite small and it would have been most unlikely for someone to contact HIV through gay sex with Blacks or

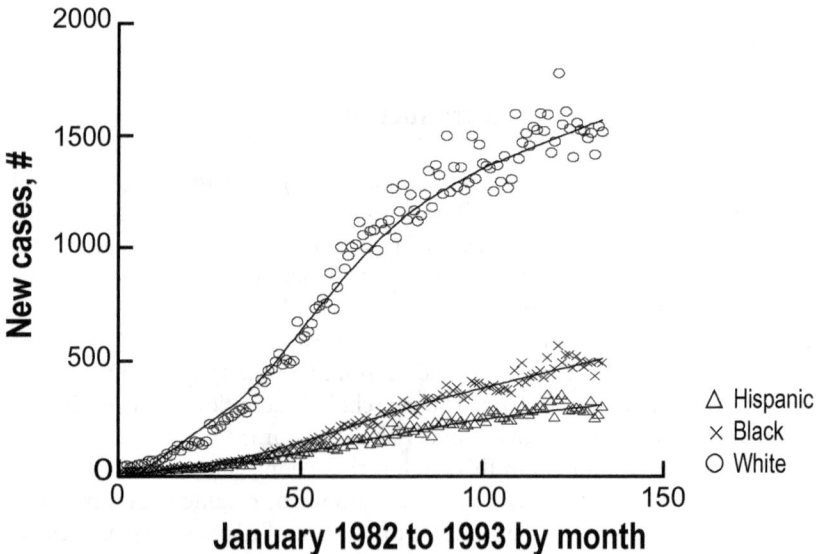

**Figure 9.1** National AIDS cases diagnosed by month.

Hispanics. In fact, from 1982 until the end of 1984, 943 cases of AIDS were diagnosed among Blacks, 664 among Hispanics, and 4834 among Whites. If these represent 10 percent of those people seroconverting between 1978 and 1981, and White cases were highly concentrated in high-risk communities, the differential objective risks attached to cross-ethnic partnering were substantial for ethnic minority gays.

Moreover, given that GRID broke out within the White, urban (and largely middle to upper-middle class) gay communities in New York City and San Francisco, and then other major cities, *the consequences of racial exclusivity in partnering behaviour under conditions of risk uncertainty should have been to insulate ethnic minority gays from HIV infection*, constraining the rise in their incidence rates in the mid- to late 1980s.

An immediate problem that may be raised with this prediction is that Blacks and Hispanics are reported to have substantially higher incidence rates than Whites. DiClemente (1992), for instance, reported that, "Blacks and Latinos are over-represented among AIDS cases.... [D]ata indicate Blacks and Latinos have significantly higher rates relative to White males.... Black and Latino males had annual rates of 92.4 and 71.9, relative to a rate of 27.4 for White males (325)" in 1991. The CDC (1996) reports that Whites now comprise a minority of the new cases of AIDS diagnosed in the U.S. Clearly, Black and Hispanic gays were not insulated from exposure to HIV. Although minority group rates may have initially been higher than those for Whites and may remain so to this day, the question posed by the hypothesis at stake is whether the spread of HIV among minority gays may have been constrained for the period of exposure when risks were known but of uncertain origin – constrained in relation to the preceding rate of growth and constrained in relation to the rate of growth among White gays.

## Effects of regional variation in size of ethnic population

Where ethnic minority populations are unevenly distributed in relation to the majority of the population, population-wide incidence rates may not provide appropriately comparable information about progression in the AIDS epidemic within minority populations. Specifically, the proportional size of a minority racial/ethnic population may have important consequences for sexual transactions where risk is uncertain, originates in the majority population and multiple partnering characterizes the behaviour of many individuals. In general, the smaller the size of the minority population, the greater the probability of cross-ethnic partnering for minorities. If majority and minority populations are not isolated, but proximate and commingling, the opportunity for cross-ethnic partnering is much greater for members of the minority than majority, and especially higher where minority populations are quantitatively small compared with where they are larger. The probability of cross-ethnic partnering for minority members will, of course, be greater, the more that multiple partnering is practised and greater where, for instance in the absence of risk, ethnic preference is less important in transactional partnering. This rather simple observation has interesting implications for HIV transmission among homosexuals.

First, it may be noted that multiple partnering was common within the urban, White gay communities of the United States in the late 1970s and early 1980s, partly a reflection of the success of the gay liberation movement in creating at least islands of toleration and freedom within the broader society. The infamous Patient Zero (Shilts 1987) illustrates this early vector of HIV transmission, directly accounting for more than one hundred cases of AIDS. Second, although as Kayal (1993) points out, racism within gay communities parallels patterns in the larger society, racism and ethnic preferences have not historically prevented sexual trans-actions across racial/ethnic lines, even where reproductive consequences were involved. Given the presence of multiple and cross ethnic partnering in sexual transactions among gays, the probability of contacting HIV by members of small ethnic minorities would be greater than the probability for members of large eth-nic minorities because (1) they were more likely to partner with Whites, where most HIV was concentrated, and (2) they were more likely to partner with very high risk Whites – that is, those with the greatest number of partners (e.g. in the bath houses of San Francisco). In short, for any given level of partnering, the chances of exposure to HIV would be greater among racial/ethnic minorities, the smaller the proportionate size of the minority population.

With AIDS overwhelmingly concentrated among Whites in the early 1980s, clearly the probability of exposure to HIV was greater for the minority partner of any cross-ethnic sexual transaction than for the majority group partner. This dif-ference would have been enhanced if multiple partnering was not evenly distrib-uted within the White gay population, but concentrated among a small group of urban, socially liberal, middle class individuals, as it was. This differential risk of exposure would have been greater yet, if homosexuality was more negatively sanc-tioned within ethnic minority cultures, particularly if those cultures were rela-tively small and close knit. It is arguable that there was at least far less tolerance of homosexuality within the Baptist-based Black culture and the Catholic-based His-panic culture than within society as a whole (Kayal 1993). Prohibitions and sanc-tions against "coming out" within minority cultures would have had the effect of increasing the rate of cross-ethnic partnering for minority gays, simultaneously increasing the probability that they would engage in sexual transactions with high-est risk Whites.

## Theoretical expectations

Three implications follow logically from this discussion. First, under conditions of unknown risk from 1978 to 1981, in which HIV prevalence was almost exclusively confined to White gays, *the incidence rate of AIDS would have grown much faster within ethnic minority populations*. Second, *incidence rates would have been higher, the smaller the proportional size of the ethnic population*. Indeed, in the latter respect, such differences in incidence rates would provide evidence supporting differential underlying rates of cross-ethnic partnering as a function of population size, reflecting differential rates of exposure to HIV carried so overwhelmingly by White gays during that period. Third, under conditions of known but uncertain risk 1982 to 1984, and given evidence of differential rates of cross-ethnic partnering depending on size of minority population, *the impact of a change in transactional behaviour toward greater ethnic preference upon ethnic minority incidence rates would be much greater, the smaller the ethnic population.* In short, the adoption of racial/ethnic preference, by either or both majority and minority group members, would impose greater constraints upon the epidemic within small ethnic minority populations. It is, therefore, appropriate to consider the conditional effects of size of ethnic population in an evaluation of the research question.

## Research design and methodology

It is not possible to test directly the hypothesis of ethnic preference under conditions of uncertain risk, due to the absence of observational data allowing contrasts of behaviour before and after the mechanisms of HIV transmission became known. Epidemiological data bases on the AIDS epidemic available to researchers do not identify personal sources of exposure, only means of exposure. However, inferences regarding the underlying theoretical model may be drawn by testing predicted effects upon observations of AIDS incidence rates. Data on case incidence were drawn from the Centers for Disease Control (1993) *AIDS public information data set* (AIDSPIDS) and include all cases of AIDS in the United States reported to the CDC until June 1993.

### Ethnicity

For this study, three racial/ethnic groups were considered: Whites, Blacks, and Hispanics. There are not enough cases, as distributed over time, to support generalizations for other ethnic groups.

### Exposure

Only AIDS cases with a "male-sex-with-male" single-source exposure to HIV coded by the CDC were considered. This category was selected because it involves significant multiple partnering behaviour, is unaffected by reproductive consequences to transactions, and avoids the complicating socio-economic influences of intravenous drug use. Cases with both drug use and gay sex as multiple exposure sources were also excluded on the same grounds and with the effect of keeping many prostitution-related cases out of the data analysed.

### Risk conditions

The cognitive setting of risk varies through three periods in the AIDS epidemic. First is the period from 1978 until the end of 1981, during which the presence of an epidemic was unknown. The first media report of what became known as AIDS was on 3 July 1981. Organizational efforts among gays developed over the next year and knowledge of risk became increasingly widespread during the 1982 to 1984 period, at least within the White gay community. Among Blacks and Hispanics, there was little ethnic-based media attention until the very late 1980s (Kayal 1993, p. 65). Knowledge about "safe" sex began to affect behaviour in 1984 (Stall et al. 1988) and risky behavior declined through the mid-to-late 1980s (Adib et al. 1991; Sittitrai et al. 1990; Winkelstein et al. 1988). Thus, a third condition of risk describes the period from 1985 to the present. In sum, the first period, 1978 to 1981 was one of *unknown risk*; the second period, 1982 to 1984, was one of *uncertain risk*; and the third period, since 1985, was one of *known risk*.

No doubt, setting plausible time frames for the impact of changes in knowledge of risk on AIDS rates is problematic, given the long and variable periods between sero-conversion and clinical diagnosis with AIDS. Of those infected around 1984, 10 percent were diagnosed with AIDS within four years (Curran et al. 1988; Phair et al. 1992). There was a median latency period of about nine years, but high HIV-1 virulence, perhaps interacting with immunological suppression from other sexually transmitted diseases (STDs), speeded up the progression to AIDS among those gays infected early and in association with multiple partnering (Ewald 1994). Ewald argues that multiple partnering created facilitative conditions for the evolution of virulence in HIV strains. It also created a setting facilitating multiple exposures to HIV and simultaneous infection from different strains accelerating progression to AIDS.[1]

There is no question that "unknown risk" would have characterized the context of exposure for those diagnosed throughout 1985. Exposure under conditions of "uncertain risk" would become a significant component of new AIDS cases beginning in 1986 and increasingly characteristic of cases diagnosed until the end of 1990. With increasing adoption of safe behaviors in 1985, the emergence of less virulent strains of HIV-1, and AZT drug treatment in the very late 1980s, the third risk condition would be increasingly characteristic of cases diagnosed from 1991 onwards.

Knowledge of "safe" behaviour would have been available at the time of exposure to very few of the people diagnosed with AIDS in the late 1980s. On these bases, we assume that (1) AIDS cases diagnosed until 1985 were exposed under conditions of unknown risk, (2) cases diagnosed from 1986 until the end of 1990 were exposed under conditions of unknown and uncertain risk, and (3) that subsequent cases were exposed under all three cognitive risk conditions. As risk was unknown from 1978 until 1982 and behaviour was not modified, we predict no reduction in incidence rates until 1985. Any observed changes in incidence rates between 1986 and 1990 are interpretable as reflecting behavioural adaptations to uncertain risk. Changes in rates after 1990 are interpretable as influenced by behavioural adaptations to known risk.

## Data base

Data for this study involve monthly reports of new cases of AIDS diagnosed and reported to the CDC and observations were utilized on the date of diagnosis, not the date of reporting. Data for the last six months in the 1993 AIDSPIDS release were excluded on the assumption that many cases diagnosed during that period had not yet been reported. Observation of race/ethnicity were utilized for the categories of White (not Hispanic), Black (not Hispanic), and Hispanic. Additional observations were recorded on the region of the U.S. in which the cases were diagnosed. The latter information is only made available by the CDC for cases diagnosed in Metropolitan Statistical Areas (MSAs) with greater than 1,000,000 population in the 1980 census, as a means of ensuring case confidentiality. We have utilized U.S. census data for the regional MSAs on the size of White, Black and Hispanic male populations aged fifteen to forty-four in 1980 to normalize case frequency counts to rates of incidence (e.g. new cases diagnosed per 100,000 population). In sum, this study utilized CDC data on date of diagnosis of White, Black and Hispanic cases of gay-related AIDS from large MSAs by month, starting with January 1982, when the CDC monthly counts began, until the end of January 1993. Although the CDC included data for Puerto Rico in the Southern regional category in the 1993 AIDSPIDS, we were able to identify these case counts from state/territory-level tables and removed them from the regional time series for Hispanics in the South.

## Findings

### National incidence data

Monthly incidence rates reported in Figure 9.2 are smoothed by a three point moving average over the 1982 to 1992 period. Curves were applied to each series using SYSTAT's (1993) "lowess" method. These data show that despite the great and growing disproportion in the White base of the AIDS epidemic among gays, the inci-

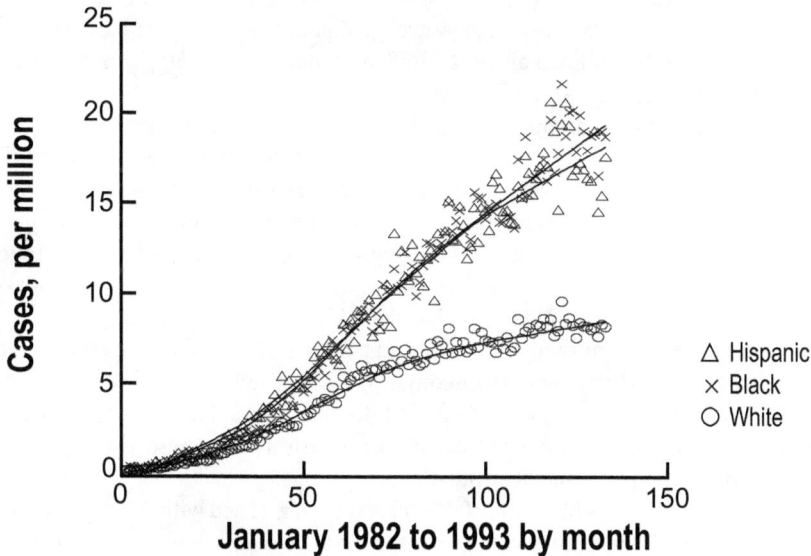

**Figure 9.2** National AIDS incidence rates.

dence rates for minorities began to exceed those for Whites by mid-1983, although the differences did not become striking until 1986. The quickness with which minority rates reached and surpassed the White rate is indicative of cross-group partnering. The divergence of minority rates from White rates in 1983 describes a higher rate of contact with HIV for minorities during the period of unknown risk throughout 1981. The clear implication of these data is that a good deal of cross-group partnering was going on, setting up the possibility for a racial/ethnic exclusivity adaptation during the subsequent period of uncertain risk.

That adaptation apparently did not take place. Instead, the progression of the AIDS epidemic among Blacks and Hispanics, month by month and year by year, is virtually unfettered throughout the decade. Indeed, the rates for Blacks and Hispanics show very little dampening even for the third period associated with known risk, while White rates begin to flatten out in 1986, consistent with behavioural adaptations instituted during the 1982 to 1984 period of uncertain risk (Kayal 1993; Kirp and Bayer 1992; Shilts 1987). Without access to scientific knowledge of prevention, it appears that White gays began to change their behaviour in ways that constrained HIV transmission, presumably in response to interest group warnings and media exposure. Blacks and Hispanics, just as clearly, did not, quite possibly because they lacked similar access to these sources of information and were more likely behaving under cognitive conditions of unknown risk.

## Multiple partnering and AIDS-related KS incidence rates

In the absence of knowledge about prevention, a most obvious response to news of GRID would have been to limit the number of sexual partners. Knowledge was already widely available that having multiple partners was associated with increased risk of exposure to hepatitis and other STDs. It is estimated that in the late 1970s and early 1980s urban gays averaged about ten different partners in a six- month period (Koblin et al. 1992). In San Francisco, some 50 percent of male homosexuals are estimated to have been HIV+ in 1985.

Studies of Kaposi's sarcoma in association with AIDS have found that it was especially prevalent among people who had many different partners (Beral 1991; Montgomery and Joseph 1989). Although different explanations have been proposed, Ewald (1994) comments that the association may result, "at least in part from infection with viruses that evolved high rates of replication in response to high sexual partner rates (p. 136)."[2] The CDC data include observations on physical conditions diagnosed in conjunction with AIDS, including Kaposi's sarcoma. Diagnoses were distinguished as definite and possible. We extracted cases from the CDC data base in which Kaposi's sarcoma (KS) was diagnosed "definitively". Frequencies of cases, by month, with KS for Whites, Blacks and Hispanics were calculated and averaged by the 1980 census populations for these three groups (expressed as rates per 100,000 population).

Smoothed time series of KS monthly incidence rates related with AIDS diagnoses are presented in Figure 9.3. They show White rates to be slightly higher than those for Blacks from 1982 until the end of 1987. White rates, however, begin to level off in 1986, while Black and Hispanic rates continued to grow until 1989. Rates in all three

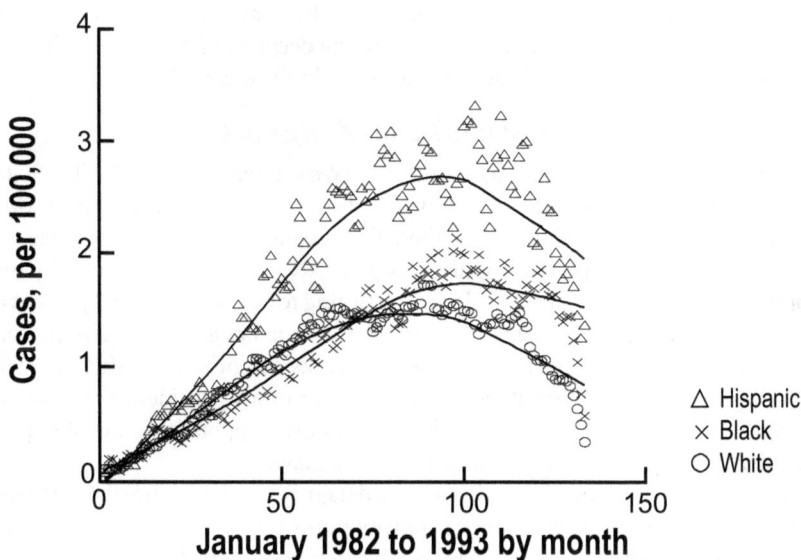

**Figure 9.3** Incidence of Kaposi's Sarcoma with AIDS.

groups plummet toward zero during 1992. We may infer that Whites began to reduce their number of partners almost immediately after hearing about GRID and Gay Plague – that is, during the period of uncertain risk. Black and Hispanic rates were equally modified, but the curves show that they lagged Whites by two years.

The first hypothesis of this study was that individuals would express ethnic preference in transaction partners under conditions of uncertain risk. Apparently Whites did reduce their total number of partners, during the uncertain risk period. There is no evidence that Hispanics or Blacks reduced their number of partners, quite to the contrary, multiple partnering appears to have continued unabated in these groups. We have argued that a reduction at this time by Blacks or Hispanics would indicate a reduction in cross-ethnic partnering by these ethnic minorities, because Whites were the principal source of HIV and the locus of multiple-partnering activities was located within the White urban gay communities. The unique conditions associated with KS suggests that very virulent strains of the virus were being passed back and forth between Whites and ethnic minorities. Assuming very similar tendencies for people to engage in multiple partnering across ethnic groups, the failure of Black and Hispanic rates to decline along with those for Whites, reveals that there was no systemic ethnic preference displayed by either majority or minority population gays in response to awareness of transactional risk.

In the absence of information that Hispanics and Blacks engaged in the wholesale adoption of condoms and other safe practices, what appears likely to have happened is that Blacks and Hispanics maintained multiple-partnering behaviour until the institutional settings of bath houses, weekend houses, parties, etc. were shut down or closed down and gays engaging in the most high risk behaviour became sick and died. Adaptations within the White gay community are likely to have brought about the conditions leading to the decline of KS and the extinction of those strains of HIV closely associated with it in the early 1990s.

## Regional AIDS incidence rates

We include data on the North-east, South and Western regions of the United States both because the AIDS epidemic was primarily occurring within these areas during the 1970s and 1980s and because these three regions provide clear contrasts in proportional size of minority populations. In the North-east, Black and Hispanic populations are similarly modest sized, accounting for 11 percent and 7 percent of the population in the 1980 census. In the West, Hispanics account for 16 percent and Blacks about 5.75 percent. In the South, Blacks comprised almost 17 percent and Hispanics about 9 percent. We theorized that minority incidence rates would be higher, the smaller the proportional size of minority populations, and also more sensitive to changes in cross-group partnering behaviour.

The regional AIDS incidence time-series data presented in Figure 9.4 lend support for our hypothesis that size of minority populations affects incidence rates. Black rates are highest in the West, where they represent a small proportion of the population, and low in the South. Hispanic rates are highest in the North-east, where their relative frequency is 7 percent, and lowest in the West; their rates in the South are also low. In both minority populations, culture may play a key role by virtue of the intolerance of homosexuality within the Black Baptist culture in the South, and Hispanic Catholic culture in the West and South-west.

The importance of region as an intervening variable is apparent when the overall rates for different subpopulation groups are compared. Although the data in Figure 9.2 demonstrated higher and more rapidly increasing AIDS rates for minority populations nationwide, this pattern does not apply where minority populations were larger. In the South, Black rates were not only low but lower than White rates all the way through the mid-1980s. In the West, Hispanic rates were not only low, but lower than White rates until the 1990s. These data challenge the validity of claims about group-based patterns of sexual behaviour that would place some racial/ethnic groups at higher risk of HIV infection. Where minority culture is strongest and most stable, for both Blacks and Hispanics, "at risk" behaviour was either less frequent for minority gays than for White gays, or minorities enjoyed a lower probability of contacting HIV in any given sexual transaction than did minority gays in, for instance, the North-east.

The lower rates for Blacks in the South and Hispanics in the West could be taken as providing support for the hypothesis of ethnic exclusivity in partnering behaviour were it not for the dramatically higher rates for the proportionately smaller minority group. Where Hispanic rates were constrained in the West, Black rates were skyrocketing. Where Black rates were constrained in the South, Hispanic rates were both greater and rising faster as a product of infection during the period of uncertain risk. Thus, cross-group partnering continued unabated during the period in which the hypothesized adaptation would have occurred.

North-eastern AIDS
incidence rates

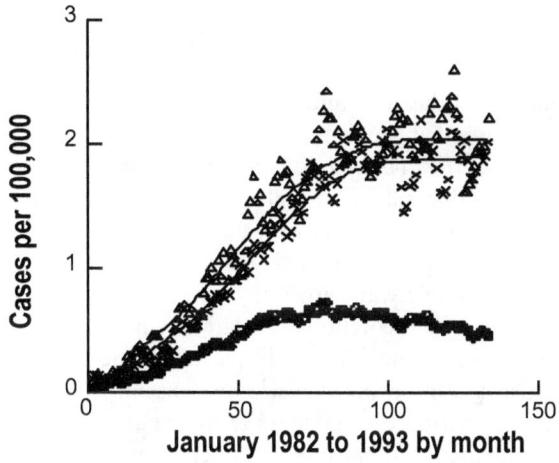

Southern AIDS
incidence rates

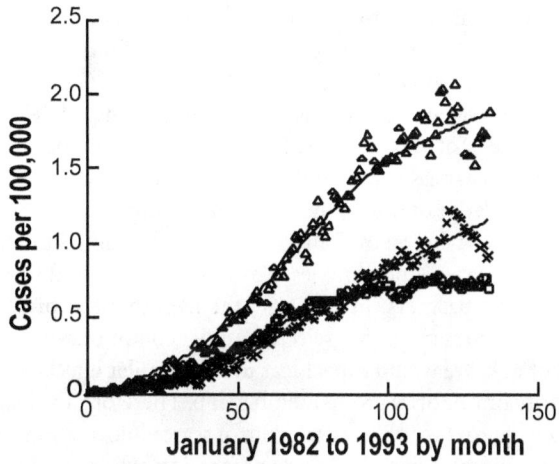

Western AIDS
incidence rates

△ Hispanic
× Black
○ White

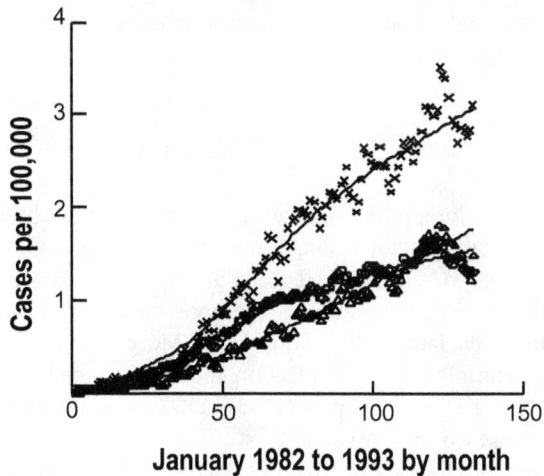

**Figure 9.4** Regional variation of AIDS incidence rates.

## Discussion

The main hypothesis examined in this chapter has two components. One involves the prediction that people modify their partnering behaviour under conditions of transactional risk. The second component is the expectation that change in partnering behaviour will favor racial and ethnic similarity in partner choices. The data we examine supports the first expectation. White gays responded to risk during the period of uncertainty by reducing their number of partners. That the data show this pattern so clearly, and especially with respect to KS rates, lends credence to our test of the second theoretical expectation. On the one hand, Whites responded to risk by trusting no one during the period of uncertainty, regardless of racial/ethnic similarity. On the other, Blacks and Hispanics with less access to information during this period did not modify their partnering behaviour, although they clearly benefited from the overall reduction in partnering by Whites.

Differential access to information by majority and minority group gays may be important for understanding the relationship of our findings with the themes of this book. The discovery of so-called GRID by the CDC in 1981 and media coverage of Gay Plague was accompanied by a good deal of unqualified fear within the urban gay communities of this country. Fear is a primary emotion that causes behavioural inhibition. Fear associated with knowledge of the risk of AIDS and, for many at that time, knowledge of friends and associates being diagnosed with AIDS, may well have activated behavioural inhibitions in those who thought themselves to be HIV-positive that overwhelmed any less emotionally intense disposition to seek out more trustworthy partners. In this case, the hypothesized preference for indications of trustworthiness in partner selection under conditions of risk is conditional upon the level of risk. We would expect fear to have similar effects on behaviour, regardless of majority or minority group membership. Therefore, the lagged response for minority gays appears very likely a product of scarce information. In sum, our findings support the premise that risk affects partnering behaviour, but poses a qualification to the thesis of this book – namely, that trust and kin mechanisms are not likely to affect partnering behaviour when the level of risk is quite high.

## References

Adib, S.M., Joseph, J.G., Ostrow, D.G., Tal, M., and Schwartz, S.A. (1991). Relapse in sexual behavior among homosexual men: A 2–year follow-up from the Chicago MACS/CCS. *AIDS*, **5**, 757–60.

Beral, V. (1991). Epidemiology of Kaposi's Sarcoma. *Cancer Survey*, **10**, 5–22.

Curran, J.W., Jaffe, H.W., Hardy, H.M., Morgan, W.M., and Selik, R. (1988). Epidemiology of HIV infection and AIDS in the USA. *Science*, **239**, 610–16.

Centers for Disease Control (1993). *AIDS public information data set.* Centers for Disease Control, Atlanta.

Centers for Disease Control (1996). *HIV/AIDS Surveillance Reports*, **8**(1). National Center for HIV, STD and TB Prevention, Atlanta.

DiClemente, R.J. (1992). Epidemiology of AIDS, HIV prevalence, and HIV incidence among adolescents. *Journal of Public Health*, **62**, 325–30.

Ewald, P.W. (1994). *Evolution of infectious diseases.* Oxford University Press, New York.

Herrnstein, R.J., and Murray, C. (1996). *The bell curve: Intelligence and class structure in American life.* The Free Press, New York.

Kayal, P.M. (1993). *Bearing witness: Gay men's health crisis and the politics of AIDS.* Westview Press, Boulder, Colo.

Kirp, D.L., and Bayer, R. (eds) (1992). *AIDS in the industrialized democracies.* Rutgers University Press, New Brunswick, NJ.

Koblin, B.A., Morrison, J.M., Taylor, P.E., Stoneburner, R.L., and Stevens, C.E. (1992). Mortality trends in a cohort of homosexual men in New York City, 1978–1988. *American Journal of Epidemiology*, **136**, 646–56.

Montgomery, S.B., and Joseph, J.G. (1989). Behavioral change in homosexual men at risk for AIDS: Intervention and policy implications. In *The AIDS epidemic: Private rights and the public interest* (ed. P. O'Malley). Beacon Press, Boston, MA.

Phair, J., Jacobson, L., Detels, R., Rinaldo, C., Saah, A., Schrager, L., and Munoz, A. (1992). Acquired immune deficiency syndrome occurring within 5 years of infection with human immunodeficiency virus type-1: the multicenter AIDS cohort study. *Journal of Acquired Immune Deficiency Syndrome*, **5**, 490–6.

Rushton, J.P. (1995). *Race, evolution and behavior: A Life History Perspective.* Transaction, New Brunswick, NJ.

Shilts, R. (1987). *And the band played on: Politics, people and the AIDS epidemic.* St. Martins, New York.

Sittitrai, W., Brown, T., and Sterns, J. (1990). Opportunities for overcoming the continuing restraints in behavior change and HIV risk reduction. *AIDS*, **4**(Supplement 1), s269–s276.

Stall, R. D., Coates, T.J., and Hoff, C. (1988). Behavioral risk reduction of HIV infection among gay and bisexual men: A review of results from the United States. *American Psychologist*, **43**, 878–85.

SYSTAT (1993). *SYSTAT 5.02 for Windows.* Systat Inc., Evanston, IL.

Winkelstein, W., Wiley, J.A., Padian, N.S., Samuel, M., Shiboski, S., Ascher, M.S., and Levy, J.A. (1988). The San Francisco Men's health study: Continued decline in HIV seroconversion rates among homosexual/bisexual men. *American Journal of Public Health*, **78**, 1472–4.

# Notes

1. Paediatric cases in Romania with multiple exposures to HIV showed very rapid onset of AIDS (interview with Dr Joanna Strauss, Chief, National Hospital for Infectious Disease, Bucharest).
2. Reports at the 1996 World AIDS Conference indicate that KS may be associated with a Herpes virus. In this case, presumably, both HIV and Herpes were being exchanged.

## CHAPTER 10

# DIALECT, SEX AND RISK EFFECTS ON JUDGES' QUESTIONING OF COUNSEL IN SUPREME COURT ORAL ARGUMENT

## James N. Schubert, Steven A. Peterson, Glendon Schubert, and Stephen L. Wasby

❧ ❧

Simply phonetics. The science of speech. That's my profession: also my hobby. Happy is the man who can make a living by his hobby! You can spot an Irishman or a York-shireman by his brogue. I can place any man within six miles. I can place him within two miles in London. Sometimes within two streets. [Henry Higgins] George Bernard Shaw (1916), *Pygmalion*, Act I

## Theoretical concerns

This study examines the effects of dissimilar dialect and sex upon Justices' questioning and examination of counsel during appellate court oral argument. The symposium reported in this book examined the proposition that people prefer ethnic similarity in their selection of transaction partners under conditions of risk. This study considers dialect to be important as an indicator of group membership and geographical origin, providing cues to ethnocultural similarity. In the United States Supreme Court, oral argument is an interactive, face-to-face stage in a much longer and more complex process in which the judges ultimately form a coalition in support of one of the sides in a case. Treatment of counsel representing the parties during oral argument is relevant to the broader theme of this book because it is an instance of the more general concern with partnership selection. Risk to the court and to judges' reputations is posed by the importance of the issues and legal questions at stake in a case. For instance, when constitutional questions are at stake, a court copes with potential risks to the constitutional foundations of government, to its own legitimacy, and to the reputational status of its individual members. Such risk is greater in constitutional cases than when the Court is dealing with other cases, for example, engaging in statutory interpretation or in review of agency rulings. In relation to the central concerns of this book it is hypothesized that Justices display anxiety arousal in their treatment of counsel who speak different dialects from their own and that this effect is enhanced where decisions are more important for the court. It should be emphasized that there is no implication of any direct effect upon the outcome of cases. Differential treatment of counsel would, at most, have indirect effects upon the information extracted by the Justices from the oral argument and subsequently brought to bear in the Court's full decision-making process.

Although the proximate mechanisms contributing to inclusivity in inter-ethnic group preferences for transaction partners may be obvious, the mechanisms for exclusivity in preferences are more ambiguous. Xenophobia, fear of strangers, is identified by Eibl-Eibesfeldt (1979, 1989) as one basis for prejudicial choices. With respect to the behaviour of infants, no doubt images of unfamiliar faces are sufficient to trigger anxiety-related responses of avoidance and withdrawal. However, when the concept of fear of strangers is generalized to older humans and apparent preferences for physiognomic similarity, the nature of stimuli triggering anxiety is less clear. It is often assumed that skin colour and the appearance of facial features are assessed comparatively and evaluated for similarity. Tajfel (1978) proposes, however, that skin colour is only one of several dimensions upon which impression formation is based. Accent or dialect is one of the dimensions that is often neglected in analyses of impression formation. Vrij and Winkel (1991), for instance, argue that "Differences in speech style and spoken fluency between ethnic groups are much neglected as a way of explaining a negative assessment of ethnic groups (1994, p. 285)." In a study of police-citizen communications between Blacks and Whites in the Netherlands, they proposed that differences in vocal nonverbal behaviours were associated with impressions of deception and reported empirical results supporting this hypothesis. The hypothesis that speech differences may underlay fears of deception and cause anxiety responses presents a partial causal explanation of why people might be more ethnically exclusive in choosing transaction partners under conditions of risk. Risk would function to heighten concerns over deception. Language is an important marker of group membership boundaries and dissimilarities may, therefore, be especially important under conditions of risk.

Interpersonal dissimilarities that do not distinguish ethnocultural differences are not expected to be associated with behavioural anxiety responses in selection of partners. In particular, differences in social class, sex, body size, age, attractiveness, intelligence, etc., are unlikely to be associated with anxiety responses *per se* because these are familiar within the boundaries of ethnocultural groups.

Measurement of the display of anxiety responses in the questioning behaviour of Justices in oral argument depends upon an underlying theory of emotion and behaviour. Gray (1987) (and see Marcus, 1988) proposes a dimensional model of emotion in which acute flight-fight responses define one dimension of extreme responses and two other dimensions, the Behavioural Activation System (BAS) and Behavioural Inhibition System (BIS), respectively describe positive and negative patterns of emotion. Threat, novelty, and uncertainty stimulate anxiety-arousal in the BIS system. BIS arousal functions to inhibit behaviour and to produce heightened alertness and attentiveness, allowing an actor to focus on the stimulus, evaluating its nature and preparing a response. Thus, an early result of anxiety-arousal is behavioural inhibition. Dialect dissimilarity might cause neurophysiological anxiety-arousal because it poses *novelty*, as unfamiliar speech, *uncertainty* with respect to objective content and subjective meaning, and *threat* to the extent that dissimilarity indicates the possibility of deception. Based on the Gray model, anxiety-arousal in the BIS in response to dissimilar dialect should be displayed by judges, first, through the inhibition in questioning behaviour directed at these counsel and, second, through greater substantive attention to their arguments. Finally, risk is regarded as a separate factor causing anxiety responses. Dissimilarity in dialect is expected to interact as a factor with risk in its effects on the inhibition of judicial questioning behaviour.

Hypotheses at stake in this analysis are that: (1) Justices display behavioural inhibition in response to (a) risk and (b) dissimilar dialect; (2) risk and dissimilarity in dialect interact in the inhibition of Justices questioning behaviour; and (3) familiar forms of social difference do not have inhibitory effects on judicial questioning behaviour.

## Methods

Observations for this study were drawn from printed transcripts and audio-tape recordings of United States Supreme Court oral arguments. These materials were available from a larger study (see Schubert et al. 1992) in which 160 cases were randomly selected from the population of cases argued during the period from the beginning of the Burger Court in 1969 through the 1974 term. During this period, the Court was composed of middle-aged to elderly males, all White with exception of Thurgood Marshall, and with origins and backgrounds in the Mid-western, mid-Atlantic, and North-eastern regions of the country, with the exception of Hugo Black, whose background was Southern and who served on the Court during the first two of the five terms under consideration.

Oral argument is, with rare exceptions, the first occasion in the processing of a case in which the Court meets face-to-face in consideration of the issues. Counsel representing the competing parties to a case each have thirty minutes in which to present their "argument" to the Court. The side that goes first (petitioner or appellant) has the option of reserving a few minutes for rebuttal, after the argument for the second side is presented. Rarely, more than one attorney takes a turn in presenting for a side and also rarely, counsel representing other parties, *amici curiae*, are heard in addition to opposing counsel. Although counsel attend oral argument with prepared monologues, Justices interrupt with questions at will, often within seconds after counsel has begun to speak. Justices' questions may serve different purposes. Some seek to clarify matters of fact, some seek to clarify meaning in the presented arguments, and others are more overtly competitive, challenging or supporting the validity of an argument or the substance of claims by counsel. In short, for the Justices, oral argument is an open, relatively unstructured, spontaneous setting in which observable verbal and vocal nonverbal behaviour is exchanged between judges and attorneys. The purpose of the interactions for Justices is to acquire information relevant to their process of reaching a decision in a case. Supreme Court Justices commonly report their perceptions of the importance of oral argument in their collective decision-making process.

Observations were recorded on the dialect and sex of counsel by listening to periods of argument for each side for each of the one hundred and sixty sampled cases. The coding of sex, based on voice, is straightforward. Eight cases were identified in which female counsel presented the argument for one side of a case, while male counsel presented for the other side. Dialect poses the possibility of theoretically defined choices, given regional, ethnic and racial variation. However, not only did few women argue before the Supreme Court during this period, but also few Blacks, Hispanics or even non-native speakers presented argument before the Court. The only source of substantial variation in language was found to be Southern regional dialect. Southern regional dialect functions as a social marker of geographic origin in the United States. It demarcates individuals as members of a culturally distinct subnational population group, kept alive during the twentieth century through such symbols of Dixie as the Confederate flag, a position not necessarily represented by all the Southern-dialect advocates before the Court and certainly not the position of Justices Black and Marshall, the two members of the Court with Southern dialects. Southern dialect serves as a group identity badge in American culture and is, therefore, an appropriate distinction to observe in operationalizing the model under consideration in this study. Fourteen cases were identified in which one attorney presented argument displaying a Southern dialect, while the other attorney did not.

Although risk might arise under a variety of different conditions, there is no doubt that the Court faces heightened risk when it considers constitutional questions. The role of the Court in interpreting the Constitution is not only contentious within national politics, but also within the Court, as revealed in the tension between activism and restraint. On the whole, cases raising constitutional questions involve more risk for the Court than cases that do not, and for many of the individual Justices as well. Four of the eight cases with female counsel contained constitutional legal questions, as did eight of the fourteen cases with counsel arguing in Southern dialect. Data on legal questions at stake in cases were available in the United States Supreme Court Judicial Data Base, 1953 to 1989 (Spaeth 1991). In short, it was possible to examine each of the independent dissimilarity variables under both high- and low-risk conditions and to test for interaction effects in a balanced analysis design.

Observations on Justices' treatment of counsel were drawn from the larger data base on oral argument (Schubert et al. 1992). The theoretical model discussed above proposes inhibition and attention as behavioural responses to the presence of dissimilar dialect. Inhibition was observed with respect to the total amount of questioning behaviour directed at counsel. The amount of questioning behaviour includes both aspects of frequency of questions by Justices and their duration. As judges might ask fewer, but longer questions of one side, or vice versa, both aspects of behavior were observed. The number of questions asked of counsel was observed from the official transcripts of the arguments, previously edited and corrected by listening to the audio tapes, while duration was timed on a stop-watch for all questions from the audio recordings. Based on the assumption that inhibition could also be expressed in the length of questions asked, a third variable was defined as the average duration of questions directed at counsel, measured in seconds of elapsed time.

Differential treatment was defined in terms of the quality of attention to counsels' argument. Two categories of qualitative variation were considered. One involved affective content in the judges' behaviour. In general, justices seldom display positive affect toward counsel; rather, questions range from affectively neutral to negative. Negative verbal affect was observed, first, in the form of explicit verbal expressions of disagreement with counsel. Such disagreements might address matters of fact or interpretation in the comments of counsel, for instance, regarding material in the case briefs, the application of a precedent case, or the relevance of a legal doctrine. Affect display may also take personal forms, as sarcasm, ridicule and invective, on a negative dimension, or praise and flattery on a positive dimension. We recorded observations on negative personal affect display in questioning behaviour.

A second qualitative category involves the function of questions. Some address matters of fact, others seek clarification of meaning, while a third form deals with acceptance or rejection, support or challenge, of the validity of claims by counsel. Observations on these functional properties of questions were recorded in the data base, with acceptable intercoder reliability (Schubert et al. 1992).

Data on judges' questions were aggregated to the level of the half-hour periods associated with each lawyer's presentation of one side of a case. The aggregated data on quantity of questioning represent the frequency of questions asked of each lawyer and the amount of time the Justices spoke to counsel. Frequency counts for the qualitative variables were expressed as percentages of the total amount of the behaviour occurring throughout the entire sixty minutes of argument for both sides in the case. Thus, data on disagreements reveal each counsel's share of the total number of disagreements expressed by the Justices in the complete argument of the case.

Extraneous factors that might well bear upon the interactions observed include whether counsel ultimately won or lost, whether they represented a liberal or conservative position on the issues, and whether, in many of these cases, they represented the prosecution or defence side of cases. Of the fourteen lawyers speaking Southern dialect, one half represented the petitioner/appellant side, appearing first and usually representing the defence. These counsel represented the liberal position in eight of the fourteen cases and were ultimately winners in five cases. In short, these extraneous factors are fairly evenly distributed across the target and control group conditions of the design. Female counsel represented the petitioner/appellant side in three of their eight cases, the liberal position in five cases, and were winners in six cases. The disproportionate wins for female counsel is the only potentially confounding factor in this portion of the research design.

In general, the research design provides for Southern/non-Southern dialect and male/female contrasts, equally under conditions of the presence or absence of a constitutional question, with counsel pairs matched on case issues and, substantially, in other case characteristics as well. Although sample sizes are unavoidably small, the framework for comparative inference is nonetheless rigorous. A quasi-experimental structure is, therefore, employed that provides a "balanced" design in terms of the sample group sizes, as defined by the grouping factor and the high/low risk conditions, and that warrants a straight forward analysis of variance (ANOVA) approach to hypothesis testing.

# Results

ANOVA results presented in Table 10.1 for dialect and the quantity of behaviour reveal statistically significant effects for the risk condition presented by a constitutional question at stake in a case for duration and frequency of questioning, as well as the interaction of risk and dialect on average length of questions – taking 0.10 as a plausible alpha level with so few degrees of freedom. The interaction term approaches significance with respect to the frequency of questions. Effects fail to meet critical values for significance on the quality of attention variables, although they reveal substantial differences with respect to both negative personal affect display and questions probing matters of fact.

Figure 10.1 presents the group means under the high- and low- risk conditions. With respect to duration and frequency of questions, particularly the average length of questions, the data reveal a clear and substantial inhibitory effect for Southern dialect that is generally greater under the high-risk condition. Without a constitutional question at stake, the differences in quantity between questioning of Southern and other counsel are quite small, although in the predicted direction.

Although the Justices expressed disagreement with counsel equally when a constitutional question was at stake, otherwise there is a consistent pattern of less emotional display toward Southern counsel. Moreover, given substantially more challenges to the validity of arguments and claims made by Southern counsel, it is unlikely that Justices were less negative because they were more satisfied with the answers of Southern counsel. Taken together, these findings point toward an inhibition in emotional expression that is quite consistent with the theoretical model

**Table 10.1** The effects of dialect on questioning behaviour

Quantity of questioning behaviour

| | Dialect | Constitutional question | Dialect by const. question |
|---|---|---|---|
| **Attention:** | | | |
| Total questioning time | | | |
| F | 0.302 | 5.995 | 0.222 |
| p< | | 0.022 | |
| Number of questions asked | | | |
| F | 0.286 | 5.920 | 1.465 |
| p< | | 0.023 | 0.238 |
| **Affect:** | | | |
| Number of disagreements | | | |
| F | 0.506 | 2.848 | 0.435 |
| p< | | 0.104 | |
| Number of questions with negative effect | | | |
| F | 1.480 | 1.332 | 0.429 |
| p< | 0.236 | 0.260 | |
| **Function:** | | | |
| Number of factual questions | | | |
| F | 0.375 | 2.401 | 0.712 |
| p< | | 0.134 | |
| Number of clarification questions | | | |
| F | 0.001 | 1.827 | 0.589 |
| p< | | 0.189 | |
| Number of challenging questions | | | |
| F | 0.393 | 4.645 | 0.393 |
| p< | | 0.041 | |
| Number of repetitious questions | | | |
| F | 0.168 | 1.656 | 1.378 |
| p< | | 0.210 | 0.252 |

Proportional distribution of question behaviour

| | Dialect | Constitutional question | Dialect by const. question |
|---|---|---|---|
| **% of questioning time** | 0.050 | 0.000 | 0.222 |
| **% of questions asked** | 0.040 | 0.000 | 2.170 |
| | | | 0.154 |
| **% of disagreements** | 0.004 | 0.395 | 0.004 |
| **% of questions with negative effect** | 1.618 | 0.743 | 0.204 |
| | 0.216 | | |
| **% of factual questions** | 1.279 | 0.033 | 0.999 |
| **% clarification questions** | 0.000 | 0.000 | 1.105 |
| **% challenging questions** | 0.539 | 0.527 | 0.019 |
| **% repetitious questions** | 0.816 | 2.130 | 0.512 |
| | | 0.157 | |

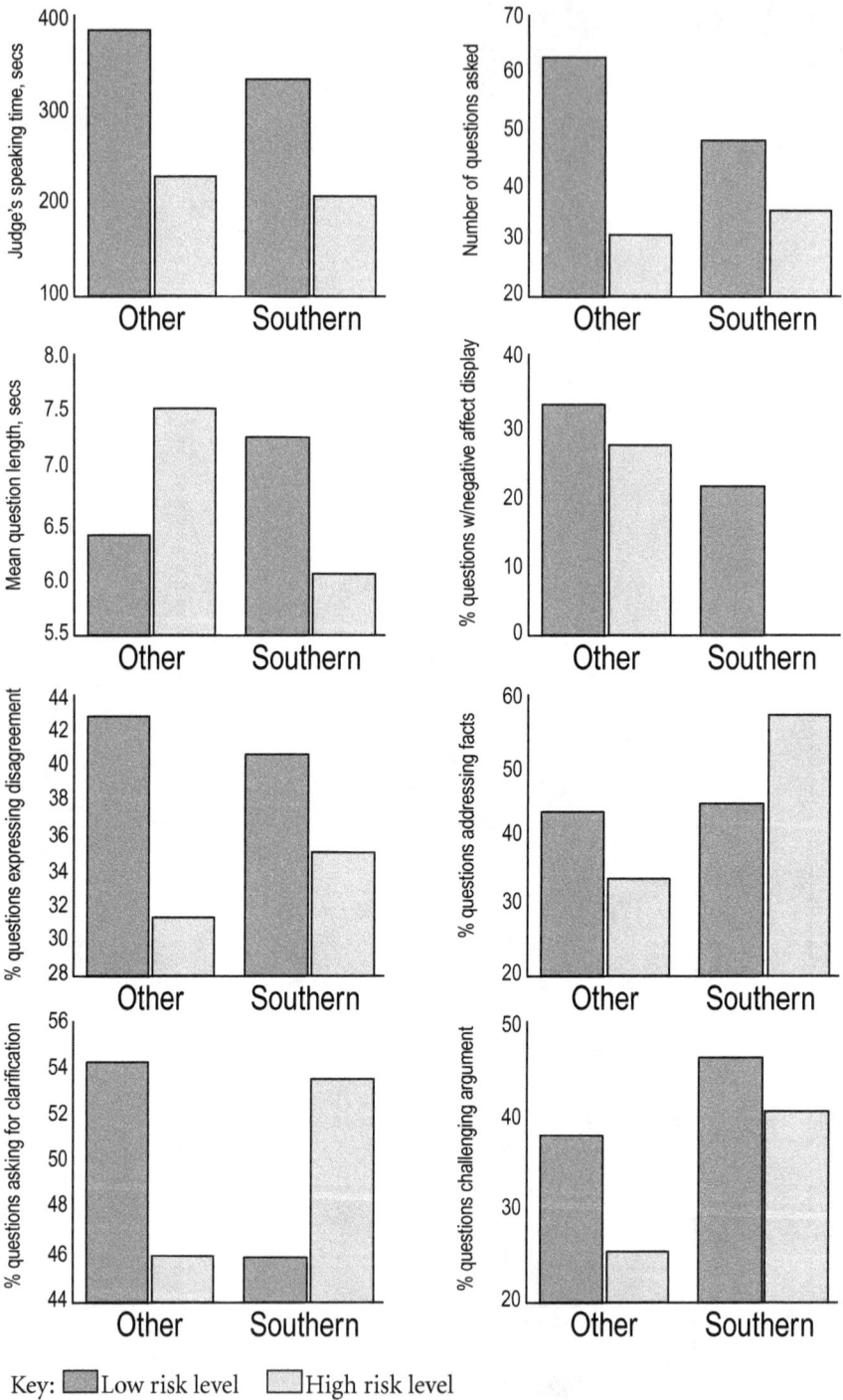

Key: ▨ Low risk level    ▢ High risk level

**Figure 10.1** The effects of counsel dialect on questioning behaviour.

of this study. The tendency to challenge Southern counsel more than others, and regardless of the risk condition, is evidence of greater substantive attention to the quality of argument by these lawyers. The impact of the risk factor on this tendency is revealed in the data on factual questions and on those seeking clarification of meaning. The greater attention to factual matters, as well as the greater effort to clarify the meaning of arguments when a constitutional question was at stake, is indicative of greater doubts about the quality of argument by counsel. The theoretical model presumes that dialect dissimilarity is important partially because of uncertainty about meaning and concern about deception or veracity in interpersonal communications under conditions of risk. The Justices in these cases displayed greater uncertainty about meaning and concern about veracity, if not deception, in the argumentation of Southern counsel when dealing with constitutional questions.

Table 10.2 presents ANOVA results for the effects of sex of counsel on Justices' questioning behaviour. There are no significant effects for sex or the interaction of sex and risk upon the quantity of questioning behaviour. The group means plotted in Figure 10.2 confirm the absence of any behavioural inhibition in the questioning of female counsel. To the contrary, Justices asked more questions and spoke longer in their examination of the women, notably when a constitutional question was present in the case.

With respect to the relative quality of attention to male and female counsel, both main effects for sex and the two-way interaction of sex and risk are statistically significant on several of the variables. The juxtaposition of results for the two affect variables are quite interesting. Males received far more verbal disagreements than female counsel, especially under the risk condition, but those disagreements were not coupled with negative personal affect displays. Female counsel received far more negative personal references than their male counterparts in these cases, and this pattern held regardless of the risk condition. The data on validity challenges also reveal less substantive attention to the claims of female counsel. This pattern appears confirmed with less attention to clarification of meaning in arguments by females, but with more attention to their command of factual matters. Taken together, these data suggest that, although the Justices spoke more to the female lawyers, giving them less time to talk, they gave more substantive consideration to the arguments of male counsel. This pattern might reflect the greater success of female counsel in ultimately winning these cases, where Justices tend to have been more active and rigorous in questioning counsel for the side that ultimately looses a case. While this extraneous factor may account for the findings with respect to disagreements and validity challenges, it does not account for the greater personal negativity displayed toward female counsel, nor the greater quantity of questioning directed toward them. Alternatively, it may reflect a pattern of social dominance in which males are characteristically less attentive to females (Henley 1977).

**Table 10.2** The effects of sex on questioning behaviour

**Quantity of questioning behaviour**

| | | Sex | Constitutional question | Sex by const. question |
|---|---|---|---|---|
| **Attention:** | Total questioning time | | | |
| | F | 0.027 | 0.647 | 0.091 |
| | p< | | | |
| | Number of questions asked | | | |
| | F | 0.295 | 4.045 | 0.000 |
| | p< | | 0.067 | |
| **Affect:** | Number of disagreements | | | |
| | F | 0.446 | 0.1 | 0.031 |
| | p< | | | |
| | Number of questions with negative effect | | | |
| | F | 0.861 | 1.601 | 0.114 |
| | p< | | 0.230 | |
| **Function:** | Number of factual questions | | | |
| | F | 0.722 | 1.270 | 0.609 |
| | p< | | | |
| | Number of clarification questions | | | |
| | F | 0.018 | 0.081 | 0.833 |
| | p< | | | |
| | Number of challenging questions | | | |
| | F | 0.134 | 4.558 | 0.163 |
| | p< | | 0.054 | |
| | Number of repetitious questions | | | |
| | F | 0.681 | 2.085 | 1.532 |
| | p< | | 0.174 | 0.239 |

**Proportional distribution of question behaviour**

| | | Sex | Constitutional question | Sex by const. question |
|---|---|---|---|---|
| **Attention:** | % of questioning time | | | |
| | F | 0.247 | 0.000 | 3.329 |
| | p< | | | 0.093 |
| | % of questions asked | | | |
| | F | 0.454 | 0.000 | 1.797 |
| | p< | | | 0.205 |
| **Affect:** | % of disagreements | | | |
| | F | 8.771 | 0.000 | 3.203 |
| | p< | 0.012 | | 0.099 |
| | % of questions with negative effect | | | |
| | F | 3.234 | 2.362 | 0.363 |
| | p< | 0.097 | 0.150 | |
| **Function:** | % of factual questions | | | |
| | F | 0.396 | 0.492 | 0.481 |
| | p< | | | |
| | % of clarification questions | | | |
| | F | 0.000 | 0.000 | 4.974 |
| | p< | | | 0.046 |
| | % of challenging questions | | | |
| | F | 0.465 | 0.000 | 0.442 |
| | p< | | | |
| | % of repetitious questions | | | |
| | F | 0.101 | 0.644 | 3.701 |
| | p< | | | 0.078 |

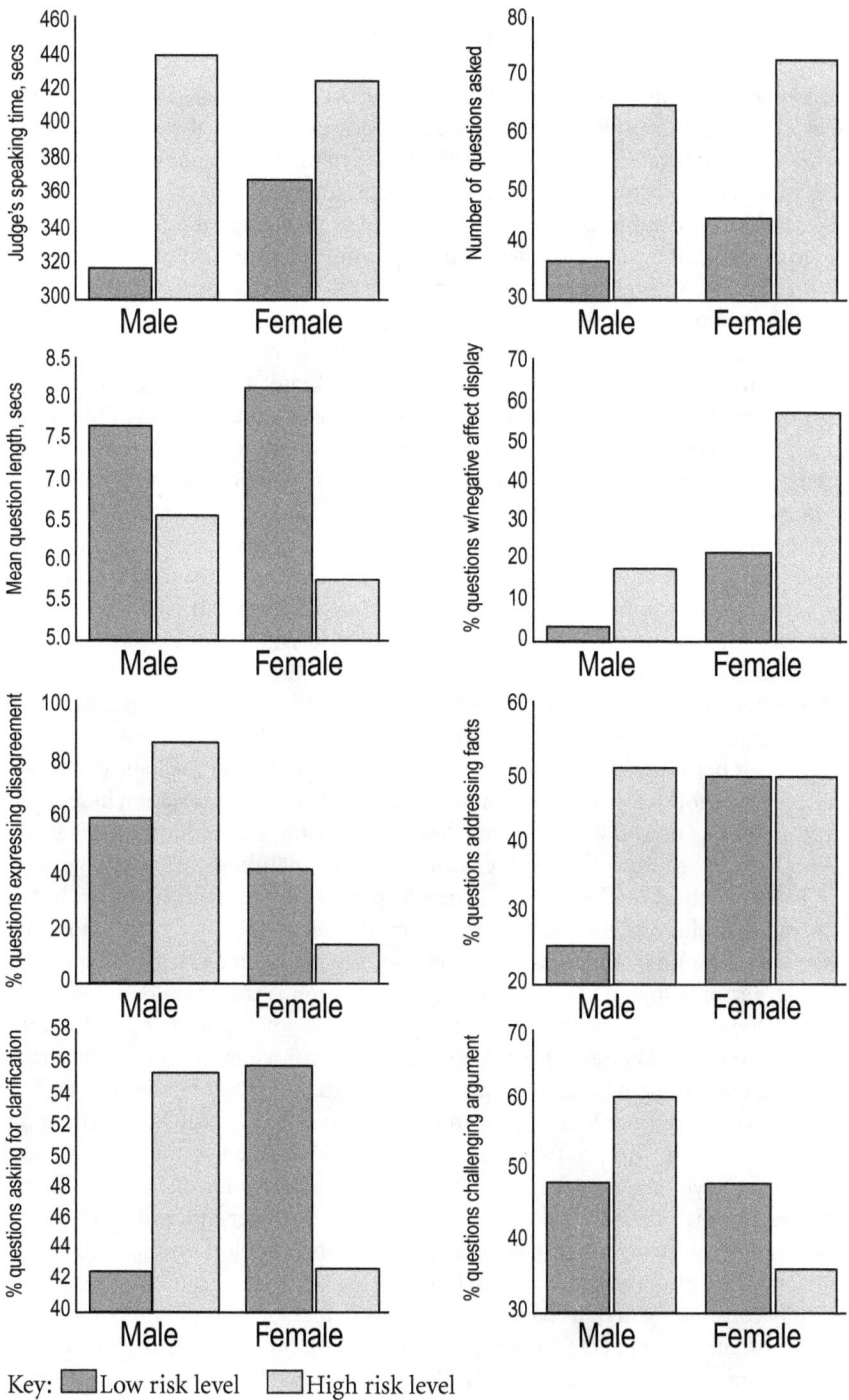

**Figure 10.2** The effects of sex of counsel on questioning behaviour.

# Discussion

At first glance, it may seem implausible that Justices of the United States Supreme Court, engaged in professional communications in the formal and ritually governed setting of oral argument, would be affected in their behaviour by such a seemingly innocuous factor as Southern dialect. Certainly the impact of differences in dialect should be minimized by the high level of professionalization involved in the interpersonal interactions occurring in Supreme Court oral argument. Thus, to find such effects in this special setting suggests the potentially greater influence of this factor upon interpersonal relations in more mundane situations.

The theoretical questions addressed in this study were raised by the announced theme of the conference reported on in this book, not by an ongoing research agenda with respect to the effects of dialect upon interpersonal relations. One implication of this origin is that, from the framing of the question through the statistical analysis of data, this study was conducted in a top down, explicitly deductive process. There was virtually no prior empirical basis for any expectation regarding the results of the analysis. For a study so purely conceived and driven by theory to yield such consistent results lends more credence to the model than might otherwise be warranted by the limitations of sample size. Sample size constraints, on the other hand, are the second implication flowing from the origin of this endeavour. Thus, rather then designing a study from scratch to address the comparative influences of dialect and sex differences upon conversational behaviour that would include a much larger data base, this study took advantage of available data that were quite limited for both dialect and sex differences. Thus, regardless of the logic of statistical inference, fourteen cases of variation in dialect and eight of variation in sex provide a tenuous basis for broad generalizations. In sum, the findings of this study may properly be regarded as both provocative and tentative.

The theoretical model at stake is one of proximate mechanisms in the broad scheme of evolutionary explanations. The model begins with the proposition that ingroup/outgroup distinctions are sometimes important influences upon qualities of interpersonal interactions. The second proposition is that these differences are likely to be more important under conditions of risk, when concerns about deception, defection and betrayal are heightened and, in consequence, greater emphasis is placed upon trust in transactional partners. Third, this pattern is viewed as affectively driven by psychophysiological arousal processes that are not dependent upon cognition. Indeed, this precognitive or extra-cognitive aspect of the phenomenon may explain why the model appears to work in the behaviour of Supreme Court Justices. A fourth characteristic is that the model does not depend, with reference to sociobiological theory, on any kin-based recognition or selection mechanisms. It does, however, propose a mechanism that predicts behavioural patterns that would be fully consistent with kin- based mechanisms in that kin recognition is undoubtedly substantially enhanced by parameters of speech. But, at the proximate level at which human beings interact in daily life, it may well be that anxiety arousal helps explain patterns of ethnic preference in partner selection under conditions of transactional risk. Under conditions of risk, actors should be concerned about deception and uncertainty in the behaviour of potential partners and the full array of verbal and non-verbal cues are activated in the presence of speech differences.

## Conclusions

Although few may approach Henry Higgins's precision in locating the origin of people from linguistic cues, there is no doubt that dialect serves to differentiate social groups and, at an earlier time for humans, among so many other species ranging from birds to chimpanzees, delineates breeding populations. Even in a post-industrial, multicultural society such as the United States, dialect remains an active social cue. Indeed, people raised in modern society whose earlier language skill acquisition occurs in diverse regional/cultural environments may be continually subject to queries regarding geographic origin throughout their lives (authors' personal observation). Current debate in the United States over the social value of promoting so-called "Ebonics," pro and con, reveals the objective function of dialect as a direct behavioural expression and marker of ethno-cultural group membership. Whatever the ultimate utility of linguistic variation for the reproductive success of breeding populations, the proximate mechanisms by which dialect may affect intergroup relations in everyday life suggest that it may play an important role in inter-ethnic social tension and conflict.

Using naturalistic data in the setting of United States Supreme Court oral argument and within the framework of a quasi-experimental design, this study tested a model in which dissimilarity in dialect was hypothesized to stimulate anxiety arousal that would be expressed through inhibition of behaviour in Justices' questioning of counsel, but increased attentiveness to the quality of the argument presented by counsel. Anxiety arousal is inferred on the dimensions of inhibition and attention, not directly observed, as a response to novelty, uncertainty and threat. Novelty is presented both by the low frequency of Southern dialect in the speech of lawyers arguing before the Supreme Court – occurring in eighteen of one hundred and sixty randomly sampled cases – as well as the dissimilarity of Southern dialect for people in the United States growing up and living outside the Southern region. Uncertainty is involved when processing information presented in dissimilar dialects, because the sounds of words are different, the structure or grammatical composition of utterances and commonplace sayings is dissimilar, and the accompanying non-verbal behaviour is also less familiar. At the very least, greater care and attention in listening – that is, greater cognitive effort – is required to understand communications in dissimilar dialects. Moreover, in the highly instrumental, adversarial setting of legal argument, verbal, vocal and non-verbal cues to veracity and deception may be especially important in the decoding and evaluation of political communications. These cues are less accessible and less decodable when presented by speakers using a different dialect from that of the listener. Thus, threat as a stimulus to anxiety arousal is also presented by the diminished capacity to detect deception and evaluate veracity. This remains a partial model in that the actual neurophysiology of anxiety arousal under these conditions is not specified and it is unclear to what extent pre-cognitive signal processing may be involved, although it certainly appears implicated.

The results of this study are that the Justices' questioning behaviour reveals significant inhibition in quantity of behaviour, comparing questioning of Southern versus non-Southern dialect speaking counsel, when a substantial risk factor is present enhancing the Justices' concern for understanding and trusting the arguments and claims of counsel. The results are also that, at the same time, Justices may be less emotional and more substantively attentive to the arguments presented in a dissimilar dialect. By contrast, no such inhibition is observed when a familiar form of physical difference, sex of counsel, is present in the characteristics of counsel arguing before the court. To the contrary, the Justices were far more active in the questioning of female counsel. These results are provocative, support the theoretical model, and generally meet criteria for statistical significance; however, they are based on a very small number of cases and should be regarded as tentative.

**Table 10.3** List of cases

| Term | Citation | Oral argument | Name |
|------|----------|---------------|------|
| **Cases with Southern dialect** | | | |
| 1969 | 3970436 | 13/11/69 | Ashe v. Swenson |
| 1969 | 3970790 | 17/11/69 | Parker v. North Carolina |
| 1969 | 3970817 | 28/4/70 | In The Matter of Spencer |
| 1969 | 4010745 | 10/11/69 | United States v. White |
| 1970 | 4010745 | 20/10/70 | United States v. White (reargued) |
| 1970 | 4010808 | 19/1/71 | Rewis v. United States |
| 1971 | 4060164 | 28/2/72 | Weber v. Aetna Casualty & Surety Co. |
| 1971 | 4070104 | 17/4/72 | Colten v. Kentucky |
| 1972 | 4090188 | 18/10/72 | Neil, Warden v. Biggers |
| 1972 | 4110001 | 12/10/72 | San Antonio School District v. Rodriguez |
| 1972 | 4110223 | 7/12/72 | Brown v. United States |
| 1972 | 4110325 | 14/11/72 | Askew v. American Waterways Operators, Inc. |
| 1973 | 4140395 | 13/11/73 | United States v. Maze |
| 1973 | 4160783 | 26/3/74 | Dillard v. Industrial Commission of Virginia |
| 1973 | 4180488 | 18/3/74 | Taylor v. Hayes, Judge |
| **Cases with female counsel** | | | |
| 1969 | 3990042 | 27/4/70 | Chambers v. Maroney |
| 1969 | 3990224 | 31/3/70 | Nelson, Warden v. George |
| 1970 | 4000309 | 20/10/70 | Wyman v. James |
| 1970 | 4000548 | 9/11/70 | Piccirillo v. New York |
| 1970 | 4020424 | 8/12/70 | California v. Byers |
| 1971 | 4040226 | 14/10/71 | Britt v. North Carolina |
| 1971 | 4060598 | 10/4/72 | Carleson v. Remillard |
| 1973 | 4140395 | 13/11/73 | United States v. Maze |

# References

Eibl-Eibesfeldt, I. (1979). Human ethology: Concepts and implications for the sciences of man. *The Behavioral and Brain Sciences*, **2**, 1–57.

Eibl-Eibesfeldt, I. (1989). *Human ethology.* Aldine de Gruyter, New York.

Gray, J. (1987). The psychology of fear and stress. 2nd edn. Cambridge University Press, Cambridge, UK.

Henley, N. (1977). *Body politics: Power, sex and nonverbal communication.* Prentice Hall, Englewood Cliffs, NJ.

Marcus, G.E. (1988). The structure of emotional responses to 1984 presidential candidates. *American Political Science Review*, **82**, 737–62.

Schubert, J.N., Peterson, S.A., Schubert, G. and Wasby, S.L. (1992). Observing Supreme Court oral argument: A biosocial approach. *Politics and the Life Sciences*, **11**(1), 35–51.

Spaeth, H.J. (1991). *United States Supreme Court judicial data base, 1953–1989.* Inter-University Consortium for Political and Social Research, Ann Arbor, MI.

Tajfel, H. (1978). *Differentiation between social groups: studies in the social psychology of intergroup relations.* Academic Press, London.

Vrij, A., and Winkel, F.W. (1991). Cultural patterns in Dutch and Surinam nonverbal behavior: An analysis of simulated police/citizen encounters. *Journal of Nonverbal Behavior*, **15**, 169–84.

Vrij, A., and Winkel, F.W. (1994). Perceptual distortions in cross-cultural interrogations: The impact of skin color, accent, speech style, and spoken fluency on impression formation. *Journal of Cross-Cultural Psychology*, **25**, 284–92.

## CHAPTER 11

# RISK AND DECEIT IN TRANSIENT, NON-REPEATED INTERACTIONS

## THE CASE OF TOURISM

## *Pierre L. van den Berghe*

Tourism, often described as the world's single largest industry accounting for U.S.$2.4 trillion in 1990 (Khan et al. 1993, p. x), is an unusual mode of interaction in that the parties to the tourist encounter are generally unfamiliar to one another and unlikely to meet again. Those are conditions likely to produce a high risk of deceit and exploitation. To be sure, many interactions in mobile, industrialized, mass societies are between strangers unlikely to repeat their transaction, and are thus fraught with risk, as any urbanite well knows. However, most of us seek to reduce such risks by avoiding such encounters. For example, the unpopularity of public transportation in large cities has much to do with such risk avoidance. When we unavoidably find ourselves in fleeting encounters with strangers, we find such situations unpleasant and we try to minimize interactions. In buses or elevators, for instance, we try to maximize distance with other passengers, to avoid eye contact, and so on. The few who seek contact, who sit too close, who stare, who strike up a conversation, are generally viewed with mild annoyance and/or mistrust, unless, curiously, some external event (an accident, a breakdown, a traffic jam, a storm) creates temporary solidarity.

Tourism, however, is different. Despite perceived risk, we positively seek unfamiliar situations where we expect to interact transiently with total strangers. Indeed, the strangeness, the exoticism of the other may even be the primary tourist attraction, as it clearly is in ethnic tourism (MacCannell 1973, 1976; Keyes and van den Berghe 1984). Even risk itself may be part of the thrill of tourism as the concept of "adventure tourism" suggests. Tourists commonly expect to be cheated, to encounter the unfamiliar, to suffer minor ailments, to eat the unpalatable, to suffer sundry discomforts, and, yet, they keep coming. Tourism is to some degree, a risk-seeking venture, or, at least, a quest for the unfamiliar (Jafari 1984, 1987; MacCannell 1976).

The question then becomes: Why did tourism become one of the most ubiquitous, enjoyable and lucrative forms of interaction in the late twentieth century, despite its vulnerability to deceit and exploitation?

Trivers in his classic 1971 article, may have suggested part of the answer. He emphasized the vulnerability to cheaters of all complex systems of "reciprocal altruism" which characterize our species (Trivers 1971). Among the conditions necessary for the control of cheaters is iterated interaction, so that detected cheaters can be punished, if only by exclusion from further exchanges. Trivers also suggested that deceit may have been a powerful, selective pressure in the encephalization of hominids. Successful parasitism of systems of reciprocity and successful survival of such systems involved a never-ending brain race between those who cheat and those who detect cheaters.

What perhaps Trivers did not sufficiently stress is the *ludic* component of deceit. Intelligence and playfulness go hand in hand, as many evolutionary theorists have noted. Thus, it is not surprising that humans are very playful animals, and, uncharacteristically for other playful species, remain playful in adulthood, one of the many aspects of our neoteny. We have a capacity and a propensity to turn practically anything into a game, and our best games or forms of entertainment have a large element of deceit, cunning or feigning: cards, chess, sports, courtship, crossword puzzles, detective stories, to name a few.

To answer the questions I posed, namely why tourism thrives despite its inherently risky nature, I would suggest that the risk element in tourism has three components:

1.  In part, tourism persists *because* of, not despite, its risky nature. Tourism, being a ludic activity, involves some risk-seeking. Some of the cheating involved is not only expected but enjoyed.
2.  In part, many risks are *avoided* or minimized, through a variety of mechanisms, especially the risks that pose a serious threat to life, health, property, freedom, privacy, autonomy or other core condition of our well-being.
3.  To resolve the tension and the contradiction between (1) and (2), much tourism involves the *simulation* of risk, the provision of carefully contrived thrills or "adventures" that only have the appearance of danger or surprise, or, if real, seem more dangerous than they are.[1]

Obviously, the relative weight of these three components varies greatly by types of tourism (e.g. beach resort vs. trekking), and by individual choice (e.g. conducted tour vs. independent travel). Indeed, degree of risk chosen or avoided is perhaps the principal consideration dictating the tourist's choice of destination, of mode of travel, and of activities, diet, and lodging on arrival.

Let us now illustrate each of the three risk components in tourism: first, the risk-seeking. Tourism is travelling for pleasure, and the essence of the pleasure is the quest for a change of place and pace from the daily routine of ordinary existence (Jafari 1987). This quest for a break from the humdrum can range from a mere change of scenery or climate to a full-blown escape to the cultural exoticism of remote parts of the Third World. A central element of this quest for the unfamiliar is the "authenticity dilemma". Many tourists seek "authentic" experiences; they want to see "real" people doing "real" things in "real" places (MacCannell 1973, 1976; van den Berghe and Keyes 1984). Yet the very presence of tourists destroys the authenticity they seek. Hence, the distaste of many tourists for other tourists. Everyone wants to be an explorer, a discoverer, at worst, a traveller, but not a tourist, because tourists "spoil" the natives, i.e., transform the "real" world into a stage show.

This authenticity dilemma can quickly become the main focus of extremely complex and subtle forms of deceit based on selective perceptions, constructions, and expectations that tourists and natives have of one another. The natives become, in effect, "tourees," that is, they literally make a spectacle of themselves based on their interpretation of what tourists want to see. If tourees, for example, have become modernized to the point that they no longer correspond to the stereotyped images that tourists have of them, they may re-create or indeed invent traditions in conformity with those images. They may construct an elaborate show of "staged authenticity" (MacCannell 1973).

Villages, such as Oberammergau in Bavaria, where tourism is the main source of revenue, may literally reinvent themselves into a "Disneylandified" image of themselves to look more authentic and attractive to tourists. Houses are elaborately painted; balconies are decorated with flowers; people dress up in *Lederhosen* and *Dirndls*, drink from oversize beer mugs and smoke Meerschaum pipes, and so on. One may legitimately ask how conscious the deceit is, how successful it is, and, indeed, the extent to which deceit is involved at all. How long can people play at being themselves without the play-acting becoming, once more, authentic? Conversely, tourists may recognize the show as a display for their consumption, but still enjoy it and appear to accept it at face value. Or, if they do not accept this "front-stage" display, they may seek to penetrate the "back stage", but the "back-stage" itself may quickly become another, yet more elaborately deceptive, front stage.

In short, the quest for, and provision of, authenticity is a collusive game of only partially conscious deceit between tourists and tourees in which the boundaries between the real and the staged frequently blur and shift. Let us return to our Oberammergau example. The main tourist attraction is a passion play whose history stretches back to well before the advent of modern mass tourism. The play involves virtually the entire population of the village in a way which is certainly real to at least some of them. Yet, the reality of that play consists in playing a role in pageant which is at once central to the religious and social life of the village and a staged performance to a paying audience of outsiders. And, since people have to make a living in the ten-year intervals between performances, they also play at incarnating a "picture-book" Bavarian village, and at providing visitors with vast quantities of "traditional" crafts, principally wood-carvings. Clearly, the line between reality and fantasy is blurred. Many tourists know that Oberammergau is less typically Bavarian than Munich, Augsburg or Nuremberg, yet they enjoy the staged authenticity of Oberammergau, and, in a sense, accept being "taken in".

One may speak of "collusive deceit," in which the touree pretends to conform to the stereotype of the tourist, and the tourist pretends to accept the deceit. Indeed, this "collusive deceit" is the pre-condition to the show being enjoyed by all. A new reality of tourist-touree interaction emerges from all this staged "authenticity."

Another arena in which this collusive deceit is expressed concerns bargaining. Most tourists expect bargaining for goods and services to be an integral part of the tourist experience. In part, this is because many tourist destinations have economies where fixed prices are the exception rather than the rule, but, even so, tourist bargaining almost invariably exceeds the limits of bargaining between locals. Again, the reason is simple enough: locals know prices and quality much better than tourists, and, therefore, the scope for price flexibility (and deceit) is much greater when the buyers are tourists.

Most tourists know they are vulnerable to paying too much, largely because, coming from affluent economies, they tend to over-evaluate the cost of local labour. Many accept being "cheated," if only because they feel exploitative for bargaining *too* hard, or because prices seem to them so low as to affect their budget only trivially. Yet most tourists also feel that they *must* bargain, however ineptly, because bargaining is part of the tourist experience, and because – they often believe – the *natives* enjoy bargaining.

It is true that native sellers frequently test the limits of tourist ignorance of both prices and quality, and enjoy taking advantage of especially naïve tourists, e.g. those on organized tours or cruise ships, but there is little evidence that natives enjoy bargaining as such, especially not under conditions of oversupply which frequently prevail on craft markets. It is also true that artists and artisans often set a value on their work that is much higher than local minimum wage and the cost of materials, and resent and reject lower bids by tourists, to the point of refusing to bargain. Despite this contrary evidence, tourists persist in the belief that their ludic view of bargaining is shared by natives. Even though they expect to be "taken in" in a game in which they are conscious of being at an informational disadvantage, they often enjoy the contest of wits and believe that the pleasure is mutual. This ludic view of bargaining on the tourist's part is clearly evidenced by the frequently desultory nature of tourist bargaining. I have even witnessed tourists pay the asking price *after* a half-hearted bargaining session in which they had driven the price down. Clearly, non-rational factors influence prices on tourist markets, and these include the tourists' view of bargaining as a game with its own intrinsic psychic rewards, beyond the acquisition of an object at whatever price. Collusive deceit is at work, much in the same way as, say, between performer and audience in a magic show.

The common denominator of these risk-seeking behaviours on the part of tourists is, of course, that the incurred risks are relatively trivial, both materially in relation to the tourists' budget, and psychically in terms of the tourists' self-esteem. Most tourists who are "taken in" by those subtle but minor forms of deceit tend to dismiss or laugh off such episodes, and even regard them as valuable learning experiences in the process of becoming a more sophisticated tourist.

By contrast, the second category of risks to which tourists are exposed are more serious, lack a ludic component, and are avoided rather than sought. Indeed, much of the tourist industry is constructed around this risk avoidance. The "serious" risks of tourism concern mostly health (due to changes in diet and sanitation, and exposure to pathogens in unfamiliar climes), life (danger of accidents, crime, terrorism, civil disorder), liberty (fear of kidnapping or run-ins with state authorities), and property (exposure to pickpockets, baggage theft, scams in money exchange, and the like). Virtually all tourists, especially to Third World countries, are concerned about all these risks, and, indeed, frequently tend to exaggerate the dangers. Tourist volume, for instance, is extremely responsive to even isolated reports of terrorism, civil disorder, strikes and the like, although the statistical probability of unpleasantness is minuscule. Hypochondria also commonly develops in otherwise "normal" tourists who literally travel with portable pharmacies.

A large insurance industry caters to a wide range of tourist risk aversions: air ambulance services, luggage loss or theft, travel cancellation, bad weather, medical coverage, legal costs, to name a few. Perhaps the greatest risk-avoidance product in the tourist industry is the organized tour, which has proliferated not only in quantity but in specialization by type of client (age, physical disability, gender, sexual preference), by destination, by mode of transport (boat, bicycle, train, motor coach, minibus, etc.), by activity (scuba diving, bird-watching, golfing, gastronomy, wine tasting, trekking, whoring, you name it) and by type of attraction (beaches, amusement parks, archeology, museums, architecture, ethnography, festivals, and so on). With just a little bit of research one can find bird-watching tours in Hawaii for young heterosexual singles, trekking tours of Nepal graded by physical stamina required, brothel tours of Bangkok for Japanese paedophiles, religious tours of the Holy Land for American Southern Baptists, tours of Burgundy for Californian vintners, and innumerable other combinations of tastes, affinities, and destinations, including tours for tourists who dislike tours.

The common denominator of this bewildering array of offerings is that all of them take "the trouble out of travelling". In the most obvious way, they arrange for transportation, lodging, meals, guide services, transfers, entrance fees, and so on. In a slightly less obvious way, they shield tourists from unwanted contact with locals, by interposing the tour guide-interpreter between tourist and touree, but also by shepherding the tourist in a sanitized capsule, sometimes stationary (the five-star hotel, restaurant, swimming pool, private beach, or, indeed, entire fenced resort like a Club Med), sometimes moving (air-conditioned bus, airplane cabin, cruise boat), but economically out-of-bounds to natives except for a few members of the élite and an army of uniformed servants.

True, some tourists actually seek contact with natives, but most do not, or, at least, only tolerate such contact as *they* initiate, in times and places of their choice. They want an inviolate retreat from the bustle, squalor, cacophony and smells of the countries they visit, even though they may enjoy a brief slumming excursion in the local market, church, bar, bullring or whatever local "scene" is defined as "colourful" and typical.

Services catering to tourists thus almost invariably involve a measure of spatial and social segregation beyond the mere selling of comfort, luxury and privacy for a price out of reach to most locals. Tourist amenities also shield tourists from a whole range of risks and annoyances: unsanitary food, unsightly beggars, importunate peddlers, confidence tricksters, pickpockets, oppressive heat, dangerous animals, unwanted noises and odours, or simply disquieting reminders of the surrounding misery. Squalor is only colourful and entertaining in small doses and from a distance. Some tourists even want to be completely shielded from the ambient society in what are in effect extra-territorial resorts, enclaves of luxury and privilege, gilded ghettos for vacationing foreigners. The "host society" simply provides the physical setting, the climate and the servants, and even the latter are as unobtrusive and invisible as possible (kept away by "do not disturb" signs on hotel room doors, for instance).

Interestingly, however, tourists keep themselves isolated from their hosts not only or simply through affluence. Often the five-star hotels and restaurants cater both to tourists and to the local élite, and, conversely, at the bottom (or near the bottom) of the scale of facilities, even the most frugal backpackers on shoe-string budgets congregate in tourist haunts. In tourist towns with many low-budget tourists, many Spartan establishments (hostels, bars, restaurants) quickly specialize in tourists, seemingly satisfying a mutual desire of both tourists and tourees to keep spatial and social distance between them, at least some of the time. Even ethnic tourists, it seems, want to retire from their touristing after hours or during meals.

Indeed all this spatial and social segregation of tourists frequently suits the locals as well as the tourists. Many locals are only too glad to see 90 percent of the tourists confined to 5 percent of the local space 75 percent of the time. Even when tourists and tourees do meet, they do so largely on pre-arranged meeting grounds that are either in everyone's public sphere (e.g. churches, markets, train stations), or in spaces especially designed for such encounters (curio shops, theatres, art shows, fairs, sound and light shows, and so on). Even in heavily touristed towns, locals seek to maintain their private space, their back stage beyond tourist reach, sometimes creating an aura of danger to keep inquisitive tourists out.

Obviously, the provision of special services and amenities specifically designed for tourists almost invariably involve a risk-reducing element. Most tourists seek to minimize not only serious risks to health, life, and property, but also seemingly more trivial risks of discomfort, missed connections, misunderstandings, embarrassment, lack of privacy, waste of time, misplaced luggage. Most of these risks can be averted or mediated through guided tours, specialized agents, and caterers who "know tourists".

The apprehensions of tourists were investigated in a sample of seventy-five subjects in Cuzco, Peru, in December 1996, with the following results. Fifteen percent of respondents denied having any fears or concerns at all; 29 percent reported one concern; 36 percent experienced two; and 20 percent more than two. Though gender differences were not large, women were, on average, slightly more apprehensive than men. The leading fear for both sexes was becoming a victim of crime, principally theft or assault: over three quarters (77 percent) of the sample expressed such fears. The second more common fear involved health, mentioned by nearly half (47 percent). Fear of unrest, guerrilla activity or civil disorder was a concern for slightly less than one fifth (19 percent). A little over one quarter of the sample (27 percent) expressed a wide variety of other fears or concerns, such as being the victim of fraud, of abuse of power by agents of the state, of misunderstandings due to language barriers, of road or airplane accidents, of adverse weather conditions or elevation, and of earthquakes.

To put these fears in perspective, it should be mentioned that Cuzco *is* a relatively risky destination. In the month preceding the study (November 1996), a severe earthquake destroyed much of the coastal Peruvian city of Nazca. During the study period (December 1996), a Marxist guerrilla group took hundreds of hostages in the Japanese embassy compound in Lima. Most guidebooks issue stern warnings about theft and assault, and, indeed, 17 percent of the respondents *were* the victims of theft or robbery. Peru has a dismal air and road safety record, due to hazardous mountain terrain and to poor equipment maintenance. Finally, high elevation (Cuzco lies at 3,400 meters above sea level), dubious water quality and poor hygiene make for high morbidity rates. Indeed, 11 percent of the sample *did* become ill on their trip, generally from altitude sickness or from intestinal disorders.

Most tourists in the sample took multiple and elaborate precautions against a variety of hazards, including some who disclaimed any fears or concerns. On average, respondents mentioned 4.2 precautions. Over half (53 percent) of the sample had taken out special travel insurance (usually covering both theft and health). Health precautions were virtually universal. Over two thirds (68 percent) took immunization shots before their trip; 41 percent were taking special drugs (such as malarial prophylaxis); and 59 percent took great care of what they ate and drank. On average, individuals mentioned taking 1.7 health precautions.

Conscious measures to protect property were likewise extremely widespread. Almost two thirds (65 percent) said they used mostly travellers' cheques and credit cards rather than cash for larger sums; a little over half (52 percent) carried their valuables in money belts, inside pockets or pouches kept under clothes; and 28 percent used hotel safes wherever possible. (Eight percent, however, considered safes unsafe, and preferred to take all valuables with them.) A long list of other safety measures was mentioned, such as using their own padlock, photocopying passports, not taking jewelry, dividing their valuables, carrying mace, taking taxis and tours, not accepting lifts, avoiding night trains, going in groups, checking bills for counterfeiting, carrying "backpacks" in front, and hiding cameras under their coats. (Over half of the sample mentioned one or more such precautions.) Clearly, almost all subjects were conscious of travel entailing special risks, and were taking special precautions to minimize these risks, even the 15 percent minority who denied any special fear of travel. Women mentioned slightly more fears than men (1.8 for women versus 1.6 for men), and seemed more cautious, averaging 4.5 precautions, versus 3.9 for men. Several women spontaneously remarked that the risks, especially of solo travel, were higher for women than for men.

Another salient dimension of risk-avoidance in tourism concerns ethnicity and kinship. This, in turn, has several different aspects: choice of destination, choice of travel companions, formation of ephemeral affinity groups on the way, and composition of tour groups are the main ones.

Choice of destination frequently has an ethnic dimension. It is true that many ethnic or cultural tourists seek not familiarity, but *dépaysement*. They thirst for the ethnically exotic. It is also true that tourism always involves a break from the humdrum of daily life. Nonetheless, there are many tourists to whom a break with the ethnically familiar is more threatening than exciting. They may want a change of climate, of landscape, of routine, yet eat familiar food and be surrounded by people who speak their language. They are quite comfortable travelling independently, so long as they can interact with locals without having to overcome too great a cultural or linguistic barrier. Many Germans of my acquaintance, for instance, travel to different destinations every year, often beyond the borders of Germany, but hardly ever beyond the limits of the German-speaking world. Their forays into Switzerland do not extend to Geneva or Lausanne; they are "at home" in Alto Adige (which they call "*Süd Tyrol*") but dare not push on to Milan or Venice. Similarly, I know of many Frenchmen who do not hesitate to travel to Tahiti, Martinique or Réunion, but who would be reluctant to go to Hawaii, Jamaica or the Canary Islands. Clearly, mastery of the local language reduces many risks and increases the psychic comfort of many tourists.

Many people make a clear distinction here between dialect and language. To take again a German example, the Germanic world is dialectically quite diverse, many spoken vernaculars verging on near-complete mutual incomprehensibility. Yet, most Germans are fluently diglossic in "High German" or "*Schriftdeutsch*" as the Swiss call their literary language, and a local vernacular. Many Germans who would not dare transcend the borders of the German-speaking world take great delight in experiencing regional dialectical diversity, a perennial subject of banter, attempts at mimicry and sub-ethnic humour among Germans. This is a way of enjoying the exoticism of regionalism, while retaining the security of the *Volk*.

For those willing and eager to venture beyond the geographical limits of their ethnic group, there are still available several ethnic- or kin-based risk-reduction strategies. There is a strong tendency for organized tours (other than locally organized day tours) to be quite homogeneous in composition, as many groups are explicitly formed around a common interest or characteristic (such as age, hobby, marital status, occupation, sexual preference, employer, club membership, and so on), but the most widespread base of homogeneity is undoubtedly ethnicity or common language. Often, the point of origin of the tour seems a sufficient explanation: a tour starting in Paris and organized by a French company will "naturally" recruit Frenchmen. Elective affinities, however, go beyond the determinism of sheer propinquity; for example, tours organized from a bilingual city such as Brussels will generally polarize into monolingual Dutch- or French-speaking groups. Indeed, many Belgians are positively irritated by hearing their "compatriots" speak the "other" language, to the point of preferring to speak English to one another.

Even "independent" travellers who assiduously avoid organized tours, resort to ethnicity or kinship as a risk-reducing strategy. This is evident both in the choice of travel companions at the point of origin, and in the loose formation of ephemeral associations during the travel or stay abroad. Solitary travel is relatively rare, and the most common travel companions are spouses or sexual partners, close relatives (even those who are not members of one's regular household, such as adult siblings) or close friends (who are generally fellow-ethnics). Clearly, the presence of someone close to one increases safety and comfort, and enhances the quality of the travel experience. Not only is the presence of a trustworthy intimate reassuring in case of accident, disease, or other mishap; it also provides a mutual audience for processing, interpreting, and enhancing unfamiliar experiences. Travel companions are prized well beyond their sheer companionship and security value in case of trouble. They are travel-experience *enhancers*. Their value is all the greater if they are close enough to one to validate one's own perceptions and confirm one's interpretations. The more exotic and unfamiliar the travel setting, the greater the need for such intimate travel companions. Indeed, so powerful, intense, and many-faceted is the shared travel experience that the latter is often a severe *test* of pre-existing relationships.

Two samples of 175 and 75 tourists, interviewed in 1990 in San Cristóbal de las Casas, Mexico (van den Berghe 1994) and in 1996 in Cuzco, Peru, report the following patterns of group membership on their current trip. Less than one fifth of them (18 and 19 percent respectively) were travelling alone; well over half (58 and 55 percent) were accompanied by a spouse, an opposite-sex companion or by blood relatives; while the remainder were either part of organized groups (9 and 5 percent), or were travelling with one same-sex friend (9 and 13 percent) or several friends of either sex (2 and 8 percent). The presumably more vulnerable women were even less likely to travel alone than were the men (8 percent versus 28 percent), and correspondingly more likely to travel with a friend of the opposite sex (27 percent versus 11 percent).

Especially instructive in this connection are the temporary groups that assemble and disperse "on the road" among "independent" tourists, for periods ranging from a few hours to a few weeks. Two of the most obvious affinity factors are age and common language. Travelling companions are not necessarily of the same nationality, but, more often than not, they have some kind of broad ethnicity in common, such as Australians and Canadians, or Danes and Swedes, or Britons and New Zealanders, or Argentineans and Chileans, symbolized by the fluent use of a common first language or of closely related ones. Such groups not only swap valuable information about lodgings, food, crafts, prices, transportation and the like, thereby reducing both cost and risks of travel, but also exchange of stories of travel experiences during the current and prior trips, and thus build on each others' perceptions of the world around them and expertness as travellers. They also recreate a microcosm of home (e.g. playing each others' favourite music and songs, telling about their regular life back home, and the like), and tend to spend much of their relaxation time together after a hard day's "work" of being tourists. Even ethnic tourists who profess an interest in the ethnic "other" often prefer to relax, drink, sing, flirt, and chat in the company of those who are ethnically close to them. Thus, they recreate abroad the predictability, safety and comfort of a familiar cultural scene, keeping the "host society" at bay. The interesting fact is that this kind of ethnic affinity grouping is found in the entire range of settings, from the decadent luxury of Club Meds and Raffles-style, post-colonial watering holes to Himalayan lamaseries catering for hardy trekkers.

Finally, we come to the intersection of the first two kinds of risks, those that are sought and enjoyed by tourists, and those that are avoided. A specialized kind of "adventure tourism" caters for a segment of the tourist market made up of clients who want to leave the "beaten path", experience the exotic and the unknown, and taste the delicious thrill of the unexpected and the adventuresome, but who lack the time, the courage, or both to undertake such "explorations" on their own. They want, in short, the thrill of adventure but on schedule and without serious risks. In the words of an organizer of adventure and ecotourism specializing in U.S. senior citizens: "How do you court adventure (without risk), experience nature (without discomfort), travel through deepest Africa (without bankruptcy)? By booking into group departures." (Note that Africa is now "deepest" rather than "darkest.") Organized adventure travel is the tourist equivalent of bungee jumping or roller-coaster rides. The successful formula is one that provides a series of experiences that seem much riskier than they are. Adventure tours must stage risk with verisimilitude.

Sometimes, this is easily done, as in African tent safaris when obliging lions and hyenas readily provide a nightly concert. A satisfied customer from Seattle who took part in an "Unexplored Serengeti Luxury Tented and Lodge Safari" enthuses as follows: "... it was wonderful. I felt comfortable and safe every step of the way. And what an experience ... hearing a lion's roar in the distance, the cool night, the stars... ." Most impressive is the hyrax, a rabbit-size relative of the elephant that sounds like a terrorized woman. Sometimes, the danger is real enough to provide a thrill, but one's exposure to it can be controlled, as in the running of the bulls in Pamplona, or the difficulty of the task can be matched to the skill of the client, as in river rafting, scuba diving or mountain climbing. Sometimes, the mere embellishment of local lore lends verisimilitude to danger, as in Scottish ghost stories, or African hunting tales. Many animals, for instance, such as lions or sharks, are much less dangerous to humans than their reputations credit them. Sometimes, the danger lies safely in the past, as when Vlad the Impaler, alias Count Dracula, continues to contribute to the grisly lure of Transylvania. Sometimes, a truly unplanned event produces a whiff of adventure, as when our Thai guide *did* get lost on a trek. (He could, of course, have been a superlative actor, but his show of fear, and later of astonished delight when we tipped him instead of asking for our money back makes that hypothesis implausible.)

## Conclusion

Tourism is, at bottom, a quest for a temporary release from the routine of daily life. Intrinsically, it involves a leap from the familiar into the unfamiliar. Equally intrinsically, it creates transient, non-repeated interactions between strangers whose behaviour is not only less predictable than that of our acquaintances, but less responsive to the norms of reciprocity since sanctions are largely unenforceable. Tourism is therefore a relatively high-risk type of interaction. We suggested that those risks fall into three categories: those that are trivial, actively sought and injected with ludic content; those that are serious and actively avoided or mini-mized; and those in the nature of thrill-seeking that are actively simulated.

Such a simple typology of risk goes a long way in explaining both the behaviour of tourists and tourees, and the supply of a vast range of goods and services in the tourist trade. Yet, risk has been little used as an analytical concept in the study of tourism. For instance, the three-column, sixteen-page, fine print subject index of a 1,007–page recent encyclopedia (Khan et al. 1993) does not contain a single entry on crime, risk, victimization, or fear, and treats "hazards" almost exclusively in the context of pathogens in food. Not only is tourism an inherently risky activity, but tourists are quite risk-conscious. This risk consciousness determines many tourist choices of destination, mode of transportation, style of travel, and the like. Equally importantly, the vast tourist industry is profoundly affected by its risk manage-ment in response to tourist concerns.

# Bibliography

Berghe, P.L. van den (1994). *The quest for the other: Ethnic tourism in San Cristóbal, Mexico.* University of Washington Press, Seattle.

Berghe, P.L. van den, and Keyes, C.F. (1984). Introduction: Tourism and re-created ethnicity. *Annals of Tourism Research*, 11(3), 343–52.

Jafari, J. (1984). Unbounded ethnicity. *The Tourist Review*, 39, 4–21.

Jafari, J. (1987). Tourism models, the sociocultural aspects. *Tourism Management*, June, 151–9.

Keyes, C.F., and Berghe, P.L. van den (eds) (1984). *Tourism and ethnicity.* Special issue of *Annals of Tourism Research* 11(3), 339–501.

Khan, M.A., Olsen, M.D., and Var, T. (1993). VNR's *Encyclopedia of hospitality and tourism.* Van Nostrand Reinhold, New York.

MacCannell, D. (1973). Staged authenticity. *American Journal of Sociology*, 79(3), 589–603.

MacCannell, D. (1976). *The tourist: A new theory of the leisure class.* Schocken, New York.

Trivers, R.L. (1971). The evolution of reciprocal altruism. *Quarterly Review of Biology*, 46(4), 35–57.

# Note

1. A definition of risk is appropriate here. Risk can be defined as $r_a = c_a \times p_a$, where r is the risk of event a, c the cost of event a, and p the probability of event a occurring. The risk is simply the product of cost times probability. Of the above three types, type 1 consists mostly of low-cost-high-probability events; type 2 of high-cost-low-probability events, and type 3 of high-cost-low-and-controlled-prob-ability events. It is an empirical question whether these three classes of events are perceived by tourists as discrete or continuous. The third type corresponds closely to the concept of "thrill," while the first partakes of gamesmanship. Perhaps only the second category could be called "true" risk, although empirically, the three types overlap, as, for instance, when a "thrill" results in a serious injury.

# EVOLUTIONARY SYNTHESES

## CHAPTER 12

# ETHNIC SOLIDARITY AS RISK AVOIDANCE

## AN EVOLUTIONARY VIEW

## *Peter Meyer*

∽〉 〔∾

After the recent breakdown of multi-ethnic empires, such as the Soviet-Union and Yugoslavia, social theorists have refocused their interest on the sources of social integration and solidarity. The impact of nationalistic and ethnic motivations has become so evident in recent wars, accompanying the breakdown of both these empires, that social theorists throughout the world felt urged to reconsider ethnic categories, as well as the impact of nationalism on the modern world. Traditionally, however, social theory was much more concerned with the spread of modernity than with ethnic and national categories, expecting that due to the dynamism of modernity, these categories would soon prove totally superfluous. Contrary to these predictions, the vitality of ethnic and related phenomena in the modern world is beyond any doubt. It is suggested that this contradiction arises from two major misunderstandings, (1) the failure to clearly distinguish system from social integration, and (2) the failure to give due consideration to the ways individuals pursue their interests. In this regard, it is suggested that due to the selective advantages of synergistic cooperation, natural selection provides human individuals with a tendency to prefer cooperation over purely selfish behaviour. It seems that in many ancestral environments the benefits likely to be gained from cooperation outweigh benefits from other behaviours. With regard to individual interests, it should therefore be a rational strategy to prefer cooperation over other options.

Turning to the distinction between system and social differentiation, according to D. Lockwood (1964, p. 245), system integration is a product of social evolution, a process of social differentiation and division of labour, providing such media as social power, money, or systems of law, which in turn serve as foundations for large-scale society. Recently, R. Münch, drawing upon Lockwood's distinction, has made it clear that successful system integration is, however, no long-time guarantee for the survival of any large-scale organization, unless its individual members sense some degree of allegiance toward this organization (Münch 1995, p. 11). In similar manner to Münch, this paper proceeds from the assumption that an improved understanding of social integration requires due consideration of the causes underlying individual allegiance to large-scale associations such as the state. More specifically, this chapter suggests that human individuals, being concerned about their well-being and safety, are willing to cooperate with others, particularly with kinsmen, and establish associations suited to safeguard their private, as well as their common interests. In ancestral environments, human beings could not have overcome the risks posed by dangerous predators or inimical groups, unless they cooperated to a certain extent.

From an evolutionary point of view, it seems to be a reasonable assumption that any organism should be interested in his own survival, as well as in that of his progeny. Furthermore, this is in keeping with kin selection theory, according to which the evolution of social behaviour can be accounted for in terms of genetic reproduction strategies. As will be pointed out, the willingness to cooperate is, however, not restricted to biological relatives but, given certain conditions, can include non-relatives as well. Nevertheless, it may be hypothesized that solidarity among kinsmen was the prevailing social pattern over the most extended period of human history. It is suggested that natural selection favoured the evolution of human cooperation because, due to the synergistic effects of coordinated behaviour, individuals are likely to benefit from such behaviour. The causes underlying the human willingness to cooperate with kinsmen or other persons cannot be fully understood unless their evolutionary rationale, as well as various layers of proximate causes, are taken into consideration.

The relation between system-integration and social-integration is still a conundrum of social theory. This paper specializes in the causes underlying social integration, more specifically it suggests that an evolutionary approach may shed some fresh light on these causes. It is further suggested that "kin selection theory", i.e., one of the major foundations of evolutionary biology, can account for some of the causes underlying the vitality of ethnicity in the modern world. Regarding social integration, kin selection theory predicts cooperative behaviours to evolve along kinship lines. Despite the fruitfulness of kin selection theory there are strong indications that individuals are willing to cooperate with non-kin as well, provided they may reasonably expect enhancement of their interests from such behaviour.

The foregoing leads to the hypothesis that natural selection provides human individuals with various detector mechanisms, indicating to them when and if the net benefits of cooperation are likely to exceed the benefits to be expected from purely selfish behaviour. Due to a number of behavioural mechanisms to be dealt with in later sections, there is, however, the strongest likelihood for highly benefi-cial social relations whenever close kin are involved, whereas there is a compara-tively lower likelihood for benefits from exchange with non-relatives. Despite this lower probability, there are many environments in the modern world, as well as in primitive times, when cooperation most likely will also be more beneficial to the individual in terms of individual interests than purely selfish behaviour. Recently, Maynard Smith and Szathmáry (1995, p. 261) presented a succinct formulation of this view: "If an individual can produce, say, two offspring on its own, but a group of $n$ individuals can raise $3n$ offspring if they cooperate, then it pays each of them to cooperate. Such synergistic effects are often invoked to explain cooperation [author's italics]." Regarding such effects, individual expectations are, however, dependent upon the reliability of detector mechanisms, signalling cheaters to them. Unless these conditions are met, cheaters would win out in the evolutionary contest, monopolize benefits and therefore would leave major numbers of off-spring. Regarding the reliability of detector mechanisms, Maynard Smith and Sza-thmáry suggest that once rowing, i.e., an environmental arrangement favouring cooperation, "is common, cooperation is evolutionarily stable. A possible answer is that cooperation starts between relatives, and later, once it is common, spreads to non-relatives" (Maynard Smith and Szathmáry 1995, pp.261–2). Eibl-Eibesfeldt makes the same point concerning the evolution of nurturent behaviour (1970). Regarding cooperation with non-relatives, it may be inferred from the foregoing that similar behaviour is likely to exert a positive influence upon the preparedness for cooperation even among biologically unrelated individuals, because similarity is understood as indicating a basic harmony of interests. This brings me to the con-cept of interests.

## Two types of individual interests

Viewed against the evolutionary background, the concept of interests needs to be defined in a broad and embracing fashion, including both subconscious, as well as conscious behavioural strategies. According to Darwinian evolutionary theory, evolution may be understood as a process of competition between conspecifics for basically the same resources, i.e., mainly territories and other resources, potentially meaningful in the competition for mates. Obviously this theory presupposes any individual organism to take an active interest in his own survival, more specifically his survival in a short-time perspective, as well as survival via offspring in a long-time perspective. According to evolutionary theory, natural selection will favour the reproduction of those organisms who have whatever minor physical or behav-ioural advantages over competitors on their side, and differential reproduction is the outcome of this process. With respect to the concept of interests, it may be gathered that the evolutionary process favours numbers of offspring as the crite-rion of the successful pursuit of interests, irrespective of the human value of consciousness on the part of the individual organism. From the evolutionary point of view, with its emphasis on the long-time perspective, it should be expected that individuals are going to strive hard to gain control over any type of resource conducive to their interests.

In fact, recent findings indicate that conflicts of interest are likely to arise even in situations when one would not expect them, for instance in the relation between the human mother and her foetus. According to Haig, human "offspring may be selected to take more from a parent than the parent is selected to give" (Haig 1993, p. 497). Later in ontogeny, "around the age of four or five," children "start to engage in deception, or the misrepresentation of information to others" (Gazzaniga 1992, p. 119) in order to serve their interests. According to these studies, human individuals pursue different sets of interests, depending on their respective age, sex, fecundity status, as well as a few other variables (Wang 1996, p. 13). With respect to the notion of interests, these considerations emphasize the need for a concept that can integrate both subconscious genetic strategies, as well as conscious behaviour and the rational pursuit of interests.

Returning to the concept of interests, G. Lenski proposed a broad and embracing formulation some time ago, that seems suited for the present purpose. According to him, "the great majority of men have always accorded survival the highest priority" (Lenski 1966, p. 37), i.e., survival is the main interest of human beings. It should be added that from an evolutionary point of view, the concept of survival must include leaving progeny, because this is what evolution is all about. With respect to the impact of kinship and ethnicity in the modern world, it may be suggested that people, whenever they are free to choose, are likely to pursue their vital interests, i.e., they will defend their own lives as well as those of their closest relatives, and will also try to preserve their right to raise children in their own ways. Shaw and Wong have formulated similar views, according to which "social scientists are only beginning to reconsider the hypothesis that ethnicity is rooted in descent, real or putative, and that this is an extension of kinship" (Shaw and Wong 1989, p. 125). This chapter subscribes to the notion that ethnicity is an extension of kinship, a view which has been succinctly formulated by van den Berghe: "If we accept that kinship and marriage (and the social organization derived from them) are rooted in the human biology of mating and reproductive behavior, then it is only a small additional step to recognize in ethnicity an extension of kinship. An ethny is basically a group whose solidarity is based on common descent" (van den Berghe 1983, p. 223; Shaw and Wong 1989, p. 125). As an example, the recent wars in former Yugoslavia have furnished proof of the ongoing impact of ethnicity on social behaviour. According to some newspaper reports, war erupted in this country when it became clear that the multi-ethnic state would not survive. It seems that various politicians succeeded in convincing sizeable numbers of citizens, in the various nations and ethnic groups, that individual interests could not be preserved unless full harmony with their ethnic group was ensured, and that military action was a legitimate means against external groups. Therefore it may be suggested that, from the individual's point of view, ethnic unity is not an end in itself, rather it seems to be regarded as a sort of safeguard for one's interests in a potentially inimical environment.

With regard to the concept of ethnicity, there is, unfortunately, no universally accepted definition available in the literature. Rather there is an ongoing discussion between followers of primordialism and ethnic nepotism theory (Salter 1997, p. 1) basically on the question whether common biological descent is a precondition for the emergence of ethnicity, or whether putative (potentially fictive) descent is a sufficient condition. In this regard, it should be emphasized once again that ethnicity's motivating force is owed to two major causes, namely, (1) real common descent, and (2) putative descent (van den Berghe 1983). From an evolutionary point of view, it seems obvious that kin selection theory can account for the origin of solidarity among people of common descent. Regarding the adaptability of ethnic sentiments to large-scale associations, and people's willingness to accept the notion of putative descent in some situations, seems to be established upon the feasibility of making "extensions of kinship". According to Tajfel, there is a general preparedness "for negative stereotyping of outgroups" (Tajfel 1981; Salter 1997, p. 29). So it should be expected that people who have been adopted into networks of reciprocity and who signal their willingness to reciprocate in future situations by adopting cultural markers, are likely to be more easily accepted in times of intergroup enmity. Some observations suggest that this preparedness to adjust to stereotypes, is a fitness-maximizing behaviour, common among primates.

According to Preuschoft and Preuschoft (1989, p. 564), young rhesus monkeys kept in captivity, who had never seen a snake in their lives, "learned from conspecifics who had grown up in the wilderness, avoiding snakes within eight minutes' time, showing all signs of fear." Similarly, human willingness to adopt "negative stereotypes" may increase fitness by intensifying bonds between group members. It seems that these tendencies inherent in human behavior easily lend themselves to integrating individuals into social groups. If this is a common descent group, the adoption of cultural markers comes naturally during early ontogeny, not to mention biological markers. When, however, it comes to larger ethnic groups, appeals to similarity of biological markers underlying a common cultural heritage, i.e., notions of common descent, seem to facilitate arousal of ethnic unity.

With regard to the evolutionary causes underlying these behaviours, Maynard Smith and Szathmáry (1995, p. 261), as well as Corning (1983) suggest that since synergistic effects of cooperation are likely to enhance individual survival, "negative stereotyping", as well as support of one's group may be concomitants of these more general causes. Due to the fitness-maximizing effects of synergistic cooperation, natural selection provided human individuals with various cues indicating to them when acts of solidarity towards one's kinsmen, or towards the larger ethnic group are likely to further one's interests best. In addition to the ultimate causes underlying the preference for cooperation, there must be a number of proximate causes which enable human actors to decide when their individual interests are likely to be served best by cooperative behaviour, or when deceit is likely to provide more benefits. With regard to the nature of these cues it is assumed that most of them are of a subconscious and non-rational nature, and that a better understanding of human behaviour presupposes due consideration of the non-rational and emotional bases of behaviour.

## Some proximate causes of cooperation

Turning to reciprocity, Gouldner suggests the norm of reciprocity holds that "people should help those who have helped them" (Gouldner 1960, p. 171) and therefore, those who have been supported have an obligation to help the original donor. Reciprocity prevailed as a time-honoured behavioural pattern because as a subtype of time-delayed cooperation, it helped human individuals to collect and keep for future use obligations from previous assistance. Similar to the synergistic effects referred to by Maynard Smith and Szathmáry, as well as by Corning, storing obligations seems to be a species-specific way of securing such effects for partaking individuals. Regarding its evolutionary underpinnings, it should be noted that in addition to the ultimate causes generally underlying cooperation, there must be proximate causes as well, helping the individual to decide when obligations should be stored or not. Contrary to the games theoretical approach with its emphasis on rational "tit-for-tat" exchange patterns as the basis of reciprocity (Axelrod 1984, p. 13), it is assumed that this basis is in fact provided by emotional, mostly non-rational processes (Miller 1993, p. 229). It will be pointed out that "bonding", i.e., one of the major emotional categories, is favoured over alternative emotional states and it will be shown how this relates to the general preference for cooperation.

To sum up, human beings, in their striving for survival, pursue different strategies in order to enhance their major interest, i.e., individual survival. Due to the various selective advantages of synergistic cooperation, a general preference for cooperation is instilled in human individuals inducing them to seek actively to establish the conditions for a basic harmony of interests with others. As has been mentioned, reciprocity and the storing of obligations have been conducive to creating a basic harmony of interests among individuals. It seems that living in comparatively small groups of kinsmen combines the selective advantages of synergistic cooperation with a capacity for controlling deceit and free riding. These may well be some of the causes for the survival of ethnic patterns over the most extended period of human history. Undoubtedly, these simple groups of kinsmen "when pitted against" more advanced societies were no real match, since "the simpler society always invariably succumbs to the more complex one" (Carneiro 1987, p. 113), and therefore modern societies have forced the simpler societies back to the remote areas of the world. Despite these advantages of the more complex societies which rely upon new technologies, as well as on novel patterns of system integration, the breakdown of multi-ethnic empires has drawn attention to the strong impact of kinship and ethnicity on social integration in times of rapid social and political change.

Regarding the evolutionary underpinnings of social integration, it should be stressed once more that, despite the universal trend toward higher levels of systemic integration, social integration is established upon some very ancient behavioural tendencies of human beings. Due to these behavioural tendencies, human individuals pursue their interests, and strive hard to establish coordinated social behaviour in a wide range of environmental conditions. Thereby they hope to prepare for risks posed by inimical forces in their respective environments. This is not to deny, however, that there are conflicts of interest which at times cause individuals to engage in various kinds of infragroup strife. Quite to the contrary, since evolutionary theory serves as the point of departure for the following considerations, its inherent emphasis on competition and conflict must be taken into account. Despite evolutionary biology's emphasis on competition, it is suggested that human individuals in most environments take an active interest in the establishment and stability of solidarity groups, and that this behavioural tendency is in keeping with evolutionary reasoning.

With respect to the causes underlying individual needs for solidarity, evolution has favoured life in small band-type associations. According to kin selection theory, individuals are likely to gain in fitness if they cooperate with their own kin. Viewed from the perspective of this theory, individuals should therefore prefer living in small groups of kinsmen over solitary existence, as well as over life in large-scale associations. As for the causes underlying the origin of this preference, it is further suggested that unless individuals in ancestral populations were willing to cooperate in defence against predators, humankind could hardly have survived. Therefore cooperation and other patterns of social integration must have been selectively favoured in ancestral environments. These causes can be accounted for in terms of kin selection theory, according to which cooperation and mutual aid should be favored, whenever reproduction of close kin is at stake. Regarding the origin of social integration, it may be summarized that common biological descent is a cause for the evolution of strong foundations for social life, and that this cause can be accounted for by kin selection theory. However, this theory fails to identify causes for the social integration of biologically unrelated individuals. With respect to the origin of solidarity among unrelated individuals, it is suggested that due to the general preference for small band associations, human individuals actively search to establish such associations in the most varied situations of modern life, particularly in risky situations. For instance, American soldiers in combat, according to a study by Little, sought to establish "buddy relations" with a very limited number of individual soldiers, in order to create an atmosphere of being "in the same family" (Little 1964, p. 199). Individuals exposed to an extremely risky situation tried to enhance their chances of survival by establishing quasi-kin relations.

Turning to some of the proximate causes underlying human behaviour, natural selection designed human emotionality as a set of parameters, indicating to the individual the degree to which behavioural alternatives are likely to serve his interests. In general, the individual is likely to prefer such environments which serve his interests, especially his need for safety. There is no need for pointing out in detail that, although individuals acquire most of their relevant knowledge via ontogenetic learning, these learning processes are in turn based upon hard-wired genetic programmes. For instance, according to some recent findings, individuals can increase their supplies of emotional energies by bonding with others (Masters 1986; Miller 1993, p. 238), i.e., there is a feedback loop between overt social behavior with ultimate genetic causality, as well as with proximate emotional causality. According to Masters (1986), "bonding" is a major category of emotional processes and its role is essential for an understanding of the causes underlying human cooperation. Given the general scarcity of time and energy stressed by evolutionary theory, it should be expected that human emotionality has been designed by natural selection in such a fashion that cooperation of individuals is favoured whenever there is a congruence of interests, because on the one hand, individual human beings could not have survived the threats posed by inimical groups, predators and other forces, unless they cooperated to some extent, and on the other hand, because each individual is likely to benefit in terms of his interests from coordinated behaviour.

In summary it is suggested that natural selection has designed a number of proximate mechanisms which help ascertain the survival value of different behavioural options. For instance, some mechanism will indicate to the individual whether the expected pay-off, in terms of time and energy, is likely to be higher from compliance with or deviance from social rules. Given that individuals' interests are guarded against free riders, individuals should tend to reciprocate favours (Trivers 1978, p. 190) from their fellow group members because by reciprocating they serve their own interests. According to Alexander, systems of direct reciprocity, where the debtor pays back to the original creditor, are likely to be supplemented by "indirect reciprocity" in the human species. Individuals observing reciprocal exchange may feel compelled to take over the debts of the original debtor when both are members of the same group (Alexander 1987, p. 77). Therefore, in the long run, complex systems of obligations are likely, according to Wiessner, "to store the debt until the situation of have and have not is reversed" (Wiessner 1982, p. 67). Particularly in risky transactions, individuals will tend to regard the storage of obligations as a guarantee against all kinds of external threats, and thus will most likely refrain from deviant behaviour.

## Some evolutionary concepts

Turning to evolutionary theory, a few remarks will suffice to refer to those parts and concepts that are directly relevant for the present purpose. Since small-scale human social behaviour is the primary concern of the following considerations, some major disagreements between evolutionary theorists will be left aside here. With regard to the evolutionary underpinnings of human social behaviour, there seems to be consensus among evolutionary biologists and other evolutionarily minded theorists that "differential reproduction" is the main issue of the natural process. According to E. Mayr, one of the most influential advocates of the modern "synthesis", evolutionary theory proceeds from the assumption of a general scarcity of resources, and the ensuing competition of individuals over access to these resources. It is thought that natural selection favours the reproduction of those individuals who are even slightly better adapted to the environment (Mayr 1982, pp. 479–80) and that the ensuing difference in numbers of offspring brings about gradual changes in the genetic composition of populations.

If differential reproduction is in fact the pivotal point of evolution, it should be expected that natural selection will favour the spread of behaviours, as well as their underlying genetic information, which are most likely to result in maximum numbers of offspring. While there may in fact be "no intelligence to the variation" as Gazzaniga suggests, "over evolutionary time, however, complexity accumulates in the organism as it comes to adapt to more and more new challenges" (Gazzaniga 1992, p. 18). Due to the evolution of complexity, the behaviour of the higher phyla is much less dependent on the "blind variation" and "selective retention" system of information storage, typical of simpler life forms, since they can put to use novel systems of information storage and processing, i.e., mental systems. Due to the availability of mental systems human beings may further economize their time-energy budgets, by learning to avoid previously unsuccessful behaviours and by even instructing the oncoming generation to avoid such behaviours. Furthermore, the oncoming generation is likely to be informed about existing patterns of reciprocal obligations, thereby providing social relations with a certain extent of reliability.

While there may be little dissent among evolutionary theorists on the general relevance of mental and cultural processes for an understanding of human behaviour, there is, however, an ongoing discussion between advocates of kin selection and of group selection as to whether these cultural processes can override individual "genetic interests". This discussion began with W.D. Hamilton's rule, according to which "behaviours that enhance the reproductive fitness of others at the expense of the individual's personal reproductive success will be favoured by natural selection if, and only if, $k > 1/r$, where k is the ratio of other's benefit to actor's cost and r is the coefficient of genetic relatedness between the participating individuals" (Crippen 1994, p. 313). Undoubtedly, this is one of the strongest and heuristically most fruitful concepts put forth in recent decades for explaining in terms of differing genetic interests phenomena such as parental investment and infanticide, which had previously been little understood. As is well known among evolutionarily interested scientists, the concept of "inclusive fitness" was established as a "bulwark of sociobiology" (Barash 1978, p. 17) on Hamilton's rule and played a decisive role in this discipline's explanatory successes. If "inclusive fitness is the sum of individual fitness and genetic representation through relatives" (Barash 1978, p. 17), then any type of evolved social behaviour could be understood as a fitness-maximizing strategy of individuals' genetic interests.

The concept of group selection, i.e., "the evolution of traits that while being detrimental to the individual, provide benefits to the social unit" (Barash 1980, p. 8) which was the object of severe criticisms in sociobiology's early years, has recently been seriously reconsidered. According to Alexander, Darwin did in fact advocate group selection (Alexander 1987, p. 170); whereas, Smillie points to the conflict between what he terms Darwin's "variational" and his "Malthusian" (Smillie 1995, p. 232) paradigms. According to Smillie, this conflict is responsible for some of the confusion over kin vs. group selection. Smillie finds the origin of the confusion in Darwin's Malthusian paradigm which exaggerates the role of competition (Smillie 1995, p. 253) because it has an insufficient understanding of the process of genetic heredity (Smillie 1995, p. 235). However that may be, the present paper assumes that the concepts of kin selection and group selection may in fact coexist (Bloom 1996, p. 3), unless group selection presupposes inclusion of support for individuals and social groups who are inimical to one's own interests. As stated by Bloom, individuals are "biologically programmed to fit in" (Bloom 1996, p. 8), i.e., due to the selective advantages of synergistic cooperation they are likely to prefer cooperation over overt conflict, whenever mutual benefits are likely to ensue. Therefore, whenever mutual benefits are likely to result from cooperation, individuals should prefer it over conflict behaviour, irrespective of their genetic relatedness.

Recently, Wilson and Sober have reviewed various criticisms against kin selection theory. According to their view, a major shortcoming of the Hamiltonian tradition is to regard the gene as "the fundamental unit of selection" (Wilson and Sober 1994, p. 589), since this view does not provide a satisfactory solution to the problem as to whether "genes differ within a single individual in fitness" (Wilson and Sober 1994, p. 591). These authors' criticism draws upon West-Eberhard's critical views, according to which part of the problem arises from confusing genes with phenotypes: "[O]ne set of researchers thinks in terms of facultatively expressed phenotype, and the other contemplates a phenotype underlain by a particular allele" (West-Eberhard 1988, p. 123). This confusion can be partially solved by adopting Maynard Smith's and Szathmáry's (1995, pp. 261–2) view, according to which "cooperation starts between relatives, and later, once it is common, spreads to non-relatives.... . The important point is that cooperation must sometimes pay." Unlike some other formulations of the problem, these authors draw attention to the fact that cooperation is not necessarily restricted to relatives, but can be extended to non-kin if mutual benefits are likely to enhance individual interests.

To summarize, it is suggested that "kin selection" and "group selection" are mutually compatible concepts, both of which are conducive to improving our understanding of the ultimate causes underlying the evolution of social life. While the concept of kin selection cannot weather all the criticisms put forward, it certainly enhances our understanding of the role of genetic factors in the evolution of social life. With regard to the evolutionary underpinnings of human social life, Wilson and Sober's point should be given due consideration that:

> human adaptations can evolve two pathways
> (1) by increasing the fitness of individuals relative to others within the same social group and
> (2) by increasing the fitness of social groups as collectives, relative to other social groups (Wilson and Sober 1994, p. 600).

Both pathways might have been important causes underlying the evolution of proximate mechanisms, causes that are directly relevant to human preference for living in small-scale social associations.

Turning to some of the proximate causes underlying human social behaviour, it should be emphasized once again that "natural selection does not select directly for behaviors, it selects for the psychological processes that in conjunction with the environment, underlie behavior" (Brown 1991, p. 83). These psychological processes in turn are established on the interaction of a multitude of genes which determine through development various neurological and physiological processes, and finally bring about psychological dispositions. All of these processes have been designed by natural selection in such a fashion, so as to fit the product of their interactions into a specific range of physical and social environments. With regard to the survival of ancestral human populations, it may be inferred that psychological and cultural adaptations to environmental conditions must have played a decisive role. Recent discussions provide numerous examples of populations which subordinate individual predispositions toward maximization of their fitness to group level rules. As an example, Wilson and Sober refer to the behaviour of the Hutterites who are "as explicit as they can possibly be that their members should merge themselves into a group-level organism" (Wilson and Sober 1994, p. 603). Similarly, MacDonald's study on the spread of monogamy points out that Christianity, very similar in this regard to the Hutterites, put "high emphasis on the goals and needs of the group rather than on individual rights" (MacDonald 1995, p. 10). Wilson and Sober's analysis also indicates that "Hutterite social organization is not a unique product of the sixteenth century but reflects an evolved human potential to construct and live within such group-level vehicles" (Wilson and Sober 1994, p. 605). This evolved potential is the foundation for the preference for life in small bands. While Wilson and Sober propose group selection as the cause of this behaviour set, it is also fully compatible with kin selection theory. It is a common behavioural pattern in the human species to expect reciprocation for previous help. Depending upon environmental conditions, peculiar patterns of reciprocity are likely to arise and to be stored in cultural memories. According to Wiessner (1982, p. 68), these patterns of reciprocity "are not economic contracts with set terms, but rather bonds of mutual help".

## Proximate causes of social behavior: The role of emotions

The term "proximate" denotes any sort of assumptions about the goals and motivations of individuals, directly preceding overt behaviour. This kind of theorizing is indispensable because, as Daly and Wilson put it, nobody believes that individuals in any direct sense pursue the goal of fitness maximization (Daly and Wilson 1988, p. 7), as some of the considerations in terms of ultimate causality seem to suggest. Rather individuals have for instance sexual dispositions that may eventually lead to the maximization of fitness for some individuals. While explanations in terms of ultimate causality tackle the problem why "certain goals have come to control behavior at all" (Daly and Wilson 1988, p. 7), they cannot predict how these goals will be pursued in a given situation because human behaviour embraces a wide range of possible reactions to environmental stimuli. It would be a misunderstanding, however, to regard these behavioural reactions as entirely free and accidental, since their very existence is owing to causality deriving from previous selective tests. For instance, a human individual may decide for himself whether a sexual mood suits a particular situation, but he cannot decide whether sexuality should be part of human existence at all. The sexual disposition is a proximate cause of certain behaviours, but the ultimate goal of reproduction has been decided upon millions of generations ago.

It should be expected that natural selection has designed the system of human emotions in such a way that the individual will immediately receive an evaluation of his behaviours by some sort of feedback, indicating the degree to which his basic interests are likely to be affected. If the preservation of physical and psychic integrity is in fact a primary human interest, then pain and pleasure may be understood as feedback mechanisms, indicating "immediate costs and benefits" (Alexander 1987, p. 110) of any particular behaviour, as well as the degree to which individual interests are being subserved. Viewed against the background of the general scarcity of time and energy, which is characteristic of evolutionary processes, individuals should tend to "seek events and repeat acts" (Alexander 1987, p. 110) that increase benefits, such as feeling pleasure, and avoiding painful events. By putting to use these very simple parameters, the human organism may, according to Badcock (1991, p. 96), evaluate the degree to which his major interests are being served by his own or by others' behaviour.

According to Masters, human emotionality can be classified into three major categories, i.e., bonding, attack and flight (Masters 1986, p. 234). Leaving aside suggestions for more differentiated categories, it may be expected from an evolutionary point of view, as Alexander puts it, that emotions should instruct individuals to prefer behaviours that result in benefits, so as to secure their most basic interest, i.e., preserving their lives, as well as serving their fitness. Obviously, however, the system of emotions is much too undifferentiated to provide the individual organism with sufficient information to secure his survival even in rather primitive societal settings. In this regard, ontogenetic learning provides individuals with numerous learned standards, adapting them to prevailing conditions in the social and physical environment. While these standards undoubtedly belong to the system of cognitions, it should be emphasized that the criteria of evaluation employed in cognitive systems pertain to human emotionality, which is a product of human evolution. Viewed against this background, Gray's view seems convincing, according to which the dichotomy between cognitions and emotions must be regarded as entirely artificial (Gray 1985, p. 110), and can only be upheld for analytical purposes. Keeping this in mind, some distinctions between cognitive and emotive processes follow:

1. All human beings are born with a hard-wired emotional system.
2. Emotional processes are located in peculiar regions of the human brain.
3. Certain neurotransmitters and other substances play a decisive role in emotional processes.
4. While the system of cognitions is closely linked to the system of emotions, the former system is, however, less intimately related to the hard-wired foundations of behaviour.

With regard to (1), psychological and other studies have demonstrated, time and again, that human infants are born with a fully developed emotional system. According to MacLean, emotional processes typically are located (2) in the "reptilian brain" (MacLean 1972, p. 137) which is, as the term suggests, one of the phylogenetically oldest regions of the human brain. Recent findings indicate that certain substances, such as benzodiazepine (3), have similar effects in humans, rats and even in fish (Gray 1985, p. 101). Diverse drugs, heroin, cocaine, amphetamine and alcohol, "all have in common that they cause the release of the neurotransmitter dopamine" (Gray 1990, p. 283), a substance that plays a decisive role in aggression. Leaving aside implications for cognitive processes, these findings point to a homology of neurological causes underlying both basic human emotional patterns, as well as those of other creatures, hence to a far-reaching similarity of proximate causes. According to Hendrichs (1988, p. 98), isolated animals show higher levels of general excitement, as compared to their more gregarious conspecifics. These findings may not be easily applicable to human behaviour in the modern world; the situation may, however, have been quite similar in ancestral environments. Like Hendrich's animals, isolated human individuals, exposed to extreme conditions such as ethnic strife or modern warfare, turn to their kinsmen or to their "buddies", trying to reduce the level of excitement.

With regard to the ultimate causes underlying the evolution of human emotionality, it is suggested that in addition to the forces favouring kin selection there must also have been factors at work "increasing the fitness of social groups as collectives" (Wilson and Sober 1994, p. 600). As pointed out by Maynard Smith and Szathmáry, "rowing may be a better model than skulling of the situations in which cooperation evolves. Once it is common, cooperation is evolutionarily stable" (Maynard Smith and Szathmáry 1995, p. 261). As indicated above, unless human individuals cooperated in order to defend their caves or camp sites against predators and against inimical social groups, they could neither have survived under ancestral conditions nor could they have succeeded in hunting down large prey.

According to Ghiglieri, it is likely that in the hominids, as well as in other primates, the cooperative defence of territories dates back as far as two million years (Slurink 1994, p. 464). Similar findings, regarding successful hunting, also emphasize the functional need for cooperation. According to Corning, cooperation in hunting ensures "per capita food acquisition that is greater than each participant can obtain alone" (Corning 1996). Viewed against this time-horizon, it seems reasonable to suggest that cooperation preceeded any deliberate, self-conscious and rational type of decision making. It may therefore also be reasonable to assume that the causes underlying human cooperation must be much older than cognitive processes and are in fact to be found in the phylogenetically much older system of human emotionality. Therefore, it should be expected that by cooperating, i.e., by a form of bonding, individuals are likely to enjoy higher yields of emotional energies as compared to non-cooperative individuals. As stated by Alexander, the emotion of "pleasure" exists in order to stimulate individuals to repeat "beneficial actions" (Alexander 1986, p. 108), i.e., actions which are in the respective individual's interest. From a behavioural point of view it should be stressed once more that human individuals do not always pursue their interests in a rational manner, and neither do they calculate their inclusive fitness. Rather they are induced by "deep-seated emotional dispositions" (Crippen 1994, p. 316) to prefer some behavioural alternatives over others. "The desire to pursue activities that engender pleasure to maximize leisure, ... partake of reproductively inconsequential sexual activity, inter alia may be construed as a proximate condition that overrides the ultimate motive for fitness maximization" (Crippen 1994, p. 323).

Viewed from an evolutionary perspective, the interconnection between various levels of proximate causality, i.e., the neurological processes and the actual behaviours, is in keeping with one's expectations. If groups are in fact, as has been argued here, "vehicles of selection" (Wilson and Sober 1994, p. 600) then it should be expected that natural selection has designed various levels of proximate causality in such a fashion that their combined effects bring about higher yields of emotional energies to partaking individuals than could be obtained by solitary individuals. The following observations seem suited to further endorse the notion of the group as a vehicle of selection. While the first point applies to increases in individual emotional energies during certain types of social interaction, particularly to bonding behaviour, the second point deals with group- level defence against deviant individual members, namely the practice of ostracism.

## In defence of cooperative systems

To understand why some interactions bring about increases in individual supplies of neurotransmitters, such as serotonin, attention should be given to the ritualistic manner of these interactions. As to the increase in neurotransmitters, it has often been observed that close proximity of individuals tends to synchronize individual biorhythms. Given a certain degree of congruence of individual interests, by establishing bonds between any two individuals, both are likely to gain in terms of serotonin and other substances. These observations comply with what one would expect from an evolutionary perspective: If selection favours cooperation, then there must be some sort of proximate causal mechanism inducing individual organisms to search actively to establish bonds with other individuals, preferably with their biological relatives. There are, in fact, some ethological studies, according to which newly born infants actively strive to establish social bonds (Eibl-Eibesfeldt 1984, p. 62), and as Marcus observes, this search is definitely empathic in nature (Marcus 1991, p. 224). The neurological mechanism underlying this empathic search may well be based on levels of serotonin and functionally related neurotransmitters which seem to underlie sensations such as self-confidence or pleasure. According to Alexander (1987, p. 110), pleasure can be regarded as an indicator signalling a positive assessment of any behaviour in terms of reproductive success, therefore the infant should "seek to repeat acts" that are likely to engender pleasure. The infant's empathic search for bonds is in keeping with predictions from kin selection theory, because securing further parental investments certainly is in the child's best interest, whereas from a parent's point of view the child represents a large investment which, in order to enhance inclusive fitness, must be safeguarded. Regarding some more general implications for social life, it is interesting to note that this pattern of emotional processes is not confined to dyadic relations; quite the contrary, it is a common characteristic of most types of social relations.

Turning to the ritualistic character of certain types of social interaction, there seems to be an interesting causal link between the repetition of acts, the perception of reality and the orientation towards future social behaviour. It seems that the stereotyping that is part of ritualistic processes evokes "a single definition of reality and a mutually reinforced emotion" (Collins 1975, p. 95). Given the neurological mechanisms underlying bonding it may be hypothesized that by ritualistic behaviour, individuals are likely to enhance their share of neurotransmitters. Moreover, "single definitions" of reality tend to reduce the time and energy each individual has to invest in trial-and-error behaviour and this is basically why these individuals will be prepared to defend their proximity.

If human individuals do in fact favour living in collectives, in a world of competition they should be prepared to defend these collectives against deviant group members, as well as against external foes. In fact, a number of studies endorse the view that people are prepared to defend the cohesion and integrity of their collective against individual members who by their acts "disrupt the cooperative system of a group" (Barner-Barry 1986, p. 143). Barner-Barry draws this conclusion from studies on the behaviour of school-children who ostracized individuals who, for instance, were overly aggressive. She also suggests that "natural selection tends, in the long run, to pick as real winners the individuals, and then the species, whose genes provide the most inventive and effective ways of getting along" (Barner-Barry 1986, p. 143).

This view is further endorsed by two studies of the practice of blood revenge and ostracism among the Pathan tribes of Pakistan and Afghanistan, as well as by the people of Montenegro. According to Mahdi, the Pathan tribes who are well-known for their bellicosity would ostracize an individual "who is likely to provoke reprisals" (Mahdi 1986, p. 153). Boehm presents similar findings about the practice of ostracism among Montenegrins. These warlike people were likely to reject individuals who would not comply with rules. "The net effect of clan execution was to enhance the reproductive and therefore the political success of the clan, as a group of closely related males who constituted the primary political subunit within the tribe" (Boehm 1986, p. 170). Boehm stresses that while chimpanzees will also avoid individuals, they lack the moral codes that underlie the practice of ostracism and blood revenge in human societies.

Regarding the origins of human cooperation it may be inferred from these studies that people take an active interest in upholding the cooperative system. Unlike individual members of some animal species, human individuals are prepared to ostracize certain group members even prior to the decisive violation of social rules, as the following report on the practice of ostracism and warfare among the Pueblo Indians of the south-western part of North America demonstrates. According to Ellis, "even recently an unusually beautiful woman or successful hunter might be killed – quietly and accidentally – or someone's fine horse be found dead or his big house despoiled" (Ellis 1951, p. 178). In further following Ellis's analysis, the reasons for this peculiar practice of ostracism were: "The imposition of village-sanctioned punishment of competition and individualism no doubt has aided tremendously in dissipation of hostilities officially permitted little other expression" (Ellis 1951, p. 178).

From a theoretical point of view, these ostracism practices may be classified into Alexander's concept of "indirect reciprocity", which occurs "when interested people observe direct reciprocity between others and use the observations to determine who will be their own future associates and how they will interact subsequently with the observed parties" (Alexander 1986, p. 107). Obviously, the practice of ostracism embraces rational calculations of the costs group members may inflict on the group by their behaviour, as well as strategies of avoiding such costs. It is quite evident that this sort of reasoning underlies the Pueblo Indian practice of ostracism: Since the unusual beauty of a woman may cause troubles, why not get rid of her? While from a modern point of view this may seem a very high price for upholding cooperation, these people obviously were prepared to pay it.

A second point worth considering is that the practice of ostracism provides benefits not only to individual members of the respective group, but stabilizes the group's social system as well. It is suggested that the practice of ostracism, as demonstrated in the examples before, seems to be accepted by every individual, because he expects to gain from it. It is as if everybody understands that he would be better off if he would not have to take over the debts caused by other members of the group. On this view, individuals practice ostracism because they expect, by avoiding fights, to benefit by saving time and energy. Furthermore, by practising ostracism, individuals demonstrate an active interest in keeping the group's system of cooperation and obligations alive.

From the viewpoint of kin selection theory, these proximate mechanisms are fully in keeping with this theory's predictions. Individuals are willing to cooperate because they may expect benefits from this behaviour, and in cases when other individuals are likely to endanger these benefits, they are ostracized. In this type of situation individuals behave as if they were totally aware of their major interests and would pursue them in a rational manner.

In order to defend their individual interests, they join with others pursuing similar interests, while ostracizing individuals who are likely to conflict with them: "The net effect of clan execution was to enhance the reproductive and therefore political success of the clan, as a group of closely related males.... This means that capital punishment was being used in a political and legal context to assure the biological and political integrity of the group – just as is done by modern nations when they are at war" (Boehm 1986, p. 170).

Everybody in the clan is likely to be more secure if individuals are ostracized who by their behaviour are likely to impose debts upon the group. For instance, the institution of blood revenge poses a real danger to every member of a traditional society, burdening him with the obligation of washing off a kinsman's blood. Therefore, pre-emptive ostracism serves as a safeguard against people likely to embroil the group in costly conflicts with reckless behaviour.

## In defence of individual interests

The foregoing has made clear that due to the selective advantages of cooperation, groups are something real. Taking the "reality" of the social group as a given, the following section will raise the question as to why certain types of social groups prevail universally, such as small band-type associations, whereas others do not. While many social scientists may agree with the notion that small band-type associations were ubiquitous in the evolutionary past, many deny their vitality in modern society, as is obvious in social scientists' adherence to the *Gemeinschaft* vs. *Gesellschaft* dichotomy.

Concerning the impact of small bands on modern life, T. Crippen (1994, p. 318) suggests that "behavioral dispositions that, in hunter-gatherer environments, may have enhanced inclusive fitness no longer necessarily serve the reproductive interests of the individual." While it cannot be denied that there are major differences between reproductive behaviour in "primitive" as compared with "modern" society (p. 320), as well as numerous differences in societal complexity and other peculiarities of modern social life, a preference for small band-type associations prevails. Below the surface of "sociocultural environments that are vastly different from our hunter-gatherer forebears" (p. 318), modern everyday people prefer to live in small associations over the anonymity of large-scale social associations, just as much as their ancestors did. To be sure, nobody in modern society can avoid becoming the object of mass organizations which, due to their economic and political power, control most resources. Nevertheless, it should be emphasized once more that even the most powerful large-scale organizations have to rely on their members' allegiance. According to a number of studies, individuals tend to establish "informal" or "primary" relations even within the boundaries of the most dispassionate and strictly objective organizations of the modern world (Meyer 1991). Regarding the purposes pursued by individuals in informal relations, most students agree that by stressing the intimate and emotional nature of their relations, individuals hope to stabilize their position *vis-à-vis* formal authorities of large-scale organizations. Typically, social power and authority are located in the upper echelons of modern organizations, depriving individual members of most means of exerting countervailing power.

Since from an evolutionary point of view, safeguarding one's interests is the single most important objective of individual behaviour, it should be expected that individual members of large-scale organizations strive hard to establish some sort of countervailing power against formal authority because this is the only way they can hope to secure their interests. Of course, humans pursue power politics in many ways, sometimes in a more rational way, sometimes in a less rational manner, establishing temporary or lasting alliances, in order to curb the power of élite groups. As compared with some of the more conscious and rational strategies, it seems that the establishment of informal groups relies mostly on subconscious and emotional motives, calling into existence social patterns designed as if their instrumental usefulness had been known from the beginning. It should be emphasized once again that despite this instrumental usefulness, the existence of these patterns is not due to the rational pursuit of interests, but to some general principles of human emotionality. One of the proximate causes underlying this paradoxical social effect may be that in contrast to large-scale associations, there usually are no major differences among individual members of these unplanned social structures in terms of interests. Another proximate cause may be that members can reassure themselves of their common interests *vis-à-vis* the external social world, by exchanging cultural markers in a ritualistic manner.

A study that sheds some light on these preferences asked "with whom the respondents had close emotional ties" (Ike 1987, p. 221). Respondents named a limited number of people, which averaged 10.9. While there is some disagreement as to the numerical limitations to membership in this type of association, there is nearly unanimous agreement that the number of members should not be below ten, and not much higher than thirty individuals.

There is an interesting coincidence with the average number of people living in hunter-gatherer societies, where, according to Ike, numbers range between twenty and forty individuals (Ike 1987, p. 223). In summarizing it may be suggested that, according to these findings, human beings universally seek to establish intimate and emotionally rewarding social relations. It is further suggested that this preference is established upon biological programmes, parts of which have been dealt with in this paper.

# Conclusions

Returning to the main topic of the role of kinship and ethnicity in risky transactions, this paper provides some clues as to the universal preference for living in small groups. According to numerous studies, this preference prevailed throughout most of human history. Obviously, however, the onset of the Neolithic Revolution brought decisive changes in its wake, favouring life in highly differentiated and very complex societies. While the trend towards complexity must have been caused by the selective advantages of such novel types of systemic integration as the state (Carneiro 1987), the general evolutionary causes underlying social integration prevailed. In some of the more remote areas of the world, however, social evolution never brought complexity above that found in tribal organization. For instance, neither in the case of Afghanistan, nor of Pakistan, have central governments gained full control over the Pathan tribesmen (Mahdi 1986), whose system of law and other traditional ways have prevailed in their tribal areas. The recent upsurge of ethnically motivated strife in some parts of former Yugoslavia illustrates that people in Europe, too, are willing to return to ethnicity as the major foundation of their political organization, whenever the weakening of central governments poses a threat to their security, i.e., to one of their major interests. In view of these recent social developments the question may be raised, as to why progressive social differentiation was the course of development for some societies, if the time-honoured patterns of traditional society, with kinship and ethnicity as the major sources of solidarity, prove to be more successful in some respects?

It seems that the views of some of the classics of sociology, such as H. Spencer and E. Durkheim, still offer valid insights: Social differentiation and growing complexity prevail over traditional society because their efficiency in terms of time and energy is much higher than that provided by traditional social patterns. Due to the large quantities of time and energy released by complex social organization, modern society can employ specialists in such fields as science or military organizations, who in turn provide the means for the domination of traditional societies. Paradoxically, however, the larger yield of time and energy typical of progressive systemic integration, is often accompanied by decreases in social integration, a problem that modern society tries to cope with by establishing increasingly complex systems of social control. These systems of control, however, have to employ ever larger amounts of social power, as well as other means of manipulation, in order to secure the loyalty of members. Despite the complexity of these systems of control, they are extremely vulnerable in risky situations, as will be pointed out in the following section.

According to some social studies on the behavioural reactions of soldiers exposed to combat during the Korean war, individual soldiers tended to concentrate their social interactions on one particular individual: "Everyone was a buddy, but one man was usually more so. The one man toward whom the choice was directed, however, did not usually return the choice verbally. Buddy choices were private decisions and consequently never threatened the solidarity of the squad or platoon" (Little 1964, p. 198). In these extremely risky situations individuals tended to rely on dyadic cliques, thereby, consciously or not, trying to reduce uncertainties about their buddies' behaviour to a minimum. As one of the soldiers put it: "That way we got to feel that we were in the same family" (Little 1964, p. 199). In a manner similar to that of the tribal people mentioned above, individual soldiers behaved as if they were rationally planning to enhance their greatest interest, i.e., their security, by establishing the most reliable type of social relations with one particular individual. Military authority would certainly have opposed buddy relations, unless it was made quite clear that these relations were no danger to the solidarity of the military unit as a whole. According to Little, individual soldiers, as well as army echelons, seem to have realized that it was both in the individual's interest, as well as in the army's interest, to reduce as much as possible the risks imposed by combat. "The primary basis for solidarity in the platoon and company was the recognition of mutual risk. A set of norms so regulated their behaviour as to minimize that risk" (Little 1964, p. 218). With regard to the general problem of human behaviour in risky situations three lessons may be inferred from this study:

1. That human individuals will actively strive to reduce risks to their major interests. One way to reduce risks is to harmonize individual interests by establishing emotionally tightly knit social groups, if environmental circumstances allow.
2. Despite the evolutionarily favoured size and structure of social relations, they are extremely flexible, both with regard to size and to structure.
3. Individuals will try to find means of adapting their actual social behaviour to environmental conditions.

Returning to kin groups in risky transactions, these considerations may well shed some light on the modern situation. It seems that minority groups in modern society, due to their relatively small numbers, continue to enjoy all the advantages in terms of emotional and social stability that have been pointed out in this paper. Due to their tightly knit normative infrastructure, firmly established on ethnic, sometimes also on religious foundations, ethnic groups immigrating into foreign countries often are quite successful in "middleman" activities (Landa 1981), and are also easily adaptable to any kind of clandestine operations. Viewed against the background of evolutionary reasoning, the growing complexity of economic and political relations may be understood as a process that adds new niches which in turn can be settled by populations, specializing in the sort of activities favoured by prevailing conditions. Given the evolutionary background of human sociality, it may be legitimate to predict that despite the dynamic impact exerted by modern individualism, ethnicity, as well as small-band behaviour will often prevail because immigrant groups expect more benefits from this behaviour than from adopting the ways of the general population.

The evolutionary causes underlying human social behaviour are, however, not restricted to social interactions based on kinship and ethnicity in the modern world. As illustrated by the behaviour of soldiers in combat, human individuals seek to establish quasi-kin, or family-like relations, whenever such relations hold out a prospect of enhancing individual interests. Individual soldiers strove hard to establish intimate relations with a few, very reliable people because in this most risky situation, this seemed the best way of providing for one's interest in surviving the risks posed by the combat situation. As pointed out above, the military organization despite its urge for total control of social behaviour accepted buddy relations, because it realized that this behaviour served its requirements to some extent too.

Returning, finally, to the relationship between system-integration and social-integration, it may be summarized that an evolutionary view reveals some of the causes underlying human willingness to cooperate. In this regard it should be stressed once more that human preparedness for cooperation must take human striving for survival into consideration. People actively seek to establish mutually reliable social relations, because in a world of competition this seems to be the best way for them to secure survival. Once reciprocity has been established, individuals may enjoy various emotional benefits, as well as other advantages of synergistic cooperation provided that they manage to mutually reassure their partners of a basic harmony of interests. Obviously, however, individuals are willing to ostracize even kinsmen if they seem to pose a danger to their interests. With regard to the emergent properties of normative phenomena which are being emphasized by the Durkheimian tradition, there are some interesting implications. Unlike this tradition, an evolutionary view brings causal impacts into focus that are much older than the normative phenomena themselves. It follows that evolutionary biology and other life sciences can shed some light on these causal impacts and should therefore be integrated into a new paradigm of the social sciences that will provide fresh insights into the underpinnings of the universal preference for living in small bands, as well as for various aspects of kinship and ethnicity.

# References

Alexander, R. (1986). Ostracism and indirect reciprocity: The reproductive significance of humour. In *Ostracism: A social and biological phenomenon* (eds M. Gruter and R.D. Masters). *Ethology & Sociobiology*, **7**(3/4) (Special issue), 105–23.

Alexander, R. (1987). *The biology of moral systems.* Aldine de Gruyter, New York.

Axelrod, R. (1984). *The evolution of cooperation.* Basic Books, New York.

Badcock, C. (1991). *Evolution and individual behavior. An introduction to human sociobiology.* Blackwell, Oxford.

Barash, D.P. (1978). Evolution as a paradigm for behavior. In *Sociobiology and human nature* (eds M.S. Gregory, A. Silvers, and D. Sutch). Jossey-Bass, San Francisco, pp. 13–33.

Barash, D.P. (1980). *Soziobiologie und Verhalten.* Parey, Berlin/Hamburg.

Barner-Barry, C. (1986). Rob: Children's tacit use of peer ostracism to control aggressive behavior. In *Ostracism: A social and biological phenomenon.* (eds M. Gruter and R.D. Masters). *Ethology & Sociobiology*, **7**(3/4) (Special issue), 133–47.

Berghe, P.L. van den (1981). *The ethnic phenomenon.* Elsevier, New York.

Berghe, P.L. van den (1983). Class, race and ethnicity in Africa. *Ethnic and Racial Studies*, **6**, 221–36.

Bloom, H. (1996). Beyond the supercomputer: Social groups as self-invention machines. Paper presented at the 19th Annual Meeting of the European Sociobiological Society, Alfred, New York, 23–25 July 1996.

Boehm, C. (1986). Capital punishment in tribal Montenegro: Implications for law, biology, and theory of social control. In *Ostracism: A social and biological phenomenon* (eds M. Gruter and R.D. Masters). *Ethology & Sociobiology*, **7**(3/4) (Special issue),157–73.

Brown, D.E. (1991). *Human universals.* McGraw Hill, New York.

Carneiro, R.L. (1987). The evolution of complexity in human societies and its mathematical expression. *International Journal of Comparative Sociology*, **28**(3/4), 111–28.

Collins, R. (1975). *Conflict sociology. Toward an explanatory science.* Academic Press, New York.

Collins, R. (1986). How to incorporate sociophysiology into sociological theory. Paper presented at Stanford University, California.

Corning, P.A. (1983). *The synergism hypothesis. A theory of progressive evolution.* McGraw Hill, New York.

Corning, P.A. (1996). Holistic Darwinism: Group selection and the bioeconomics of evolution. Paper presented at the 19th Annual Meeting of The European Sociobiological Society, Alfred, New York, 23–25 July 1996.

Crippen, T. (1994). Toward a neo-Darwinian sociology: Its nomological principles and some illustrative applications. *Sociological Perspectives*, **37**, 309–35.

Daly, M., and Wilson, M. (1988). *Homicide.* Aldine de Gruyter, New York.

Dawkins, R. (1986). *The blind watchmaker*. Longman House, Burnt Mill, Harlow, Essex.

Durkheim, E. (1980). *Die Regeln der soziologischen Methode*. Luchterhand, Neuwied/Darmstadt.

Eibl-Eibesfeldt, I. (1972/1970). *Love and hate: The natural history of behavior patterns*. Holt, Rinehart & Winston, New York. Original German edn (1970): *Liebe und Hass. Zur Naturgeschichte elementarer Verhaltensweisen*. Piper, München.

Eibl-Eibesfeldt, I. (1984). *Die Biologie des menschlichen Verhaltens. Grundriß der Humanethologie*. Piper, München.

Ellis, F.H. (1951). Patterns of aggression and the war cult in South-Western Pueblos. *South-Western Journal of Anthropology*, 7, 177–201.

Gazzaniga, M.S. (1992). *Nature's mind. The biological roots of thinking, emotions, sexuality, language and intelligence*. Penguin, Harmondsworth, Middlesex.

Gouldner, A. (1960). The norm of reciprocity: A preliminary statement. *American Sociological Review*, **25**(2), 161–78.

Gray, J.A. (1985). A whole and its part: Behaviour, the brain, cognition, and emotion. *Bulletin of the British Psychological Society*, **38**, 99–112.

Gray, J.A. (1990). Brain systems that mediate both emotion and cognition. *Cognition and emotion*, **4**(3), 269–88.

Haig, D. (1993). Genetic conflicts in human pregnancy. *The Quarterly Review of Biology*, **68**(4), 495–532.

Hendrichs, H. (1988). *Lebensprozesse und wissenschaftliches Denken*. Alber, Freiburg.

Ike, B.W. (1987). Man's limited sympathy as a consequence of his evolution in small kin groups. In *The sociobiology of ethnocentrism* (eds V. Reynolds, V. Falger, and I. Vine). Croom Helm, London and Sydney, pp. 216–35.

Küppers, B.-O. (1986). *Der Ursprung biologischer Information. Zur Naturphilosophie der Lebensentstehung*. Piper, München.

Landa, J.T. (1981). A theory of the ethnically homogeneous middleman group: An institutional alternative to contract law. *Journal of Legal Studies*, **10**, 349–62.

Lenski, G. (1966). *Power and privilege. A theory of social stratification*. McGraw Hill, New York.

Little, R.W. (1964). Buddy relations and combat performance. In *The new military. Changing patterns of organization* (ed. M. Janowitz). Russell Sage Foundation, New York, pp.195–225.

Lockwood, D. (1964). Social integration and system integration. In *Explorations in social science* (eds G.K. Zollschan and W. Hirsch). Routledge, London, pp.244–57.

MacDonald, K. (1995). The establishment and maintenance of socially imposed monogamy in Western Europe. *Politics and the Life Sciences*, **14**(1), 3–24.

MacLean, P.D. (1972). Cerebral evolution and emotional processes: New findings on the striatal complex. *Annals of the New York Academy of Sciences*, **193**, 137–49.

Mahdi, N.Q. (1986). Pukhtunwali: Ostracism and honor among the Pathan Hill tribes. In *Ostracism: A social and biological phenomenon* (eds M. Gruter and R.D. Masters). *Ethology & Sociobiology*, **7**(3/4) (Special issue), 147–57.

Marcus, G.E. (1991). Emotions and politics. Hot cognitions and the rediscovery of passion. *Social Science Information*, **30**, 195–233.

Masters, R.D. (1986). The biology of social participation. In *Ostracism: A social and biological phenomenon* (eds M. Gruter and R.D. Masters). *Ethology & Sociobiology*, **7**(3/4)(Special issue), 231–47.

Maynard Smith, J., and Szathmáry, E. (1995). *The major transitions in evolution.* W.H. Freeman/Spektrum, Oxford, New York, and Heidelberg.

Mayr, E. (1982). *The growth of biological thought. Diversity, evolution and inheritance.* Harvard University Press, Cambridge, MA.

McGuire, M.T., and Raleigh, M.J. (1986). Animal analogues of ostracism: Biological mechanisms and social consequences. In *Ostracism: A social and biological phenomenon* (eds R.D. Masters and M. Gruter). *Ethology & Sociobiology*, **7**(3/4)(Special issue),53–67.

Meyer, P. (1991). Soziale Gruppen. In *Basale Soziologie: Hauptprobleme.* (eds H. Reimann et al.). Westdeutscher Verlag, Opladen, pp. 75–90.

Miller, T.C. (1993). The duality of human nature. *Politics and the Life Sciences,* **12**(2), 221–41.

Münch, R. (1995). Elemente einer Theorie der Integration moderner Gesellschaften. Eine Bestandsaufnahme. *Berliner Journal für Soziologie,* **1**, 5–24.

Preuschoft, H., and Preuschoft, S. (1989). Protokultur: Zur Evolution der menschlichen Kultur. In *The nature of culture.* (ed. W.A. Koch). Brockmeyer Studienverlag, Bochum, pp. 542–77.

Riedl, R. (1975). *Die Ordnung des Lebendigen. Systembedingungen der Evolution.* Parey, Berlin/ Hamburg.

Salter, F.K. (1997). A defence and extension of Pierre van den Berghe's theory of ethnic nepotism. Unpublished paper.

Shaw, R.P., and Wong, Y. (1989). *Genetic seeds of warfare. Evolution, nationalism, and patriotism.* Unwin Hyman, Boston.

Slurink, P. (1994). Causes for our complete dependence on culture. In *The ethological roots of culture* (eds R.A. Gardner et al.) Kluwer, Amsterdam, pp. 461–74.

Smillie, D. (1995). Darwin's two paradigms: An 'opportunistic' approach to natural selection theory. *Journal of Social and Evolutionary Systems,* **18**(3), 231–55.

Spencer, H. (1974). *The evolution of society.* Selections from Herbert Spencer's *Principles of sociology* (ed. R. Carneiro). Chicago University Press, Chicago.

Tajfel, H. (1981). *Human groups and social categories: Studies in social psychology.* Cambridge University Press, Cambridge, UK.

Trivers, R.L. (1978). The evolution of reciprocal altruism. In *Readings in sociobiology* (eds T.H. Clutton-Brock and R.H. Harvey). W.H. Freeman, Reading and San Francisco, pp. 189–227.

Wang, X.T. (1996). Evolutionary hypotheses of risk-sensitive choice: Age differences and perspective change. *Ethology & Sociobiology,* **17**, 1–15.

West-Eberhard, M.J. (1988). Phenotypic plasticity and "genetic" theories of insect sociality. In *Evolution of social behavior and integrative levels* (eds G. Greenberg and E. Tobach). Lawrence Erlbaum, Hillsdale, NJ, pp. 123–33.

Wiessner, P. (1982). Risk, reciprocity and social influence on !Kung San economies. In *Politics and history in band societies* (eds E. Peacock and R. Lee). Cambridge University Press, Cambridge, UK, pp. 61–84.

Wilson, D.S., and Sober, E. (1994). Reintroducing group selection to the human behavioral sciences. *Behavioral and Brain Sciences,* **17**, 585–654.

## CHAPTER 13

# ETHNIC NEPOTISM AS A TWO-EDGED SWORD

## THE RISK-MITIGATING ROLE OF ETHNICITY AMONG MAFIOSI, NATIONALIST FIGHTERS, MIDDLEMEN, AND DISSIDENTS

### *Frank K. Salter*

Intergroup antagonism is thus the inevitable concomitant and counterpart of ingroup solidarity. (G.P. Murdock, *Social Structure*[1])

Since altruism will evolve more rapidly the greater the relatedness of individuals in a group, this model would suggest that self-sacrifice and xenophobic aggression are two sides of the same evolutionary coin, certainly a familiar enough picture in human history. (R. Fox and U. Fleising, *Human Ethology*[2])

You know, he's not sure of me 'cause I'm not, I'm not, I'm not Italian. You know what I mean? (Eliot Weismann[3])

The Anglo-Saxons do it, the Jews do it, so do the Hindus and the Muslims... . Networking is the natural thing to do. (Lee Kuan Yew[4])

Let the saints be joyful with glory: let them rejoice in their beds.
Let the praises of God be in their mouth: and a two-edged sword in their hands;
To be avenged of the heathen: and to rebuke the people;
To bind their kings in chains: and their nobles with links of iron.

(Psalm 149, v. 5)

# Introduction

In this chapter I argue that ethnic solidarity can be turned to offensive as well as defensive purposes because loyalty mitigates the risk of many kinds of group enterprises. I illustrate this thesis – that ethnic nepotism is a two-edged sword – using the literature on ethnic mafias, nationalist fighters, ethnic middlemen groups, and ethnic dissidents. I discuss possible methods for structuring societies so that they gain the benefits of solidarity without the costs of aggressive behaviour towards minorities and other societies. Evolutionary theory features throughout the discussion, since it is an aid to understanding the double-edged effect and designing social structures to deal with it.

# Risk of defection and ethnic nepotism theory

It is well recognized in the social sciences that ties, notably between kith, kin and co-ethnics, increase trust and trustworthiness, and thus mitigate breach of agreement. Intuitively, the strength of a tie is indicated by the "amount of time, the emotional intensity, the intimacy (mutual confiding), and the reciprocal services" characterizing relations between two individuals (Granovetter 1977/1973, p. 348). Granovetter observes that ties produce trust. Bond partners are not only trusted, but are usually trustworthy, because of the altruism – unreciprocated giving – that is cued by emotional bonds. Tie partners show some non-calculative commitment to each other, a tendency to support, to take risks for, and to show emotional commitment for one another or group interests as a whole. As such, ties are useful where contract law or other methods of enforcement do not apply or are weak, such as in illicit business and middleman trading (Bonacich 1973; Landa 1981, 1994; Williamson 1996). Even weak ties, such as those between acquaintances, can become the basis of some level of trust and reliability. "Leaders … have little motivation to be responsive or even trustworthy toward those to whom they have no direct or indirect connection" (Granovetter 1977/1973, p. 361). Evolutionary theory helps enlarge this insight to the many kinds of risky transactions facilitated by ethnic ties.[5]

It is a commonplace that kinship increases altruism, a willingness to share resources, and even sacrifice personal welfare on the other's behalf. Sociobiological theory explains this as the product of the evolutionary mechanism of inclusive fitness. According to this theory, nepotistic favouritism was adaptive in primordial environments because it increased the reproductive fitness of copies of the actor's genes found in close kin. All the copies of an individual's distinctive genes found in his own and other genomes and shared by common descent comprise his inclusive fitness. At the genetic level of analysis, close kin have significant genetic interests in each other's reproduction.

> [H]umans like other organisms[s] are so evolved that their "interests" are reproductive. Said differently, the interests of an individual human (i.e., the directions of its striving) are expected to be toward ensuring the indefinite survival of its genes and their copies, whether these are resident in the individual, its descendants, or its collateral relatives.... . We need not be concerned with the possible argument that interests are only definable in terms of what people consciously believe are their interests or intentions. Biologists continually investigate the life interests of nonhuman organisms while lacking knowledge on this point and nonhuman organisms live out their lives serving their interest[s] without knowing in the human sense what those interests are (Alexander 1995/1985, pp. 182–3).

Pierre van den Berghe has extended inclusive fitness theory to argue that under some conditions it also explains trust between co-ethnics. In *The Ethnic Phenomenon* (1981), van den Berghe developed a sociobiological theory to explain several aspects of ethnic affairs. He argued that ethnic and racial groups are attenuated forms of kinship, real or putative. Favouritism shown towards other group members is thus explicable as nepotism, manifested in emotions and commitment homologous to those found in familial affairs, which van den Berghe had previously analysed sociobiologically (1979). Elsewhere I review the criticisms that have been made of the theory, and find them generally misdirected or erroneous (Salter 2001). Even cultural and constructionist accounts of ethnic change, offered as strong refutations of biological social theory in general, are on closer scrutiny amenable to van den Berghe's analysis (see below under "Social technology"). I conclude the review thus:

> Pierre van den Berghe's ethnic nepotism theory is supported by ethnographic data on the centrality of kinship as an organizing principle able to release altruism in hunter-gatherer societies. Unlike instrumental models, the theory explains the powerful emotions, both positive and negative, that punctuate ethnic affairs. By drawing on evolutionary theories of social evolution, the theory offers ultimate explanations of the proximate mechanisms analyzed in the nonevolutionary social science literature. It is compatible with a version of constructionism that builds upon, instead of ignoring, the reality of innate universals of human nature. As such, ethnic nepotism theory can explain rapid changes in ethnic mobilization, but predicts slower changes in ethnic boundaries. It also allows for arbitrary content in ethnic identity, but posits a ranking of group markers as an evolved mechanism for excluding free riders from altruistic relationships. Ethnic nepotism theory is thus compatible with the cross-cultural semiotics, especially the ethology of ethnicity. Highest priority is given to markers of high heritability, explaining the invidious nature of inter-racial relations compared to intercultural relations.... . Despite possible incompleteness, ethnic nepotism theory is parsimonious in explaining several key features of ethnic and race relations, and is compatible with or falsifies different approaches held by various critics

to be inimicable to it. It is unique in offering an evolutionary causal analysis that also explains kin altruism in non human species, thus achieving a level of generality not achieved by nonevolutionary theories. In addition it explains central aspects of the macro-phenomenon of ethnicity in terms of the micro levels of kin selection. The theory is thus unique in offering vertical as well as horizontal generality; vertically by extending causal analysis from the macro to micro levels, thence to phylogeny and natural selection; horizontally by virtue of its cross-cultural scope. Ethnic nepotism theory provides insights that constrain and refine nonbiological theories of both ethnic change and primordialism (Salter 2001, pp. 68–9).

As noted, one strength of ethnic nepotism theory is that it draws on biological theory so general that it encompasses the sociality of nonhuman animals, including apes and social insects (E. O. Wilson 1975). By comparison, non-biological social science theory is limited to a single culture or era or, rarely, to the species. Despite its generality, the modern evolutionary approach recognizes humans to be a special case by virtue of their strong reliance on culture, a theme to be developed below in the section on "Social technology".

## The hierarchy of bond and tie-strengths

The evolutionary approach predicts, rather than merely acknowledging, a hierarchy of tie-strength and trust in which risk of defection increases with decreasing relatedness, going from the relatively strong altruism engendered by familial bonds, through moderate altruism between extended kin, to local community (Landa's clan and village layers of trustworthiness – this volume), then the weaker altruism engendered by ethnic identification (perceived similarity of descent), to the even weaker but ubiquitous altruism shown between individuals merely on the basis of physical, cultural, or psychological similarity, and finally decreasing to relations between anonymous individuals drawn from different races and cultures. Ethnic nepotism theory allows ethnicity and similarity to be placed on a continuum with kinship because it holds that the underlying motivations are homologous, though differing greatly in strength. They are all instances of kin selection evolved in the small-group hunter-gatherer milieu.

Evidence for evolved gradients in tie strength is widespread. The gradient between nuclear family and extended family is evidenced by the universal tendency of extended families to decompose into nuclear families under economic and social pressures. This occurs as traditional societies industrialize, and new economic pressures arise that disadvantage large family units, for example state and industrial policies that place a premium on work-force mobility. At the same time, individuals are freed of familial responsibilities by changing mores and government welfare, and the process can continue to atomize society to one-person households. However, the nuclear family has proved an attractive social unit, for which individuals are willing to make considerable sacrifices. Even in the most individualistic of societies, such as the late twentieth century United States of America and Britain, altruism decreases as kinship recedes, as measured by the value of gifts; simultaneously, the likelihood of peer reciprocity increases with closeness of kinship (Caplow 1982). Further evidence comes from anthropology. When hunter-gatherers experience sparse resources, as during the dry season in the Kalahari, bands disperse into nuclear family groups (Wiessner 1981). Perhaps the best-known alleged case of environmentally induced atomization is Turnbull's (1961) reports of the Ik, an African tribal people who had been driven off their land and had their way of life severely disrupted. Turnbull reported radical individualism and breakdown of social bonds, to the extent where children were left to care for themselves. Yet in revealing passages he describes nurturance, such as parents carrying their children.

A striking example of the gradient between familial and friendship bonds comes from an ingenious analysis of risk-taking in a life-and-death emergency. The study suggests the existence of a tie (or altruism) gradient between kith and kin. A fire in a large holiday complex on the Isle of Man in 1973 killed fifty people, because the exits became choked with the sudden rush. Of groups separated at the time the alarm was given, 50 percent of families took the risk of finding one another before emerging, while none of the non-family groups did so. Initially, 66 percent of the families and 54 percent of the non-family groups were together. While over two thirds of the families emerged intact, only one quarter of the non-families did so (Sime 1983). Sime's analysis bypasses the epistemological problems of deception and justificatory self-deception inherent in the self-report method (Alexander 1979; Lockard and Paulhus 1988). When it came to the "crunch", the people caught in this emergency showed a greater willingness to take risks for kin than for kith.

The gradient in tie-strength between extended family and local community is attested by anthropological evidence that village conflict and fissioning in small-scale societies tend to occur along kinship lines (for Yanomami see Chagnon 1980; for New Guinea see Koch 1974; W. Schiefenhövel personal communication[6]). The next tie gradient, between intra- and inter-ethnic relations, is evidenced by a mass of examples, including those of mafias, nationalism, ethnic middlemen, and ethnic dissidents, to be discussed in this chapter.

Self-report studies conducted by Burnstein and colleagues have compiled evidence indicating that the more biologically important a decision, such as that involving a life-and-death risk or the allocation of large resources, the more likely individuals are to take account of relatedness in apportioning support (Burnstein et al. 1994, also this volume). These findings are consistent with a hierarchy of tie strengths based on relatedness. They also help explain the tendency of ethnic solidarity to rise in response to perceived threat. A clear and present danger to an ethnic group as a whole is analogous to a threat to a whole primordial band. In both cases there is a large fitness risk to the typical member[7] despite varying relatedness within the group, a reason to suppose that group loyalty is especially adaptive in times of crisis. The hierarchy of ties is most likely to map relatedness when each tie-gradient is tested under conditions of risk to actors' inclusive fitness.

The gradient between intra- and inter-ethnic relationships has been challenged by Silverman and Case (1998) on the basis of historical and social psychological research. Elsewhere, I offer a detailed critique of their position (Salter 2001). Suffice it here to remark that the strongest part of their argument derives from a social psychological experiment that found only weak ethnic nepotism among a sample of Canadian university students. Given the multicultural ideology now dominant in Canada, it is surprising that any ethnic loyalty was voiced at all, even though confidentiality was assured. In such matters, behavioural research is more reliable than a questionnaire. There is much indirect behavioural evidence that altruism is stronger within such groups than between them. For example, economists have documented the reluctance of taxpayers to contribute to public goods such as schools, libraries, and welfare when other ethnic and racial groups will make use of them (Alesina et al. 1997; Easterly and Devine 1997). Nevertheless, Silverman and Case make the important point that ethnic solidarity can be quite weak. Inter-ethnic and interracial relations can be neutral or amicable, and friendships and marriages can span group boundaries; but ethnic solidarity can rise to overwhelm these ties in a short period of time, as demonstrated by the dismemberment of Yugoslavia in the 1990s. Still, ethnic ties are not nearly as fixed as family bonds, indicating a powerful role for culture. This theme will be taken up presently.

At the weak end of the tie continuum, several studies have found that similar individuals are more likely to marry than dissimilar individuals. Marriage predicts or is due to bonding and altruism. Among the traits on which spouses positively assort two components of ethnicity – race and religion – are among the most predictive (Thiessen and Gregg 1980; Rushton 1995). The bonds of marriage are much stronger than any resulting from similarity alone; but the similarity effect is strong enough to result in assortative pairings. The same appears to be true of friendship which, like marriage, also predicts altruism. Rushton (1989) found that in an English sample, friends were more genetically similar than were non-friends. The effect even holds within families, identical twins being more cooperative than non-identical twins (Segal 1988). The similarity effect could be due to a type of kin recognition (see comments by Hepper and Tooby, and Cosmides in Rushton 1989). The attraction of similar individuals to form altruistic relationships could operate to prop up group cohesion and firm up group boundaries when there are substantial group differences along assortative characteristics (Rushton 1995, pp. 85–8).

## Social technology version of ethnic nepotism theory

Members of a family usually develop trusting relationships in the absence of special cultural institutions. Despite great cultural diversity, the family unit – nuclear or extended – proliferates in all social systems. Friends also negotiate relationships of trust and altruism, though as we have seen, friendship is usually less binding than familial bonds. Ties tend to weaken as kinship recedes. In anonymous mass societies, commercial and bureaucratic interactions are usually conducted between non-kin and are often impersonal, with relatively little role for social ties (Eibl-Eibesfeldt 1989, Section 8.2; Weber 1964). The weakness of ties in mass-market economies creates a need for legal guarantees (Williamson 1975; Landa 1994).

Hence culture influences and can substitute in specific ways for evolved social ties, allowing community (*Gemeinschaft*) to give way to contract-based society (*Gesellschaft*; Tönnies 1887).

Ethnic middleman groups, mafias, and nationalist movements place considerable reliance on *Gemeinschaft*, which is interesting because, by itself, ethnic identity elicits only weak group solidarity. Group identity is a necessary but not a sufficient condition for heightened solidarity. How then does solidarity get raised high enough to become a reliable basis for trust in risky group endeavours? The answer I want to suggest is artifice.

Solidarity rises and falls with circumstance, mainly threats to the group, but solidarity must be organized if it is to be maintained at high levels during periods of intermittent threat. Ethnic identities by themselves require less artifice. Primordial ethnic identities – groups with consciousness of shared descent – are self-organizing and have developed and persisted in small communities over the millennia. Since they exist objectively, they can be discovered. The ethnic identities forming the core of the modern nation-state also have objective origins but have been articulated back to the people by intellectuals, who tend to edit, homogenize, and elaborate their group's history and cultural traditions (Anderson 1983; Smith 1986). While aspects of modern ethnic identity are "imagined", to use Anderson's term, ethnic boundaries usually have a basis in fact. By comparison, solidarity is much more sensitive to cultural and organizational factors (Salter 2001; Spicer 1971). As an example, consider perceived threats to the group, the most efficacious of mobilizing agents. These can be delivered situationally. Members of an ethnic or racial group might personally experience discrimination or other aggression directed at them on the basis of their group identity, or they might receive reports of an insult directed at the whole group from some outside antagonist. Threats can also be fictive, in the form of false reports, or be delivered culturally in the form of folk stories and rituals commemorating great victories or defeats. In his study of persistent ethnic identities Spicer (1971) found that these groups reproduced myths and rituals containing accumulated symbols of challenges to the group, "oppositional symbols". Leaders can also be decisive in mobilizing a people by reporting real or fictive threats, and amending the group's tradition to include oppositional symbols.

The foregoing can be interpreted in the parlance of social technology theory (Salter 1995). Social technologies are ideologies, rituals, organizations, and symbols that shape social behaviour in a functional or goal-directed manner. They are deliberately constructed for a purpose or selected in cultural evolution because they have some functional outcome.[8] Although social technologies are culturally produced and disseminated, they manipulate innate behaviour patterns that are genetically reproduced. Techniques for raising ethnic solidarity operate by releasing kin altruism and directing it towards the wider group. This might begin by demarcating or clarifying a group's identity when it is fragmented or poorly articulated. Rituals and ideology define group membership by reference to cultural or physical markers. These group markers are analogous to the markers found in other animal species that facilitate recognition of kin and species members (van den Berghe 1981). Markers are shared by most or all group members. Non-racial markers include shared territory as well as shared cultural features such as language and religion (Shaw and Wong 1989). Ancestral homeland is a recurring feature in persistent ethnic groups (Connor 1985). Markers often designate relatedness via shared group membership and ancestral group myths, including founding heroes and gods, ancestral saints and wise men, originating tribes, cousin peoples, shared blood, common appearance, language and habits. The resulting group identity is that of a greatly extended family, evidenced by the ubiquitous role in tribal and ethnic cultures of origin myths and beliefs about common descent (Connor 1993, 1994; Eibl-Eibesfeldt 1989; Horowitz 1985).

By the time of the ancient Greeks and Romans, some principles of ethnic nepotism were being deployed in diplomacy, helping to forge alliances (Jones 1999). Group identity as extended family opens the way for other social technologies that mobilize solidarity by portraying threats of various kinds, mitigating individual competition and mistrust, and facilitating joint action. These effects make origin myths and other genealogical beliefs grist for ethno-nationalist ideology (Smith 1986). Nationalist social technologies redirect familial altruism towards co-ethnics who are only distantly or putatively related (Eibl-Eibesfeldt 1972).

Arguably, origin stories and other ethnic social technologies are more likely to establish an ethnic identity when a group does in fact have a shared lineage, since people are fascinated with family trees and relatedness in general, leading to detailed knowledge of the origins of the groups forming their social environment. Ethnic ideologies thus tend to find a home with objectively existing ethnic groups (van den Berghe 1981, 1995; Smith 1986), organizing altruism in genetically self-interested directions.

Ethnic solidarity can be raised or lowered by cultural and situational factors. The former include social technologies. This is why there are times of general indifference about ethnic differences as well as times of intense emotions, self-sacrifice, and intergroup aggression.

## Non-affiliative social technologies

States invest considerable resources in legal systems that control transaction risks, lowering them for activities deemed licit and increasing them for those deemed illicit. These systems rely on social technologies that manipulate behaviours involved in dominance and reciprocity. Since these behaviours are universal components of the species' repertoire, social technologies that deploy them are applicable to populations of any ethnicity or ethnic mix. Techniques involve monitoring and punishment of defectors, rest more on calculative than emotional commitment, and do not elicit altruism as do affiliation-based techniques. While recognizing the presence of other risk-reducing social technologies, this chapter is devoted to the affiliative type that is of particular relevance to ethnic solidarity.

## Solidarity as a two-edged sword

The evolutionary approach provides a further insight. Evidence from a number of disciplines indicates that ties can be used aggressively as well as defensively. If there is such a two-edged effect it should also be strongest with families, so empirical testing properly begins there.

In small-scale societies kin solidarity is deployed defensively in exchange networks (Wiessner 1982, also in this volume). Kin are more likely than non-kin to reciprocate a favour, and more likely to extend a favour "on credit". Solidarity is deployed offensively as well as defensively in interlineage and intercommunity conflict (Chagnon 1980, 1988; Keeley 1996; Konner and Shostak 1986). It is a universal of human communities that they are defended by groups of related males (van der Dennen 1995; Wrangham and Peterson 1996, p. 25). In attack, too, the primordial unit consisted of brothers (and cousins and brothers-in-law) in arms, whose cooperative bonds were also useful for big-game hunting.

> A kinship density factor appears to be involved in revenge raids. It is difficult for a small or heterogeneous Yanomamö group to put together a raiding party. The risks are high and men are willing to take them in proportion to the amount of mutual support they receive from comrades.... Lone raiders do not exist. The higher the kinship density in a local community, the greater is the likelihood that a large number of mutually supportive individuals will take such life-threatening risks and that retaliation will occur if one of the members of the group is killed (Chagnon 1988, p. 989).

A further example is group homicide in the modern-day United States. Murder is risky because it attracts the close attention of police and apprehended offenders suffer severe penalties. Daly and Wilson (1988) show that in the United States, when a homicide is committed by a group, members are usually more closely related to each other than they are to the victim. Indeed, joint killers are six times more likely to be blood relatives than are killers and victims. M. Daly has recently explained this difference in terms of risky transactions:

> We don't know how much people interact with relatives and nonrelatives. But whatever that distribution is, if the opportunity to form cooperative alliances in dangerous endeavours is distributed according to interaction frequency, the opportunity to come into conflict is similarly distributed. By a pure opportunity-model these two things ought to be similar. But it doesn't work like that. People tend to collaborate with their relatives and they tend to do damage to nonrelatives (M. Daly, quoted by Roes 1996).

An advantage of group solidarity for aggressive purposes is that it mitigates the risk of retaliation. Solidarity increases the ability to resist counter-attack and prevent defection under duress. Thus groups that have developed a solidary defensive strategy may also be well positioned to deploy that solidarity in aggressive ways for acquiring resources. Bonded human males often conceptualize their relationship in familial terms and consequently to bond more intensely (Tiger 1989/1969; Tiger and Fox 1989/1971). Brothers-in-arms, often men who grew up together in the same village, make more effective fighting units than unbonded aggregates because their close ties give them great coherence in the fearsome risks of war (Creveld 1982).[9] It is clear that the relatively intense affiliative bonds uniting close kin can be turned to aggressive ends, but what of more diffuse ties such as those binding ethnic groups?

In the following sections I argue that ethnic solidarity also tends to be two-edged, though culture plays a critical role in determining the sharpness of those edges. While the aggressive side of ethno-nationalism is well recognized, accounts of minority ethnic solidarity often overlook its offensive deployment. The affiliative side of ethno-nationalism is also often overlooked, in which a society works together for common goals and class competition is ameliorated to some degree. In the following section I discuss several examples of two-edged deployment of ethnic solidarity drawn from ethnic mafias, nationalist fighters, ethnic middleman groups, and ethnic dissidents. All these groups use kin and ethnic bonds defensively as insurance against defection from risky transactions, but mafias, middlemen and rebels also use their solidarity actively to create risks for opponents.

## Ethnic mafias

Ethnic mafias use a mix of strategies for reducing the risk of illicit transactions. Criminal transactions such as selling illicit drugs can carry inordinate risk from police and competing criminals. There are various ways of minimizing that risk, such as choosing categories of interactants unlikely to contain police officers or informants, maintaining anonymity, and keeping the transaction as fleeting as possible. The last two strategies are compromised when a risky transaction is repeated, especially when it forms part of a continuing relationship, such as is found in the networks that distribute illicit drugs. Police or other antagonists are more likely to detect a series of transactions between the same individuals, and the risk of defection by one of the interactants increases by virtue of loss of anonymity and the emergence or discovery of opportunities for profitable defection.

The risk of risky relationships is reduced by increasing reliability or trust. Strategies for building trust can be discussed under two headings.

1. Deterrence. An interactant can attempt to increase reliability by convincing his partner that defection will incur a cost greater than the benefit so derived. The behavioural systems available for delivering such a threat are dominance and reciprocity. An interactant might be threatened with harm – to status or self – instilling a degree of anxiety or fear, or promised material reward or its withdrawal, inducing willingness to cooperate or anxiety about defection. Organized criminal groups use both methods, licit businesses only the latter in modern capitalist economies. In modern economies contracts are enforced by the state authorities using both types, though harm is usually limited to loss of status and liberty.
2. Bonding. A second class of techniques, not necessarily exclusive of the first, works to increase trust by virtue of a pronounced non-calculative element. Partners can be chosen who are already bonded, such as friends or family, and thus unlikely to defect even when it is profitable to do so; or analogous interpersonal and corporate ties can be created through the use of rituals, work practices, and ideologies. This is a feature that distinguished mafias from other organized criminal enterprises.

Ethnic mafias certainly impose severe penalties on informers, and reward loyalty, as do other forms of organized crime, but they also rely on familial and (minority) ethnic trust and loyalty (Blok 1974; Edwards 1990; Ianni 1972, 1974). mafias are usually built around biological families; but they also socially define members as kin as a means of strengthening ties. As Blok points out in this volume, the Sicilian mafia emphasizes the tie of blood, a belief that extends the metaphor of family to all members of a local organization.

The central role of kinship and ethnicity in mafias makes kin and ethnic nepotism a plausible (partial) explanation for their solidarity, though van den Berghe does not include mafias among the many ethnic phenomena traversed in his book. Perhaps this contributed to his underemphasizing the risk-mitigating potential of nepotism as well as the offensive capacity of minorities in business.[10]

Some of the violence practised by mafias could be due to the security afforded by solidarity, including the code of silence. Economists apply the term "moral hazard" to the tendency of individuals protected from bearing the negative consequences of their actions to indulge in what would otherwise be immoral and risky behaviour. An example is the lapse of security-mindedness in some people well covered by theft insurance. The ethological literature reports analogous phenomena in coalitional behaviour (Harcourt and de Waal 1992). A child will behave more boldly towards a stranger when it is in proximity to a parent. Dogs do the same when close to their human master. It is possible that moral hazard is a general tendency in species with strategic intelligence when supported by a solidary group.

A nice confirmation of the importance of tie-gradients in organizing ethnic mafias is the way that family solidarity can be used aggressively against co-ethnics, in the same way that ethnic solidarity can provide a competitive edge in inter-ethnic competition.[11] In this situation, a clan or criminal brotherhood uses its inside knowledge of fellow-ethnic trading practices, their vulnerabilities and language, to extort. The same criminal groups can evolve into predators of other communities and protectors of their own when the scale of operations grows so large that they require alliances with the community's legitimate élites (Kleinknecht 1996). In the early 1900s, the mobster Jack Zelig was hailed as "the great emancipator of the East Side" for beating back Italian criminal depradations against that New York Jewish community (Kleinknecht 1996, p. 34). Zelig's gang, which had connections among the local élite, actually posted guards on the neighbourhood approaches. Similarly, Mafia-controlled districts of contemporary New York are reputed to be relatively safe from street crime.

## Nationalist fighters

The idea that group solidarity is an important determinant of military and political power has been the practical knowledge of leaders since at least Alexander the Great, who forcefully integrated his growingly multi-clan forces to maintain a unitary group identity. But the first analysis of the power-political implications of communal affiliation came much later, from the Islamic historian Ibn-Khaldun

(1332–1406), in *The Muqaddima* (Hill 1993). Ibn-Khaldun argued that new states and political movements founded by conquering tribes challenged more civilized élites on the basis of superior *asabiyya* or social solidarity. As a new society forms, the group with the strongest solidarity dominates. But over the generations the victors' cohesion is eroded by complacency and internal divisions. Chiefdom gives way to kingdom and rule is rigidified through coercion. Natural solidarity declines and with it, the power of the kingdom. Disintegration is exploited by a relatively primitive group possessing fresh reserves of solidarity, a strong communal ethos, which dominates the decaying social structure. The process is recapitulated. Ibn-Khaldun's account is amenable to sociobiological interpretation. Without reference to Medieval sources, Hamilton (1975, p. 149) conjectured along inclusive fitness lines:

> It may even be suggested that certain genes or traditions of the pastoralists revitalize the conquered people with an ingredient of progress which tends to die out in a large panmictic population … I have in mind altruism itself, or the part of altruism which is perhaps better described as self-sacrificial daring… . Thus civilization probably slowly reduces its altruism of all kinds, including the kinds needed for cultural creativity… .

Ibn-Khaldun's thesis assumes the dual defensive and offensive potential of tribal solidarity. Nationalist fighters are similarly a clear example of the double-edged effect. Implicit or explicit in nationalist sentiment is greater loyalty to fellow ethnics than to others. Patriotic and nationalist sentiments are, in the first instance, expressions of love of country or people, as evidenced by associated literature and memorials (Anderson 1983). In support of this view Bar-Tal (1993; and see Hogg and Abrams 1987, p. 7) argues that patriotism serves valuable integrative and identity functions for populations sharing territory and can be distinguished from the aggressive elements which he identifies with nationalism. Individuals with confident patriotic beliefs based on clear group identification experience emotions of love, care, and devotion toward the group. This contributes to cohesiveness and altruism. Gurr and Harff (1994) find that strong communal bonds, robust group identification, and shared territory, increase a group's readiness to resist oppressive governments, either through protest or armed struggle.

Billig (1993) argues that Bar-Tal's positive picture of ethnic solidarity ignores considerable invidious features. He maintains that there are other forms of community, that ethnic identity need not demand loyalty, that some groups such as traditional Jews and Gypsies got by without attachment to a country, and advances post-modernist theory to suggest that the nation is obsolete. His conclusion is that patriotism has inevitable aggressive components. In other words, ethnic bonds are not necessary for cohesion and tend to be dangerous. The last point agrees with the ubiquitousness of the double-edged effect, while the others do not contradict the proposition that patriotism, though perhaps not necessary to produce the positive results Bar-Tal describes, can be sufficient to do so. At least two of Billig's assertions, though true, when taken together undermine his disparagement of ethnicity as a basis for communal solidarity, especially in multicultural societies. Ethnic identity can indeed be so unmobilized that it does not amount to group loyalty; and Jews and Gypsies have indeed managed without a country. Traditionally, however, they managed with ethnic identities that demanded powerful loyalty. Both of these ethnies were traditionally endogamous and lived in separate communities. In effect their ethnic solidarity substituted for territory. As Jews began to assimilate in the nineteenth century, many of those who retained a secular ethnic identity felt the need for a country, giving rise to the Zionist movement. This hardly confirms Billig's view that ethnic loyalty and countries are simultaneously dispensable.

Caton (1998) argues for a still wider interpretation, that group identity *per se* is beneficial to group members: "My claim that indoctrination is a positive thing refers in the first instance to the positive affect that the acquisition of a strong group identity has on people. It instills pride, energy, commitment, a sense of power and well-being, and operational competence. These rewards create a craving for indoctrination... ." A compatible view is that the ethnic type of identity is a powerful need: "The need to belong deeply and intimately to an ethnic aggregate is a powerful motivation" (Fishman 1996/1980, p. 68). Finally, van den Berghe interprets ethnic affiliation as an extended form of family relations:

> The deep emotional attachment to one's ethny is the outcome of a multiplicity of previous beneficial associations with one's kinfolk, in-laws and other intimates... . They are not only intimate and based on a trust born out of a long-standing experience; they are also diffuse – that is, they extend over the whole range of one's life and activities. Ethnic ties, in short, constitute an all-encompassing matrix of intimate, affective relationships, conferring the multiple benefits of both kin selection and reciprocity. An ethny is a social womb, largely coterminous with one's closest, longest-lasting and most functionally significant ties (van den Berghe 1981, p. 257).

Billig's concern about the offensive potential of nationalism, and I think of territorially based patriotism, are well founded. In both defence and offence, countries' solidarity, whether ethnically or territorially oriented, is usually defined in opposition to neighbours, at least in part, and is readily turned to producing a willingness to fight for group interests. As noted above, small-group bonding is enhanced by the socially defined kinship of "brothers in arms". As a diluted form of kinship, ethnicity usually yields weaker commitment than that possessed by brothers-in-arms, but one that can mobilize larger populations. The kinship marker of shared territory similarly can be turned to defence and offence. Nationalist and patriotic rhetorics are rich in kinship terminology (Connor 1993; Holper 1996; Johnson 1987). Nationalist and patriotic sentiment can be disseminated to a whole society, lowering resistance to military recruitment and often producing volunteers. In Gurr and Harff's (1994, p. 84) theory of rebellious minorities, a strong predictor of armed revolt is dense communication networks joining leaders with people, allowing inculcation of a war mentality and readiness to subordinate personal preferences to group needs. A study of 25,000 letters from soldiers on both sides of the American Civil War found that love of homeland and of comrades were prominently featured as motivations for taking or justifying the risks of war, in addition to the motives of honour and duty (McPherson 1997).

The value of ethnic nepotism and ethnic hostility in promoting cohesion and a willingness to kill the enemy respectively has not been lost on propagandists in the great wars of the twentieth century. Propaganda has expanded from a pep talk before a battle, to a massive sustained campaign conducted via the mass media and special military agencies (Ballard and McDowell 1991; Bartov 1989; Messer-schmidt 1969; Sillman 1943). When nationalist war propaganda is successful, it radically exaggerates the social distance between the ingroup and outgroup, in a manner described by Erikson (1966) as cultural pseudospeciation. When carried to an extreme, the enemy is no longer conceptualized as human, and the inhibition against killing is suspended. Moral hazard may also play a role in increasing the violence of bonded military units.

Nationalist armies resemble mafias somewhat in their mix of social technologies. These include disciplinary methods combined with rituals and ideologies that elicit loyalty, though mafiosi loyalty is probably less self-sacrificial.

## Ethnic middleman groups

The two-edged solidarity of ethnic middlemen is not as obvious as that of mafias or nationalist fighters and has not been as well analysed. A more extensive treatment is thus required here. When contract law is weak, as in international trading before the advent of commercial treaties, family and ethnic networks can be the only effective means of conducting some types of risky transactions. A famous example is the Rothschild family which opened banks in several capitals of Europe, relying on familial bonds in place of (nonexistent) international law to invent the bond market and become the most important bankers for much of the nineteenth century (Ferguson 1999). An efficiency advantage can also accrue to ethnic middlemen from reduced transaction costs. It was the original insight by Coase (1937) that the profitability of an enterprise is affected by the cost of conducting transactions. Analysts of ethnic middleman groups argue on this basis that the trust engendered by kinship and ethnic ties tends to lower the risk of transactions and hence the cost of enforcing contracts (Bonacich 1973; Landa 1981, 1994; Light and Karageorgis 1994). Even in a law-bound environment such as the United States, it is easy to see how trust could cut costs. A middle-sized building project entails thousands of transactions. A typical $100 million project generates 150,000 separate documents, including technical drawings, legal contracts, purchase orders, and information requests (*The Economist* 15 January 2000, p. 75).

A strict Coasian approach attributes the advantage in effectiveness enjoyed by the Rothschilds to savings in transaction costs, which reduce prohibitive costs to tolerable ones. A problem with this interpretation is discussed below but the broader Coasian proposition seems secure, that solidarity can become an economic resource that increases the competitiveness of members of solidary groups (Landa 1981, 1994; to some extent Light and Karageorgis 1994; for a general treatment see Williamson 1975, 1996).

A leading analyst of middleman minorities is J. Landa (1981, 1994, and in this volume) who conceptualizes them as "Ethnically Homogeneous Middleman Groups" (EHMG). Landa's approach is institutional economics drawing on findings from anthropology and evolutionary theory. Her analysis of ethnic-Chinese middlemen in Malaysia takes into account the ethnic identities and solidarities of actors in a heterogeneous market. Ethnic middleman monopolies, Landa argues, enjoy a competitive advantage over individual competitors when market conditions are such that contracts cannot be enforced, or only enforced at great cost. The trust existing between ethnic Chinese traders lowers transaction costs, including the risk of reneging. Trade between co-ethnics can be expedited by extensions of credit, while that conducted with other ethnic groups tends to be handled in cash as a means of eliminating the risk of reneging. Though Landa, like van den Berghe, finds discrimination directed towards outgroups to be a salient aspect of middleman minority economic behaviour, this is not emphasized as a cause of their economic dominance. Yet it is at least intuitively plausible that a cohesive group whose trading strategy is systematically discriminatory towards other groups could in principle drive competitors out of a niche. This becomes more plausible if one focuses on non-economic behaviours.

> If the Chinese middleman refuses to trade with "outsiders," he must incur the opportunity costs of exclusion, the costs of foregone profits. So long as the opportunity costs of excluding outsiders from trade exceed transaction costs, a trader has an incentive to cross ethnic boundaries to incorporate outsiders into his trading network (Landa 1994, p.106).

But EHMGs are by definition homogeneous, indicating a tendency to exclude other groups despite an individual-profit incentive to incorporate outgroup members. Williamson (1996) suggests how this might occur. He notes that strong bond relationships are almost non-calculative, and are treated by participants on an "all-or-none" basis, rather than by continuous updating of costs and benefits. The result is that "personal/trust relations and commercial/calculative risk relations differ in kind" (Williamson 1996, p. 97). This suggests that group-loyal individuals often maintain solidarity even during periods when not profitable for them.

It is thus reasonable to impute an important non-economic basis for middleman ethnocentrism. The rule is not, "discriminate only when necessary to maintain profitability", but "discriminate in favour of the ingroup unless doing so incurs too great a cost". Such a rule will often be economically harmless to the discriminator, but not to the excluded ethnic group. For example, when an employer chooses to recruit ingroup employees from an ethnically mixed group of equally qualified candidates his business is not harmed, but the unemployed outgroup members are. In both van den Berghe's and Landa's analysis, the pronounced group solidarity of middleman minorities leads to favouritism towards the ingroup and, by implication, aggression in the form of invidious discrimination against outgroups. The two-edged sword of group solidarity is indicated.

Landa's analysis dwells on risks posed to the middleman group. But it is possible that middlemen contribute to the riskiness of their niches, at least as experienced by outgroups. Middleman groups, simply by being ethnically homogeneous and monopolizing an economic niche, have some characteristics of a group strategy directed both to defence and aggressive competition against the host population. Competitive strategies facilitated by solidary behaviour include price manipulation, cooperative bidding at auctions, and the sort of discrimination discussed in the previous paragraphs. Such tactics render economic niches more risky for competitors than for the ingroup. If true, this would be an important cause of ethnic monopolies, even where the monopolists are not more efficient as individual competitors. Of course, an edge in efficiency for whatever reason, including the lower transaction costs of trusting relationships would, as Bonacich, Landa and van den Berghe argue, make the trend to ethnic monopoly even more pronounced.

Looking beyond ethnic middlemen, transaction cost economics is inadequate to explain the spontaneous mutual support found within cohesive groups, or the emotional commitment that can result in personal sacrifice. Even Weber discounted economic explanations of patriotic "fervour", though critical of notions of blood ties as an objective cause of national solidarity (Gerth and Mills 1958, p. 171). Some kinds of transaction, such as those undertaken by criminals and nationalist freedom fighters, are so risky that they are only feasible between bonded individuals. Thus the analysis needs to shift from consideration of relative efficiency to the relative effectiveness of group defence, and the transaction-cost approach loses force. Williamson acknowledges that monopolies avoid transaction cost effects (1996, p. 87). Members of solidary groups can attempt certain transactions not because they are more efficient than other groups due to lower costs of keeping members loyal, but because intense trust is the only way to overcome fear of these risky transactions. This is true of élite troops, dissidents from oppressive regimes, and probably long-lived crime organizations. Schelling (1960) described a bond as one type of commitment device, without which risky cooperation cannot get started. Frank (1987, p. 594) notes that trust is important in overcoming the commitment problem, when honesty is "impossible or prohibitively costly to monitor". It is a matter of effectiveness rather than efficiency. In some situations what would be the most efficient method does not work, is unavailable, or is not tried for prudential or emotional (fear) reasons. As Meyer points out in this volume, emphasis needs to be put on the emotional dimension of social processes (and see Hirshleifer 1984, quoted by Frank 1987). Doing so helps illuminate all the roles played by group solidarity, both defensive and offensive.

The nature of ethnic economic aggression and its intimate connection to defensiveness is implied by Light and Karageorgis's (1994) analysis of trust as an ethnic resource in the late twentieth-century United States. Trust helps some groups develop a strong entrepreneurial economy (and see Bonacich 1973). Another ethnic resource is the widespread aspiration to self-employment. "Typical ethnic resources include kinship and marriage systems, trust, social capital, cultural assumptions, religion, language, a middleman heritage, entrepreneurial values and attitudes, rotating credit associations, relative satisfaction arising from nonacculturation to prevailing labor and living standards, reactive solidarities, multiplex social networks, employer paternalism, an ideology of ethnic solidarity, and underemployed and disadvantaged co-ethnic workers" (Light and Karageorgis 1994, p. 660). These resource types include several forms of solidarity, and it becomes clear from Light and Karageorgis's examples that they are resources partly because they facilitate discrimination and collusion, allowing group members to "help one another", "follow one another into the same trades", "combine easily to restrain trade", "utilize rotating credit associations", and "deploy multiplex social networks to economic advantage". Entrepreneurial ethnic leaders are often inspired by a desire to advance the prestige of their groups and assist individual members. They do so partly by employing coethnics on a discriminatory basis. "Ethnic solidarity requires the group's entrepreneurs to adopt a paternalistic attitude toward co-ethnic workers, offering them entrepreneurial training, sponsorship, and patronage they would not accord an outsider" (Light and Karageorgis 1994, pp. 660–1). This economic solidarity derives largely from the employer, who actively seeks to favour fellow ethnics. And co-ethnic employers combine to "restrain trade", that is, act collectively to disadvantage outgroup competitors. For their part, co-ethnic employees work long hours for low or nil wages, trusting in the long-term reciprocity of their employers (Bonacich 1973, p. 586; Light and Karageorgis 1994).

In addition to their solidarity, ethnic groups with long experience of middleman economic roles – a subset of minority ethnic economies – have an additional type of cultural capital accumulated in the form of social technologies specialized for manipulating customers and political masters alike. These techniques belong to the larger category of skills typically possessed by ethnic middlemen, including specialized crafts, literacy, bookkeeping, some understanding of market processes as well as the organization of trade, distribution and credit (van den Berghe 1981, pp. 139–40; Bonacich 1973). Ethnic capital is passed on by parents and by the wider ethnic community. Even in a modern economy such as the United States with blurred ethnic boundaries, income and sociocultural mobility is significantly affected by intra-ethnic transmission of skills (Borjas 1992).

Van den Berghe draws on Bonacich (1973) to describe some of the typical middleman minority manipulatory techniques that he believes are forced on them as self- defence against a hostile population. Many of these techniques are also potentially hostile. Ethnic middlemen must learn the language and culture of the host population. They must assess and, if need be, create demand for products. They must understand and adapt to the buying behaviour of the natives, know when to extend credit, know how to deal with government officials, know how and when to "bribe, cajole or manipulate", and be able to negotiate their way around legal restrictions. Successful ethnic middlemen must be adept at public relations, remaining inconspicuous and hiding wealth. Van den Berghe adds some behavioural detail to Bonacich's analysis. Ethnic middleman demeanour is, optimally, "blandly affable" while hiding feelings and opinions. Towards the powerful it is "subservient and sycophantic" and, except towards one's fellow ethnics, "one must be coolly calculating, ever alert and watchful" (van den Berghe 1981, p. 145). Ethnic middleman nepotism is developed in self-defence, kinship and ethnic ties being cultivated across the reaches of diasporas for essentially the same reasons that hunter-gatherers maintain extended kinship nets – as life insurance in case of inclement seasons and hostile neighbours. Sales tactics are adapted to local customer behaviour, for example by raising asking prices in anticipation of haggling, or using short weights to reduce the cost of a "free" gift thrown in with the purchase (van den Berghe 1981, pp. 145–6).

Although ethnic middleman tactics are effective for a time, the larger populations they manipulate invariably detect elements of the strategy, and the trading group gains a reputation for being "clannish, underhanded, dishonest, sly, disloyal, greedy, avaricious, exploitative and unassimilable ..." (van den Berghe 1981, p. 139), much of which can be true, at least from the point of view of the host population. "Each party to the conflict has a 'reasonable' point of view which arises from the interaction" (Bonacich 1973, p. 589). As van den Berghe points out, the capacities for these characteristics are universal, and they are only brought out in exaggerated form in ethnic middleman groups because of the latters' need to cope with economic and political challenges. It is very difficult for a group to develop trusting relationships with a population known to hate it, and to threaten it periodically (van den Berghe 1981, p. 146). Both sides' solidarity is deployed defensively as well as offensively. Elsewhere, van den Berghe remarks the unifying effect of external threat (e.g. 1981, p. 187), and his analysis is consistent with Spicer's (1971) emphasis on ethnic solidarity as reactive in the face of actual or symbolic threat. Spicer studied several persistent ethnic groups and found that they all had "oppositional" symbols and rituals embedded in their traditions. Bonacich (1973) also finds that ethnic middleman solidarity is partly a reaction to antagonism from the host population but adds that this antagonism is triggered by economic competition from the middleman group. Intergroup competition exacerbates the universal human predisposition to evaluate outgroups negatively and positively evaluate and affiliate with ingroups (see discussion of social identity theory later in this chapter).

It does appear as though the most intense group solidarity requires for its genesis a perception of threat to the group. As argued earlier in this chapter, cohesiveness in the face of risky transactions is maintained by recurring experiences of actual threat, and/or by fictive threat coded in traditions. However, it is clear from innumerable cases that, once established, ethnic solidarity can be used for initiating aggression, whether of the economic or martial kind. This conclusion is supported by examining the middleman tactics described by van den Berghe. Defensive and offensive methods can be distinguished. Not all harm done to outgroups can be attributed to hostile intent. For example, the kin and ethnic favouritism exhibited by all ethnic economies is invidious to groups thus excluded from jobs and fair terms of trade (Light and Karageorgis 1994), but the invidiousness is collateral damage, and can even be an unwanted side-effect of extending special favours. The cause is not a positive act of aggression, and neither is the motive aggressive. By comparison, methods for cheating and exploiting outgroups are predatory. The maintenance of kin and ethnic safety nets can be seen as part of a two-edged strategy since they facilitate aggression by providing support and, in the final resort, bolt holes, should retaliation for aggressive economic tactics become unmanageable. As argued above, it is missing an important factor to rely exclusively on defensiveness as an explanation of aggressive ethnic trading tactics, since these tactics pay, and are used as initiatives as well as responses in inter-ethnic relations. They rely on a double ethic of amity and trust for the ingroup, and enmity and mistrust for the outgroup (Keith 1947/1968; MacDonald 1994; Spencer 1892; Sumner 1906; Weber 1963). Ethnic middleman groups have the same human nature as other groups, and thus are as likely to be motivated by competitive and aggressive sentiments; often more so, since they initiate group competition and their endogamy and other social-avoidance behaviours maintain a wide social divide between them and other groups (Bonacich 1973; MacDonald 1994).

Arguably, such distance allows opportunistic acts of "enmity", to use Keith's (1947/1968) term for intergroup hostility. Maintenance of a separate ethnic identity can thus be profitable because it facilitates calculative, opportunistic transactions, even if it also incurs costs of endemic hostility and intermittent conflict. The multiple defences described by van den Berghe are on hand to counter these risks. Ethnic middleman groups can establish monopolies so deeply entrenched that even authoritarian governments find it difficult to open up the affected industries to other groups.

> The difficulty of breaking entrenched middleman monopolies, the difficulty of controlling the growth and extension of their economic power, pushes host countries to even more extreme reactions. One finds increasingly harsh measures, piled on one another, until, when all else fails, 'final solutions' are enacted (Bonacich 1973, p. 592).

Bonacich also points out that the hostile reaction of the host population polarizes ethnic relations, and legal countermeasures aimed at breaking minority monopolies can further the latter's occupational concentration, increasing their isolation, externally reinforcing their endogamy strategy, and selecting for further refinement of the middleman group's manipulative social technologies. It tends to be a self-reinforcing process.

Group solidarity can be economically disadvantageous by inhibiting aggressive tactics against fellow ethnics. I have already noted that a prime function of minority ethnic collusion is to restrain competition between fellow ethnics. By the same logic, business people with ties to the majority ethnic group in an economy are likely to be more constrained in deploying aggressive manipulatory techniques than are members of cohesive minority business groups. This puts a twist on Max Weber's stark distinction between capitalist and precapitalist economic behaviour. Weber argued that modern industrial capitalists treat employees and associates in a strictly impersonal, rational manner (Weber 1958, 1964). In Weber's view, the weakness or absence of interpersonal attachments has boosted economic development by permitting the rational treatment of manpower. Thus the individualism found in Protestant Europe gave them an advantage over the Catholic South in developing the capitalist mode of organization. Pre-capitalist economies are characterized by blood and religious ties that prevent business from treating individuals on a purely instrumental basis. Capitalist rationalism is so pronounced, Weber believed, that in economic affairs the businessman treats his own family members as dispassionately as he does strangers (Weber 1958, p. 21). Although Weber's ideal-type analysis captured an important characteristic of capitalist instrumentalism, it distorts reality. Nepotism is rife in Western business practice (Light and Karageorgis 1994). Weber also underestimated the ways in which ethnic nepotism is functional in modern economies, namely in ethnic economies (Weber 1958,

p. 21). He noted the economic disadvantages of "pariah" status, but not the advantages of ethnocentrism, which he referred to as the "double standard."

> The legally and factually precarious position of the Jews hardly permitted continuous, systematic, and rationalized industrial enterprise with fixed capital, but only trade and above all dealing in money.... As a pariah people, they retained the double standard of morals which is characteristic of primordial economic practice in all communities: what is prohibited in relation to one's brothers is permitted in relation to strangers (Weber 1963, p. 250).

Yet as we have seen, discriminatory trading based on blood ties can be effective when practised by minorities against individualist competitors (Bonacich 1973; Landa 1981; Light and Karageorgis 1994; MacDonald 1994). Particularism can score over universalism.

One likely advantage of minority particularism lies in its unsentimental approach to the population forming the bulk of the market. Majority businessmen are more prone to be burdened by a social conscience based on ethnic identification with most of the population. A similar case has been made with regard to feudal and colonial societies, whose élites and traders often had familial or religious obligatory ties with the people. Bonacich (1973, p. 584) agrees with Park (1939, p. 14) that in feudal and colonial societies merchants with affiliative ties to customers and competitors were disadvantaged compared with minority traders who could be more "objective" or instrumental in the market-place, except when dealing with members of their own group.

## Ethnic dissidents

A comprehensive study has yet to be written of the internal dynamics of groups that publicly dissent from the policies of an authoritarian state on the grounds of ethnic independence or equality. However, Gurr (1993) and Gurr and Harff (1994) survey global occurrences of "non-violent protest" as one type of ethnic conflict, between 1945 and about 1990. Their analysis does not consider the risk factor of collusion between dissidents, but offers indirect support for the hypothesis that overcoming the risk of defection facilitates collective dissident behaviour against repressive regimes. For example, they argue that individuals rarely challenge institutions or society alone, but usually join with others to do so. Groups of like-minded individuals with shared grievances are more likely to take action (Gurr and Harff 1994, p. 84). Another group factor that facilitates rebellion is cohesion, marked by dense networks of communication. "Group cohesion increases to the extent that groups are regionally concentrated, share many common traits and grievances over long periods of time, and have widely accepted autocratic leaders" (ibid.). Gurr and Harff do not discuss defection, but the thrust of their analysis implies that members of cohesive groups are less likely to betray each other than are less cohesive groups. In line with Spicer's (1971) analysis of long-lasting ethnic groups, Gurr and Harff's (1994, pp. 98–9) survey indicates strongly that groups become mobilized, and thus more cohesive, when discriminated against by other groups and governments – what Spicer calls oppositional events.

The role of shared ethnicity in mitigating risk of defection is also strongly indicated by Gurr and Harff, though again indirectly. They argue that the stronger an individual identifies with a persecuted group, the more likely he is to take action in its defence, whether by peacefully dissenting or by armed rebellion. This strongly suggests that individuals are more willing to run risks for co-ethnics than for others. Gurr and Harff (p. 89) note that group identification is increased the more group members share a common language, religious beliefs, visible racial characteristics, a shared history of at least a century, and a common culture consisting of identifiable social and legal customs. In their case studies of dissident minorities they note the importance of belief in shared descent. All these factors are group markers for ethnicity (van den Berghe 1981; Shaw and Wong 1989).

Ethnic dissidents are like nationalist fighters in motivation, except that they employ peaceful tactics. When challenging authoritarian regimes, the similarity can be grim. Dissidents can face imprisonment, torture, and death, often administered by security forces trying to extract information about fellow dissidents or a public denunciation of them. Sometimes members of a group find themselves forced into the role of dissidents in passive support of group members who have taken up armed struggle against the government. Here is part of the testimony of a young Kurd whose family was persecuted by the Iraqi government in the late 1970s and early 1980s because his father was a guerrilla fighter. The ties of kinship were put to the test, apparently without breaking.

> They put my family in prison because my father was a peshmerga – a fighter for the Kurds… . [T]he government started to catch Kurdish families again and unfortunately they caught my grandfather and beat and tortured him so badly that half his body was paralysed. They tortured him to find out where my father was hiding… My mother and brothers and I had to leave our house … to go to live in the mountains of Kurdistan near where my father was (quoted by Gurr and Harff 1994, pp. 27–8).

Ethnic loyalty can hold individuals back from informing on or denouncing their fellow dissidents. Consider the case of Natan Sharansky (1988), an academic in the Soviet Union who subsequently served as a cabinet minister in an Israeli government. Soviet anti-Semitism accelerated after the Second World War with a purge of Jewish intellectuals, artists and party functionaries initiated by Stalin following widespread Jewish enthusiasm for the new Jewish state of Israel (Goldberg 1996, p. 143; Kostyrchenko 1995). A second intense phase began after the 1967 Israel-Arab War, when Soviet Jews *en masse* began protesting against institutional anti-Semitism and demanding the right to emigrate to Israel (Kowalewski 1981, p. 178). For his support of dissident causes, Sharansky was arrested by the KGB and charged with espionage and treason. He spent nine years in prison, of which four hundred days were spent in punishment cells, and over two hundred on hunger strike (Sharansky 1988, p. ix). He was interrogated for prolonged periods. "They wanted to use me to destroy the two groups I worked for – Jews who hoped to leave

for Israel and dissidents who spoke out on behalf of human rights." This coura-
geous man combined a concern for human rights and a powerful ethnic loyalty.

> In those days the beginning and the end of my Jewishness was an awareness of anti-
> Semitism. As an adolescent I had come across some lines of Julian Tuwim, a Polish-
> Jewish poet who wrote after the Holocaust that he felt himself Polish by virtue of the
> blood flowing in his veins (by which he meant Polish culture and literature), and Jew-
> ish by virtue of the blood that flowed *out* of his veins. In other words, when Jews were
> attacked he felt a solidarity with them. I felt that Tuwim was speaking for me. I loved
> Russian culture, ... [b]ut I was a Jew because of anti-Semitism. If it had ever disap-
> peared, I would have been happy to declare myself a Russian (Sharansky 1988, p. xii).

To conclude, ethnic dissidents are a distinct category that fits the risky transactions analysis. The risk of being informed on to the police for expressing proscribed
ideas resembles the risk of illicit trading (see "Ethnic middleman groups" above). In
both cases the actor depends on his partner not to defect, sometimes under great
pressure. There is also a resemblance to the risk of unenforced contracts. The differences lie in the incentives to defect. Hence risks suffered by dissidents in authoritarian regimes have the same structure from their perspective as risks posed to
traders in volatile and hard-to-regulate industries. In all three types of risky transactions a prudent strategy is to choose to deal with trusted categories of friends, kin,
and ethnic ingroups. Ethnic dissidents also resemble nationalist fighters in being
motivated by ethnic affiliation; but fighters take up arms while dissidents adopt the
peaceful approaches of protest and martyrdom, as exemplified by the non-violent
methods of protest pioneered by the Indian leader Mohandas Gandhi. Dissidents
are not completely unaggressive, since they deliberately set about embarrassing and
discomforting their opponents; and since their peacefulness is often due to a lack of
military capability. Nevertheless, for whatever reason, dissidents are usually not
aggressive and this is the closest example we have of a competitive group strategy
that mitigates the double-edged sword of ethnic nepotism.

## The Soviet Union and National Socialist Germany

The turbulent history of the Soviet Union has been influenced by differential
group solidarity. In this respect it is instructive to compare Soviet and National
Socialist German social control techniques aimed at instilling affiliation towards
the regime. These two systems entered a close-run military contest that entailed the
mobilization of much of the population where victory partly depended on citizens'
willingness to make sacrifices for the war effort.

Ethnic mafias and nationalist fighters figured in the breakup of the USSR in the
late 1980s, not causally but opportunistically. Before that, ethnic dissidents took
their toll of Soviet legitimacy, as did the ethnically organized underground economy (Alessandrini and Dallago 1987; Simis 1982) and the refusal of subordinate
nationalities to give up their identities despite concerted attempts at universalization and Russification (Khazanov 1995). All of these groups, though lacking the

power derived from state institutions, enjoyed great superiority in the group resource of ethnic solidarity. The Chechens, for example, are a clan-based society with intense tribal solidarity compared to Russians (Handelman 1995). The success of nationalist rebels, including the Chechens in their war of liberation of the mid-1990s, would have been impossible without the willingness of rebels to die for their people.

Other pivotal events of Soviet history were influenced by differential solidarity in accordance with Ibn-Khaldun's theory. One well-known example is Stalin's rediscovery of patriotism at the nadir of Soviet fortunes in the face of the German onslaught of 1941. The officially Marxist Soviet regime had, since the 1917 revolution, extolled extreme egalitarianism and condemned national distinction in favour of the solidarity of the international proletariat. Yet when faced with the seemingly unstoppable German invasion, the same regime rehabilitated czarist generals, resurrected traditional rank insignia, and reinstituted the ancient kinship language of "Mother Russia" to fight the "Great Patriotic War". Czarist heroes and Orthodox saints were recalled in official propaganda (Kohn 1960). It was a race to reinvoke primordial willingness to run risks for the group. In effect it was an arms race, not of guns, but of the social technologies for producing cohesive fighting groups, a race in which the Germans held the lead with their ethno-nationalist doctrine and communal-based military practices. The National Socialist state invested heavily in indoctrinating soldiers with its racial world view, especially German chauvinism, an investment that continued throughout the Second World War (Messerschmidt 1969; Bartov 1989). A comparison of national fighting effectiveness in the Second World War found that German units were more cohesive and as a consequence more effective due to management practices that kept bonded individuals together (van Creveld 1982). Although both the Nazis and the Allies attempted to whip up hatred for the enemy (e.g. Sillman 1943), a willingness to kill is distinct from the willingness to die for one's comrades. German punishment was also meted out in a manner calculated to preserve trust within fighting units. On the eastern front both sides resorted to summary executions of stragglers and other miscreants to preserve order in the face of extreme conditions including chaotic retreats that affected first the Soviets and later the Germans; but the Russians compromised group ties by having locally attached commissars administer the worst punishments. The ethos of mass killing honed in the NKVD was incorporated into conventional Soviet military formations. The Germans were careful to insulate their mass killing apparatus from the general population, and continued the practice within the military. Military police units with powers of summary execution operated under separate command from local units and were not attached to them. The result was to drive stragglers back into the relative protective care of their officers, even if the effect was to lose their lives in the next battle. The Soviets attempted what is probably the impossible: forging trusting reciprocal bonds between individuals, one of whom is liable to inflict harsh punishment on the other (Salter 1995, p. 454, fig. 12.16).

Communist social technology did not overlook the need for group ties, but its universalism was incompatible with the mobilization of ethnicity. From its conception, Bolshevik social control had a pronounced affiliative dimension. The proletariat was conceptualized not just as an interest group but as an international bond of brothers and sisters. "Fraternity" has long been used by socialists and unionists to describe their associations. The Bolsheviks also suppressed loyalties perceived to compete with affiliation to the party. Both communism and fascism were jealous about ties of loyalty. At the height of their revolutionary fervour in the 1920s and early 1930s, the Bolsheviks demanded that citizens subordinate all other loyalties to the party, including ethnic and familial ones (Heller 1988). While fascist ideology asserted the precedent of state over family ties, it incorporated the ideal and symbolism of the family while communism, especially the Lenin-Trotsky model, competed directly with familial piety.

In the 1920s and early 1930s, the Bolsheviks attempted to replace family loyalty with allegiance to the overall Soviet society. The methods were indoctrination by schools and press, as well as by radical family policies that allowed sexual freedom and easy divorce and abortion, resulting in a decline in the Soviet family as an economic and socializing unit. The cost, however, was perceived to be too high and Stalin, in an attempt to revive the Russian family, adopted pro-natalist policies by 1936 (Goldman 1993; Heller 1988). In addition to the breakdown of the family, original Bolshevik social policy also suffered from the continuous and often disruptive effort needed to indoctrinate people away from their self-organizing primary bonds. Competition between state and familial loyalties was hardly new. Ethno-nationalism is a kinship ideology (van den Berghe 1981; Connor 1993) and tensions over dual familial loyalty can arise. Consider this injunction issued during the radical Terror of 1793 by the *ad hoc* revolutionary authority of Lyon, urging citizens to denounce Federalists:

> Friends, nothing can, nothing should constrain your ardor here: former servants must not forget that the Motherland is their sole mistress; nor relatives forget that it alone is their mother; nor citizens forget that they owe themselves utterly to this Motherland which rewards their zeal so effectively, but which would sanction without pity their negligence and punish their criminal silence (quoted by Lucas 1996, p. 768).

Marxism is thoroughly universalistic, disapproving of all particularisms. Despite official universalism, the Bolsheviks won a new lease of legitimacy due to their leadership of the country in what Stalin called the Great Patriotic War of 1941–1945. The party came to be identified as the defender of the Russian and allied peoples, in addition to the representative of the proletariat of all lands. To defeat Hitler, Stalin had his propaganda agencies mirror aspects of National Socialism with a doctrine of socialism in one country, thus reaping the self-sacrificial altruism of ethnic nepotism. Ethnic Russians occupied pride of place in this new national Bolshevism, minority nationalities being relegated to an unofficial peripheral status and subjected to Russification in the guise of modernization and integration.

What of reciprocity as a source of legitimacy? The economic inefficiency of the Soviet command economy contributed to the strain on the regime by weakening its ability to buy loyalty. Consequently, control tended to fall back on dominance and the patriotic capital built up in the Second World War, the latter sustained reactively by the Cold War. Whatever the fortunes of its affiliative political technologies, the regime always invested heavily in policing and censorship, and as if obeying an Ibn-Khaldun's edict, this assumed a greater role as organic solidarity and the legitimacy that goes with it broke down. This totalitarian drift to greater coercion was less marked in fascist Germany, which focused on suppressing minorities rather than the majority group's religion and local traditions. The opening of the East German political police (Stasi) files following the collapse of the German Democratic Republic regime in 1989 allows a comparison of Nazi and Communist control techniques applied to the same ethnic group. The equivalent to the Stasi in Nazi Germany was the Gestapo, which had less than 15,000 staff for the whole of Germany, Austria and Czechoslovakia. The Stasi had 85,000 staff for the surveillance of East Germany. Incidentally, it is interesting to compare these figures with Britain in the 1990s, where MI5 and the Special Branch staff together numbered 4,000 (Annan 1997). Clearly Hitler's was a repressive regime, but achieved greater administrative efficiency than its pre-war Bolshevik counterpart by mobilizing the majority ethnic group.

As the repressive Soviet social control technology began to crumble with the corruption and loss of will of the ruling élite, differences in solidarity became decisive in determining the outcome of group competition, and the Soviet economic and political system fissioned along kinship and ethnic lines (Khazanov 1995).

## Is it possible to design stable one-edged group cohesion? Constraints on engineering ethnic affairs

Analyses of social phenomena are often pregnant with ideas for change or preservation. In *The Republic* Plato (*c.* 428–347 BC) recommended authoritarian rule by a philosophical élite, involving rigorous education of candidate rulers and censorship and job-demarcation for the ruled. The Italian political theorist Niccolò Machiavelli (1469–1527) offered his analysis of political power as advice for princes on how to control subjects and compete with peers. The English philosopher Jeremy Bentham (1748–1832) assessed human motives as ruled by self-interest, and this, conjoined with his utilitarian ethics, inspired various legislative and administrative recommendations, including the extension of democracy, the use of punishment only for deterrence, and most famously the blueprints for the panopticon, a privately-run prison designed to maximize observation of prisoners. The analysis of capitalism by the German social theorist Karl Marx (1818–83) informed his recommendations for accelerating its inevitable progress to socialism. Closer to the present subject, the Scottish economist Adam Smith (1723–90) defended his individualist economic analysis by arguing that affection is little more than habitual sympathy produced by proximity. As evidence he claimed that siblings educated apart lose some of their original affection for one another (Smith 1759/1808 II, pp. 68–70), and that people care little for misfortune befalling strangers (I, p. 317). Enlightenment thinkers in general favoured political systems designed by rational planners, with the partial exception of the social

Darwinists and free market economists, who have opposed state intervention in society and the economy except for the purpose of maintaining competition. Perhaps there is a tinkerer in even the most abstract social thinker. It is as though ideas about how a system works, especially human society, prompts a desire to test that idea in the real world.

So what policy recommendations can be drawn from this chapter's analysis of how ethnic solidarity, like kin solidarity, can be turned to offensive or defensive purposes? My value assumption in the following remarks is that, if possible, defensive solidarity is to be preserved, but the offensive kind curbed. Returning to a previous example, Hitler's Germany produced greater cohesion and public altruism than did Lenin's or Stalin's Soviet Union prior to the Second World War; but it was also more aggressive towards minorities and neighbouring states. Cohesive societies might have some benefits, but cohesiveness is not worth a Hobbesian war of all against all. Can a ploughshare be so fashioned that it resists being beaten into a sword, or to use the two-edge analogy, can ethnic nepotism's offensive edge be kept selectively blunt?

I believe it is possible, though by no means certain given the present state of theory, that the two-edged effect can be skewed. The ethnic dissidents discussed earlier offer some hope in their mainly defensive solidarity, even though their powerlessness precluded offensive tactics. Also promising is the art of diplomacy. Experiments in international governance, multilateral agreements, and the emergence of a "world opinion" that censures aggressive states, or at least some of the smaller ones, are valuable cultural developments. Another approach is through arms limitation treaties and pacifist movements, which keep military culture a small part of the social fabric. Nazi Germany's aggression was not only due to its ethnic solidarity, but was the outcome of years of militarization of the culture, through organs such as the Hitler Youth and the wearing of uniforms by national leaders on ceremonial occasions, together with the acceleration of arms manufacture. An ethnic cohesion separated from militarism would be inherently less capable of being motivated to wage aggressive war.

Despite preventative measures, wars still occur, and differences in ethnic interests and aspirations are a major cause (Gurr and Harff 1994). Often the conflict is due to an ethnic minority seeking independence, which is a reasonable aspiration, but this is opposed by the majority group wanting to retain the territory that would be lost through partition, which is also understandable. Picking the just side in such disputes is not always simple, and often beside the point for the purpose of saving lives and reducing misery. The latter goal would be furthered by dampening aggressive ethno-nationalism while satisfying the need for affiliation with moderate ethnic solidarity.

Our species is capable of seemingly miraculous contrivances, especially when intuition is replaced by scientific understanding of the properties of materials. Perhaps there is some new social device, or a novel arrangement of traditional ones, that will reliably circumvent the two-edged effect of group solidarity. Social engineering has its limits. At the most general level social technologies are limited by the species repertoire. Fox (1971, p. 281) was perhaps the first to make this point:

[E]very species has a complex of social behavior made up of recognizable units – a complex which distinguishes it from other species – but these units may well be put together in different ways by different populations adapting to different environments. But one does not find a baboon troop, for all its ingenuity, adapting like a herd of horses and vice versa. The baboons can only adapt with the material at hand in their stock of behavior units, and the same is true of man.

Do such limitations apply to the double-edged effect in humans? The following review of social technology theory, which Caton names "political ethology", will help clarify the challenge awaiting researchers and philosophers (and see Salter 1995 for a review of this body of theory).

Political ethology describes behaviours used for combining individuals into political aggregations and keeping them there. It presupposes a description of hunter-gatherer behaviours, and it assumes that such behaviours are the only material available for combining men into larger aggregations (Caton 1994/1983).

Behaviour can be "stretched" to suit group goals, Caton points out. However, it is sufficient for a social technology to work that hunter-gatherer behaviours are able to be decoupled from their evolved small-group context and recombined into functional complexes (see also Caton 1988, Introduction; Eibl-Eibesfeldt 1972/1970; Geiger 1988; Salter 1995, chapters 1 and 12). Decoupling is dependent on a society's scale and demographics, large size facilitating role specialization; but recombination is achieved by techniques of social control which build up in cultural traditions and in the more formalized frameworks of institutions. Military organization is a paradigm case of early social technology (Caton 1988, pp. 10–11), and the command hierarchies of large organizations are rich in social technologies (Salter 1995).

Caton's analysis of the military fighting unit gives some insight into the way social technologies are constructed, and are limited by the human material with which they must work. First, a little background is necessary. Recent social technology theory is undertaken with the benefit of the pioneering human ethology of Eibl-Eibesfeldt (1979), which articulated the human behavioral repertoire. It also makes use of evolutionary anthropology in the tradition of Alexander (1979), and the evolutionary sociology of Tiger and Fox (1971; Tiger 1969), who were the first to recognize the male bond as a primordial risk-reducing relationship. The male bond is an adaptation for group hunting and intergroup conflict and lends itself to deployment within more formal military command hierarchies. Conflict between hunter-gatherer groups is conducted on a small scale and with few casualties in any one engagement. The favoured tactic is ambush, since this minimizes risk to the attackers and requires little discipline, the latter being effectively absent between adults in pre-institutional societies. I quote Caton at some length to do justice to his paradigmatic analysis of one example of solidarity being socially engineered.

Military discipline aims in the first instance at the control of force by creating units responsive to command.... . The destruction it can wreak, and the terror it can inspire, are quite beyond anything hunters can imagine.... . Great Britain held the Indian sub-continent with ten regiments and a fleet.... . The effects are achieved without any alteration of the hunter's behavioral repertory. The secret lies in resequencing individual behavior, and in combining individual action to create group action, using no other resources than those already existing in the human material. Warriors are made into soldiers by detaching hunter solidarity from the diluting influences of family and by redirecting the evolutionary function of band solidarity to the public goods of political society. Such manipulative techniques are based on the same craftsman intuition that pervades the proto-technologies of early states.... . The simple insight that natural processes, including human nature, may by deft manipulation be made to multiply their uncultivated yield, is the cornerstone of capitalization, of political organization, and of progress (Caton 1988, pp. 10–11).

Recent research in the mechanisms of cultural evolution indicate that behavioural manipulations such as those described by Caton were partly achieved using newly invented techniques, partly using techniques copied from other groups, and partly by techniques accumulated in traditions of governance (Boehm 1996; Boyd and Richerson 1985; Salter 1995; Soltis et al. 1995). Groups can imitate the practices of other groups as deliberate attempts to reproduce admired qualities. For example, it has recently been confirmed that at least one primitive horticulturalist society, the Enga of Papua New Guinea, has conducted extensive trade in cult rituals aimed at manipulating own-group behaviour (Wiessner and Tumu 1998). Groups can also undertake experiments in group living, as argued by MacDonald with regard to the ancient Spartans (1983), medieval Christianity (1995), and Judaism (1994). It is clear that humans have designed societies to meet their needs, and this gives reason to hope that the benefits of intragroup fraternity can be retained while blunting its outgroup offensiveness. It is also possible that social technologies for achieving this are unworkable by virtue of the species' evolved social repertoire, the phylogenetic raw material from which all social systems are constructed. Fox (1971, p. 282) again expresses this point with admiral clarity:

Unlike the baboon or horse, we can imagine things that are different from the plot laid down for us, and we can put our dreams into practice. The question then is, will the dream work? If you accept that all behavior is culturally learned and that man can learn anything, then the answer is yes. The only limit is human ingenuity. We can invent any kind of society for ourselves. If you believe ... that we have a species-specific repertoire of behavior that can be combined successfully only in certain ways, then the answer is no. There are definite limits to what this animal can do, to the kinds of societies it can operate, to the kinds of culture it can live with. But there is no end to its dreams and its fantasies.

In the following section I look at new developments in evolutionary theory that promise to shed new light on human nature, and consider ways in which this new understanding might be manipulated to circumvent the two-edged effect.

## Evolutionary theory and skewing the double-edged effect

Sociobiology might show the way to engineering one-edged solidarity. Evolutionary theory is not limited to analysing trust as kin selection, and indeed there is more to trust than kin and ethnic ties. Culture-based theories of group selection are contending in the market-place of ideas with the individual selectionist theories that have dominated selection theory for the last three decades (Boehm 1996; Eibl-Eibesfeldt 1982; Rushton 1989; Wilson and Sober 1994). If these theories are verified the evolutionary analysis of bonds for conducting risky transactions will need to be extended.

### *Group-as-vehicle selection and social identity theory*

Wilson and Sober (1994) distinguish between groups as replicators and as vehicles, developing the distinction made by E.O. Wilson (1975, p. 562) and Dawkins (1982). The classical criticisms of group selection have targeted the notion that groups are replicators. To produce genetic effects through differential group reproduction requires suppression of free riders and a high rate of group extinctions with little intergroup migration, the last condition being especially unrealistic in the human case given the documented exogamy of hunter-gatherer groups (Maynard Smith 1976; Williams 1966); but the last two criticisms do not apply to individual adaptations for group living. Shaw and Wong (1989) follow up this point with regard to ethnocentrism. Groups have been valuable, even crucial, vehicles for individual human survival and reproduction. This has selected for individual traits that draw individuals to groups and hold them there, such as cooperativeness, ranking behaviour, loneliness, indoctrinability, and ethnocentrism. Individuals who did not manage to fit into a group and conform to social controls on group loyalty would have been disadvantaged.

The process might have selected for indoctrinability to group identity and self-sacrifice for the group, though making a case for this requires circumventing the free-riding problem. Assuming that group discipline was inadequate to exact uniformly high levels of altruism, the risks of intergroup conflict would afflict those showing most indoctrinability and group identification. Thus, genes coding for high levels of indoctrinability and group identification would be weeded out in favour of genes that coded for selfish behaviour (Campbell 1972, p. 33). Yet indoctrinability appears to be a species universal (Eibl-Eibesfeldt and Salter 1998). Some theoreticians argue that free-riders are prevented from circumventing cultural constraints by close mutual monitoring and punishment, well-documented in hunter-gatherer groups (Boyd and Richerson 1992; Eibl-Eibesfeldt 1982). Campbell (1972, pp. 30–1) draws on Trivers (1971) and Ranulf (1938) in noting the prevalence of moralistic aggression against selfish free riders, behaviour that would have facilitated group selection by suppressing free riders. So it is possible that mutual monitoring is indeed sufficiently rigorous to punish or deter cheaters.

Campbell prefers an individual selection model based on Waddington's (1960) argument that indoctrinability has been selected because of its general utility in facilitating cultural accumulation. "Probably the overall adaptive advantage for indoctrinability, group identification, and fear of ostracism is strong enough to overweigh the negative selection produced when the most indoctrinable incur greater fatality rates in wartime" (Campbell 1972, pp. 33–4; and see Wilson 1975, p. 562). Also, if indoctrination had a fitness cost, then indoctrinating and disciplining behaviour would be selected both socially and genetically when differentially directed towards non-kin. This is an avenue for further research.

The pattern of behaviour summarized by Social Identity Theory conforms to what one would expect to result from group-as-vehicle selection. The following summary of that theory in relation to ethnic conflict is based on a review of the relevant literature by MacDonald (1998, and in this volume). The starting point of social identity theory is the finding that individuals actively engage in categorizing themselves and others in social categories or groups. These groups are then stereotyped and evaluated, more or less disjunctively and intensely depending on a number of factors including the actor's personality, objective differences between groups, and perceived competition between the groups.[12] Probably due to individual need for positive self-esteem, ingroups are positively evaluated and outgroups negatively evaluated.

Bearing on the double-edged nature of ethnocentrism is the analysis by Tajfel (1981) of group identification in which negative stereotyping of outgroups developed spontaneously, in the absence of intergroup competition. In this experiment subjects were randomly assigned to groups, with no conflict of interest and no history of hostility between groups. Even when subjects were informed that assignment was random they still attempted to maximize group differences, apparently in an attempt to outcompete other groups. At least in Western cultures, group competition is thus easily triggered.

Conflict of interest between groups lowers the triggering threshold for ethnocentrism and intensifies the double-edge effect. The seminal research in this area was conducted by Sherif (1966), who randomly assigned boys to groups and then set these groups against one another in a series of competitions. Group membership became a salient aspect of personal identity. Furthermore, the boys negatively stereotyped members of other groups and acted on these evaluations with aggressive conduct (and see Triandis 1990). Emotional attachment to ingroup and rejection of outgroup members is implicated in these processes.

Invidious stereotyping of other groups is intensified when they are perceived as impermeable (Hogg and Abrams 1987). The endogamy cited by Bonacich and van den Berghe as typical of ethnic middleman groups is thus likely to be an important source of reactive discrimination against them. Perceived intergroup competition also intensifies social distance by increasing the disjunctiveness of negative outgroup stereotyping. Individual do this by exaggerating ingroup similarity and contrasting this to an exaggeratedly homogeneous outgroup, forming a disjunct from a more continuous distribution of characteristics, and in a manner that enhances ingroup status and depresses that of the outgroup. Anthropological evidence indicates this to be a human universal (Reynolds et al. 1987). The phenomenon has long been recognized under various headings, such as Keith's (1947/1968, pp. 86–7) interpretation of it as a dual ethical code, an interpretation he also applied to the group behaviour of young children and chimpanzees. A recent review of primate and child ethology by van der Dennen (1995) confirms Keith's view, and indicates that the double-edge effect is universal and innate.

Social Identity Theory suggests a method for ameliorating intergroup hostility, or rather explaining the success of an old trick used by innumerable leaders. By providing an otherwise divided group with an imperative superordinate goal, a new group identity can sometimes be forged in opposition to some external group or challenge. Sherif (1966) found that this was the only way he could lesson antagonism between his groups of boys. The same point was made by the early sociologist Sumner (1906, p. 12): "The exigencies of war with outsiders are what make peace inside, lest internal discord should weaken the we-group for war. These exigencies also make government and law in the ingroup, in order to prevent quarrels and enforce discipline." The power of an external threat to unite peoples with otherwise competing interests is a cardinal lesson of the Cold War, which for its duration helped hold together the two multi-ethnic competitors. According to ethnic nepotism theory, while a common goal will produce some cooperation among disparate individuals and ethnies, it should produce more among related peoples. Conversely, to generate a given level of group solidarity in a multi-ethnic state probably requires stronger superordinate goals than in a more ethnically homogeneous state. Ruling élites might find an oppositional foreign policy more necessary to produce domestic unity in a multicultural than in a monocultural state.

Any use of ethnic solidarity, whether defensive or aggressive, will be curbed by forgoing ethnic appeals altogether. Perhaps the resulting loss of within-group altruism can be mitigated by territorial solidarity, patriotism versus nationalism. As already noted, identification with a home range is a recurring feature of tribal and nationalist traditions. Shared territory acts as a recognition marker (Shaw and Wong 1989) on which some ingroup affiliation and outgroup antagonism can be predicated; but it also provides information for the reproduction of some forms of group identity. Simply by growing up together in the same territory individuals might develop cooperative relationships and a shared sense of identity with relatively little reliance on cultural identity devices. Perhaps a stable community locality helps reproduce ethnic solidarity without recourse to dedicated cultural devices for reproducing group identity. One avenue of research for testing this possibility is to look at territorially defined organized criminal groups. It is possible that criminals have patriotism, or that bonding necessary for high-risk ventures can occur without the glue of kinship or ethnicity. The picture is probably complex, with different kinds of bonds overlapping.

Barth (1969) argued that ethnic identity is a matter of boundary definition. In his theory, boundaries between groups are more important to identity than the contents of group culture *per se*. This is compatible with ethnic nepotism theory, for which gradients in relatedness are boundary features of special relevance to defining ethnic identity. It is also relevant to the way territory provides physical boundaries. In contrast to long-resident groups, mobile ethnic groups such as diaspora peoples use cultural and ritual devices, often entailing reaffirmation of a wish to return to an ancestral homeland (Connor 1985; Spicer 1971). Great flexibility is shown in choice of ethnic and racial markers, though difficult-to-fake features such as dialect and especially lineage are given priority over easily acquired cultural features such as dress (van den Berghe 1981). For most of the species' existence, co-residence has been a reliable guide to band membership. Perhaps a long history of territorial stability and panmixia results in the atrophying of cultural mechanisms for marking group boundaries between communities. Family and clan names are one such mechanism. Until the advent of the centralized bureaucratic state, family names were not the norm in Europe. German-speaking alpine communities, slow to bureaucratize, still tend to use place names in preference to family names (W. Schiefenhövel personal communication). Sedentary farming peoples living in small communities had no need of family nomenclature, even though clan and family lineages have always been of first importance in demarcating social ties and obligations.[13] Territorially identified groups are likely to be more assimilable than culturally identified ones. Even in the absence of assimilation, the redefinition of a mixed group according to common territorial boundaries should help create some unity. Thus multicultural societies can call themselves countries, and invoke loyalty to place. Territorially defined states might thus be more tolerant of cultural and racial minorities than ethnically defined ones, but it is not at all obvious how this approach could selectively blunt offensive deployment of solidarity between countries. Also, the deep racial divisions within the United States offer sobering counterevidence to these speculations. As with the common-goal strategy, territorial solidarity probably works best in a relatively homogeneous society.

## *Cultural group selection and indoctrinability*

Another group evolutionary theory that is yielding some confirmatory results is cultural group selection (Boyd and Richerson 1985; MacDonald 1994; Soltis et al. 1995). It shares some features with group-as-vehicle selection. The idea is that human groups can invent or choose changes in lifestyle, "experiments in living" as MacDonald puts it (1994). These then can have differential effects on reproductive fitness within the group, and for the group as a whole. Group members who are effective players according to the new rules will have more offspring or help their close relatives to do so. Groups that adopt functional lifestyle innovations, perhaps agriculture or a new initiation ritual that produces greater social cohesion, will tend to displace other groups or be emulated by them. Hence culture spreads and with it new selection pressures. As with group-as-vehicle selection, free riders are prevented from circumventing the cultural constraints by close mutual monitoring and punishment. Boehm (1996) argues that hunter-gatherer egalitarianism is marked by consensual decision making and was a precondition for group selection. Purposefulness was an essential feature of cultural evolution, and social arrangements contained deliberate design based on insight, argument, and planning.

The important trait of indoctrinability is predicted by both group-as-vehicle selection theory and cultural group selection theory (Campbell 1972; Eibl-Eibesfeldt 1982; Eibl-Eibesfeldt and Salter 1998; E.O. Wilson 1975). Individuals unable to conform and show loyalty to the group would come under selection pressure in both cases. Differences in indoctrination practices within and between cultures might explain the great variability shown in ethnic solidarity, from near-indifference and tolerance to extreme xenophobia. Thus, one approach to circumventing the double-edged effect might be to manipulate the process by which group identity develops. One constraint is that the process should be directed at the young, since group identification may exhibit something of a critical period culminating in early adulthood, which is capitalized upon by initiation rites in traditional societies (Eibl-Eibesfeldt 1998). The phenomenon is in need of research. It appears that initiation rituals are used to expand the boundaries of group identity, and hence cooperativeness (Wiessner 1998), suggesting that we are predisposed spontaneously to identify with the small, face-to-face groups into which we are born but must be taught to embrace a wider community. However this by itself does not show a way out of the double-edged effect.

In modern societies initiation rituals are less important for indoctrination than are the mass media and mass education, which pervade the typical young person's world. As a result it has become increasingly feasible to change the content of ideology, perhaps in such a way to frustrate the unwanted side effect of invidious stereotyping of outgroups. One candidate is the ideology of ethnic pluralism or multiculturalism in English-speaking societies in the last quarter of the twentieth century. This ideology targets majority ethnocentrism as the most potentially disruptive kind. The mass media and education system celebrate minority identities while promoting universalism among the majority ethnic group. This is reinforced with ritual affirmation of minority grievance and majority guilt, and punishment of majority particularism whether in the form of discrimination or expression of ethnic consciousness. Multiculturalism also dismantles, or consolidates the dismantling of, the institutional bases of majority ethnic identity and dominance, such as restrictive immigration laws and emphasis on the majority group's religion, culture, and history in schools and public rituals (Harrison and Bennett 1995). In immigrant societies such as the United States, Canada, and Australia the result has been the decline of majority ethnic groups' proportion of the population (for the U.S. see Day 1993; for related analyses see Bouvier and Grant 1994; Harrison and Bennett 1995). Multicultural elites downplay the displacement of the majority population as inevitable, of no importance, and even as beneficial due to the resulting diversity (Clinton 1998). At the same time, multicultural doctrine advocates loyalty to the overall multi-ethnic society, which is given the oxymoronic title "universal nation" (Wattenberg 1991). Society is held to be worthy of loyalty because of some noble social idea expressed by it, rather than because of shared ethnicity. Recently diversity has been added to the pantheon of ideals along with equality, freedom, tolerance, and so on (e.g. Kallen 1956/1916; Parrillo 1996; Walzer 1995; Wattenberg 1991).[14]

It will be interesting to see whether this marriage of minority particularism and majority universalism is sustainable within a unified democratic polity. Van den Berghe (1981, chapter 9) believes multi-ethnic democracy is feasible under certain conditions, but is less sanguine about the prospects of multiracial democracy. From an evolutionary perspective one would expect multiracialism especially to lead to a decline in public altruism that would hamper redistributive programmes, inducing less successful groups to demand forceful allocation of resources such as found in affirmative action policies. Recent cross-cultural research has confirmed the negative effects of multiculturalism on taxpayer's willingness to contribute to public goods such as welfare, libraries and schools, and despite its wealth the United States has so far found it politically impossible to institute a comprehensive welfare system comparable to those found in more homogeneous European societies (Alesina et al. 1997; Easterly and Levine 1997; Gilens 1996; Salter forthcoming). At the same time, the growing racial diversity of European states is contributing to a decline in welfare rights (Faist 1995). Whatever its faults, however, multiculturalism of the American kind has so far proven self-sustaining and its advocates can truly claim it is workable, if fraternity as well as majority ethnic identity are deemed expendable.

Universalism might present a social-engineering problem arising from the double-edged effect. Conservative commentators argue that loss of tribal (including religious) identity tends to atomize society and degrade standards of reciprocity and communal affiliation. If true, this would strike at the heart of the universalist argument that the evils of racism and nationalism can be countered by dissolving particular identities, or merging them into a national or global one, through intermarriage or cultural homogenization or both (e.g. Freedman 1979). Social planners who want rapid change might be faced with a choice between inculcating in citizens a robust sense of duty and altruism, or sacrificing this for a universalist society. Campbell has made a more general point along these lines in discussing methods for eliminating war:

> [In addition to war] our great cities and large populations are also manifestations of our termite-like capacity for complex social interdependence; they are thus also in jeopardy as we tear down the belief systems of the past and the altruistic purposes and dispositions they provided. What are grounds for optimism with regard to the problem of war may also be grounds for pessimism about our capacity to maintain the still functional aspects of complex social interdependence (Campbell 1972, p. 35).

The optimal solution might be to accept that human sympathy declines with social distance, exploit this fact to build stable, caring civic communities from relatively homogeneous ethnies, while mitigating the invidious attitudes thus generated towards outgroups. As suggested in the above discussion of social technologies, mitigation has proved reasonably successful at the institutional level, whereby states conduct educational campaigns to counter extreme xenophic ideologies and outlaw discrimination on the basis of group membership. States can also enter into binding trade and diplomatic relationships with other countries in order to build interdependency and delay the foreign policy programmes of aggressively nationalist governments that might come to power from time to time.

## Cultural constraints on social technological innovation

Social technologies are constrained culturally as well as biologically. This is evident in organizing. Innovative administrators who would create an organization must begin with the beliefs, behaviours, gender identities, and standards of legitimation existing in the population from which staff are recruited. Thus the cultural and institutional environment affects an organization's style and methods (Scott and Christensen 1995). The same probably applies to ethnic activist groups. If so, it should be relatively easy for a group to switch between mafia and nationalist-fighter activity, or between dissident and middleman economic activity; but it will be more difficult to redeploy a group conditioned for violent activity to peaceful means, and vice versa. Culture, as well as habit, will have exerted a conservative influence, limiting the rate of social technological innovation.

One example that illustrates conservation of culture is Chechens at the end of the Soviet Union. Traditionally Chechens have been "addicted to firearms as a way of settling disputes or merely demonstrating prowess" (Handelman 1995, p. 50). When the decline of the Soviet state of the late 1980s allowed organized crime to spread, violent Chechens gangs were among the most successful. Chechnia declared its independence from Russia in 1991, culminating in the first Russian invasion of the province. Many Chechen mafiosi returned to their homeland to fight. Dunn (1996, p. 65) notes that this resulted in the rapid decline in Chechen gang numbers in Russia during this period. The same attitudes, skills, and practices were similarly deployable to both organized crime and guerrilla warfare. These included weapons skills, small-group male bonds, practice in violence, but also ethnic affiliation, which structured both sets of activities. One conservative mechanism to explore in this regard is the imprinting of group values during the critical period of high indoctrinability in adolescence (Eibl-Eibesfeldt 1998).

Offensive group activity requires more organizing than defensive activity, since kin and ethnic solidarity are more automatic in defence than in offence. Spicer (1971) found that the oppositional stories that inspired persistent ethnic groups dwelt mainly on suffering caused by outside attack, rather than on victories won. Defensive solidarity is more likely to be self-organizing, a spontaneous emotional response to a real threat to the group. Solidarity is also a resource for marshalling offensive group action, but as part of a deliberate strategy. One demographic category that does tend to self-organize for offensive behaviour is young men, whether as tribal warriors, political rioters, or football hooligans (Salter et al. 1998); but this exception proves the rule, since other categories are more likely to be found in defence than attack. If culture plays a large role in shaping intergroup aggression out of solidarity, then this would be cause for hope that aggression, at least organized aggression, is sensitive to social technologies of one sort or another. Campbell again had something to say of relevance to this theme:

> [Assuming that] man's termite- and ant-like capacity for military heroism is in culturally transmitted dispositions, not genetic ones, makes me more optimistic about the possibilities of social inventions eliminating war, for such developments will have the temptations of biological selfishness on their side. However resistant culture is to change, it is probably less so than the gene pool (Campbell 1972, p. 34).

## Selection of bond types?

Something that is fascinating about the profound political changes that have con-vulsed the ex-Soviet Union and other Communist societies over the last decade has been the robustness of natural human bonds. Several examples have already been documented in this chapter: the emergence of family- and ethnic-based mafia organizations that sprang up as law and order declined; the clan-based under-ground economy of the Soviet Union; and the survival of minority national iden-tities despite concerted attempts at universalization and Russification. As artificial political structures dissolve and new ones are constructed, the phylogenetically ancient bonds of family and clan, and even their weaker form of ethnic ties, demonstrate remarkable resilience in the face of the police state and decades of indoctrination aimed at rooting them out. In the case of Soviet repression of Chechens, Jews, and others, those ties may have been strengthened (Sharansky 1988, p. xii; Simis 1982). "[T]he deportations had strengthened the very charac-teristics that made [Chechens] such a cohesive and dangerous criminal threat" (Handelman 1995, p. 50). It is as if hostile environments such as repressive regimes differentially select the strongest ties, weeding out the more ephemeral reciprocal relationships that coordinate much of the economy and society in liberal environ-ments. As repression eases, some of the surviving groups and networks find them-selves at a competitive advantage in a society that is more atomized than it was before the repression set in. Commercial and political benefits accrue differentially to these solidary groups until the broader society revives.

The idea of social selection of bond types can be extended using the argument developed so far concerning different tie strengths and their utility in risky trans-actions. I want to suggest, as a prompt for further research, that social selection can increase the salience of kin and ethnic group solidarities as organizing principles during and after oppressive regimes. Other mechanisms for increasing trustwor-thiness, such as reward and punishment, are more easily suppressed by oppressive regimes, and this could leave kin and ethnic solidary groups to sieze economic and political opportunities as oppression wanes.

Extending this speculation, there might even be a cross-generational effect, since kin and ethnic ties reproduce within lineages with greater fidelity than do other kinds of ties. Cousins, the children of a group of siblings, probably retain a corpo-rate family identity and keep in touch during their lives more than do, say, the chil-dren of a group of business colleagues. Exchange and friendship ties are like the clouds that Dawkins (1987) disqualifies as candidates for natural selection on the grounds that they do not reproduce. The few exceptions prove the rule, such as the Kalahari Bushman tradition of passing on *hxaro* exchange ties between descendants of the original partners (Wiessner 1982). Inheritance of reciprocal and friendship ties is dependent on factors that are more numerous and changeable than inheri-tance of kin and ethnic ties. Cross-generation selection requires a stable replicator on which to record and thus iterate modifications. Lineages and thus ethnic groups replicate group identities and often nepotistic ties. Ethnic-nepotistic ties are not necessarily or even usually replicated between particular descendants of the bond partners of a previous generation. Rather, bond replication occurs stochastically within successive generations of a particular ethnie. Stochastic replication is bound to be more reliable than the particular variety needed to replicate friendships and trading partners. The social technologies that intensify and exploit ethnic ties are also reproduced (culturally) cross-generationally within the group, passing either from parents to child, or between successive élites. Thus it is a case of dual inheritance, of a group identity, and the culture that manipulates it.

# Summary

Social ties, notably between kith, kin and co-ethnics, increase trust and trustworthiness, and thus mitigate breach of agreement. As such, ties have a commercial value where contract law or other methods of enforcement do not apply or are weak, such as in illicit business and middleman trading. Evolutionary theory can enlarge this insight in the form of van den Berghe's ethnic nepotism theory, which provides an ultimate explanation for the nature of ethnic ties. These ties are held to be homologous with nepotism (altruism between kin) evolved in the small-group hunter-gatherer milieu, though the ethnic variety is usually of weaker intensity. Nepotistic ties are so strong that they can elicit self-sacrifice in defence of kin, but this reduces the actor's ability to reproduce, and so depresses individual fitness. Nevertheless, kin and ethnic nepotism are human universals which must have been generally adaptive across a wide spectrum of environments in the evolutionary past. If nepotism tends to depress individual fitness, why has it not been weeded out of the gene pool? NeoDarwinism provides the answer: extreme altruism is adaptive when it preserves or increases *inclusive* fitness, the total number of copies of an individual's genome. Each individual carries a complete copy of his or her own genes. Siblings carry half of each other's genes, as do parents and children. First cousins carry one eighth of each other's genes. Thus it is adaptive to risk one's life for two siblings or for two children or eight first cousins. Ethnic nepotism theory conceptualizes fellow ethnics as distant relatives who carry some small proportion of each other's distinctive genes. The small inclusive fitness stake in fellow ethnics makes it maladaptive to show much ethnic solidarity, except when large numbers are likely to benefit, as in group defence. Ethnic ties belong to the weak end of a continuum of bond strengths correlated with degree of genetic relatedness.

A necessary addition to ethnic nepotism theory is the role of culture in the form of social technologies that regulate the intensity of ethnic altruism. Intensification is achieved by symbols and rituals that portray the group to its members as kin, redirecting intense familial altruism towards individuals who are only distantly or even fictively related. Weakening comes from avoiding or subverting these symbols and rituals so as to direct altruism away from real or putative ethnic kin. Cultural and situational factors can thus raise or lower ethnic tie strength relative to other ties. The evolutionary approach provides further insights. In small-scale societies kin solidarity is double-edged, deployed defensively in exchange networks and offensively in intergroup raiding. Ethnic solidarity also tends to be two-edged, though culture plays a critical role in determining the sharpness of the edges. While the aggressive side of ethnic solidarity is well recognized in the case of the nation state, the aggressive side of minority ethnic solidarity is often overlooked. In making this point I discussed four examples of the deployment of ethnic solidarity – ethnic mafias, nationalist fighters, ethnic middlemen, and ethnic dissidents. All these groups use kin and ethnic bonds defensively as insurance against defection from risky transactions, but mafias, middlemen, and rebels also use their solidarity to create risks for opponents.

Is it possible to design one-edged solidarity, arranging society to enjoy the benefits of cohesive and generalized public altruism but without the aggressive tendencies towards neighbouring societies? Options were discussed without reaching a definite conclusion. Factors include the ethology of social engineering, which indicates biological constraints on social-technological innovation. Another factor is the spontaneous double-edged effect implied by social identity theory. I also discussed the implications of evolutionary theories of group selection that challenge orthodox theories based on individual selection. There are also cultural constraints on social technologies that hold some promise for engineering single-edged solidarity.

Finally, I noted that kin- and ethnic-group ties are reproduced across generations with some fidelity. Fidelity is high in the case of nuclear families but lower in the case of ethnic solidarity because ethnic ties are much more contingent on the reproduction of culture and situation, especially the social technologies that define the group and regulate its level of solidarity. This dependence on culture and situation allows for dramatic fluctuations in the prevalence and average intensity of ethnic bonds as well as bonds between distant relatives. A special case is oppressive regimes suppressing weaker types of bonds by punishing their expression. I advance the hypothesis that the process is analogous to natural selection, but of relationships rather than of individual characteristics. Weaker ties are weeded out as they become maladaptive; stronger ties survive even if the individuals involved suffer because they are evolved to serve inclusive, not individual, fitness. The surviving ties are relatively intense and generally associated with real instead of fictive genetic interests. Solidarities forged in defence are then available to be deployed competitively in the economic and political realms once the oppressive regime is lifted.

# References

Abrams, D. and Hogg, M.A. (1990). *Social identity theory: Constructive and critical advances.* Springer-Verlag, New York.

Alesina, A., Baqir, R. and Easterly, W. (1999). Public goods and ethnic divisions. *Quarterly Journal of Economics,* **114**, 1243–84.

Alessandrini, S. and Dallago, B., eds (1987). *The unofficial economy: Consequences and perspectives in different economic systems.* Gower, Aldershot, UK.

Alexander, R.D. (1979). *Darwinism and human affairs.* University of Washington Press, Seattle.

Alexander, R. (1995/1985). A biological interpretation of moral systems. In *Issues in evolutionary ethics*, (ed. P. Thompson), pp. 179–202. State University of New York Press, Albany, NY.

Anderson, B. (1983). *Imagined communities. Reflections on the origin and spread of nationalism*. Verso Editions, London.

Annan, N. (1997). Secret sharers [review of T.G. Ash, 1997, *The file: A personal history*, Random House]. *New York Review of Books*, **44**(14), 22–3.

Ballard, J.A. and Mcdowell, A.J. (1991). Hate and combat behavior. *Armed Forces & Society*, **17**(2), 229–241.

Bar-Tal, D. (1993). Patriotism as fundamental beliefs of group members. *Politics and Individual Differences*, **3**(2), 45–62.

Barth, F. (1969). *Ethnic groups and boundaries*. Little, Brown, & Co., Boston, MA.

Bartov, O. (1989). Daily life and motivation in war – the Wehrmacht in the Soviet Union. *Journal of Strategic Studies*, **12**(2), 200–14.

Berghe, P.L. van den (1979). *Human family systems. An evolutionary view*. Elsevier, New York.

Berghe, P.L. van den (1981). *The ethnic phenomenon*. Elsevier, New York.

Berghe, P.L. van den (1995). "Does race matter?" *Nations and Nationalism* **1**(3), 357–68.

Billig, M. (1993). Patriotism and forms of community: A comment. *Politics and Individual Differences*, **3**(2), 63–6.

Blalock, H. (1967). *Toward a theory of minority-group relations*. Wiley, New York.

Blalock, H., and Wilken, P.H. (1979). *Intergroup processes: a micro-macro problem*. The Free Press, New York.

Blok, A. (1974). *The Mafia of a Sicilian village, 1860–1960 [Die Mafia in einem sizilianischen Dorf 1860–1960. Eine Studie über gewalttätige bäuerliche Unternehmer, translated by H. Fliessbach, Frankfurt: Suhrkamp, 1981]*. Oxford University Press, Oxford.

Boehm, C. (1996). Emergency decisions, cultural-selection mechanisms, and group selection [with peer commentary]. *Current Anthropology*, **37**(5), 763–93.

Bonacich, E. (1973). A theory of middleman minorities. *American Sociological Review*, **38**, 583–94.

Borjas, G.J. (1992). Ethnic capital and intergenerational mobility. *The Quarterly Journal of Economics*, **107**(February), 123–50.

Bouvier, L.F. and Grant, L. (1994). *How many Americans? Population, immigration and the environment*. Sierra Club, San Francisco.

Boyd, R., and Richerson, P. J. (1985). *Culture and the evolutionary process*. University of Chicago Press, Chicago.

Boyd, R., and Richardson, P.J. (1992). Punishment allows the evolution of cooperation (or anything else) in sizable groups. *Ethology and Sociobiology*, **13**, 171–95.

Bruck, C. (1994). *Master of the game: Steve Ross and the creation of Time Warner*. Simon & Schuster, New York.

Burnstein, E., Crandall, C., and Kitayama, S. (1994). Some neo-Darwinian decision rules for altruism: weighing cues for inclusive fitness as a function of the biological importance of the decision. *Journal of Personality and Social Psychology,* **67**, 773–89.

Campbell, D.T. (1972). On the genetics of altruism and the counter-hedonic components in human culture. *Journal of Social Issues,* **28**(3), 21–37.

Caplow, T. (1982). Christmas gifts and kin networks. *American Sociological Review,* **47**, 383–92.

Caton, H.P. (1988). *The politics of progress: The origins and development of the commercial republic, 1600–1835.* University of Florida Press, Gainesville.

Caton, H.P. (1994/1983). Descriptive political ethology. Griffith University, Brisbane, Australia.

Caton, H.P. (1998). Reinvent yourself: Labile psychosocial identity and the lifestyle marketplace. In *Indoctrinability, ideology, and warfare: Evolutionary perspectives,* (eds I. Eibl-Eibesfeldt and F.K. Salter), pp. 325–43. Berghahn, Oxford and New York.

Chagnon, N. (1980). Mate competition, favouring close kin, and village fissioning among the Yanomama Indians. In *Evolutionary Biology and Human Social Behavior,* (eds N.A. Chagnon and W. Irons), pp. 86–131. Duxbury, North Scituate, MA.

Chagnon, N. (1988). Life histories, blood revenge, and warfare in a tribal population. *Science,* **239**, 985–92.

Clinton, W.J. (1998). Speech on diversity. Commencement address at Portland, Oregan, State University. *The Social Contract,* **8**(4), 334–7.

Coase, R.H. (1937). The nature of the firm. *Economica,* **4**, 386–405.

Connor, W. (1985). The impact of homelands upon diasporas. In *Modern diasporas in international politics* (ed. G. Sheffer), pp. 16–46. Croom Helm, London.

Connor, W. (1993). Beyond reason: The nature of the ethnonational bond. *Ethnic and Racial Studies,* **16**(3), 373–89.

Connor, W. (1994). *Ethnonationalism. The quest for understanding.* Princeton University Press, Princeton, NJ.

Creveld, M. van (1982). *Fighting power: German and U.S. army performance, 1939–1945.* Greenwood Press, Westport, CT.

Daly, M. and Wilson, M. (1988). *Homicide.* Aldine & de Gruyter, New York.

Dawkins, R. (1982). *The extended phenotype: The gene as the unit of selection.* Freeman, Oxford and San Francisco.

Dawkins, R. (1987). *The blind watchmaker. Why the evidence of evolution reveals a universe without design.* W.W. Norton, New York.

Day, J.C. (1993). *Population projections of the United States, by age, race, and Hispanic origin: 1993 to 2050.* U.S. Bureau of the Census.

Dennen, J.M.G. van der (1987). Ethnocentrism and in-group/out-group differentiation. A review and interpretation of the literature. In *The sociobiology of ethnocentrism,* (eds V. Reynolds, V. Falger and I. Vine), University of Georgia Press, Athens, GA.

Dennen, J.M.G. van der (1995). *The origin of war. The evolution of a male-coalitional strategy.* 2 vols. Origin, Groningen, The Netherlands.

Dunn, G. (1996). Major mafia gangs in Russia. *Transnational Organized Crime*, **2**(2/3) [Special double issue: *Russian organized crime: the new threat?*], 63–87.

Easterly, W., and Levine, R. (1997). Africa's growth tragedy: Policies and ethnic divisions. *Quarterly Journal of Economics*, **112**(November), 1203–50.

Edwards, P. (1990). *Blood brothers. How Canada's most powerful Mafia family runs its business.* Key Porter Books, Toronto.

Eibl-Eibesfeldt, I. (1972/1970). *Love and hate: the natural history of behavior patterns.* (transl. G. Strachan). Holt, Rinehart & Winston, New York (Original German edn 1970, R. Piper, Munich).

Eibl-Eibesfeldt, I. (1979). Human ethology: Concepts and implications for the sciences of man. *Behavioral and Brain Sciences*, **2**, 1–57.

Eibl-Eibesfeldt, I. (1982). Warfare, man's indoctrinability and group selection. *Ethology (Zeitschrift für Tierpsychologie)*, **60**, 177–98.

Eibl-Eibesfeldt, I. (1989). *Human ethology.* Aldine de Gruyter, New York.

Eibl-Eibesfeldt, I. (1998). Us and the others: The familial roots of ethnonationalism. In *Indoctrinability, ideology, and warfare: Evolutionary perspectives*, (eds I. Eibl-Eibesfeldt and F.K. Salter), pp. 21–53. Berghahn, Oxford and New York.

Eibl-Eibesfeldt, I., and Salter, F.K., eds (1998). *Indoctrinability, ideology, and warfare: Evolutionary perspectives.* Berghahn, Oxford and New York.

Erikson, E.H. (1966). Ontogeny of ritualization in man. *Philosophical Transactions of the Royal Society of London*, **B251**, 337–49.

Faist, T. (1995). Ethnicization and racialization of welfare-state politics in Germany and the USA. *Ethnic and Racial Studies*, **18**(2), 219–50.

Ferguson, N. (1999). *The house of Rothschild: Money's prophets, 1798–1848.* Viking, New York.

Fishman, J. (1996/1980). Ethnicity as being, doing, and knowing [excerpted from "Social theory and ethnography", in Peter Sugar (ed.), *Ethnic diversity and conflict in Eastern Europe*, ABC-Clio]. In *Ethnicity* (eds J. Hutchinson and A.D. Smith), pp. 63–9. Oxford University Press, Oxford and New York.

Fox, R. (1971). The cultural animal. In *Man and beast: Comparative social behavior*, (eds J.F. Eisenberg and W.S. Dillon), pp. 275–96. Smithsonian Institution Press, Washington, DC.

Fox, R., and Fleising, U. (1976). Human ethology. In *Annual Review of Anthropology*, Vol. 5. (eds B. Siegal, A. Beals and S. Tyler), pp. 265–88. Annual Reviews, Palo Alto.

Frank, R.H. (1987). If *Homo Economicus* could choose his own utility function, would he want one with a conscience? *American Economic Review*, **77**, 593–604.

Freedman, D.G. (1979). *Human sociobiology: A holistic approach.* Free Press, New York.

Geiger, G. (1988). On the evolutionary origins and function of political power. *Journal of Social and Biological Structures*, **11**, 235–50.

Gerth, H.H. and Mills, C.W., eds (1958). *From Max Weber: Essays in sociology.* Oxford University Press, New York.

Gilens, M. (1996). "Race coding" and white opposition to welfare. *American Political Science Review*, **90**(3), 593–604.

Goldberg, J.J. (1996). *Jewish power: Inside the American Jewish establishment.* Addison-Wesley, Reading, MA.

Goldman, W.Z. (1993). *Women, the state, and revolution: Soviet family policy and social life, 1917–1936.* vol. 90. Cambridge University Press, Cambridge, UK.

Granovetter, M.S. (1977/1973). The strength of weak ties. In *Social networks: a developing paradigm* (ed. S. Leinhardt), pp. 347–67. Academic Press, New York.

Gurr, T.R. (1993). *Minorities at risk. A global view of ethnopolitical conflicts.* United States Institute of Peace Press, Washington, DC.

Gurr, T.R., and Harff, B. (1994). *Ethnic conflict in world politics.* Westview Press, Boulder, Colo.

Hamilton, W.D. (1975). Innate social aptitudes of man: An approach from evolutionary genetics. In *Biosocial anthropology*, (ed. R. Fox), pp. 133–55. Malaby Press, London.

Handelman, S. (1995). *Comrade criminal: Russia's new Mafiya.* Yale University Press, New Haven, CT.

Harcourt, A.H., and Waal, F.B.M. de, eds (1992). *Coalitions and alliances in humans and other animals.* Oxford University Press, New York.

Harrison, R.J., and Bennett, C.E. (1995). Racial and ethnic diversity. In *State of the union: America in the 1990s. Volume Two: Social trends* (ed. R. Farley), pp. 141–210. Russell Sage Foundation, New York.

Heller, M. (1988). *Cogs in the Soviet Wheel. The formation of Soviet Man.* Collins Harvill, London.

Hill, E. (1993). Ibn-Khaldun. In *The Oxford companion to the politics of the world* (ed. J. Krieger), Oxford University Press, New York.

Hirshleifer, J. (1984). The emotions as guarantors of threats and promises. University of California Los Angeles. Department of Economics Working Paper 337.

Hogg, M.A., and Abrams, D. (1987). *Social identifications.* Routledge, New York.

Hogg, M.A., and D. Abrams (1993). Toward a single-process uncertainty-reduction model of social motivation in groups. *Group motivation: social psychological perspectives.* M.A. Hogg and D. Abrams. Harvester Wheatsheaf, London.

Holper, J.J. (1996). Kin term usage in *The Federalist*: evolutionary foundations of Publius's rhetoric. *Politics and the Life Sciences*, **15**(2), 265–72.

Horowitz, D.L. (1985). *Ethnic groups in conflict.* University of California Press, Berkeley.

Ianni, F.A.J. (1972). *A family business; kinship and social control in organized crime.* Russell Sage Foundation, New York.

Ianni, F.A.J. (1974). *Black Mafia: Ethnic succession in organized crime.* Simon & Schuster, New York.

Ibarra, H. (1992). Homophily and differential returns: Sex differences in network structure and access to an advertising firm. *Administrative Science Quarterly*, **37**, 422–47.

Johnson, G.R. (1987). In the name of the fatherland: An analysis of kin terms usage in patriotic speech and literature. *International Political Science Review*, **8**, 165–74.

Jones, C.P. (1999). *Kinship diplomacy in the ancient world*. Harvard University Press, Cambridge, MA.

Kallen, H. M. (1956/1916). *Cultural pluralism and the American idea: An essay in social philosophy*. University of Pennsylvania Press, Philadelphia.

Keeley, L. (1996). *War before civilization: The myth of the peaceful savage*. Oxford University Press, New York.

Keith, A. (1947/1968). *A new theory of human evolution*. Philosophical Library, New York.

Khazanov, A.M. (1995). *After the U.S.S.R. Ethnicity, nationalism, and politics in the Commonwealth of independent states*. University of Wisconsin Press, Madison.

Kleinknecht, W. (1996). *The new ethnic mobs. The changing face of organized crime in America*. Free Press, New York.

Koch, K.-F. (1974). *War and peace in Jalémó. The management of conflict in Highland New Guinea*. Harvard University Press, Cambridge, MA.

Kohn, H. (1960). *Pan-Slavism*. Vintage Books, New York.

Konner, M., and Shostak, M. (1986). Ethnographic romanticism and the idea of human nature: Parallels between Samoa and !Kung San. *The past and future of !Kung ethnography*. M. Biesele, R. Gordon and R. Lee. Buske, Hamburg, pp. 69–76.

Kostyrchenko, G. (1995). *Out of the red shadows: Anti-Semitism in Stalin's Russia*. Prometheus Books, New York.

Kowalewski, D. (1981). National rights protest in the Brezhnev era: Some determinants of success. *Ethnic and Racial Studies*, **4**(2), 175–88.

Landa, J.T. (1981). A theory of the ethnically homogeneous middleman group: an institutional alternative to contract law. *Journal of Legal Studies*, **10**(June), 349–62.

Landa, J.T. (1994). *Trust, ethnicity, and identity. Beyond trading networks, contract law, and gift-exchange*. Michigan University Press, Ann Arbor.

Light, I. and Karageorgis, S. (1994). The ethnic economy. In *The handbook of economic sociology*, (eds N.J. Smelser and R. Swedberg), pp. 647–71. Princeton University Press, Princeton.

Lind, M. (1995). *The next American nation: The new nationalism and the fourth American revolution*. Free Press, New York.

Lockard, J.S. and Paulhus, D.L., eds (1988). *Self-deception: An adaptive mechanism?* Prentice Hall, Englewood Cliffs, NJ.

Lucas, C. (1996). The theory and practice of denunciation in the French Revolution. *The Journal of Modern History*, **68**(4), 768–85.

MacDonald, K.B. (1983). Production, social controls, and ideology: toward a sociobiology of the phenotype. *Journal of Social and Biological Structures*, **6**, 297–317.

MacDonald, K.B. (1994). *A people that shall dwell alone: Judaism as a group evolutionary strategy*. Praeger, Westport, CT.

MacDonald, K.B. (1995). The establishment and maintenance of socially imposed monogamy in Western Europe [with peer commentary]. *Politics and the Life Sciences*, **14**(1), 3–46.

MacDonald, K.B. (1998). *Separation and its discontents: Toward an evolutionary theory of anti-Semitism*. Praeger, Westport, CT.

Maynard Smith, J. (1976). Group selection. *Quarterly Review of Biology*, **51**(2), 277–83.

McPherson, J.M. (1997). *For cause and comrades: Why men fought in the Civil War*. Oxford University Press USA, New York.

Messerschmidt, M. (1969). *Die Wehrmacht im NS-Staat. Zeit der Indoktrination*. R. v. Decker's Verlag/G. Schenck, Hamburg.

Murdock, G.P. (1949). *Social structure*. Macmillan, New York.

Park, R.E. (1939). The nature of race relations. In *Race relations and the race problem*, (ed. ET. Thompson), pp. 3–45. Duke University Press, Durham, NC.

Parrillo, V.N. (1996). *Diversity in America*. Pine Forge Press, Thousand Oaks, CA.

Ranulf, S. (1938). *Moral indignation and middle class psychology*. Levin & Munksgaard, Copenhagen.

Reynolds, V., Falger, V. and Vine, I., eds (1987). *The sociobiology of ethnocentrism. Evolutionary dimensions of xenophobia, discrimination, racism and nationalism*. Croom Helm, London.

Roes, F. (1996). Killers and victims. Interview of Martin Daly and Margo Wilson on homicide. *Human Ethology Newsletter*, **11**(4), 5–8.

Rushton, J.P. (1989). Genetic similarity in male friends. *Ethology and Sociobiology*, **10**, 361–73.

Rushton, J.P. (1995). *Race, evolution, and behavior*. Transaction Publishers, New Brunswick, NJ.

Salter, F.K. (1995). *Emotions in command. A naturalistic study of institutional dominance*. Oxford University Press Science Publications, Oxford.

Salter, F.K. (2001). A defence and an extension of Pierre van den Berghe's theory of ethnic nepotism. In *Evolutionary theory and ethnic conflict* (eds P. James and D. Goetze), pp. 39–70. Praeger, Westport, CT.

Salter, F.K. ed. (forthcoming). *Welfare, ethnicity, & altruism: New data & evolutionary theory*. Frank Cass, London.

Salter, F.K. (in preparation). *Ethnic infrastructures and elite ethnic competition in America: An evolutionary-Blalock analysis*.

Salter, F.K., Kruck, K. and Adang, O.M.J. (1998). Urban rioters and tribal warriors: The madding crowd, rationality, and justice. In *Research in public policy analysis and management*, Vol. 9. (ed. S.S. Nagel), pp. 185–209. JAI Press, Stamford, CT.

Schelling, T.C. (1960). *The strategy of conflict*. Oxford University Press, New York.

Scott, W.R. and Christensen, S., eds (1995). *The institutional construction of organizations. International and longitudinal studies*. Sage, London.

Seagrave, S. (1995). *Lords of the rim: The invisible empire of the overseas Chinese*. G.P. Putnam's Sons, New York.

Segal, N.L. (1988). Cooperation, competition, and altruism in human twinships: a sociobiological approach. In *Sociobiological perspectives on human development* (ed. K.B. MacDonald), pp. 168–206. Springer-Verlag, New York.

Sharansky, N. (1988). *Fear no evil*. Random House, New York.

Shaw, R.P. and Wong, Y. (1989). *Genetic seeds of warfare: evolution, nationalism, and patriotism*. Unwin Hyman, London.

Sherif, M. (1966). *In common predicament: The social psychology of intergroup conflict*. Houghton-Mifflin, Boston, MA.

Sillman, L.R. (1943). A psychiatric contribution to the problem of morale. *Journal of Nervous Mental Disorders*, **97**, 283–95.

Silverman, I. and Case, D. (1998). Ethnocentrism vs. pragmatism in the conduct of human affairs. In *Indoctrinability, ideology, and warfare: Evolutionary perspectives*, (eds I. Eibl-Eibesfeldt and F.K. Salter), pp. 389–406. Berghahn, Oxford.

Sime, J.D. (1983). Affiliative behaviour during escape to building exits. *Journal of Environmental Psychology*, **3**, 21–41.

Simis, K.M. (1982). *USSR: The corrupt society. The secret world of Soviet capitalism*. (transl. J. Edwards and Mitchell Schneider). Simon & Schuster, New York.

Smith, A. (1759/1808). *The theory of moral sentiments, or an essay toward an analysis of the principles by which men naturally judge concerning the conduct and character first of their neighbours and then of themselves*. (11th edn). Bell & Bradfute, Edinburgh.

Smith, A.D. (1986). *The ethnic origins of nations*. Basil Blackwell, Oxford.

Soltis, J., Boyd, R. and Richerson, P.J. (1995). Can group-functional behaviors evolve by cultural group selection? An empirical test [with peer commentary]. *Current Anthropology*, **36**(3), 473–94.

Spencer, H. (1892–3). *Principles of ethics*. Vol. 1. D. Appleton & Co., New York.

Spicer, E.H. (1971). Persistent cultural systems. *Science*, **174**(November), 795–800.

Sumner, W.G. (1906). *Folkways*. Ginn, Boston.

Tajfel, H. (1981). *Human groups and social categories: Studies in social psychology*. Cambridge University Press, Cambridge.

Thiessen, D., and Gregg, B. (1980). Human assortative mating and genetic equilibrium: An evolutionary perspective. *Ethology and Sociobiology*, **1**, 111–40.

Tiger, L. (1989/1969). *Men in groups*. Marion Boyars, New York and London.

Tiger, L. and Fox, R. (1989/1971). *The imperial animal*. (2nd edn). Henry Holt & Company, New York.

Tönnies, F. (1887/1955). *Community and association (Gemeinschaft und Gesellschaft)*. (transl. Charles P. Loomis). Routledge & Kegan Paul, London.

Triandis, H.C. (1990). Cross-cultural studies of individualism and collectivism. In *Nebraska symposium on motivation 1989: Cross cultural perspectives*, University of Nebraska Press, Lincoln, NB.

Trivers, R.L. (1971). The evolution of reciprocal altruism. *Quarterly Review of Biology*, **14**, 35–57.

Turnbull, C.M. (1961). *The forest people*. Chatto & Windus, London.

Turner, J.C. (1987). *Rediscovering the social group: A self-categorization theory.* Basil Blackwell, London.

Vine, I. (1987). Inclusive fitness and the self-system. The roles of human nature and sociocultural processes in intergroup discrimination. In *The sociobiology of ethnocentrism* (eds V. Reynolds, V. Falger and I. Vine), University of Georgia Press, Athens, GA.

Waddington, C.H. (1960). *The ethical animal.* Allen & Unwin, London.

Walzer, M., ed. (1995). *Toward a global civil society.* International political currents. Berghahn, Oxford.

Wattenberg, B.J. (1991). *The first universal nation: Leading indicators and ideas about the surge of America in the 1990's.* Free Press, New York.

Weber, M. (1958). *The Protestant ethic and the spirit of capitalism.* Scribner, New York.

Weber, M. (1963). *The sociology of religion.* Beacon Press, Boston, MA.

Weber, M. (1964). *The theory of social and economic organization.* (transl. A.M. Henderson and Talcott Parsons). Free Press, New York.

Wiessner, P. (1981). Measuring the impact of social ties on nutritional status among the !kung San. *Social Science Information,* **20**(4/5), 641–78.

Wiessner, P. (1982). Risk, reciprocity and social influences on !Kung San economics. In *Politics and history in band societies,* (eds E. Leacock and R. Lee), pp. 61–84. Cambridge University Press, Cambridge, UK.

Wiessner, P. (1998). Indoctrinability and the evolution of socially defined kinship. In *Indoctrinability, ideology, and warfare: Evolutionary perspectives* (eds I. Eibl-Eibesfeldt and F.K. Salter). Berghahn, Oxford, 133–50.

Wiessner, P. and Tumu, A. (1998). *Historical vines: Enga networks of exchange, ritual, and warfare in Papua New Guinea.* (transl. Nitze Pupu). Smithsonian Institute Press, Washington, DC.

Williams, G.C. (1966). *Adaptation and natural selection: A critique of some current evolutionary thought.* Princeton University Press, Princeton.

Williamson, O.E. (1975). *Markets and hierarchies: Analysis and antitrust implications.* Free Press, New York.

Williamson, O.E. (1996). *The mechanisms of governance.* Oxford University Press USA, New York.

Wilson, D.S. and Sober, E. (1994). Reintroducing group selection to the human behavioral sciences. *Behavioral and Brain Sciences,* **17**, 585–654.

Wilson, E.O. (1975). *Sociobiology: The new synthesis.* Harvard University Press, Cambridge, MA.

Wrangham, R., and D. Peterson (1996). *Demonic males: Apes and the origins of human violence.* Houghton Mifflin, Boston, MA.

# Notes

1. Murdock (1949, p.83).
2. R. Fox and U. Fleising (1976, p. 280).
3. Quoted by Bruck (1994, p. 118).

4. Quoted from Seagrave (1995) by *The Economist*, 11 November 1995.
5. "Bond" is best applied to relatively intense individualized attachments, such as between family members and friends. It is often too strong a designation for the ethnic variety, for which the broader concept of "tie" is more appropriate.
6. W. Schiefenhövel has observed kinship alliances during intra- and inter-village conflict among the Eipo of Highland New Guinea, and has compiled Koch's descriptions of conflict from the same area. As with Chagnon (1980) with the Yanomami, Koch (1974) found that alliances during conflict usually ran along kin lines. He recorded eleven conflicts (three intra-village, seven inter-village, and one inter-regional). The risks of participation were real, since a total of thirty-one men and five women were killed in these disputes. The causes were mainly over sex (seven conflicts), social problems (two), and highly valued pigs (two). In nine of the eleven conflicts, protagonists took the side of kin.
7. In the case of the hunter-gatherer band, the fitness risk is loss of status, life or territory for close relatives numbering in the tens. In the case of an ethnic group, the risk applies to distantly related, generally anonymous individuals numbering in the thousands or millions.
8. Cultural evolution is not necessarily selective, and can involve random processes as in biological evolution. However, it is extremely unlikely that a cultural item (ideology, ritual, symbol) could manipulate group behaviour in some functional way without having emerged through selection or being deliberately invented for the purpose, or both.
9. Ethnic economic solidarity might also entail male bonding. Some evidence for this exists in findings of gender-specific work networks (e.g. Ibarra 1992).
10. However, van den Berghe does implicate inter-ethnic risk as an important determinant of ethnic middleman solidarity (e.g. 1981, pp. 145–6).
11. It is tempting to advance the general proposition that group solidarity can be deployed most effectively, in either defensive or aggressive mode, down the tie-strength hierarchy but not up it. The idea is that when group cohesiveness is a competitive factor, strong bonds will give an advantage over weaker ones. Thus nuclear family bonds should provide an edge in solidarity when organizing competition against all other types of bonds and ties, extended family ties to provide an edge against all other types except those of the nuclear family and extended family, and so on. Ethnic ties are of variable strength, but generally will provide an edge in solidarity over multi-ethnic groupings. One problem with this idea is that solidarity is not the only element of power. The most tightly knit and highly motivated groups can be overwhelmed by competitors who are fragmented and less committed to their groups, but who possess superior numbers or resources. Concentric circles of receding kinship contain geometrically growing numbers of individuals. When considering military or voting capacity, overall group strength will be maximized at the intersection of decreasing tie strength and increasing group size. A social technology able artificially to elevate tie-strength among members of a large group will greatly increase military or political power. This is essentially Blalock's analysis (1967; Blalock and Wilken 1979) of relative group power (Salter in preparation), and a plausible explanation at the macro level for the success and spread of nationalism based on ethnicity broadly defined.
12. MacDonald cites Abrams and Hogg (1990), Hogg and Abrams (1987, 1993), Tajfel (1981), and Turner (1987), together with Vine (1987) and van der Dennen (1987) for evolution-oriented reviews.
13. The sociobiological theory of ethnic markers suggests that diaspora peoples should have a longer history of family and clan names than stable populations.
14. Lind (1995) offers a dissenting typology: America is both multi-ethnic and a nation by virtue of a shared culture. Its unity would be best maintained by a strong central government, free social mobility, liberalism on sex, religion and diversity, rigid separation of church and state (meaning keeping the state a neutral referee of ethnic competition), and a strong sense of national identity. Lind thus discounts the historical argument that nations have an ethnic origin and core (Connor 1994; Smith 1986). In the context of the present discussion, his model will be most likely to succeed if national identity is defined in opposition to other identities, i.e., by using an aggressive foreign policy stance to keep a continuous string of superordinate goals before the population.

# SUBJECT INDEX

# NAME INDEX

**A**

Abella, I., 154, 167

Abrams, D., 158, 161, 166, 168, 254, 272, 280, 284, 289n12

Abric, J. C., 74, 88, 99

Adib, S. M., 180, 186

Adorno, T. W., 164

Africa, 22, 28, 33, 35, 38, 39, 155, 157, 214, 239, 247, 283

Albania, 116

Albrecht, F., 73, 101

Alderman, G., 163, 167

Alesina, A., 248, 276, 280

Alessandrini, S., 264, 280

Alexander the Great, 253

Alexander, R. D., 10, 14, 48, 67, 72, 88, 99, 156, 167, 226–34, 239, 245, 247, 269, 280–81

Allai, M., 61, 67

Altman, J., 25, 38

Anderson, B., 249, 254, 281

Annan, N., 267, 281

Arlacchi, P., 6, 14, 113, 122, 124n2, 125nn4–6, 12, 126nn18, 20–22, 25–26, 127nn27, 34, 39, 42, 128nn43, 45–46

Asch, S. E., 74, 99

Axelrod, R., 48, 67, 72, 77, 88, 99, 224, 239

Azerbaijan, 4

**B**

Badcock, C., 230, 239

Baer, Y., 162, 167

Bahuchet, S., 25, 37, 38

Balch, S. H., 59, 67

Bales, R. F., 73, 99

Balikci, A., 37, 38

Balkan, 13, 118, 120, 123, 127n40, 159

Ballard, J. A., 256, 281

Barash, D. P., 227, 239

Barnard, A., 37, 38

Barner-Barry, C., 233, 239

Barnes, M. F., 75, 100

Bar-Tal, D., 254, 281

Barth, F., 273, 281,

Barton, C. A., 37, 38, 115, 122

Barton, C. M., 23, 38

Bartov, O., 256, 265, 281

Batson, C. D., 77, 90, 99

Baumeister, R. F., 166, 167

Bayer, R., 182, 187

Beaty, J., 164, 167

Becker, G., 93, 99

Bedouins, 115, 116, 123

Benjamin, L. S., 73, 99

Bennet, C. E., 275, 284

Bentham, J., 267

Benveniste, E., 122, 125n10